WEB OF LIFE

Nostalgia Jewishness is a lullaby for old men

gumming soaked white bread.

J. GLADSTEIN, *modernist Yiddish poet*

CONTRAVERSIONS

JEWS AND OTHER DIFFERENCES

DANIEL BOYARIN,

CHANA KRONFELD, AND

NAOMI SEIDMAN, EDITORS

The task of "The Science of Judaism"

is to give Judaism a decent burial.

MORITZ STEINSCHNEIDER,

founder of nineteenth-century

philological Jewish Studies

WEB OF LIFE

FOLKLORE AND MIDRASH IN
RABBINIC LITERATURE

GALIT HASAN-ROKEM

Translated by Batya Stein

Stanford University Press • *Stanford, California*

Stanford University Press
Stanford, California

© 2000 by the Board of Trustees of the Leland Stanford Junior University

This revised edition of *Web of Life: Folklore and Midrash in Rabbinic Literature* was originally published in Hebrew in 1996 as *Riqmat hayim: ha-yetsira ha-ammamit be-sifrut hazal.*
© Am Oved Publishers Ltd., Tel Aviv, 1996

Printed in the United States of America on acid-free, archival-quality paper.

Library of Congress Cataloging-in-Publication Data

Hasan-Rokem, Galit.
  [Rikmat hayim. English]
  Web of life : folklore and midrash in rabbinic literature / Galit Hasan-Rokem ;
translated by Batya Stein.
    p. cm. — (Contraversions)
  Includes bibliographical references and index.
  ISBN 0-8047-3226-4 (alk. paper) — ISBN 0-8047-3227-2 (paper : alk. paper)
  1. Midrash rabbah. Lamentations—Criticism, interpretation, etc.   2. Folklore in
rabbinical literature.   I. Title.   II. Contraversions (Stanford, Calif.)
BM517.M74 H3713   2000
296.1′4206—dc21   00-041049

Original printing 2000

Last figure below indicates year of this printing:
09   08   07   06   05   04   03   02   01   00

Designed by Sandy Drooker
Typeset by Keystone Typesetting, Inc. in 10/14.5 Minion

In memory of Amitai, my firstborn

(1973–1990)

CONTENTS

PREFACE

THIS BOOK DEALS with rabbinic literature—the largest textual body in Hebrew literature, as well as the most influential in Jewish life since its creation and until today. The modern reader, and particularly one lacking religious erudition, may construe the world of the Talmud and the Midrash as strange and inaccessible. In truth, however, rabbinic aggadic literature includes many fascinating and complex works, capable of moving and enchanting contemporary readers.

Lamentations Rabbah, the Midrash that will be at the focus of attention in this book, was composed in Palestine, approximately in the middle of the first millennium C.E. This Midrash weaves a rich and varied web of life, beautiful and poignant, around the biblical Book of Lamentations. It conveys experiences of loss and destruction but also of love between men and women, parents and children, as well as details of everyday life—food, clothing, trades, and pastimes.

Some approaches claim that patterns of study prevalent at the academies, reflecting the scholars' intense exegetical concerns, had a decisive influence on the artistic form assumed by the texts. Other approaches emphasize the influence of the public sermon at the synagogue—an institution that stressed such values as public education and oral artistic communication. My own approach is to show how both of these formative bodies—the academy and the synagogue—were also open to other socializing institutions, above all, the family, rural and urban public spaces, and the political, commercial, and artistic discourse of the time.

The voices expressed in the text represent both the elite and the broader layers of society. Multivocality and collective articulation, characteristic features of rabbinical literature, are also conveyed in the rich representation of genres and forms of discourse usually identified with folk literature. The marks of oral creativity are revealed as the building blocks of the written text. Contemporary thinking, particularly cultural and literary theory, provides the starting point for my study of Jewish ancient literature as a manifold and multicontextual system of artistic communication.

∾

This book is the product of years of study and research at the Department of Hebrew Literature at the Hebrew University in Jerusalem. My teachers, colleagues, and students at the Department were my partners at various stages of the research. I was privileged to be a student of Dov Noy, who pioneered the study of Jewish folk literature in Israel in a unique and trailblazing endeavor. I found inspiration and support in his extraordinary human qualities at all stages of my work. Jonah Fraenkel, who formulated a unique scholarly vision of the poetics of aggadic literature, has indelibly imprinted my research, both as a teacher and as a partner in dialogue. The late Joseph Heinemann directed our attention to the art of ancient Palestinian sermons in his lectures and writings. Among my other teachers in the faculty of the Institute of Jewish Studies at the Hebrew University, I wish to mention with great appreciation the late E. S. Rosenthal and Yaakov Sussman.

I thank my colleagues for their advice and comments: Tamar Alexander, Haya Bar-Itzhak, Dan Ben-Amos, Yoram Bilu, Yaakov Elbaum, Oded Irshai, Joshua Levinson, Yehuda Liebes, Daniel Schwartz, Anat Shapira, David Shulman, David Stern, Haim Weiss, Eli Yassif, Sara Zfatman. Special thanks to Ariel Hirschfeld, Raanan Kulka, Avigdor Shinan, and Dina Stein. Pinhas Mandel generously shared with me his philological findings on *Lamentations Rabbah*, and I thank him in the body of the text whenever I made use of them. Without the help of Ariela Avni, Yehudit Avraham, Ahuvah Cohen, and Ilana Mautner, of the Hebrew University, I could not have completed this work.

I wish to thank Sarah Japhet and Shlomo Naeh, who carefully read the

Hebrew edition of this book and made useful corrections, which I incorporated into the English translation. The remaining mistakes, however, are mine.

Thanks to the editor of the Hebrew version of this book, my friend Avraham Shapira, for his trust, patience, and persistence. Thanks to Daniel Boyarin, the editor of the Contraversions series, which is publishing the English version of this book, who has been a challenging and encouraging friend and a brilliant intellect. The National Foundation for Science, the Israeli Ministry of Education, and the Memorial Foundation for Jewish Culture have supported me in studies that contributed directly and indirectly to the writing of this book. Thanks to the Charles Wolfson Fund at the Institute of Jewish Studies of the Hebrew University of Jerusalem for its contribution to the costs of the translation. Thanks to Helen Tartar and Stacey Lynn at Stanford University Press, to copy editor Ruth Steinberg, and to Batya Stein, the most creative, attentive, and patient translator I have ever met.

Through my studies of Hebrew literature and Jewish folk literature I am preserving the tradition of my forefathers and mothers, Talmudic scholars of Lithuania and Hasidim of Poland.

Thanks to my husband, Freddie Rokem, who shares my life and my research, and to my children Naama and Ariel, cherished partners to dialogue and study, beloved beyond words.

G. H.-R.

Translator's Note: The translation was carried out with the cooperation of the author.

"assembling shreds unto a whole . . ."
—HAYYIM N. BIALIK

". . . if the text is subject to some form, this form is not unitary, architectonic, finite; it is the fragment, the shards, the broken or obliterated network—all the movements and inflections of a vast 'dissolve' which permits both overlapping and loss of messages."
—ROLAND BARTHES

1 THE STUDY OF FOLK NARRATIVES IN RABBINIC LITERATURE

THE CONCERN OF this book is with the presence of folk literature and folk culture in Palestinian aggadic literature in Late Antiquity. This time is known in intracultural Jewish terms as the period of the Mishnah and the Talmud, or the rabbinic era, and in regional political terms as the period of Roman and Byzantine domination in Palestine. In this fateful era for Jews in Palestine and throughout the world, together with the destruction of the Temple and due to it, Judaism shaped cultural patterns that have partly been sustained up to our own times. It was in this period that Judaism began its complex cultural negotiation with the world.

The scholarly concern with aggadic literature is rich and manifold. Scholars have focused on the contents and the forms of Aggadah, on its language and its versions, on the thought it encompasses. They have illuminated it from historical and literary perspectives. The research foundations laid from the nineteenth century onward by outstanding figures such as Leopold Zunz, Zecharia Fraenkel, Wilhelm Bacher, and others, have enabled more recent scholars to develop their explorations and understanding in many directions. In our own time, research concerns have also focused on the literary forms of Aggadah, including its languages and versions, and on its characteristic patterns of thinking.[1]

All scholars of aggadic literature have acknowledged that folk literature was an aspect of the spiritual and cultural creativity of the rabbis. Whereas some view it as a central element of the cultural polysystem represented by the literature of the Talmud and the Midrash, others consider it less important. This book makes folk narrative research the starting point for the study of rabbinic literature, and thereby continues the work of Sigmund Fraenkel, Hayyim Nahman Bialik and Yehoshua Hana Ravnitzky, Micha Josef Berdyczewski (Bin-Gorion), Louis Ginzberg, Bernhard (Bernát) Heller, Raphael Patai, Immanuel Bin-Gorion, Alexander Scheiber, Dov Noy, and Dan Ben-Amos.[2] This approach views folk narratives as woven into the very fabric of rabbinic Aggadah and rabbinic literature in general and not merely as an amusing digression providing relief from heavier and more important matters. As will emerge from the chapters of this book, folk literature deals with the most important issues of its time.

How should the place of folklore in the literature of the *tannaim* (first and second centuries C.E.), and particularly in that of the Palestinian *amoraim* (over the next three hundred years), be understood? In all forms of literature known to us—certainly Hebrew literature, and perhaps world literature as a whole—nothing resembles the aggadic Midrash in its multiplicity of simultaneous perspectives, which range from descriptions of everyday life to prophetic visions, from proverbs bearing the group's experience in generalized terms to the most private scream of pain. Locales shift from uppermost heaven to market alleys and even below. The rabbis' unparalleled literary endeavor stands before us as a textual repository, constructing a total representation of a culture that is no longer. No human detail is too small or too negligible to be included and perceived as a necessary part of the whole. What concerns us here, then, is a gigantic, collective cultural operation, whose motivations are close in essence to what anthropologist Clifford Geertz defined as "thick description."[3] The assumption here, then, is that the rabbis were concerned with the comprehensive ethnographic recording of their culture, hence their serious approach to folk literature and to folk creativity in general—an approach that led to the varied and frequent appearance of these bodies of culture in all realms and genres of the rabbinic endeavor.

"An attempt to survey Jewish folklore in all its aspects within the limits of a single lecture would be not only presumptuous but also futile," wrote Louis Ginzberg in the opening sentence of his 1938 lecture celebrating Harvard's three hundredth anniversary.[4] Whatever is true of Jewish folklore in general is also true of folklore in the largest textual corpus of Jewish culture, rabbinic literature, and whatever is true of one lecture is also true of the introductory remarks to this book. Nevertheless, I do see myself obliged to begin this book by relating, on the one hand, to the previous research of folkloristic and folk-literary aspects of rabbinic culture, as these can be inferred from those of the rabbis' writings that have reached us and, on the other hand, to the theoretical and methodological tools serving us today.

The study of folklore as a scientific discipline offers a range of research methods enabling a scholarly hermeneutical approach to bodies of knowledge and creativity in all eras, both ancient and modern, and in varied channels of communication—oral, written, through words, pictures, movement, voice, and ritual and symbolic behavior.

The scientific study of Judaism and the study of folklore begin at the same time; both are rooted in the awakening of national consciousness among the peoples of Europe and in philological research methods.[5] Nineteenth-century scholars, who were mainly concerned with the study of rabbinic literature from a philological perspective, tended to relate to the presence of folk narratives in this corpus by noting their parallel universal versions. This was then the predominant trend in the study of European folklore. Known as the geographic-historical school, it combined philological inspiration with Romantic notions about a search for the ancient sources of culture. This was the approach of such scholars as Sigmund Fraenkel, Abraham Tendlau, Max Gruenbaum, Josef Perles, Max Grunwald, Leopold Dukes, and others. Interest in the folk literature found within the rabbinic corpus grew at the beginning of the twentieth century due to its clear association with the cultural and ideological spirit of the times. Introducing his anthologizing project in the essay "On the Anthologizing of Aggadah," and his blueprint for a Zionist Hebrew culture in another essay, "The Hebrew Book," Bialik referred to aggadic literature as the classic belles-lettres of the Jewish people, as well as a worthy and desirable replacement for the folk literature of Exile (for him, mainly in Yiddish).[6] Bialik's contemporary, Berdyczewski, also engaged in the research and anthologizing of rabbinic folk literature, choosing the pen name Bin-Gorion for this endeavor.[7] Berdyczewski's approach was more patently folkloristic than Bialik's. This emphasis came to the fore both in his expansion of compilation efforts beyond rabbinic literature to include medieval fiction and in his citing of parallel versions of the same story from different sources.

Like Berdyczewski, Louis Ginzberg also approached rabbinic literature with an awareness of available research methods in folklore. This shows in several of his articles, as well as in the research culminating in *The Legends of the Jews*, first published in English during the 1920s. More than Berdyczewski, however, and certainly more than Bialik, Ginzberg adhered to scientific research methods. He also placed stronger emphasis on the intercultural character of rabbinic aggadic literature by citing parallel motifs from Greek and Roman literature, and particularly from Christian literature, throughout.

Studies by Israël Lévi were also being published at the same time. Although these studies appear to continue the nineteenth-century tradition of the *Wissenschaft des Judentums*, they actually relate mainly and more distinctively to the intercultural communicative dimension embodied in comparative research.[8]

This concern with rabbinic folk literature as part of the concern with folklore in general and with the folk literature of Semitic languages in particular, was also typical of the approach endorsed by Bernát Heller. He and his disciple Alexander Scheiber were among the leaders of the Hungarian school, which was very active and influential in the study of folk literature.[9]

The focus on folklore in rabbinic literature also led to an interest in the relationship between the text and other institutionalized cultural contexts, such as folk religion as it emerges from the studies of Avigdor Aptowizer. By the time he conducted his studies, functionalism had already become a dominant trend in the study of culture and society and had also affected the geographic-historical school, which had so far been at the center of folkloristic research. The crux of this theory entails a shifting of focus from the text per se to the text in its cultural context, and to the functioning of every cultural expression within the general context of culture as a system. Questions about local cultural adaptations and specific ways of implementation and performance in every work replaced comparisons between versions and a search for the source.

Raphael Patai was among the first to approach rabbinic (as well as biblical) literature with a theory and a methodology that had been tried in the study of folk literature elsewhere. He followed the research approach of James Frazer who, in *The Golden Bough*, compiled folk-literary material from all over the world in order to point out the developmental links between myth and ritual.

The thinking of Yitzhak Heinemann and Max Kadushin inspired the study of folklore in rabbinic literature by suggesting that specific categories of thought and creativity, traditionally considered popular, should be viewed as the basic infrastructure of rabbinic creativity in general, whether scholarly or popular. Heinemann's "organic thinking," for instance, is close to the "savage mind" of Lévi-Strauss, who argues that this type of thinking unites the creations of *l'esprit*, the human spirit, everywhere. Whereas Lévi-Strauss remained within the confines of primitive cultures, Roland Barthes exposed the "mythologies" of Western industrial culture.[10] Clearly, then, a concern with folk culture does not demand that we confine ourselves to the endeavors of "simple folk." Torah scholars and Talmudists, ancient and modern, just like contemporary professors, have folk creativity channels of their own, some unique to them and some that they share with other social groups.

As a student of Aptowizer, and equipped with the research tools of the scientific folkloristic discipline he had acquired in the United States, Dov Noy combined a geographic-historical approach and a moderate functionalism in his studies of rabbinic aggadic literature. He was the first to bring into the study of aggadic literature the experience acquired in folkloristic field research, which he also applied to his main research enterprise, the Israel Folktale Archives. The Archives bring together the oral narrative traditions of ethnic and religious groups in the State of Israel.

Oral performance, which is a characteristic feature of folk literature, was a dimension that concerned Joseph Heinemann, followed by his disciple, Avigdor Shinan. Rather than studying oral performance from the perspective of folk literature, he dealt with this dimension by stressing the centrality of the synagogue as the powerhouse of rabbinic literature.

By assuming, as I do above, that folk literature is not an endeavor limited to the "simple" or "lower" classes, we might argue that, in principle, the same academy in which Jonah Fraenkel locates the creation of rabbinic literature also produced folk literature, and even of the oral kind.[11] Fraenkel, although distancing his own discussion from folklore, eventually affected scholars dealing with folk literature in the rabbinic corpus when his influence blended with that of the formalist school, originating mostly with Vladimir Propp.

Dan Ben-Amos was one of the leaders of the new folkloristic school prevalent, mainly in the United States, from the end of the 1960s until the mid-1980s. In his studies of rabbinic aggadic literature he included neofunctionalist aspects, which focus mainly on the immediate context of perfor-

mance and on the communicative interactions sustaining oral folk literature, rather than on the general context of culture as a system. He also placed
the concept of the genre at the center of the discussion, introducing formal
and structuralist research models that examined the dynamic between permanent and contingent elements in folk literature. His approach, rather
than being philological or content-oriented, as in the geographic-historical
school, or concerned with functional adaptation, focused on the structure of
plot development.

Genre is also at the center of Eli Yassif's research. Most of his studies are
devoted to Hebrew fiction in the Middle Ages and the early modern period,
but in the book where he presents the Hebrew folk narrative within a
historical continuum, the longest chapter is devoted to rabbinic literature,
thus stressing its importance and its formative effect on later developments.

Contemporary folkloristic research on rabbinic literature draws from
this scholarly tradition and enhances intradisciplinary approaches through
interdisciplinary theorizing, which is a growing phenomenon within the
humanities as well as between the humanities and the social sciences. Research today is also influenced by a sharpened hermeneutical consciousness
that, to some extent, has replaced positivistic certainties. Scholars are thus
more conscious than ever that they neither reconstruct nor describe things
as they are or were, but, rather, interpret them according to data that is
a priori limited, and according to their own paradigms of knowledge and
experience.

The traditional comparative methods continue to turn our attention to
cultural interfaces and, in the broadest sense, also to the fact that, even in the
corpus of rabbinic literature, the most unique of all textual modes in the
whole of Jewish culture, we are not "a people who dwell alone."

By directing our attention to social bases that are broader than those acknowledged in standard scholarly practice—the synagogue and the academy—this book sheds light on the text from a multivocal perspective regarding gender, age, and class.

The traditional character of folk culture allows the rabbinic aggadic scholarship attuned to it to develop a long-term perspective, the *"longue durée"*
suggested by historians of *mentalité* such as Jack Legoff, Natalie Davis,
Robert Darnton, and others. The concentration on folk creativity also paves
the way for a social history that is not confined to political events. Instead, it
establishes a picture of the past that also includes fragments of everyday life

(in the wake of Michel de Certeau), and broader concepts of *habitus* (in the wake of Pierre Bourdieu), the environment and the activities creating the identity of the carriers of the culture.

Comparative studies based on such premises do not focus, then, on a search for direct links between Jewish texts and those of another culture, be it Christian, Roman, or Persian. Concepts of cultural exchange between Jews and Christians, at least until the fourth century, can thus be understood more broadly. Rather than being construed solely in terms of a polemic, they can include a wider spectrum of possibilities, partly of dialogue, partly of dispute. Delving into the materials of popular culture leads us to the assumption that polemics were mainly typical of the leadership stratum, whereas everyday life was characterized by softer and more open modes of intercultural communication.

Folk literature is interwoven at various levels of explicitness in rabbinic aggadic literature. Scholars addressing folk narrative deal with the multi-layered and heterogeneous origins of the authority articulated in rabbinic Aggadah. They thereby point to a distinctive source for a crucial stylistic and structural feature of this literature, its tendency to convey complex meanings through multivocal modes of discourse.

Folk literature is conceptualized as *collective*. Its authors and performers generate it through a persistent link with the community that creates this literature together with them. They have no exclusive rights to it, nor do they stake claims of sole ownership. It is *traditional* and transmitted from one generation to another. Its main and original mode of existence is *oral*, and its artistic features are the result of its *re-creation in the course of performance*, which is one of its distinctive features.[12]

The folk literature included in the rabbinic corpus therefore reaches us as an echo of an ancient form of folk creativity, in most cases totally severed from its contexts of composition and performance and as part of a text. Yet, the texts sometimes give us an opportunity to learn about these circumstances through a comparison with what is known to us about the creation of folk literature, its performance and its contexts, in later periods as well as today.[13]

A concern with the folk literature found in the rabbinic corpus will turn our attention to aspects that are not necessarily at the center of traditional scholarly interest with rabbinic literature. The focus suggested here will highlight everyday life as a cultural category rather than as the background or the setting for more important, "historical" events. Light will thus be shed on groups that have so far been in the shadow of the sages—the scholars of the academy, the spokesmen, and the social leaders; this approach to the study of folk literature leads us to women, children, uneducated people, and strangers of all kinds, and conveys their contribution to the polysystemic character of rabbinic culture.[14]

The methodological approach to rabbinic literature applied in this book is, therefore, innovative, reflecting its focus on folk literature. The folk narratives in various rabbinic writings are not perceived here as representing the totality of rabbinic folk literature, nor all its themes, motifs, and genres. The updated conclusions of philological research concerning the circumstances of the writing and the copying of various Midrashim, compel us to acknowledge two facts. First, it is absolutely impossible to access the original versions of the texts as they were produced by their authors, orally and in writing[15]; and second, the phenomenological circumstances surrounding the writing of rabbinic works closely resemble those of folk literature in general—that is, most of the material was accessible as a reservoir of general knowledge to the various partners in the creative process, the transmission into writing remained inconstant and often casual, and the versions that have reached us are partial and somewhat fortuitous, particularly in all that concerns the folk-literary parts of the corpus.

This study is largely based on one work of aggadic literature from the period of the Palestinian *amoraim* (third to sixth century C.E.). The work is the Midrash *Lamentations Rabbah*, which expounds upon the biblical Book of Lamentations. Research dates the compilation of this Palestinian Midrash to the fifth century. Nevertheless, what we know about the circumstances of the creation and transmission of works in that period indicates that *Lamentations Rabbah* certainly includes earlier fragments, while later materials were apparently added to it in the course of its various transmutations.[16]

Lamentations Rabbah, like other classical Palestinian aggadic Midrashim, and particularly *Genesis Rabbah* and *Leviticus Rabbah*, includes a great deal of folk-literary material. Like *Genesis Rabbah*, *Lamentations Rabbah* was edited according to the order of the verses, in the form generally known as "exegetical" Midrash. In contrast, the editing of *Leviticus Rabbah* follows a selection structured according to the order of the Torah readings in the synagogue at the time, in a form generally known as a "homiletic" Midrash.[17] This terminology seems to suggest a close association between the "exegetic" type of Midrash and the academy—where writings are explained or interpreted—and between the "homiletic" Midrash and the synagogue—where these interpretations are expounded to the public. It would be wrong, however, to conclude that each one of these institutions exerts exclusive influence over a particular kind of Midrash. Scholars differ regarding the dominant influence of these two important institutions on midrashic literature. Unquestionably, both have left an indelible mark on the structure of midrashic discourse and its modes of literary composition.

The present study adds a new dimension to the intellectual and experiential sources of creativity found in aggadic Midrash by highlighting the contribution of such social institutions as the family, the market and commerce, female society, rural and urban public spaces, and others. The emphasis on a folk-literary perspective stresses the fact that these institutions rely solely, or almost exclusively, on oral discourse. Indeed, most of the creativity in the academy and the synagogue at this time was also oral. These institutions, however, possessed the cultural instruments for developing processes for the canonization—fixation and institutionalization—of the text, and for setting it in writing.

Some of the folk-literary characteristics woven into midrashic literature, such as its traditional and collective nature, partially overlap those of Midrash in general. Explicit quotes in the name of a specific sage, worded as "Rabbi so-and-so said," may appear in another context in the name of another rabbi, and a multigenerational chain is often pointed out, formulated as "Rabbi so-and-so said Rabbi so-and-so said." Oral transmission was a feature that folk literature shared with midrashic writings at the time of their composition. Nevertheless, in the written version available to us today, the distinctive oral features emerge as an antithesis to the written formulation. The contrast between these two forms, however, is moderated because of the numerous manuscripts and printed versions available for every midrashic work. The process of re-creation in the various contexts can thus be made explicit, by bringing to the surface the oral creativity of folk literature.[18]

The focus on folk literature will also lead us to reevaluate the identity of the social groups to whom we should ascribe the creativity of midrashic literature. Whereas previous assumptions had viewed this literature as the exclusive endeavor of a male establishment, the account that follows will significantly change this perception.

⌒

The structure suggested for this book is meant to create and substantiate methods for analyzing and interpreting folk-literary material in aggadic Midrash. The most crucial and specific feature of folk literature is, in my view, its constant re-creation in changing contexts. I have therefore chosen to analyze the folk-literary material in relation to the relevant cultural contexts where this re-creation process takes place. In principle, all the material is obviously linked, to some extent, to all the contexts introduced into the discussion. For the sake of clarity, however, I have tried to place each text discussed here in the specific context that best illuminates its characteristics, as well as its uniqueness of form and content.

The separate analysis of the various contexts is not meant to challenge the approach underlying this study, which views culture as a complex and encompassing system. The discussions of the different contexts are meant as heuristic steps, aiming to show the complexity and the comprehensiveness of the culture through an analysis of folk literature, informed by the scholarly and hermeneutical approaches outlined as the theoretical background of the study.[19]

The order of the discussion that follows proceeds from what I considered the most easily discernible contexts to those that seemed more subtle to infer. In determining this order, I did not take a stand on the importance of the contexts for the understanding of these texts, or on the extent of their impact on the creation of these texts. Each discussion is preceded by an exposition of the central concepts used in the presentation and analysis of the text in that particular context, highlighting the relevant theories and research methods.

Chapter 2 introduces the literary context, which seems to be the most visible within the general framework encompassing the folk literature included in aggadic Midrash. A discussion of this context requires us to consider, as background, the interpretation of literary works in general. The text at the center of the discussion was thus chosen because of its literary qualities. The novelistic folk narrative of a tragic human destiny at the time of the destruction of the Temple—which in the course of the chapter will emerge as "anti-novelistic"—unfolds in the Midrash, after its literary re-creation, as a masterful work of art.

Chapter 3 presents the genre context. The example I chose to consider allows for a complex approach to the subject, because the text involves a chain of stories, all of them linked to a non-narrative folk-literary genre, the riddle. A rich intergeneric cluster is thus created. The generic character of the text is examined in its formal aspects, as well as in the meaning it bestows on the general literary context of the Midrash.

Chapter 4 examines folk literature in its comparative context. More than all others, this context may have determined the traditional methods of folk-literary research: the narrative type and the folk motif used in intercultural comparisons. The riddle stories discussed in Chapter 3 from the viewpoint of genre will be examined here from a comparative perspective. The comparison serves to establish the perception concerning cultural links and an intercultural discourse.

Chapter 5 presents the folkloristic context of folk literature, which maintains close links with other expressions of folk creativity: practices, beliefs, texts, and arts. The folkloristic context illustrated here is the practice of dream interpretation. Texts of stories about dream interpretation are examined here in the specific cultural context of the spiritual world of Palestinian *amoraim*, in a culture where dream interpretation is part of the interpretation of Scripture. This chapter thus addresses the operation of a powerful cultural mechanism directed to the search and articulation of the subtle border between the known and the unknown.

In Chapter 6 we encounter the social context of folk literature. Folk literature is created at all layers of society, by all ages, genders, and classes. In this chapter, folk literature in aggadic Midrash is presented as opening up options for changing the conventional picture of rabbinic literary creativity as an institutionalized male expression of academy scholars. In the representations of folk literature in aggadic Midrash we also hear the varied voices of people who are not part of the establishment creating the written text, the voices of those whose contact with the authors of the text is through oral literary channels. The chapter focuses specifically on the female voices speaking in the folk narratives included in the work. Through that perspective, the narrative interaction between various religious traditions, in this case Jewish and early Christian, is also set in focus.

Chapter 7 is devoted to the religious context of aggadic folk literature. At the center of rabbinic literature is a religious experience, conveyed through the sustained relationship with the texts that present God's revelation to the people of Israel: the Scriptures. Even events that occurred during the lifetime of the creators of this literature are interpreted in these texts as evidence of God's presence in the world. The religious attitude of the authors of the Midrash is not unquestioning. It exposes a complexity that includes belief, doubt, love, awe, and anger. The striking quality of the imagery on the subject results from the frequent use of intimate language and family relationships to portray religious experience.

The final context, discussed in Chapter 8, is the historical context of the aggadic Midrash. Folk literature has traditionally functioned as an important source for the history of the period. In the course of exposing the distinctive features of folk literature in the midrashic stories, this chapter sheds light on the complex mutual relationships between characters and images, between events and narrative plots, between memory and history, between vision and reality.

Aggadic literature, and Palestinian aggadic literature in particular, is suffused with materials that work through the experience of loss and mourning following the destruction of the Second Temple, and the pain of the oppression caused by the conquerors and rulers of Palestine. *Lamentations Rabbah*, as a Midrash that bestows new meaning on the Book of Lamentations for the destruction of the First Temple in the context of a second catastrophe, is particularly rich in such materials. The folk literature in this work reflects the experiences of destruction and oppression directly and in a variety of transformations.

The study from which the present work grows, like many other studies by contemporary scholars, conveys the encounter between a theoretical focus on a cultural-spiritual subject and the hermeneutical focus on one particular midrashic work.[20] This combination characterizes the introduction of a phenomenological perspective into historical research, a combination that appears to be a distinctive feature of contemporary literary studies of Aggadah.

Lamentations Rabbah is made up of two main parts which were created separately, according to the conclusions of philological-historical scholarship.[21] The first part comprises thirty-six homilies, usually brief and known as proems, and is mostly later than the other part of the book, the body of the Midrash. All thirty-six proems follow the homiletic structure common in Palestinian Midrashim, ending with the verse of the text that is read on a particular day at the synagogue. The verse that concludes almost all the thirty-six proems is the first verse of the Book of Lamentations: "How [*eikha*] does the city sit solitary" (the numerical value of the Hebrew letters making up the word *eikha* equals thirty-six).[22] The second part of the Midrash comprises five chapters parallel to the five chapters of the biblical Book of Lamentations, and follows them verse by verse. The first chapter is the longest, and includes most of the folk-literary material found in *Lamentations Rabbah*, whereas the others are progressively shorter.

The entire text of *Lamentations Rabbah* reacts to the events of the destruction and its aftermath on a human, personal, experiential level. Ambiguity and tension toward values we tend to see as representing "Judaism" or "rabbinic literature" are poignantly expressed at this level. One such value, illuminated in the text from several angles, is reward and punishment as part of a theodicy, particularly regarding the relationship between the sins of the people and the destruction of the Temple. The motto of most of the proems is the phrase "Because they sinned, they were exiled; because they were exiled, Jeremiah [whom tradition considers the author of the biblical Book of Lamentations] began to lament over them, *Eikha*." This phrase categorically formulates the theodicy principle, and takes a stand concerning the literary response appropriate to the destruction of the Temple. The proems, which are later than the body of the Midrash, are partly a moralistic response, reconciling ideological and emotional gaps emerging in the text itself. Folk literature, which is interlaced through the body of the Midrash, is inherently closer to the experience, and plays a key role in allowing expression to the less normative side of the tense dialogue conveying the collective consciousness.

The study of the folk literature included in the Palestinian aggadic Midrash may, therefore, expand and deepen our understanding, both concerning the literary quality of works from this period, and concerning the world-views of the people living in Palestine in Late Antiquity. I do not suggest reading this text literally, inasmuch as reality is not self-evident. And who better than R. Akiva embodied this insight in his life and his work:

R. Gamaliel, R. Joshua, R. Eleazar b. Azariah, and R. Akiva were on their way to Rome, and heard the mobs in Rome, one hundred and twenty miles away. While they began to weep, R. Akiva was laughing. They said to him: "Akiva, we weep and you laugh?" He said to them: "Why are you weeping?" They answered: "Should we not weep? When these heathens who worship idols and bow down before images live safely and content, and the footstool of our God has become cinders and turned into a haven for the beasts of the field, should we not weep?" Said he: "That is why I laugh. If they who offend Him fare so, how much better will they who do His will." Once again they went up to Jerusalem. As they reached Mount Scopus, they rent their clothes. And they reached the Temple Mount when a fox was leaving the Holy of Holies. They began to weep and R. Akiva began to laugh. R. Gamaliel said to him: "Akiva, you always amaze us, we weep and you laugh." He said to them: "Why are you weeping?" R. Gamaliel said to them: "See what Akiva is telling us! When in a place of which it is written, 'And the stranger that comes near shall be put to death' (Numbers 1:51) a fox roams, should we not weep? On us were the verses fulfilled: 'For this our heart is faint. . . . Because of the mountain of Zion, which is desolate, foxes prowl over it'" (Lamentations 5:17–18). Said he: "That is why I laugh, because it is written: 'And I took to myself faithful witnesses, namely, Uriyah the priest, and Zekhariah the son of Jeberechiah' (Isaiah 8:2). And what does Uriyah have to do with Zekhariah? What did Uriyah say and what did Zekhariah say? Uriyah said: 'Zion shall be plowed like a field, and Jerusalem shall become heaps and the mountain of the house as the high places of a forest' (Jeremiah 26:8). Zekhariah said: 'Thus says the Lord of hosts; Old men and women shall yet again dwell in the streets of Jerusalem, and every man with his staff in his hand for very age. And the streets of the city shall be full of boys and girls playing in its streets' (Zekhariah 8:4–5). The Holy One, blessed be He, said: 'There are these two witnesses, if the words of Uriyah are fulfilled, the words of Zekhariah will be fulfilled, and if the words of Uriyah are revoked, the words of Zekhariah will be revoked.'" So they said to him in these words: "Akiva, you have comforted us, may you be comforted by the comforters."—
Lamentations Rabbah 5:18

This is the last narrative text in *Lamentations Rabbah*, and it appears very near the closing remarks, which are also comforting, following a widespread convention in midrashic literature as a whole. The well-known folk motif appearing in the story, of amazing deeds that the protagonist explains through theodicy, is told in midrashic and folk tradition about the prophet Elijah, about the angel of death, and about Asmodeus.[23] Here, it assumes special form because the hero behaving in amazing fashion is R. Akiva, who is known for a method of expounding Scriptures that ascribes numerous and unexpected meanings to the verses. The riddle is apparently solved through homilies characteristic of R. Akiva's method. Nevertheless, as in many other midrashic stories, the solution of the riddle is accompanied by the strengthening of its darker partner, the paradox, which points to an ambiguity that is not fully resolved. This is the pain involved in this midrashic text, but also its sublimity. The riddle of laughter at a time of mourning is embroidered with the subtle, colorful, and artistic threads of folk narrative woven into the web of life of the Midrash. The theodicy stands beside the profound tragedy that subverts any justification, acceptance, or understanding of the verdict. The artistic power of the midrashic work successfully bears this contradiction, as well as others. Through its unique literary form, which allows expression to many voices, the rabbinic Midrash presents a multiplicity of narratives rather than a single authoritative one. The text, which originates in the exegesis of the Bible, is available to the modern reader for reinterpretation. It allows interpreters in every generation to establish their cultural identity through an understanding of this text. Undoubtedly, this is what is meant by an eternal text.

2 THE LITERARY CONTEXT OF FOLK NARRATIVES IN THE AGGADIC MIDRASH

INTERPRETING NARRATIVE STRUCTURE

The code is a perspective of quotations, a mirage of "structures,"
we know only its departures and returns.
—ROLAND BARTHES

AGGADIC TEXTS OF the Rabbis are often of unique literary quality.[1] Many folk narratives in this corpus tend to be artistically well wrought, in a manner more typical of written literature than of verbatim records of orally transmitted narratives.[2] The following analysis may serve to highlight artistic features and literary forms of folk narratives peculiar to the Palestinian aggadic Midrash.

A literary text is a multivalent system of various levels of expression. For the purposes of the analysis, the language of transmission may be viewed separately from the content messages, namely, the complex of meanings expressed through the text.[3] This artificial separation is intended for analytical purposes only since, in fact, the message has no pre-linguistic or translinguistic existence, and no meaningful combination of words can possibly emerge without carrying some message. The analysis of the text may address several levels of language: sounds, words, and sentences. In works longer than the stories found in aggadic Midrashim, attention should also be paid to larger units, such as paragraphs and chapters. These three levels are interdependent and create a cumulative effect: the level of sounds provides the building blocks for the level of words, while the level of words builds the level of sentences.

Several specific levels can also be discerned in content messages, as Roland Barthes has shown.[4] Barthes was mainly concerned with nineteenth and twentieth-century literature, focusing on long works with complex plots and many characters. In his analysis, he applied more message levels (or codes in his terminology) than those needed for our discussion, although the possibility of expanding the realm of the discussion concerning the messages of the midrashic story beyond the present suggestion should not be ruled out. I have chosen to focus on two levels that seem to me particularly dominant in the stories of Palestinian aggadic Midrashim, namely, the clash between the psychological and the ideological messages, which is at the heart of the tension and the multivocal complexity so characteristic of these stories.

Let us return to the conditions of interpretation discussed in the introductory chapter and elaborate on some of them. The interpretation of ancient texts may stress them as set in their own time or as given in our own reality as contemporary readers. The former approach has led to a number of exemplary studies in the tradition of historical philology. The aim of these studies was to establish, as far as possible, the "original" composition of the text based on concrete details of reality known to us from the study of history, languages, and archaeology. Paragons of this type of study are Saul Lieberman's books.[5] As Steven Fraade has pointed out, there are, however, variations in literary and historical approaches to rabbinic texts within the philological-historical school itself.[6]

A systematic formulation of a literary approach dictating detachment from the Midrash text while perceiving it as exclusively contained within its time of production, was suggested by Jonah Fraenkel:

> The second is the way of scientific research, for which the forefathers' world is no longer the homeland of the spirit but a historical object. Scientific consciousness requires detachment from the ancient text, and a distance established with full awareness. Thereby, the spiritual creations of the past are no longer the obvious contents of the present, but rather testimonies, enabling us to understand in the present what was created in the past.[7]

In light of Fraenkel's sweeping claim that this is the only "way of scientific research," his approach should be understood as relying on the hermeneutical theory of Emilio Betti, who suggests ways of "objective interpretation."[8] But further developments within hermeneutics have paved the way for including in the study of ancient texts and their interpretation a perception that seems to me almost self-evident, namely, that such texts as the Bible, the Midrash, and the Talmud are, indeed, *also* part of the obvious content of the present. The study of these texts, then, should take into account the variations of their reception in our culture throughout history. My own view, which interprets ancient cultural creativity within its time but assumes that no interpretation is possible without including the present in complex modes, is indebted to some central trends in contemporary hermeneutics, in addition to the basic inspiration of structural folkloristics and critical theory of literature and culture.

Hans Georg Gadamer traces the historical gap between us and the ancient texts we are interpreting to the history of these texts' resonance in the culture. We do not merely analyze the text itself but the process of its reception, and thus also the history of its influence on the culture. Transcending the boundaries of "pure" textual interpretation, his suggestion leads to a historical sociology of literature. Gadamer assumes the possibility of "stepping into the shoes" of the author, in the sense of adopting the perspective adopted by the early authors in their work. This enables the interpreter, through understanding and participation, to touch upon a meaning shared by both author and reader. At the same time, Gadamer is highly critical of the Romantic perception of interpretation, whereby understanding the shared meaning implies reconstructing the original moment of creation. Gadamer also claims that the true meaning of the text does not emerge through the temporal relationship between the authors and their original audiences, and that the act of interpretation must also take into account the historical position of the later interpreter. Rather than being mainly concerned with the reconstruction of the original conditions of authorship, interpretation is perceived as a new and unique creative act. For Gadamer, the time gap is not a necessary evil that we should seek to overcome by resorting to philological and historical means as precise as possible. Studying the process of the text's reception and resonance opens the way for a deeper understanding of its meaning, an understanding altogether impossible at the moment of its creation, namely, the meaning involved in the historical process of the text's life.[9]

On this issue, Gadamer's argument comes close to the proposition of Claude Lévi-Strauss that the structure of the myth emerges through a study of all its versions. Accordingly, in his structural analysis of the Greek myth of Oedipus, Lévi-Strauss also includes the "version" represented by Freud's interpretation of this myth.[10]

On this point, Gadamer's theory poses a problem. Gadamer argued that the historical process of the reception of the text results in the elimination of interpretation errors and in the emergence of new sources of interpretation. He failed, however, to give a clear answer concerning the possibility of discerning, at any given moment, erroneous knowledge that could lead to an erroneous interpretation, from correct knowledge that could lead to a correct interpretation.

Jürgen Habermas sharpened the definition of the conditions of interpretation when he said that, in the humanities, contrary to the natural sciences, "access to the facts is provided by the understanding of meaning, not observation,"[11] ruling out the possibility of objective interpretation. In his view, the interpreter exposes the original meaning only to the extent that she manages to clarify her own world at the same time. There must be communication between the world of the interpreted and that of the interpreter. Habermas refers to this attitude as a "practical" interest in knowledge, as opposed to a "technical" interest in the sciences. Habermas's plea for "self-reflection" in the act of interpretation demands recourse to extratextual models, such as Marxism and psychoanalysis. According to these models, interpretation releases both the text and the interpreter from the controlling apparatus of the institutions wielding interpretive power. Similar tendencies have become central in cultural studies inspired by most modern theories grounded in the philosophy of Foucault, and developments in anthropological research.[12]

Paul Ricoeur increased our awareness of the interpreter's role. For Ricoeur, the interpreter's awareness of the distance between the interpreter and the interpreted text is a vantage point enabling us to bridge the problematic gap between the wish to tell the truth and the research method chosen to study it. The question of whether the sources of interpretation are in the text itself or in the interpreter's subjectivity is transformed by Ricoeur into a hermeneutic procedure that establishes a convergence between the interpreter and the text. Interpreters trace the course of the text from the time of its inception until they encounter it, but they also draw on contemporary ideological, psychological, and historical influences.[13]

Ricoeur addresses the problem concerning relevant sources of interpretation by resorting to cognitive models crucial to the interpreter's culture. Ricoeur himself bases his work on psychoanalysis as well as on literary structuralism and on the phenomenology of religion.[14] But what characterizes his approach to every one of these methods is self-reflection: the psychoanalytical inquiry is, at the same time, the critique of psychoanalysis; his phenomenological speculation also hints at its own limits, while his literary structuralism is marked by a very deep critique of this school, directed mainly at its failure to relate to historical processes.

Relying on this background, the analysis that follows will deal with the text both as "a projection of the world" and as "communication of self-understanding."[15] The psychological and ideological messages that we will discern in the story convey our understanding of the narrators' world, and of the platform that we share with them as human beings. Our appreciation of these messages does focus on the motivations and the behavior of the characters in the story. It is formed, however, by the impressions created by the language levels described above, together with our knowledge of the historical process inscribed in the story, with reference to both the assumed period of its creation and the historical perspective that has emerged between then and now.

The text reproduced below is a translation of Solomon Buber's edition of *Lamentations Rabbah*, which is based on a manuscript of this Midrash found at the Casanata library in Rome. A brief comparison with the rendition of the same story in the printed version will follow.[16]

This is a story about the two children of Zadok, the High Priest, who were taken captive, one male and one female. This [child] fell to one officer and this [child] to one officer. This [officer] went to a harlot, and gave her the male in payment, and this [officer] went to a merchant and gave the female in payment for wine, to fulfill what is written, "and they have given a boy for a harlot, and sold a girl for wine" (Joel 4:3). After several days, the harlot went to the wine merchant and said: "I have a Jewish man [Ms. version: "slave"] who looks like the girl you have, let us wed them to one another and let us split their offspring." They did so, closed them both in one house and locked them in. The girl began to weep, and the boy said: "Why are you weeping?" She said: "Woe to this daughter of the High Priest, going to marry a slave." He said: "Who is your father?" She said, "Zadok [Ms.: "Yehoz," shortened from Yehozadak] the High Priest." He said: "Where did you live?" She said, "In Jerusalem." He said: "In which street?" She said, in such and such a street. He said: "In which courtyard?" and she said in such and such a courtyard. He said: "What was the sign in your courtyard?" She said such and such a thing above such and such a thing. He said, "Did you have a brother?" She said yes. "What sign did he have?" She said: "He had a mole on his shoulder, and when he would come back from school he would uncover the mole and I would kiss it." He said, "And were someone to show you this mole, would you know?" [it? him?]. She said, "Yes." He uncovered his shoulder to her. She saw [addition in Ms. version: "and recognized it"] and they recognized ["knew"] one another, embraced one another, and kissed one another, and wept to each other until their souls departed. And the Holy Spirit cries out and says, "for these I weep."—*Lamentations Rabbah*, 1:16

I wish to point out several prominent differences between Buber's version, which represents mainly an Italian and Ashkenazi tradition, and the printed version, which represents mainly a Sephardic tradition. Since the publication of this Midrash from one of the many manuscripts that preceded the invention of print, the printed version became the best known and the most popular among readers. In several places, the text of the printed version is more poetical and richer in its assonances than the one in the Buber edition. Missing from the Buber version, as opposed to the printed text, is the assent of the wine merchant to the deal offered by the harlot; in contrast, missing from the printed version is the emphasis on closing the room where the boy and the girl were placed. Crucial differences are revealed in the dialogue between them. Buber's version begins by concealing information from the readers in the girl's answer to the fourth question—"in such and such a market"—and again resorts to this device in the fifth question. The printed version reserves the unique formulation "such and such" for one answer only.

Some of the subtleties of the language cannot be explored in detail in the translation, and I confine myself to a broad outline. The Midrash is written in Hebrew up to the quotation of the verse from Joel, and from then on in Aramaic until the Hebrew closure—"and then the Holy Spirit . . .". This closure is not really part of the story but rather an editorial formula that recurs in several stories appearing both before and after this one, creating a sequence of martyrological tales.[17]

The sounds making up words represent the most concrete level of language in literature. The story about the two children of Zadok the priest is marked by a sophisticated play on similarity. Roman Jakobson and Benjamin Hrushovski have discussed the role of similar sound sequences in literary texts in the context of structuralist theory, suggesting that sounds are not signifiers per se.[18] Directing attention to them as a result of their position in sequences, and stressing the similarities or differences between them, draws attention to the literary character of the text (Jakobson's "aesthetic function of language"), which chooses words not only by their meaning but also by the phonological and aesthetic impression they create.

In the present text we note a strong emphasis on the use of sound sequences, which serve to intensify the aesthetic impression of the terse prose. The conciseness of the aggadic story is a literary context that produces enhanced creativity in matters of sound, rhythm, and structure.[19] Puns, rhymes, and other sound devices, are a significant component of the artistic strategy of folk narrators in the oral transmission of stories, signaling the kinship between the craft of the writer and that of the storyteller before a live audience.[20]

The original language of the story we are considering abounds in rhymes and assonances, some of them unusual and suggesting a literary register of language.[21] The repetition of identical or similar words functions, in principle, like the repetition of sounds. Most of the words recurring in this text are mainly demonstrative adjectives, or such that determine the status of words in the text as definite or indefinite. The recurring words thus serve to point to the status of the characters as known or unknown, and play a role in shaping the central theme of the story—establishing the identity of the protagonists, on which more below. At the same time, the recurring words generally serve to build the unique specificity of the event described in this text.

Because of the gender distinctions typical of both Hebrew and Aramaic, some of the words are identical in meaning but are actually sexual opposites, such as *ehad ha-hu* [this one (male)] and *ahat-ha-hi* [this one (female)], or brother-sister. In most cases, however, the opposition is not merely grammatical but points to actual sexual antitheses. Relations of opposites are created even more prominently at the level of words, between such words as male/female, harlot/merchant, and parallels between such words as male-merchant and harlot-female.

We also find sequences of words representing different signs with identical signifieds: male–child–Jewish man–brother; female–girl–sister (the last word does not appear in the text). The order of the sequence is from an impersonal sign, when we do not yet know anything about the characters (male/female), through the stage when youth and fertility are important (boy-Jewish man/girl), and up to the stage when the actual interpersonal relationship between them is clarified (brother/sister).

The limited scope of the story highlights the role of yet another literary device, which is the use of word-roots with double or multiple meanings. Thus, for instance, the Aramaic root ŠRI appears once to mean "begin," in the sentence "the girl began to weep," and once to mean "live," in the sentence "where did you live?" The ambiguity of the word "know" in this story, however, is essentially different. It does not stem from the double meaning of the root itself but from the metaphorical use of the Hebrew verb "know," beginning with Genesis 4:1 "And the man knew Eve, his wife," which I discuss below.

When shifting from the level of words to the level of sentences, note must first be taken of the sentences recurring in the opening episode. The opening sentence joins brother and sister to create one indiscriminate entity "the two children of Zadok, the High Priest, who were taken captive," without even pointing out the sexual differences between them. In the first action of the plot they still remain united—"were taken captive," namely, both together, but the rest of this sentence exposes the first difference between them, one male and one female. From here on, the tight form of the syntactic structures concretely conveys the thematic element of the siblings as captives, limited and confined. "This [child] fell to one officer, and this [child] to one officer." Although the contents of this sentence clarify that each one fell to a different officer, the officers are not differentiated or characterized in any specific way either, so that the main distinction between the two children of the priest is still one of gender. From here on, their ways part more sharply.

The sentence "This [officer] went to a harlot, and gave her the male in payment, and this [officer] went to a merchant and gave the female in payment for wine . . ." creates an additional opposition: each one of the captives is sold to a buyer of the opposite sex.

In the episode where brother and sister are brought together we find a sequence of three verbs, as is common in the prose of folk narratives (but not only there): "did . . . closed . . . locked." Here we see the clear difference between the siblings: only the girl begins to cry, in accordance with the cultural perception that was also prevalent in Palestinian aggadic Midrashim, whereby expressing feelings of weakness and sorrow is more acceptable for women than for men. In the dialogue between them, a sequence involving three questions times three follows: "Why are you crying? . . . Who is your father? . . . Where did you live? . . . In which street? . . . In which courtyard? . . . What was the sign of your courtyard? . . . Did you have a brother? . . . What sign did he have? . . . And were someone to show you . . . ?" The questions, beginning with a general identification through a location of the exact address and up to the body, build up a dynamic resembling that of a mystery story, where we move from zero knowledge to a solution of the riddle.

The closing sentences are also a stylized repetition of the syntactic patterns built from two triads of actions: "uncovered . . . recognized . . . and they knew one another." The first two are actions each one of them performs separately: he uncovers and is exposed and she sees; immediately afterwards, the shared activity of recognition takes place. After that, three shared physical activities are reported: "they embraced . . . and kissed . . . and wept." The whole sequence is bound together and intensifies the sense of an inevitable catastrophe by means of the "one another" construct, which acts as a connecting link between the third action of the first sequence—"knew one another"—and the three physical actions that follow. The dissociation between the end of the sequence of recognition activities and the beginning of physical contact emerges from the syntax as well as from the content. The word "embraced" is not connected to the previous one through the "and" conjunction, and thus marks the beginning of a new series of actions. The concluding sentence of the story—"until their souls departed"—is a powerful final accord unifying the multiple activities and hinting to the varied meanings of this phrase at the level of the messages, as noted below. The story began by creating total oneness between "the two children of Zadok, the High Priest," and the circle now closes with the united departure of their souls, connecting brother and sister, man and woman, in life and death.

Let us now consider the messages transmitted in the story's language. The opening sums up in a few words many preceding circumstances and hints to others. The text duration is highly compressed relative to the story duration.[22] The protagonists are mentioned right at the beginning, in line with the conciseness characterizing aggadic stories of the rabbinic period, and are identified as children of the High Priest. In the context of a cycle of martyrological stories, special importance is attached to the identity of the protagonists as children of the High Priest, who had been assured a privileged position and defined ritual roles in the Temple service. Through the figurative device known in classical poetics as "synecdoche," they represent the entire priestly class, now dispossessed, and, perhaps, even the exiled people of Israel as a whole. The priests have been exiled from their city and their Temple, and deprived of their social and religious status. They thereby lose their special power to mediate between the worldly and the sacred, between the people of Israel and the holy. This story is part of a sequence of stories about the decline of the Jerusalem elite prior to the destruction of the Temple, from the zenith of wealth and rank to the nadir of hunger, torture, and exile.

Historical research, which enables us to consider the story's details in the context of the times, indicates that priests seem to have preserved some of their privileges even after the destruction of the Temple. The *tannaim* had ordered that priestly offerings should continue, although the priests no longer had any role. The priests themselves continued to adhere to a strict code of purity regarding food and sexual relationships, as the Talmudic saying tells us: "From the day the Temple was destroyed, the priests became very punctilious about themselves" (TB Kiddushin 78b).[23]

Through the priest's children, a whole realm of associations about the holiness of the Temple in Jerusalem and the calamity of the devastation that befell the *axis mundi*[24] enters the story. In complete contrast, the officers are introduced through a foreign word (*istratiot*), which brings into the story a whole realm of Roman military associations. The contrast is sharpened even further when we read immediately afterward that the soldiers sell the representatives of priestly ritual purity to the quintessential representatives of defilement, the harlot and the wine merchant. They represent the two domains against which priests were explicitly warned in the Bible: "They shall not take a wife that is a harlot, or profaned; neither shall they take a woman put away from her husband: for he is holy to his God" (Leviticus 21:7); "Do not drink wine or strong drink, thou, nor thy sons with thee, when you enter the Tent of Meeting" (Leviticus 10:9); "Thou shalt not bring the hire of a prostitute, or the price of a dog, into the house of the Lord thy God for any vow: for both these are abomination to the Lord thy God" (Deuteronomy 23:19).

The opposition between defiled sexuality and priestly purity presented in this story is also found in another story about R. Zadok, where he refrains from sex with a harlot precisely on the grounds that he is a member of a priestly family.[25] A comparison between the various versions of *Lamentations Rabbah* indicates that the name of the siblings' father in the story under consideration is R. Zadok in one of the manuscripts, and R. Yehozadak in another. According to tradition, two R. Zadoks lived in the period close to the destruction of the Temple: one was a disciple of Shammai and the other was apparently the disciple's grandson, who was captured when the Temple was destroyed.[26] The sources have not proved helpful in establishing the identity of the R. Yehozadak (Zadok) in this story.

The act of selling the two children of the High Priest to a harlot and a merchant points to the degradation of human life that obtains when one nation conquers another and turns its children into chattel. They are sold for the favors of a harlot and for wine, thus creating a kind of degrading parity between the boy and the harlot's favors, and between the girl and the wine. The new combinations, merchant and female, harlot and male, which the phonological structure of the text stresses, create two impure and humiliating matches that more than hint at the possibility of sexual exploitation.

Quoting the verse from Joel, which joins together the boy sold for the harlot's favors and the girl sold for the wine, functions as a kind of symbolic key, setting the tone for the renewed encounter between brother and sister. The biblical quotation transposes the single, ephemeral event to a general level, transcending the specific narrative. This is a direct consequence of the paradigmatic, systemic role that biblical texts play within the rabbinic discourse.[27] A dialectical tension emerges between the personal event, whose transience is emphasized through numerous artistic devices in the *Lamentations Rabbah* story, and the quotation of the verse. Details of style, such as the demonstrative adjectives mentioned above, point to a personal, unique fate, while quoting the verse indicates that the story actually concretizes a cultural principle given permanent form in the verse. Biblical verses often serve as generative nuclei, sources of narrative plots in rabbinic literature, as Avigdor Shinan has shown regarding several other stories.[28] If we follow the *amoraim* in their way of thinking, the story *fulfills* the words of the prophet Joel, in the sense of "fulfilling what was said." The addition of the verse thus gives the story a further ideological dimension, as corroborating evidence of the faith in the power of true prophets to predict the future.

The greed of the prisoners' purchasers or, more precisely, the harlot's business initiative, saves the youths from the impure mating into which they had been trapped, the boy with the harlot and the girl with the wine merchant. The degradation of human life becomes real in the harlot's attitude to the two youngsters as animals to be mated for reproduction, whose offspring can be allotted mechanically, and without consideration for the parents' feelings.

As the plot proceeds, the separation between the siblings leads to information gaps between the various characters, creating situations of dramatic irony. In these circumstances, it is the resemblance between the two youths that serves as an excuse for the harlot to mate them![29] The story presents a marionette theatre, as it were, with the slave owners handling the two youngsters on the stage, namely, the room where they are placed. Contrary to the owners' expectations, yet in complete agreement with those of the readers, the puppets come to life and realize their own human individuality.

The girl acts first, and bursts out crying. A certain parallelism thus emerges between the initiative of the two women, the harlot in the offspring deal and the girl, whose weeping brings the rest of the plot to unfold. Yet the girl's "activity" is basically static and introverted. It puts her in a position of weakness vis-à-vis the boy, but also enables communication, with the boy immediately shifting to an active role by asking questions. The balance of activity and passivity between them remains tense and undecided, because it is actually the girl who, through her answers, provides most of the information that builds the pre-plot or background circumstances.

The situation turns ostensibly melodramatic—a boy and a girl before sexual intercourse, and the girl bursts into tears, seemingly expressing her virginal anxiety. Her answer to the boy's first question reveals, however, another reason for her sorrow, linking her personal situation to the historical context—a daughter of the High Priest, exiled and enslaved after the destruction of the Temple. The girl weeps because she foresees the danger of a mésalliance, a "bad match" unsuitable to her standing—a descendant of priests will be defiled and married to an ordinary slave who, for all she knows, may not even be a Jew. Dramatic irony evolves into tragic irony: the girl foresees catastrophe in a marriage to a slave totally different from her. But the true source of catastrophe is what she does not know, that he is in fact too much like her, actually her own brother. The disaster she is mourning pales before the one that will indeed happen because of their mutual ignorance. This moment in the story highlights the almost banal truth that, in every situation of sorrow and adversity, a new and even worse fate may still be in store.

At this point, readers may begin to ask themselves how incest will be avoided, if at all. The dramatic situation, where a brother and sister are brought to the threshold of marriage and/or sexual intercourse without knowing they are related, is not unknown in the literatures of antiquity. The motif of sibling marriage, indeed only to half-sisters, appears, for instance, in a work by Roman playwright Plautus, *Epidicus*.[30]

The balance between holiness and defilement in the story reaches here its most delicate and fragile equilibrium. The readers already know that the circumstances are potentially incestuous, but the characters themselves are still unaware. Both of them are led to the tragic understanding through the boy's questions, arranged in a carefully constructed sequence that opens with a query addressing the concrete situation, "Why are you weeping?" The girl replies, and in her answer reveals her ancestry. From here onward, the boy's knowledge is shared with the readers, and the girl is the only one who remains in a situation of dramatic irony. The boy's restraint, holding back full disclosure, suspends the course of the plot. At the level of the characters, it emerges as a subtle tenderness in his attitude to his sister, whom he will slowly lead to the harsh realization, at her own inner pace. From a psychological perspective, the questions-and-answers episode shows awareness of the connection with childhood as a crucial key to the individual's identity and ability to cope with present problems. Similar to the process of self-understanding, the sequence of questions begins outside and leads inward: the city, the neighborhood, the courtyard, the sign on the courtyard, the brother, the sign on his body.

This picture strongly resembles the episode of the meeting between Orestes and his sister Electra in Aeschylus's *The Libation Bearers*, where the brother also identifies his sister before she identifies him. Here, too, final identification is made by means of questions through which the readers and the audience, as well as the sister, steer closer to certainty.[31] The quest for identity is one of the central literary traditions of Eastern Mediterranean cultures in antiquity, found in both literary and folk-literary contexts, in myths, legends, plays, and poems.

The key sentences in the *Lamentations Rabbah* story, representing the transformation of two apparent strangers into brother and sister as we had known them at earlier stages of the story, are: " 'And if someone were to show you this mole, would you know?' [it? him?]. She said, 'Yes.'" The literary and emotional effect of this text derives from the use of a particular type of punning that, as noted, is quite widespread in the poetic language of stories appearing in aggadic Midrashim and in the Talmuds.[32] Words that are almost similar are placed so as to stress the slight change involved in the transmutation from one situation to another, manifest at the linguistic level in slight changes in only one or two syllables. These small changes in the form of the word parallel the process of change in the plot or in the character. Here, the act of seeing the bodily sign is what causes the shift from ignorance to knowledge. The physical act embodies the growing knowledge in the course of the gradual, inward-leading questions, and turns it into certainty.[33]

The sharpest change focuses on the word "know," which bears the full ambiguity of the root *YD'* (know) in biblical Hebrew, linking conscious, reflective activity to the sexual act. The pendulum representing the meaning of this word, oscillating between body and soul, is joined by another pendulum added in this sentence: the verb "to know" shifts from one to another possible object in the sentence, according to the various interpretations that follow from the verb's multiple meanings. The movement is from male to female (the mole, which is grammatically female in Aramaic as well as in Hebrew), and from the lost brother to the mole on his shoulder. The sentence, therefore, may denote any one of these meanings: "And if someone were to show you this mole, would you know it?"—namely, the mole; or "And if someone were to show you this mole, would you know him?"— namely, whoever shows it; and also "And if someone were to show you this mole, would you join him in sexual intercourse?" This last possibility may be somewhat contrived, since conventionally the subject of this verb in its sexual usage can only be a male. Therein lies, however, some of the subversive power of the narrative.

Gender changes, particularly in an attempt to pass for someone of the opposite sex, are a set feature in stories and plays of the period and the region, where lost siblings come close to the brink of incest. It could thus be viewed, according to the discussion in the previous chapter, as a motif belonging to a system of signs characterizing a relatively stable narrative topos within the culture. As is often the case in Talmudic-midrashic narratives, only a slight hint of this motif remains here.

The motif of a physical sign as a key to the discovery of identity is also well known in Mediterranean literature. The *locus classicus* is the return of Odysseus (Ulysses) to Ithaca and the nurse identifying him through a scar.[34] In the story of the two siblings in *Lamentations Rabbah*, the identification mark is expanded from the human body to include a house. The metaphorical association between the house and the human body is quite prevalent in rabbinic literature. It is manifest, for instance, in the frequent substitution of "his home" for "his wife,"[35] or, in another form, in the perception of the Temple as the body of a national entity that was harmed and eliminated with its destruction.[36]

The sign as a key to identification is also a characteristic motif in the folk-narrative genre of novellae of fate.[37] The story actually preserves, at least in formal terms, the basic plot structure of the tales of fate: separation, trial, and reunion. In many other regards, however, this story is the antithesis of a novella of fate, a kind of anti-novella. If we define the novella as a narrative plot bringing together the remote lovers who are meant to unite, the present story brings together those who are close and not meant to unite. Unlike the novella of fate, therefore, it does not end in a happy marriage but in a tragic death. It thus resembles the finale of many ballads, which end with the lovers' death in what is known as *Liebestod*, or, in Hebrew imagery, a "kiss of death."

In chapter 16 of his *Poetics*, Aristotle discusses "recognition" (*anagnorisis*) and, as usual, distinguishes between less and more refined forms of this dramatic device.[38] The lowest form of "recognition" is through a visible token, better is that construed by the poet or the narrator, and even better is a discovery relying on memory. Still better is recognition by reasoning, even if mistaken. Best of all is recognition ensuing from the events themselves. It would appear that all these forms are integrated in the story before us in quite wondrous ways. The reader partakes in the recognition construed by the poet, the boy reaches his by inference, while the girl's, although made possible through a visible token, is actually a consequence of the events (which, for Aristotle, nullifies the importance of visible signs). The complex use of focalization in the story's various stages is thereby exposed. Points of view shift between the narrator, the reader, and the two characters.[39] At some stage, the text even appears to imply that the boy and the girl share information undisclosed to the reader, when signs identifying the market and the house are given as "such and such." Obviously, it must be assumed that for identification to be at all possible, the girl must have provided some more definite pointers. The reader is thus placed at an ironical disadvantage, knowing less than the characters in the story, who become more and more intimately connected.

The association between the recognition and the sexual union, which emerges at the linguistic level in the ambiguity of the verb "to know," becomes even more significant because of the tragic context bringing the siblings together in one room. They have been brought together to engage in sexual intercourse, but without their knowledge. In other words, they were sent there as unknowing creatures without free will, to comply with the wishes of their greedy owners. At the start of their encounter, they have no knowledge about their identity and about the links between them. Knowledge of their true identity is the reason for the catastrophe lurking in the other, sexual type of knowledge. Nevertheless, the message of the narrative regarding the possibility of a sexual act between them remains equivocal throughout. In fact, the tension between the longing and the prohibition intensifies throughout their discourse, never precluding the option of their acting on their desire.

Both the language and the syntax of the story point in this direction. Obviously, at the overt level of the plot, the multiple meanings in the ambiguous sequence of sentences—"He uncovered his shoulder to her. She recognized the mole and they knew one another"—imply, first and foremost, "they recognized each other." To this literal interpretation, however, further levels of meaning (or "surplus meanings," in Ricoeur's terms) are immediately added, which broaden the general message of the story and particularly its psychological dimensions. The act of disclosure or, more precisely, the stripping, reconstructs an act from the past mentioned previously in the text: "He would uncover the mole and kiss it." The text is vague concerning the identity of the kisser, but this can hardly be construed as a narcissistic display of the boy kissing himself, and other versions spell out more clearly that the kisser was actually the sister. The printed version of *Lamentations Rabbah* cites the sister as explicitly saying: "And when he would return from school I would bare it [or him] and kiss him [it]," namely, the mole, the shoulder, the brother, in this order of expanding meanings, from the physical detail to the person identified through this sign.

A psychoanalytical interpretation might infer here that an act entailing guilt for actual incest is lurking in their past. In the context of the historiosophic assumptions prevalent among the rabbis, this act could be seen as a personal expression of collective guilt for the destruction of the Temple and of Jerusalem. This interpretation accords with the wish to contend with an existential and historical situation entailing tremendous suffering without renouncing the moral support of a doctrine of retribution, although it does not fully exhaust the meaning of the act. A fundamental feature of rabbinic literature is revealed here conveying, through the double or multiple messages contained in the narratives, the outline of an alternative historiosophy to the one ideologically supported by a doctrine of retribution. The personal fate of the protagonists fully discloses the power of an experiential interpretation of history, which refuses to accept the ideological justification of suffering as self-evident.

The kiss from the past, which in the course of the story leads to a kiss of death, serves to reify the world as it had been prior to the destruction in the imagination of the stories' narrators and of their later listeners still affected by the consequences. The world of the past appears to them as one where love had been possible, in circumstances other than the inhuman ones described in the narrative present.

The possibilities of interpretation suggested by the sentence "they knew each other" are particularly rich and intricate. We begin to unravel its complexity through the semantics, by tracing the multiple meanings of this word that, as noted, date back to biblical tradition. *Lamentations Rabbah* certainly preserves this multiplicity of meanings in the phrasings characterizing the text on dream interpretation, which is discussed in Chapter 5. In the interpretation of one of the dreams we are told "and he knew his mother" (*Lamentations Rabbah* 1), namely, he had sexual relations with his mother. Complexity is enhanced in the story because of the location of this sentence in the passage, as suspended between two sequences, suggesting two inter-pretations of its meaning. On the one hand, this sentence ends the passage that describes identification through a sign, its meaning thus being "they recognized each other." But a semantic problem is thereby created, since the brother had already identified his sister through the information she herself had provided in the course of the dialogue, and is here acknowledging the mutual identification. We may therefore interpret this identification also at a non-cognitive level. The first possible option is identification by sight, which is stressed through the assonances mentioned above. The second option is sexual union, which is reinforced by the joining of this sentence to the sequence of actions denoting physical closeness: "and they knew one an-other, embraced one another, and kissed one another, and wept to each other." The absence of the conjunction "and" before "they embraced" sug-gests that a new unit begins, detached as it were from the verb "know," whereas the identical syntactic structure suggests a close link with what will come later. The singular male form of this verb in the Aramaic version, as opposed to the plural forms that follow, is puzzling. This form would seem to suggest that, rather than the siblings knowing one another, he knew her, although according to what we are told at the level of identification, he had already recognized her and identification was now left to her.[40] This is a small-scale example of how rabbinic literature uses the intensity of linguistic opposition and cognitive contradiction as a central means of expression, a device that significantly contributes to its literary quality and its human credibility.

The ending of the story is marked by a double message, which includes a dialectical contrast: "until their souls departed." On the one hand, the con-flict imposed on the siblings by the greed of their owners is now solved because death releases them from a union involving incest, and the so-ciocultural entanglement is prevented by avoiding a forbidden marriage. On the other hand, a deep erotic yearning for death is revealed. Death itself could be perceived here as the ultimate erotic realization, but the joint departure of their souls—the embrace, the kissing, and the weeping, which could be viewed as a detailed enumeration of "they knew each other"—could simply be interpreted as an erotic climax. We might say that the clash between the psychological and the ideological messages in the finale suggests that incest, which was avoided in reality so as to preserve the purity of the priestly descendants, is actually performed in the language so as to allow expression to their yearnings.

∿

As is true of many other stories in *Lamentations Rabbah*, and particularly the martyrology stories in this Palestinian Midrash, this tale also appears in another version in the Babylonian Talmud. The interaction between the two messages, the ideological and the psychological, is slightly different in the latter version:

> It is told that the son and the daughter of R. Ishmael b. Elisha were taken captive by two masters, who happened to meet after a while. One said, I have a manservant, in the entire world no man is his equal in beauty, and the other said, I have a maidservant, and in the entire world no woman is her equal in beauty. They said: Let us wed them to each other and share the children. They placed them in one chamber, where he sat in one corner and she sat in another. He says, "Am I, a priest descended from high priests, to be wed to a slave?" And she says, "Am I, a priestess descended from high priests, to be wed to a slave?" And so they wept through the night. As the day dawned they recognized one another and fell on each other and wept sorrowfully until their souls departed. For them Jeremiah lamented, "for these things I weep, my eye, my eye runs down with water" (Lamentations 1:16).— TB Gittin 58a[41]

The comparison between the story in the Babylonian Talmud and the version in *Lamentations Rabbah* reveals several differences, some touching on marginal details and some concerning central issues. First, the difference in the father's name. R. Ishmael is known to have belonged to a priestly family, and we are also told that he was exceedingly handsome (TB Avodah Zarah 11b). Differences are also visible in the artistic form of the narrative. Absent from the TB story are most of the sound, verbal, and syntactic devices enumerated in the *Lamentations Rabbah* story. On the one hand, the TB story opens with a distinction between the two characters, "the son and the daughter"; on the other, we find no individual characterization of them in the rest of the story. The tension between their union and their separation throughout the story is thereby toned down. Both are described as good-looking, apparently following what is known about R. Ishmael their father, and this description actually plays the same role as the harlot's remark in *Lamentations Rabbah* that the siblings look alike. The verse from Joel and the two mediators, the merchant and the harlot, have all disappeared. In the central scene, in the room, their behavior is almost completely symmetrical. The TB story thereby detracts from the psychological portrayal of the characters as convincing depictions of individuals. Even the discovery scene lacks the tension ensuing from the dramatic irony of *Lamentations Rabbah*. The gradual progress in the sequence of questions from ignorance to knowledge is replaced by a simple statement: "As the day dawned they recognized one another." The encounter itself lacks the erotic emphasis of *Lamentations Rabbah*, and the description is rather flat: "they recognized one another and fell on each other and wept sorrowfully until their souls departed."

Even the connecting verse, between the story and the homiletic context, which is the same verse from Lamentations also found in *Lamentations Rabbah*, is tempered in the TB story because it is presented from the perspective of the grieving prophet rather than God's: "For them Jeremiah lamented, 'for these things I weep . . .'" The direct perspective of God contemplating the concrete fate of two human beings is thereby removed from the story. Absent is also the tragic irony entailed by the omnipotent God beholding his creatures being destroyed and weeping, as is the acknowledgment of human impotence in the face of catastrophe, an impotence we cannot escape by finding solace in omnipotence or absolute justice, even as projected onto God.

This comparison between the *Lamentations Rabbah* and TB versions of the story is not meant to suggest a chronological order between them. The Babylonian narrator or editor may have erased the strong psychological overtones so as to focus on the compelling ideological message of martyrology. It is equally possible, however, that the Palestinian narrator poured his subtle artistic talent and his profound psychological insight into an existing, simpler narrative frame. I still prefer to think that the directness of the experience described in the *Lamentations Rabbah* story, as well as its roots in historical events that took place in Palestine, attest to the Palestinian origins of the story in the form closer to the *Lamentations Rabbah* version, including its psychological intensity and its complex messages.

Nor is this comparison intended to make a general statement about the psychological depth of stories in the Babylonian Talmud as opposed to Palestinian aggadic Midrashim. On the same page that features the story about the children of R. Ishmael b. Elisha, there is a beautiful and poignant story about the carpenter's apprentice who committed a "tragic mistake," a true *hamartia* in Aristotelian terms.[42] He divorces his wife, but having borrowed the money needed to pay off her marriage settlement, he ends up serving his ex-wife and his lender at their feast.[43] Nevertheless, those stories in the Babylonian Talmud with parallel versions in the Palestinian aggadic Midrash tend to emphasize ideological biases prevalent among Babylonian Jews toward the Holy Land, the destruction of the Temple, and the historical reality in Palestine prior to the destruction. Gedalyah Alon pointed this out clearly regarding the story about R. Yohannan b. Zakkai leaving the besieged city of Jerusalem in a coffin. The main Palestinian versions of this story appear in *Avot de-Rabbi Nathan* and *Lamentations Rabbah*, while another version is found in the chain of destruction stories at the end of Gittin in the Babylonian Talmud. Alon rejects the prevalent interpretation which claims that, a priori, the story favors the move from Jerusalem to Yavneh as a conscious ideological choice, preferring to save the tradition of learning rather than the city.[44] In his view, the Palestinian versions are closer to a realistic description of the Roman conquerors' approach toward their subjects. In contrast, the ideological trend noted above gives us the Babylonian angle on the story, whereby the value of learning is balanced against the holiness of the land of Israel and of Jerusalem.

The hermeneutical reading of the tale about the children of Zadok the High Priest in *Lamentations Rabbah* illuminates the interaction between the structure of the story—as manifest in the linguistic form, the words and the sentences—and the messages of the story. The analysis indicated that complexity at each one of these levels is a function of their mutual dependence. The art of the narrative was presented as it is revealed through the creation of psychological and ideological messages that could be involved in rather complex relationships. The story in *Lamentations Rabbah* is marked by the tension between these two messages, sometimes to the point of open conflict. At the ideological level, the priestly descendants preserve their purity even at the cost of their lives, but at the psychological level, the kiss of death is the ultimate representation of the siblings' incestuous yearnings, and perhaps even the punishment for it. This death, then, fulfills Ricoeur's pointed remark, following Freud: "The dualism of Eros and Thanatos appears as a dramatic *overlapping of roles.*"[45]

The story thus prompts us to think about the dimension of guilt that Freud, as we know, considered the underlying foundation of the entire system of cultural meanings. One could be tempted to view this as a story about the guilt attached to incest, and thus add it to the tales about sins explaining the catastrophe, such as the series of stories in TB Gittin beginning with "because of Kamtsa and Bar-Kamtsa Jerusalem was destroyed," and others about various offenses between fellow human beings. Yet the singular power of this story seems to stem from its subversion of the guilt perception generated by rabbinic literature regarding the destruction of Jerusalem and the Exile, at both the collective and conceptual levels. Rubenstein, who also writes about rabbinic literature from a psychoanalytical perspective, pointedly argued that: "Rabbis apparently preferred self-blame to the possibility of an irrational universe devoid of correlation between virtue and good fortune."[46] An approach of "self-reflection," where culture is perceived from the vantage of time, informs these stories with guilt feelings. This is equally true of the TB story and of the *piyyutim* written on the subject, all based on the TB version of the story. But the versions closest to the telling of these stories as historical legends, which shaped the historical event from the perspective of the individuals who lived through it, may suggest a subversive interpretation. This interpretation refuses to accept the point of view implied in the statement "How, my city, have I sinned against Heaven," in the words of the *piyyut* based on our story. It is only natural that, in a literary corpus named after sages and halakhists, this subversive message would be left to genres considered part of folk literature. The voice we are exposed to, then, is "the voice of the people," in the words that the Romantic poet and philosopher Johann von Herder used to define folk literature.

This refusal does not appear as an explicit ideological message in rabbinic literature, but resonates clearly in the psychological message. Hence, the story we have discussed is a story about the existential plight at catastrophic times, when people standing at the brink of the abyss are forced to contend with the very foundations of their self-definition as human beings and as civilized individuals. The danger of losing one's humanity looms large, and the greater the danger the greater the heroism required from individuals, the story's protagonists, in order to cling to their humanity and their civilization. As contemporary Jews, we look back to the fire that consumed a third of our people in an event devoid of all meaning, except for feelings of abomination and terror that cannot be conceptualized. For us, the rabbis' artistic creativity spans the complexity between granting meaning and refusing to accept it. A study of hermeneutical devices, which focused on the possibility of interpreting an experience lying at the foundation of an ancient work from the perspective of present-day reality, has thus led us to the story's most specific meaning. The story emerges as a miniature wonder when it succeeds in turning the maximal concentration on the fate of an individual into a defined cultural attitude with a unique and distinct voice.

3 THE GENRE CONTEXT OF FOLK NARRATIVES IN THE AGGADIC MIDRASH

RIDDLES ABOUT THE WISE PEOPLE OF JERUSALEM

Wherever a Jerusalemite would go, a chair of learning
would be offered to him.
— *Lamentations Rabbah* 1

ONE OF THE ways to identify a folk narrative within the midrashic corpus is to place it under a specific genre rubric. As a way of illustrating this approach, we will deal with a group of tales closely similar in genre. The genre context cuts across the linear sequences of the midrashic text, creating a hermeneutical association between different tales belonging to the same genre as a complement to their existence within the universally conceptualized realm of folk narratives.

A question that scholars have considered is whether a genre, including the definition of its form and content, is a creation of narrators and their audiences, or rather, draws from the analytical terminology of scholars busy dissecting folk literature. In other words: Does the narrator of a folktale—let us say about a woman falling in love with a monstrous animal—know that this is a folktale? That, being a folktale, it transcends time and place and involves motifs of transfiguration and magic? Does the narrator of a legend about the magical healing powers of a saintly rabbi know that this genre is characterized by its embedding in reality, by its attachment to concepts and beliefs current in the narrating society, and by the inclusion of devices meant to persuade the audience about its authenticity? Dan Ben-Amos has systematically considered this topic. He has pointed to the many views on genres in the research literature, ranging from a perception of genres as "natural" on the one hand, or as an analytical device totally divorced from the reality of narrators and their audience on the other.[1]

The notion of genre has played a highly significant role in the study of folk literature throughout the short life of this discipline.[2] I assume that the presence of folk narratives in the flow of everyday speech was the main impetus behind this scholarly concern. A system of genres methodically described by scholars thus provided a kind of safety net, enabling orientation concerning material that could at times seem almost boundless. Scholars of folk literature are constantly aware of the fact that they cannot cover, through empirical methods, all the material that is available on any of their research subjects. Written literature is fundamentally a closed group of texts, at least retrospectively. It is possible to encompass the entire oeuvre of a particular writer, even when access to all the versions and items of his work might be a complex and time-consuming task. With regard to folk literature, however, the situation is clearly different. Its immaterial existence, its totally transient nature, as well as its presence in varied forms of narrative, completely rule out the possibility of covering it in its entirety. We could perhaps say that there is no complete body of folk literature, and its manifestation is altogether marked by incompleteness and fragmentation. The study of folk literature is, by definition, the study of an endless phenomenon, whose entirety cannot be fathomed.

The question concerning the narrators' awareness of the existence of folk-literary genres could also be asked about the authors of Midrash. The material found in *Lamentations Rabbah* seems to indicate that the editors of the Midrash were aware of genre distinctions, and even resorted to them in their editing.[3] In this chapter we will discuss texts that in folk-literary studies have been classified as folktales.

The classic description of folk prose genres suggested by the Grimm brothers at the beginning of the nineteenth century—the myth, the legend, and the folktale—continues to guide the work of many twentieth-century scholars of folk literature. The interpretations and characterizations of the genres, however, have changed according to the scholars' theoretical points of departure. In the formalist school, genres are determined by formal characteristics, in the functionalist school by function, and in the comparative one by contents. Structuralist schools deal with in-depth structures of meaning and do not, as a rule, view genre determination as an important issue. Recent approaches focus on narration and on the artistic performance of folk literature, including precise distinctions concerning the specific conditions of narration, the personality of the narrator, and his/her mutual relationships with the audience, proving the division into three main genres to be too general and usually inadequate.[4]

In the present discussion of folk literature as part of an ancient literature preserved in writing, genre is an important element, pertaining to the choice of texts as well as to the understanding of the function, the form, and the meaning of folk narratives. My approach to genres in this work assumes a continuum of folk prose, ranging from folktale to legend, which is informed by the division introduced by one of the most important scholars of folk literature qua literature, Max Lüthi.[5] I do not consider the third component in Grimm's triad, myth, as a genre. Instead, it is best understood, on the one hand, as a comprehensive structure of thinking that inspires the various expressions of a given culture, including its perception as a group, and on the other hand, as the a posteriori construct of the most fundamental and formative of a culture's narratives.[6]

Following Lüthi, the folktale, and even more so the legend, is described here according to poetic and formal criteria, and according to epistemic features typical of the mode of representation adopted within each genre. The world represented in the folktale, as opposed to that of the legend, is imaginary, fictional, and fantastic. Unlike the legend, which tends to articulate social issues as norms and rules of behavior, the folktale is a symbolical articulation of the individual's inner world.[7] Scholars with a psychological and psychoanalytical orientation have, therefore, compared folktales to dreams,[8] relating to folktales as symbolical reflections of the individual's mental reality from a variety of perspectives.[9]

The folktale often resorts to stylistic and structural devices that are ornamental, thereby consistently distancing itself from reality. The events of the folktale unfold at an imaginary, fictitious time, just as its location lacks identifying signs. The opening formulae characteristic of folktales also help to convey their distance from reality: "Many, many years ago, beyond the mountains and the sea, in a far-away land . . ." in many European and Mediterranean folktales, or even: "Once upon a time, in a land beyond the sun and the moon . . ." in Scandinavian folktales. At times, real but exotically distant places serve as the location of the folktale, such as Arabia or India in European folktales.

This distance enables the narrators as well as the audience, through their identification with the heroes of the folktale, to experience in symbolic terms the extreme events, both positive and negative, which affect the protagonists. Thus, motifs of extreme violence or unconventional forms of sexuality, mostly within the family, are quite common in folktales. These motifs are fantastic, imaginary realizations of hidden wishes and powerful taboos.

Characters in the folktale are typological and even stereotypical, and lack individuality. Thus, in many folktales, heroes and heroines have no names and are called "boy," "girl," "old man," and so on, as necessary. When the protagonists do have names, they are often typological names pointing to a specific trait, such as "Snow-White" or "Briar-rose" in the Grimm stories, or names that recur time and again, such as "Little Ivan" in Russian folktales, or "Smida Rmida" (Cinderella) among Moroccan Jews.[10] The protagonists of the folktale are presented within family contexts, which they leave for trials, struggles, and ordeals, in order to form a new family at the end. Often, the folktale symbolically overlaps the process of adolescent maturation.[11] The social context is not defined, and everything happens in a world beyond time and place. Nature is essentially friendly, and its representatives—the animals—aid the heroes. The generalizing nature of folktale characters makes them available objects of identification for every listener and narrator.

Folktales can be classified as symbolic, supernatural, or realistic. In symbolic folktales, the heroes are often animals behaving like human beings and, in many cultures, these folktales became direct metaphors of the human world. This is true of the European folk literature related to the Greek tradition associated with the name of the legendary fabulist Aesopus, as well as of many rabbinic narrative texts.[12] In symbolic folktales animals have fixed characteristics, such as the slyness of the fox (in Europe), or the porcupine (in North Africa), or the ape (in India). In supernatural folktales there are other stock characters, such as wizards and witches, fairies of both genders, dwarfs, giants, dragons, and so on. In the plot of the supernatural folktale, heroes and their opponents resort to various magic devices—objects or animals, and reversals of form and character—in order to achieve their aims. In realistic folktales, the powers of the heroes do not exceed regular human powers, and the mechanisms activating the folktale are from the realm of fate (a couple separated by fate is reunited), the cleverness of the characters, and miracles performed by the divine power in the religion within which the story is narrated or by its emissaries (such as Elijah in the Jewish folktale).

As Lüthi showed, makers and narrators of folktales—particularly supernatural ones—emphasized the text's aesthetic dimensions. In many cultures, such as Arab culture, folktales are sometimes told in rhymed prose. Their plot structure may be complex, and may also include a frame narrative and subplots. Non-narrative genres, such as riddles, may also appear in them. Folktales are usually long and told by particularly gifted narrators. In European literature, they have been transformed into the literary art form known as "the artistic folktale" (*Kunstmärchen*).[13]

The folktale is also characterized by a clear focus on aesthetic aspects of the contents, including lavish descriptions of the heroes' clothing, a bright palette of colors, and glittering and rich metals. The result is a representation of a world declaring itself "artistic" and denying a direct connection between the real world and its representation.

The mode in which the chain of tales discussed in this chapter is presented within the midrashic corpus clearly attests that the editors of *Lamentations Rabbah* were aware of the genre connections between them. The analysis of the tales will point to both formal and content aspects in the concept of genre. The presence of these tales in a midrashic work so deeply focused on the destruction of the Temple sheds light on the notion of the genre from a further angle, namely, the unity of the spiritual and emotional experience spurring the creation of a genre in folk literature. This approach was most concisely formulated by André Jolles in his *Einfache Formen*.[14] Jolles described the emergence of a genre as a process whereby linguistic materials originating in individual and collective experiences coalesce into simple, fixed forms, each one bearing the mark of the dominant experience that prompted it in the first place. Jolles formulated these basic experiences as a series of simple questions. The myth's concern is—*where from?* The legend addresses the question—*who?* And the riddle deals with the question—*how?*

Loss and destruction are central themes in rabbinic literature. Stories about individual lives often turn into cosmic accounts about the destruction of the Temple, much as the story of the Temple's destruction can perhaps be told only through the personal experiences of individuals. The sages of the Midrash and the Talmud may have displayed a special stroke of genius when they succeeded in translating these harsh experiences of personal and collective loss into an artistic form including a uniquely powerful element of play.

Tradition has pointed to "rules of the game" in midrashic discourse, and refers to them as "rules for drawing inferences from the Torah." The rules of the game in aggadic Midrash are looser than those imposed on halakhic inferences. The behavioral and legal rules of Halakha are inferred through Hillel's seven rules, through R. Ishmael's thirteen rules, but never through all the thirty-two rules ascribed to R. Eliezer b. Yose ha-Gelili (and even these do not exhaust all the rules found in aggadic Midrash).[15] The last in the latter series of rules are specific to aggadic homilies, and definitely suffused with elements of play, puns, and games of meaning. For instance, included in the list ascribed to R. Eliezer b. Yose ha-Gelili are parables, allusions, *gematria* (the numerical value of letters), and *notarikon* (acronyms or the breakup of words). Saul Lieberman has already shown that these rules, as well as more "serious" ones used in the drawing of halakhic inferences, such as *gezerah shavah* (comparisons between similar expressions) or *binyan av* (a construction posing a premise as a basis for inferences), are all close to the hermeneutical techniques prevalent in Greek and Hellenistic culture.[16] The playful structure of the discourse thus points not only to the sophisticated creativity of the Hebrew Aramaic authors of Late Antiquity, but also to their openness to the cultural creativity in the world surrounding them, and to their ability to draw from it new elements for their own game.

Lamentations Rabbah is, naturally, the midrashic text where the experiences of loss and destruction are expressed most directly, as its basic text is the biblical Book of Lamentations. In the open and creative spiritual world reflected in Palestinian midrashic literature, the severe mourning experience does not mar the amusement with narrative creations that include more than a sprinkling of fun.

At the core of this work of sorrow is a chain of stories cleverly and artfully designed, made up of eleven riddle tales. Only readers who are totally oblivious to the playful dimension of aggadic Midrash could consider their presence here bizarre. The following reading of these tales is informed by the insight that play and humor may be the most powerful modes of spiritual survival at times of extreme sorrow and loss.[17] Hence, the riddle tales in *Lamentations Rabbah* should not be considered "comic relief" meant to sweeten the bitterness of the rest of the Midrash, which includes tales of martyrdom and great suffering. Nor should they be seen as deviating from the main theme of the book. In their own playful way, they deal with the central issue of the Midrash, namely, with the question "How?" (*Eikha*). This question is transformed into a series of riddles dealing with the central themes of human existence. One of the versions of this question (at the beginning of chapter 1 and, in a more minor way, in proem 4) carries echoes of God's hide-and-seek with Adam among the trees of Eden, by extrapolating the orthographic identity of the two words in Hebrew (*Eikha?* [How?] and *Ayeka?* [Where are you?]). Through this parallel, the first chapter of *Lamentations Rabbah* outlines the historiosophical argument that locates the destruction within a moral system of crime and punishment, as a response to human sins resembling those of Adam. This argument, however, does not remain unquestioned in the course of the riddle tales, as we will see below.[18]

Folk narratives are a powerful instrument for offering a valid spiritual alternative to the doctrine of retribution as an interpretation of the historical plight of the times. Anonymity and the collective character of folk literature, together with its capacity to allow expression to "other," non-elitist groups, turn it into a convenient instrument for conveying feelings and opinions that are not necessarily compatible with ideological trends dominant in the textual establishment of rabbinic literature. One instance of such a trend is the historiosophic argument that views the destruction of the Temple, the loss of political independence, and the human suffering caused by these historical events, as part of a justified causal chain of crimes and punishment.

A sequence of eleven riddle tales is introduced in the first section of *Lamentations Rabbah* to praise the wisdom of Jerusalem's inhabitants. The common denominator of the stories is their association with a riddle. The interpretive sequence is directly prompted by a question regarding a possible double meaning in the first verse of the Book of Lamentations: "How does the city sit solitary, that was full of people! How is she become like a widow! She that was great among the nations and princess among the provinces, how is she become a vassal!" (Lamentations 1:1). If it has already been said "full of people" (*rabbati am*), why the need for "great among the nations" (*rabbati ba-goyim*)? The hermeneutical poetics of the rabbis, which assumes that the Bible has already said it all with supreme conciseness, clashes here with the conventions of biblical poetry, which uses parallelism as one of its main devices.[19] This encounter between the different historical poetics is one of the most fruitful rabbinic instruments for drawing expanded meanings from biblical texts. The stories' original language was Aramaic:

(1) There was a man from Jerusalem who went to Athens to stay with a friend for several days. His time came [to die] and he entrusted his belongings to the man he was staying with. He told him: Should my son come to you and desire these belongings, don't give them to him unless he does three wise acts [things]. They [the Athenians] had [an agreement] that none of them would point the way to another person's house for a traveler. The son heard [of his father's death] and went there, knowing the name of the man. He came and sat at the city gate, saw a man carrying a load of wood and said, "Are you selling that wood?" He said: "Yes." He said: "Take payment and go unload it [at so-and-so's house]." He followed him until they arrived at the man's house. He [the woodcarrier] began calling for him. [The master of the house] looked through the window and asked: "What do you want?" Said he: "Come out and take the wood." He said to him: "Did I tell you to bring it to me?" He said: "It's not yours; but belongs to the one sitting behind it." He came down to ask who he was and said: "Who are you?" He said to him: "I am the son of the man from Jerusalem who died at your house." He took him in and prepared him a meal. The man had a wife, two sons, and two daughters. They sat down to eat and they brought him five young birds. He said to him: "Take them and serve." He said to him: "It is not my [role] since I am a guest." He said to him: "Give me the pleasure." He took one bird and set it before the master of the house and his wife, took another and set it before the two sons, took another and set it before the two daughters, and took two for himself. He said to him: "How have you served?" He said to him: "I said to you, did I not, that I am a guest and that it is not my [role], but I have served well in any case—you and your wife and the bird make three heads, your two sons and a bird make three heads, your two daughters and a bird make three heads, and I and two birds make three heads." In the evening he prepared a feast for him and brought him one bird. He said to him: "Take it and serve." He said to him: "It is not my [role], since I am a guest." He said to him: "Give me the pleasure." He took the head and set it before the master of the

house, took the stomach and set it before his wife, took the legs and set them before the two sons, took the wings and set them before the two daughters, and took the body and all the rest for himself. He said to him: "How have you served?" He said to him: "I told you, did I not, that it is not my [role], but I have served well in any case. I gave you the head because you are the head of the house, and the stomach and entrails to your wife because these children came from her, I gave the two legs to your two sons who are the pillars of your house, I gave the two wings to your two daughters who will take their marriage contracts and leave, and I took the body [shaped like a boat] and the rest for myself, since I will be leaving on a boat." He said to him: "Go ahead and give me my father's belongings and I will go my way." He went ahead and gave him his things and he went away.

(2) Four men of Jerusalem went to Athens and stayed with a certain man. In the evening he prepared a meal for them. While they were eating and drinking he set four beds for them, one of them damaged. After they had eaten and drunk, he said: "I have heard that the men of Jerusalem are extremely wise; I will go in and lie there among them to find out what they say." The one who was lying on the damaged bed woke up, and said: "You may think that I am lying on a bed, but I am actually lying on the ground." The second one got up and said: "Is that any wonder? The meat he gave us tasted like dog meat." The third got up and said: "Is that any wonder? The wine we drank had the taste of the grave." The fourth got up and said: "Is that any wonder? The man himself, the proprietor, is not the son of his father." At this the proprietor said: "One is telling the truth and three are lying." He rose in the morning, went to the butcher and said to him: "Take payment and give me the same meat as last night." He said to him: "I have none." He said to him: "Was there anything special about it?" He said to him: "I had a kid whose mother died and I had a nursing bitch and the kid nursed from her, and when you came in the evening and pressed me, I had no meat to give you and I slaughtered that kid and gave you the meat." At that point he said: "Two are telling the truth and two are lying." He went to the wine merchant and said to him: "Take payment and give me the same wine as last night." He said to him: "I have none." He said to him: "Was there anything special about it?" He said

to him: "I have a vine that grows on the grave of our father, and you pressed me and I had none to give you, so I gave you of that wine." At that point he said: "Three are telling the truth and one is lying." He [the proprietor] said: "This man [the proprietor himself] must go and check with his mother." He went to his mother and said to her: "Whose son am I?" She said to him: "Your father's." He said to her: "Tell me the truth, whose son am I, or I will kill you now." She said to him: "Your father could not have a child; did I not do well when I prostituted myself and brought you this property instead of letting it go to someone else?" At that point, they [the Athenians] said: "Will the men of Jerusalem come to us and make us all bastards?" They agreed that they would not take in people from Jerusalem.

(3) Some days later, another man from Jerusalem went to Athens and no one wanted to give him lodging. He went to an inn and after he had eaten and drunk he asked to sleep there. The innkeeper said to him: "We have already agreed among us that no one from Jerusalem will sleep here, until he jumps three times." He said to him: "I don't know how you jump here, so you jump first, and I will do so after you." He [the innkeeper] jumped the first time and reached the middle of the inn, he jumped a second time and reached the inn's gate, and jumped a third time and was outside the gate. The man of Jerusalem got up and shut the gate before him. Said he: "What are you doing?" He said to him: "I am doing to you what you wanted to do to me."

(4) A man from Athens went to Jerusalem, went to a school and met children there. Their teacher was not there. He asked them questions and they answered. They said to him: "We are laboring for nothing; let us agree between us that whoever is asked and fails to answer will have to give up some of his clothes." They agreed. They said to him: "You ask first, since you are an old man." He said to them: "You ask first, since you live here." They said to him: "What is this thing: nine go out and eight are complete, and twenty-four serve, and two pour, and one drinks." He could not answer so they took his clothes. He went to Rabban Yohannan ben Zakkai and said to him: "Is this how you behave in your place, stripping guests?" He said to him: "Who stripped you?" He said to him: "The children at the school." He said to him: "Did they ask you a question and you did not answer?" He told him

the story. He said to him: "Go tell them that the nine covered are the nine months of pregnancy, the eight sitting are the eight days before circumcision, the twenty-four serving are the twenty-four months that a woman nurses, the two pourers are the two nipples, and the one drinking is the baby." He went and answered them and they gave him his clothes, and they called to him: "If you had not plowed with my heifer, you would not have found out my riddle" (Judges 14:18).

(5) An Athenian went to Jerusalem and met a boy. He gave him money and said: "Go buy me cheese and eggs." When he came, he [the Athenian] said to him: "Tell me, whose eggs are these, a white hen's or a black hen's?" The boy said to him: "Tell me, whose cheese is this, of white goats or black goats?"

(6) An Athenian came to Jerusalem and met a boy. He gave him money and said to him: "Go and buy me some figs." The boy went and bought. He said to him: "Good for you." He said to him: "[Did I do this] for nothing?" He said to him: "What do you want?" He said to him: "You gave your money and I gave my legs." He said to him: "Sit down and divide them up [between us]." One was rotten and he put it aside for himself, and the good one he put aside for the guest. He said to him: "Good for you." He [the Athenian] said: "It is rightly said that the men of Jerusalem are very wise, because he knew that the money was his [mine], he chose the good one and set it aside for me." When he went, he [the boy] said to him [the Athenian]: "By your life, let us cast lots. If you win, you will take what is before me."

(7) An Athenian went to Jerusalem and met a boy. He said: "Take this money and bring me enough food so that I can eat and be satisfied and have some left to take with me." He went and brought him salt. He said to him: "Did I tell you to bring me salt?" He said to him: "You said you wanted to eat to be satisfied and have some left; by your life, there is enough for you to eat, to be satisfied, and have leftovers to take with you."

(8) An Athenian came to Jerusalem and found a broken mortar. He took it and went to a tailor. He said to him: "Sew this mortar for me." He [the tailor] took a handful of sand and said to him: "Spin threads from this, and I will sew it for you."

(9) An Athenian went to Jerusalem and met a priest. He said to him: "How much smoke will that load of wood make [when burning]?" He said to him: "When it is wet, it is all smoke, and when it is dry, a third becomes smoke, a third ash, and a third is eaten by the fire." Where had the priest learned this? From the wood of the altar.

(10) An Athenian went to Jerusalem wanting to learn wisdom. He spent three and a half years there and learned nothing. As he was about to leave, he bought a slave who was blind in one eye. The man who sold him said to him [the buyer]: "By your life, he is very wise and sees far." When they had gone some distance from the city gate, he [the slave] said to him: "Let's go that we may overtake that caravan in front of us." He said to him: "What caravan in front of us?" He said to him: "There is a she-camel blind in one eye, and she has twins in her womb, and is carrying two skins, one of wine on this side and one of vinegar on that side, and the camel-driver is a Gentile, and it is four miles away." He said to him: "How do you know that she is blind in one eye?" He said to him: "From the grass that she grazes on one side, but not on the other." "How do you know that she has twins in her womb?" He said to him: "I saw, where she lay down, the tracks of both of them." "And how do you know that she is carrying a skin of wine on one side and a skin of vinegar on the other?" He said to him: "From the dripping, since wine seeps [into the ground] but vinegar seethes." "And how do you know that the camel-driver is a Gentile?" He said to him: "Because a Gentile urinates on the road, and a Jew does not." "And how do you know that it is four miles away?" He said to him: "From the hoof-marks, since a camel's hooves can be recognized for up to four miles, but farther than four miles they cannot be recognized."

(11) There was an Athenian who made fun of Jerusalemites. They said: "Who will bring him to us?" One of them said: "I will bring him with his head shaven." He went to Athens and pretended that one of his sandals was torn as he was walking in the market. He [the man from Jerusalem] gave him one *tremis* and told him: "Go fix it for me." He [the Athenian] asked him: "Are these sandals expensive where you come from?" He told him: "When they are expensive they cost ten dinars, and when they are cheap they cost eight dinars." He said to him: "If I were to bring a stock of sandals there would I be able to sell

them?" He said to him: "Yes, but go there without me." So he did. When he came to the city gates he sent for him [the man of Jerusalem who had been to Athens]. He came out to him and pretended to be concerned about his well-being. He said: "What can we do with you? We have an agreement among us that no stranger may bring anything to sell here unless he shaves his head." He said to him: "What do I care, I'll shave my head and sell my load." He went and shaved his head. He went in, sat in the middle of the marketplace and spread his sandals before him. One man came up to him and asked: "How much is this sandal?" He said: "Ten dinars." He said to him: "Who has ever seen a sandal for ten dinars?," hit him over the head and went. He got up and sat in another place, another man came and said to him: "How much is this sandal?" He said: "Eight dinars." He hit him over the head, and he went and sat in another place. Everyone who passed by did the same to him, until they injured his head. Then he came to [the man of Jerusalem] and said to him: "Do I owe you for all this evil?" He said to him: "From now on don't ever make fun of the people of Jerusalem."— *Lamentations Rabbah* 1:1

Without question, this collection of riddles is not only one of the clearest conceptualizations of generic coherence in *Lamentations Rabbah*, but one of the most cohesive such collections in the entire corpus of rabbinic literature. The high level of cohesiveness is manifest in the style—in the repetition of certain idioms—and in the narrative art—in the recurrence of narrative situations where the people of Jerusalem present Athenians in a ridiculous or derisive light, in the marks of the genre in the riddle tales, and so forth. Their distinctly folk-literary character has drawn the attention of folklorists, and a number of studies have been devoted to them.[20] Most of these studies have dealt with comparative aspects, correlating them to corresponding traditions in other cultures, especially those of India and Arabia. Their presence in the text is thus a cogent sign of the communication between the Jews of Late Antiquity and other cultures with which they were in contact. Unlike most tales of confrontation, and especially those in *Lamentations Rabbah*, where the themes of the Roman oppression and the unsuccessful Jewish uprisings against it are central, this confrontation is designed for Jews to win.

Narratives, and especially orally transmitted ones, are often the arena where the losers in military and political struggles have the upper hand.

These tales thus convey the paradox of a narrative victory in the midst of an experience of physical and political destruction. The existential and experiential character of the riddle tale, however, manages to shatter the narrated victory of both riddlers and solvers.[21] The narrative confrontations in which Jerusalemites act out their self-image as the wisest people of Late Antiquity are consistently staged with Athenians, whose city was known as the center of cultured wisdom from days of old, and even up to that very time, rather than with Romans, who had conquered Palestine and destroyed the Temple.[22] The struggle, then, is for the crown of wisdom itself rather than as a symbol of political domination.

The riddle genre presents categories, meddles them, reconstitutes them, and constantly reenacts their inner collapse.[23] Riddles thus truly express the chaotic and desperate wavering between stable, collective self-assurance, gained through the rabbis' perception of themselves as the bearers of true wisdom—contrary, for instance, to the Athenians—and the threat of individual and collective annihilation. The riddle tales in *Lamentations Rabbah* do include intense images of loss and impotence, which in themselves are a mockery of any doctrine of retribution surely unsuited to situations where individuals have no control over their fate. It is exactly the presence of riddle tales and other genres of folk literature that makes it impossible for rabbinic literature to barricade itself behind the safety of uniform and authoritative conventions, creating a pervasively skeptical subversion against a potentially totalitarian monotheism.

❦

A discussion of these tales as part of the Midrash on the one hand, and as part of the international tradition of folktales on the other, raises questions at least along four dimensions: (1) What is the generic character of the stories? (2) What is the status of these tales in this Midrash, and in rabbinic literature in general? (3) What is the meaning of these stories within their midrashic context? (4) What is the position of these stories within the international folktale tradition?

The riddle is a specific literary and folkloric genre.[24] It is usually relatively short; the text has two parts—the riddle and its solution, performed as part of a social event in which the "riddler" presents the riddle to the "riddlee," and the "riddling" event takes place.[25]

Pagis distinguishes between the *riddle* itself, which is a text, and the *riddling*: "the fundamental characteristic of the riddle that sets it apart from other genres, for two main reasons: its function in posing a challenge, either in public or in private (this is the *riddling situation*) and its verbal design, that is, the text's ability to pose a challenge (this is the *riddling potential*)."[26]

Riddles need not always be exclusively verbal and, as Pagis shows, may include pictures—as is often the case in folk narrative and in children's riddlings—or an iconic or metaphorical act requiring explication.[27] Riddles including pictures are called "rebuses"[28] and, in the context of the Hebrew literary riddle, these were perfected into the specific form of the "emblem riddle."[29] Similarly, it is possible to use the term "action riddles" for riddles in which an act supplies the hint of the solution. In addition to riddles considered "true riddles,"[30] there are riddles where solutions do not depend on information intimated in the riddle itself but rather on general or specific contextual information. These riddles, where knowledge of the specific context to which the riddler is referring—such as Samson's riddle in the biblical Book of Judges—are known as "neck riddles."[31]

The literary and folkloristic tradition contains many stories where riddles are interwoven in various ways. Following Pagis's terminology, we may distinguish between *riddling narratives*, in which the riddler, the riddlee, the riddle, and the solution are all included in the narrative itself, and *riddle narratives*, which include only the riddle, while the riddler is the narrator and the riddlee is a character external to the story (as is the riddler himself). The riddling situation is identical in this case to the narrating situation. The solution is to become evident from within the narrative or through some external information, and it would therefore be correct to distinguish, *mutatis mutandis*, between "true" and "untrue" riddle narratives. Many "riddle narratives" are embedded in frame narratives, as in the Indian Vetala stories or "Vampire Tales."[32]

In the sequence of stories discussed here, all the stories are riddling narratives by the above definition. Some of the stories only border on being true riddling narratives since the act described in them, although closely connected to the riddle, is rather a challenge or a test. The close relation between these tests and riddles is revealed in the structural similarity between typical riddle narratives and those closer to test narratives, and in the interlacing of the two types in a single coherent story sequence. We might also mention here the links with biblical and post-biblical traditions of two typical riddling narratives: the story of Samson, and the story of King Solomon and the Queen of Sheba.

In the first story of the present chain, where the Jerusalemite first accomplishes the task of finding the Athenian's house without knowing the address and then divides up birds in two separate meals, all the riddles are non-verbal. The riddler's identity in this story remains equivocal: Is the riddler the Athenian, who assigns the tasks following the father's will, or is the riddler perhaps the son, who performs the task in a cryptic and enigmatic fashion, itself requiring solution? The story is thus very close to a "neck riddle," where the task itself sometimes involves the invention of a riddle that cannot be figured out by the person assigning the task.[33] In stories including "neck riddles," the character put to the test usually bets on his/her life or on the life of someone very close. Thus, in tale type AT 500, known as *Rumpelstilzchen* from its name in the Grimm tales, the king's wife is about to lose her son if she fails to guess the strange name of the dwarf who helped her to weave gold from linen.[34]

In fact, it is his dying father who puts the Jerusalemite to the test rather than the Athenian, who is merely an emissary. The riddling situation does not entail a bet on the son's life but on his father's legacy. Nevertheless, a further message appears to be implied here: the father, being a Jerusalemite, purposely left an enigmatic will because he knew that his son, a Jerusalemite, would be wiser than the proprietor. The father could therefore be sure that the enigmatic will would leave the fortune to his son rather than to the Athenian. The son, then, who is the ultimate solver, carries out his father's intention and solves the riddle, which is also the riddle of his own identity as a Jerusalemite and as entitled to the inheritance. The Athenian is the mediating riddler, who poses to the son from Jerusalem a series of riddles involving actions: concealing his address, serving up five birds to be divided among seven diners, and serving up one big bird to all the diners. The readers do not know for sure, until the end of the story, whether the Athenian riddler knew the correct mathematical or symbolic answer. We feel, however, that the Athenian had no idea of how his guest would perform the tasks he assigned to him, since in both meals he ended up the loser, receiving less food.

At first glance, the riddler in the story in which the four men of Jerusalem lodge at the Athenian's house would seem to be the Athenian, and the riddles once again riddles of action in the form of the bed, food, drink, and identity of the Athenian. The services provided to the guests are not what they seem: the proprietor himself offers a damaged bed and, without his knowledge, provides food—originating in a dog, drink—originating in a grave, a proprietor—whose identity is changed.

But an additional enigmatic reversal is once again created within the story, with the apparent solutions presenting the host with new riddles, which he solves with the help of contextual information. In the end, these riddles bring him to a process of *anagnorisis*, self-knowledge through the solution of riddles (in his case, knowledge that is for him tragic).[35] From this point of view, this story, more than the other stories in the cycle, exhausts the possible existential and psychological dimensions of riddle narratives, in the form of "solve the riddle and know thyself." This story, where the solution ends with self-knowledge, is essentially close to the classic riddle story of all times, where the solver of the riddle also reaches a tragic understanding of his own identity, namely, the Oedipus story.[36]

Of all the stories in the cycle, the one farthest from the riddle genre is the story of the jumps. Like the concluding tale, however, where Athenians are made to look ridiculous, it recalls the typical conclusion of the riddling situation, when the riddlee fails to solve the riddle and is expelled by the public or the riddler in shame. In societies where popular riddling developed into a ritual, this expulsion assumes a symbolic dimension, such as the expulsion to Hymylä, "land of laughter" in Finnish riddling culture.[37]

The riddle included in the story where the pupils confront the Athenian appears in later midrashic tradition in the *Midrash on Proverbs* as one of the riddles that the Queen of Sheba posed to Solomon.[38] This is the most explicit riddling tale in the sequence, as it includes a full verbal riddle and its verbal solution. This example also conveys the association between the riddles in *Lamentations Rabbah* and the classic tradition of the Hebrew riddle, through the mention of the verse from the story of Samson's riddle that was solved by the Philistines.

It is worth noting that, in Samson's story too, as well as in the story of Solomon and the Queen of Sheba, the riddling is tied to a national and cultural opposition. In addition, in the two stories originating in the Bible, the sexual opposition is prominent. In four of the stories in the midrashic chain, in addition to the national (Jerusalem-Athens) opposition, there is an age (children-adults) opposition that strongly emphasizes the superiority of Jerusalemites. The adult Athenian requires the assistance of an adult Jerusalemite to save himself from failing before the children of Jerusalem. The age opposition is so prominent in this story that it almost seems as if the two adults have a shared interest when Rabban Yohannan b. Zakkai helps the Athenian to escape the plight in which he finds himself after the encounter with the children. This stress on the age opposition at the expense of the national one suggests that the plot of this particular riddle tale is less obliged to the ideological frame binding the cycle as a whole. This exception, however, highlights even more the consistent dominance of the Athens-Jerusalem opposition in all the other stories, an opposition that actually appears in this story as well. In the three stories that follow, the superiority of the children of Jerusalem in explaining enigmatic tasks is revealed in a surprising way. In these stories—as in the two longer and more developed stories that open the series—we also find an abbreviated version of the same enigmatic turnabout in which riddlee turns into riddler and the Athenians are presented as foolish.[39]

Jerusalem is the scene of most stories in the *Lamentations Rabbah* sequence, and is consistently described as a large city of teeming markets and active schools. The wisdom of Jerusalemites is treated as a renowned sociocultural fact. In the context of a Midrash about destruction, this also suggests a great longing for the city that was destroyed. The inner world of the stories, however, does not display sadness and, instead, the city and its inhabitants are still fully alive.

When asked about the burning of wood, the Jerusalem priest bases his answer on his unique experience as a priest. The riddler is therefore presenting here a kind of reversed neck riddle, since the riddlee is the one to have sole access to the necessary information; at all events, the question raised in the story lacks true riddling potential.

The pattern in which apparent answers turn, by an enigmatic reversal, into actual questions, is also found in the story of the one-eyed slave. This pattern, crucial to these stories, reveals a fundamentally enigmatic attitude toward certainty, any certainty, toward reality, and toward truth. Although the division of roles between riddler and riddlee prevails in all the narratives, this particular reversal demonstrates the relativity of each of these roles in any given situation. It also suggests the possibility that roles might be reversed not only in riddling situations, but even in sharper and more "realistic" human oppositions, such as conqueror and conquered, victor and vanquished, and so on. A short story, the sixth in the above sequence, in which the Athenian sends a Jerusalem boy to buy figs, succinctly conveys the arbitrariness of these role reversals in human existence. The boy gave the Athenian the good fig and took the rotten one. When the Athenian applauded his wisdom, he answered: "By your life, let us cast lots. If you win, you will take what is before me." Casting lots is linked, by association, with a situation of destruction, according to the verse from Joel that was quoted in the story about the children of Zadok the priest that was discussed in Chapter 2. At a deeper level, however, casting lots is also linked to an enigma that cannot be resolved through rational means, and goes on troubling us even after its more limited and abbreviated expression in the riddle genre has been solved.[40]

Riddling situations embedded in a narrative become, therefore, a mirror within a mirror, a box within a box, a reflection within a reflection. The emphatic reflexivity revealed in riddling tales explains why, as Abrahams has pointed out: "Riddles within stories seem central to an understanding of all 'true riddles.'"[41]

In the last tale, the eleventh in the sequence, the riddle tale genre is almost completely hidden, and the pattern of the "trickster novella,"[42] leading to the Athenian's humiliation, overshadows the riddle structure almost completely. The concluding words of the story once again reconnect with the homiletic framework by expounding the first verse of Lamentations, "Great among the nations—great in knowledge."

ॐ

As noted, folk literature that is part of an ancient literature such as that of the rabbis usually lacks a concrete performance context. Nevertheless, we can communicate with a wider cultural context through texts associated with the one we are examining, *inter-texts* or *co-texts* perceived as *con-texts*.[43] Constructing the context by means of co-texts naturally begins by turning to texts that are as close as possible, and then broadening the scope to more distant ones. Brief allusions to relevant biblical texts were noted above—the story of Samson in the Book of Judges and the story of Solomon and the Queen of Sheba in Kings I.

The initial relevant co-texts concerning the riddle stories in *Lamentations Rabbah* are the parallel versions of the narrative types found in the present sequence of stories in other rabbinic works.

As mentioned earlier, *Lamentations Rabbah* is available in two printed editions, the ordinary edition of *Midrash Rabbah* and the Solomon Buber edition. The whole corpus of riddle tales is found in both editions and in most manuscript traditions, with some minor and unimportant differences in the order of presentation. Since the tales in *Lamentations Rabbah* do seem to be a coherent compilation, the examination of their separate existence as isolated stories in other texts of rabbinic literature could prove fruitful.

The most interesting text for comparison, and also the earliest of all texts outside *Lamentations Rabbah*, is in Tractate Sanhedrin in the Babylonian Talmud. In the printed version of the Talmud (104a–b), there is a story about identifying the characteristics of a camel, its burden, and its driver by their tracks. The Talmudic text in which this story appears opens with an aggadic passage that is also quoted at the opening of chapter 1 in *Lamentations Rabbah*:

> He expounded to them "How [*Eikha*] does the city sit solitary" (Lamentations 1:1). Rabba said in the name of Rabbi Yohannan: "Why were Israel punished that a lamentation [*Eikha*] was said about them—because they transgressed the thirty six prohibitions in the Torah that cut them off from God, etc."—BT Sanhedrin 104a

The numerical value of the Hebrew letters in the word *Eikha* is thirty-six. The Talmudic text includes many homilies on the word *Eikha* (which opens the Book of Lamentations), largely in the same wording as those found in *Lamentations Rabbah* in the chapter where the riddle tales appear. After expounding the verse "how is she become like a widow," the Babylonian Talmud reads:

> "Great among nations—princess of countries." Rabba said in the name of Rabbi Yohannan: "Wherever they go they are made ministers to their masters." Our rabbis taught: "Two men were taken prisoner on Mount Carmel and their captor walked behind them. One of them said to his companion: 'The camel walking before us is blind in one eye and loaded with two skins, one of wine and one of oil, and two men are driving it, one a Jew and the other a Gentile.' [Their captor] said to them: 'You stiff-necked people! How do you know?' They said to him: 'The camel eats the grass on the side it sees and on the side it does not see it does not eat, and it is loaded with two skins, one of wine

and one of oil; the one of wine drips and seeps [into the ground], and the one of oil drips and floats [on the ground], and the two men driving it, one is a Gentile and one is a Jew, the Gentile relieves himself on the road and the Jew relieves himself on the side of the road.' He ran after them and found it to be as they had said. He came and kissed them on the head and brought them to his house and made a great feast for them and danced before them and said: 'Blessed is He who chose Abraham's seed and gave them of his wisdom, and wherever they go they are made ministers to their masters.' And he let them go and [they went] to their houses in peace."

Following this story are additional passages and stories that also appear in *Lamentations Rabbah*.

When we compare this story to the parallel version in the riddle tales in *Lamentations Rabbah*, the first striking difference is that the story in the Palestinian Midrash takes place in Jerusalem before the destruction of the Temple, whereas here the scene is Mount Carmel. After the destruction of the Temple and of Jerusalem, the rabbis established study centers in the northern part of Palestine, where Mount Carmel is.[44]

The riddle tale from the Babylonian Talmud follows the stylizing tendency characteristic of many Babylonian versions of stories of the destruction. It removes them from their specific, concrete humanity and turns them into ideological summaries of the historical past, as was noted in Chapter 2 in the comparison between the Palestinian and Babylonian versions of the stories about the children of Zadok the priest. Instead of the *Lamentations Rabbah* story about a one-eyed Jerusalemite sold as a slave to an Athenian, the Babylonian Talmud tells us about "two men who were taken prisoner." Echoes of a paradigmatic summary of the history of the Jewish people can also be heard in the words of the captor, "stiff-necked people," in a clear allusion to the biblical verses dealing with the story of the golden calf. The sequence of verses including the expression begins: "And the Lord said to Moses, I have seen this people, and, behold, it is a stiff-necked people: now therefore let me alone, that my wrath may burn against them, and that I may consume them" (Exodus 32:9–10). And later: "And when the people heard these evil tidings, they mourned. . . . For the Lord had said to Moses, Say to the children of Israel, You are a stiff-necked people: I will come up into the midst of thee for a moment and consume thee" (Exodus 33:4–5). And finally: "And Moses made haste, and bowed his head toward the earth, and worshipped. And he said, If now I have found favor in thy sight, O Lord, let my Lord, I pray thee, go among us; for it is a stiff-necked people; and pardon our iniquity and our sin, and take us for thy inheritance" (Exodus 34:8–9).

The use of this idiom to describe the people of Israel recurs in the Prophets and in the Books of Kings, but it first appears in the sequence of the verses describing the story of the golden calf, and this is also the relevant association for the use of the idiom in the present story.[45] The significance of the order of the occurrences of the idiom in the story in Exodus is that punishment follows sin, but forgiveness will also bloom from the same root. This minor story thus becomes a concise reflection of the familiar rabbinic historiosophic pattern: sin and punishment, followed by repentance and forgiveness. Quoting a biblical text pregnant with known ideological implications illustrates the generative potential of a biblical verse, and here even of a mere biblical idiom, to create meanings in rabbinical texts. Verses constitute more or less fixed nuclei of meaning, and serve as foci for the various plot structures with a similar message.[46]

In some Talmudic manuscripts the story of the clever captives appears together with another story from the sequence of riddle tales in *Lamentations Rabbah*. This collocation sheds new light on the intertextual relations between the version of the story in the Palestinian Midrash and that in the Babylonian Talmud. Following is the story as it appears in the Munich manuscript, which is the oldest complete manuscript of the Talmud, dating from the fourteenth century.[47] The story appears immediately after the story about the two prisoners found in the printed version of the Babylonian Talmud.

And he would dance before them. They said to him: "It seems to us that our master looks like the king's hangman." He went and asked his mother and said to her: "If you admit, all the better, and if not, I must kill you." She said to him that her husband had left her under the bridal canopy, and the king's hangman laid with her and she conceived. He brought them meat and when they smelled it they said: "This meat tastes like dog meat." He went and asked his mother and said to her: "If you admit, all the better, and if not, I will kill you." She said to him: "A lamb's mother died and she nursed from the dog." He brought them wine and they said to him: "This wine has the taste of a dead man." He went and asked his mother and said to her: "If you admit, all the better, and if not I will kill you." She said to him: "This is wine from a vine that grows on the grave of your father." He went and kissed them on their heads and said: "Blessed be God who chose," etc.—TB Sanhedrin 104a–b (Munich Ms., chap. 11)

The comparison between this story from the Munich manuscript of the Babylonian Talmud and the parallel version in the Palestinian aggadic Midrash points to a pattern similar to that revealed by the comparison between the Babylonian version and the *Lamentations Rabbah* version of the story about the two children of Zadok the priest. The Palestinian text adopts a precise style that highlights the human uniqueness of the event described, a harmonious narrative rhythm, and a variegated dialogue, where the proprietor addresses every question to the relevant character—the wine merchant, the butcher, and the mother. In contrast, in the Talmudic version, all the questions are addressed to the mother.[48] The advantage of the midrashic story is particularly evident in the order of the narration, with the most serious flaw, the proprietor's ignoble ancestry, coming at the end of the series rather than at the beginning. This order, which recurs in most versions of the story, creates an effect of gradual increase. We may speculate that the reversal of the order in the Talmudic version, when the episode of the proprietor's ancestry is put forward, is due to the fact that the story opens with the proprietor's dance that pointed to his inherited characteristics. There is a slight, charming logical flaw in the version found in the Munich manuscript, which uses the word "bridal canopy" to describe the wedding ceremony of a woman who, according to the story, is not Jewish, a mistake that was noticed and corrected by another copier.[49] The ending in the Talmudic story is also slightly illogical—the proprietor, who has just been told of his bastard ancestry, blesses those who have disclosed it. The mother's mention of his father's grave also seems extremely inappropriate. The midrashic story, which ends with the proprietor's anger, seems better suited to human nature.

The joint appearance of two of the riddling tales from the *Lamentations Rabbah* sequence in the Babylonian Talmud may simply indicate that *Lamentations Rabbah* is the original source of these stories. It could also attest, however, to the (oral?) existence of a coherent genre tradition of riddle tales in the culture of the times, when one story creates immediate associations to additional tales in the chain sharing the same genre tradition.[50]

∽

Is there a unique ideological meaning that is attained in *Lamentations Rabbah* through the inclusion of riddle tales?

"R. Judah and R. Nehemiah—R. Judah says, 'The word *eikha* is a word of reproof' and R. Nehemiah says, 'The word *eikha* is a word of lament'" (*Lamentations Rabbah* 1). At its core, this Midrash spans these two understandings of the word *eikha*. *Lamentations Rabbah* is, above all, a Midrash of mourning and of a search for the meaning of mourning, an attempt to represent in various ways the experience of loss. The explanations lead to reproof and to the presentation of a world that is divinely, cosmically ordained; a world-view in which loss is placed within the framework of a certain logic—perhaps not always intelligible to human beings—regarding events, reality, existence. The religious answer is engaged in an effort to breathe meaning into the loss, and to make it part of a vision of the world as an ordered entity that obeys certain laws, and can be predicted and justified. The structure of the argument may therefore be compared to a riddle: an apparent inconsistency is replaced by a consistent structure once the solution is provided, to be further replaced by an enigma for which no solution exists.

Yet *Lamentations Rabbah* is also a text in which loss becomes an independent existential entity that breaks free of logic, as the lasting enigma escapes the boundaries of the solved riddle. The poetic imagery allows loss, as it were, to speak in its own language.

The first chapter of the Midrash opens with homilies on letters and *gematria*, all of which show the destruction of the Temple as a quid pro quo retribution for the sins of the people, constructing a framework of rationality, acceptance, and order. The text then moves on to a parable of a king who had a son, and then to an explication of the parable in terms of God mourning his people, his son, and resorting to human ways of mourning to give meaning to his world. The loss draws its emotional effect from the human experience, and the object of its anger and comfort is the God who destroys and orders the world. The loss also breaks the bounds of order;

human and God face each other, each reflecting the other's mourning, each one feeling the other's loss through their own. Not subject and object, but two subjects touching each other with the searing experience of loss. Through her own loss, the mourning person may come to know God, and in the reflection of the two subjects gazing at each other, she also knows herself. She thus stands before the knowledge of the No-God, dreading or serene. Dreading, serene.

Lamentations Rabbah is an exegetic Midrash. Its order is thus dictated by the order of the verses in the Book of Lamentations. But the verses are like rungs in a ladder, and those who climb from rung to rung pause in the empty spaces between, which are flooded by turbulence, irrationality, and, at times, the unexpected. Between the verses, the Midrash is not committed to any law. The rungs of the verses, providing support between the empty spaces, are safe enough for climbers to dare stretch their legs and attempt the next gaping adventure.

The subject, then, is loss. Loss takes many forms, in the world and for humanity. Life could be said to go from loss to loss, transforming one into another. When the human being turns from the darkness of loss to the glare of loss, life becomes an attempt to understand one loss through another, an attempt to understand the God within loss and the loss within God. The nothingness.

Why do the riddle stories appear in the first chapter of *Lamentations Rabbah*? Were there only a single story here, or even two, it might be possible to dismiss the entire matter as part of the anthologizing approach of the author of the Midrash, who may have been carried away by a motif. But a series of eleven stories, immediately followed by stories of dream interpretations, shows, I believe, that this is not a tangent but the very substance. The riddle stories emerge as a poetic response to the verse "great among nations," interpreting it to mean "great in knowledge." They react to the opposition between "us" and "them," between Jerusalem and Athens, between what stood and survived and what is destroyed and lost. By telling of the life of Jerusalem before the destruction, the stories recreate what has been lost, not only to enhance the pain of its absence but also to awaken joy at what once was. In so doing, the stories suggest various images of loss in the imaginary life: a father dies abroad and bequeaths his son a legacy; the son sails to a distant land to seek his inheritance. A Jerusalemite sleeps on a broken bed until he lies on the ground, which is an act of mourning. Meat that tastes like dog meat comes from a lamb whose mother died and was then nursed by a dog before being slaughtered. This image, in and by itself, is a powerful icon of orphanhood, of powerlessness, of cruel fate. Moreover, the wine that tastes of the grave grew on the grave of the vintner's father. This image brings together that which brings joy with that which destroys all joy. The fear of extinction is what moved the mother of the Athenian host to give birth to a bastard son. Ignorance brings the son close to matricide. From the moment the secret is revealed, the son will forever live with the anxiety of alienation.

The boy from Jerusalem offers salt to the Athenian as food—a substance that is a necessary condition of existence and becomes lethal when alone. Salt of the earth, but also the salt sown on the destroyed city. A pillar of salt. Salt rubbed in wounds. And the broken mortar will never be whole again— just as it is impossible to spin thread from sand. The powerful impossibility of the word "if." One does not know where one came from or where one is going, just as it is impossible to know which egg was laid by a white hen, and what cheese was made from the milk of a black goat. Fire consumes wood when it is dry, not wet. Dry and wet. Life and death. "The fire and the wood," Isaac being led to the sacrifice. The greatest riddle of them all: nine go out, eight come in, two pour, one drinks, and twenty-four serve. The solution: pregnancy, birth, circumcision, nursing, and weaning. The wisdom of many in one, one which becomes many. Filling and emptying in an endless chain. Separation after separation. From the mouths of babes, young children pose this riddle, a riddle posed to the wisest of all men by his mistress that comes from afar and then returns.[51]

The order of things is not fixed; it changes from version to version. The scenes are fixed: images of loss, icons of absence, portraits of nothingness.

Who sees farthest? The one-eyed man. Who is most free? The slave led by his master. The camel has gone, and only the tracks remain. And the man who brings expensive sandals to Jerusalem, the city of the wandering Jew, the eternal cobbler, may find his sandals remain unworn, abandoned.

"The psychological motivations are not relevant to our discussion, which concerns the nature of the genre, but they are very obvious in reality," says

Dan Pagis.[52] The psychological motivations of riddles in stories in general, including those in the Midrash, are usually exposed through the stories in which they appear. In the riddle tales in *Lamentations Rabbah*, the loss assumes form in pictures, images, and plots. The theme of loss fits the inner nature, I would even say, the logical nature, of the riddle. A riddle is a riddle as long as it has no solution. As soon as a solution is given, the riddle is gone.[53] This is an irreversible process. Yet the riddling story puts this irreversible process in a paradoxical situation that makes it almost tolerable. A story, as fiction, may be told countless times, each time bringing back the protagonist, who is the object of our identification, to a previous state in which the riddle still exists. The riddle tale allows us to oscillate between no solution and no riddle, between riddle and solution; to be in touch with all the possibilities and survive.

"Riddles have a specific relation to desire."[54] Riddles at wedding ceremonies are bridesmaids to an irreversible process: two become one, virginity is lost.[55] The two will always be, whether united or separated, touched and seared by loss. The riddle is fundamentally erotic; it is structured to join the separated, to connect the disconnected. It is built on dropping hints, flirting with the riddlee, reaching consummation and relief in momentary harmony. In this the riddle, like Eros, touches death, and has a place in the ritual of mourning. "The word *eikha* is a word of lament"—and such is the rhetoric of lamentation from earliest times, rhyming questions about what was and cannot be brought back: "Where?" "Why?" "When?" "Who?"

The Book of Lamentations also opens with a question, "*Eikha?*" (How?). The riddle tales are a continuation of this question of questions. They dissect the question of the destruction into small riddles. They turn the unbearable loss into more fragmented but more personal pictures. They comfort through riddles that can be solved, unlike the riddle of existence and loss that remains unanswered.

The *Eikha* question rhymes in the Midrash with God's question to Adam in Eden: "*Ayeka?*" (Where are you?) When question is weighed against question, the suffering is explained, as it were, as punishment for sin. Yet, from within the heart of the riddle, a question is addressed to God: the historical content of this question—why was the Temple destroyed?—is transposed to the existential level—why is there undeserved suffering? It is not only modern man who walks in the garden and calls out to his God "Where are you?" Those who created, composed, mined from within themselves the midrashic tales of *Lamentations Rabbah*, also called to their God with the question *"Eikha?—Ayeka?"*

❧

In this chapter, I discussed folk literature in Palestinian rabbinic texts focusing on genre and, in this case, on the realistic folktale that is also a riddle tale. The heroes in these tales are unnamed, almost typological (Jerusalemite, Athenian), their time beyond time and fundamentally different from the time of the narrators and editors, since it precedes the destruction of the Temple. Jerusalem goes on functioning as the symbolic never-never land of the folktales, even in the later tradition of Jewish folk narratives in the languages of exile.[56] The midrashic context, however, ex-territorializes the Jerusalem of the folktale from the fictional isolation that, to some extent, prevails in the stories, and connects it to the destroyed historical Jerusalem.

4 THE COMPARATIVE CONTEXT OF FOLK NARRATIVES IN THE AGGADIC MIDRASH

FOLK NARRATIVE AS INTERCULTURAL DISCOURSE

FOLK NARRATIVES IN aggadic Midrashim convey the immediate cultural context of the narrators, namely, Palestine at the end of the Roman and the beginning of the Byzantine periods. Yet folk narratives, recognized for their cultural and linguistic mobility, may also indicate links between their society of origin and other cultures. This chapter places the folk narratives of rabbinic literature within a broader geographic and historical perspective, focusing on the comparative context.

Dov Noy has suggested a methodological framework for the study of folk narratives in Midrashim in general, and of their comparative aspects in particular.[1] Like most scholars of folklore educated in the 1940s and 1950s, Noy was trained in the tradition of the geographic-historical school. This school, which represents the main comparative trend in the study of folk literature, dates its rise to the end of the last century, and was influenced by the evolutionary approach to culture studies, as well as by philological methods used in the research of classical and religious texts. In its systematic formulations, this school defined its goal as the study of the "tale type," an archetypal plot shared by different cultures beyond space and time. The aim of research was to determine a postulated original form of the narrative type, tracing its wanderings over languages and cultures.[2]

The emphasis that comparative research had placed on the diachronic dimension and on the changes that stories undergo in the course of time has recently lessened under the influence of other scholarly approaches. Vladimir Propp's formalism has directed attention to the narratological constructs of folk narratives, and to mechanisms characterizing specific genres.[3] Functionalism, which approaches culture in the context of social functions, has stressed social aspects in folk literature, such as the roles of the narrator and the audience in the shaping of this literature, and its dependence on the broader social system.[4] Structuralism has unveiled deep structures of the mind, leading research to focus more and more on the human and existential significance of folk literature.[5] In a seminal paper where he analyzed the adaptation of international tale type to Jewish culture, creating ecotypes (oikotypes), Noy added other theoretical influences, both formal and structural, to the geographic-historical method.[6] The "animal language" tale type becomes, in Jewish tradition, a story about the verse "Cast thy bread upon the waters." Noy examined the variation of motifs in the context of the plot, summarizing his conclusions in three "rules," purportedly typical of this adaptation, the ecotypification process: (1) the main changes appear at the opening and closure of the story; (2) through wordplay, a unique link is created between the story and Hebrew (or another Jewish language); and (3) the narrative plot is associated with Jewish cultural elements, such as the above-noted reference to the biblical verse.[7]

In this chapter, I return to the riddle tales in *Lamentations Rabbah* 1. These tales were translated verbatim in the previous chapter, where I discussed mainly three aspects: the definition of the genre, including the riddle tale and the "riddling" situation; the tales' position in the Talmudic-midrashic tradition; and their meaning in the context of a Midrash about the destruction of the Temple. In the present chapter, I situate these stories within the context of international folk literature. Relying on the assumption that popular narratives might point to connections between cultures, our comparative concern will be directed mainly toward cultures that had maintained connections with that of the rabbis of Late Antiquity. Not surprisingly, international tale types found in rabbinic literature are particularly widespread in civilizations geographically and culturally close to Roman and Byzantine Palestine. This comparative study, however, cannot ignore large gaps in the information currently (or ever) available about written texts preserved from antiquity, and even larger gaps in orally transmitted material. We have no choice, therefore, but to forgo attempts to trace direct and unilateral paths of influence. Rather than concentrating on the vertical transmission of stories (from one generation to another), atten tion will be focused on processes of horizontal transmission, intergroup communication, and cultural contact in general. We will also touch on hermeneutical questions, in line with assumptions presented and applied in previous chapters.

A comparative examination of midrashic folktales enables us to see Midrash in its broader cultural context. Traces of motifs and tale types from other cultures, over different periods, also suggest possible lines of contact between Midrash and other cultures, in addition to those discernible in the transmission of specific stories.

Two main forms of borrowing can be discerned. The first is the borrowing of an isolated story, or even an isolated motif. This type of borrowing draws attention to specific sections of the midrashic work, while stressing the dynamism and mobility of folk elements in the work as a whole. The broad intertextual links of Midrash literature are also thereby exposed, within the corpus itself, as well as with literary bodies beyond Jewish culture and the Hebrew or Aramaic languages. The focus on partial elements, such as motifs, emphasizes the essential multivocality of this text. It also highlights the fact that midrashic works, although all have been edited, at least to some extent, draw on a broad range of cultural and social sources.

The second form of borrowing is that between literary works that were particularly widespread in various types of anonymous literature, such as the rabbinical Midrashim discussed here, and anthologies of stories dating from the Middle Ages onward.[8]

∽

In the chain of eleven riddle tales in *Lamentations Rabbah*, three have parallel versions, often recorded in writing, in other cultures. The second and the tenth tales in the sequence are the most interesting for the comparative concerns raised here. The first tale also appears in the comparative material, and will be mentioned briefly below.

The second tale tells a story about four men from Jerusalem who went to Athens, dined, and stayed at an inn. The innkeeper listens to their conversation, which poses to him three riddles: the meat they ate tastes like dog meat, the wine they drank had the taste of the grave, and the innkeeper is not his father's son. The answers to the riddles: the kid slaughtered for the meal had lost its mother and nursed from a bitch, the wine was made from a vine growing on the grave of the vintner's father, and the innkeeper was born a bastard. The innkeeper solves the riddles one by one, and finally solves the most puzzling one, bearing on his own identity. The tenth tale is also often found in other cultural settings: an Athenian goes to Jerusalem seeking wisdom and learns nothing, but buys a slave blind in one eye who, according to the seller, can see far. The slave solves the riddles of the tracks and claims that a caravan is before them, with a she-camel blind in one eye and pregnant with twins, carrying on one side a sack of wine and on the other a sack of vinegar.

Out of the eleven, these two are the most typical "riddling" stories, in that they include an explicit riddle and its solution as part of the plot.[9] The story about the four men from Jerusalem is a better specimen of this genre, as it also includes the stage of testing the answers for accuracy, whereas the story about the one-eyed slave ends with the decoding of the signs.

The first story in the sequence has fewer parallel versions. The riddling mechanism in this story is particularly complex: a man from Jerusalem died in Athens and entrusted his belongings to an innkeeper to give to his son, who would be coming from Jerusalem, contingent on the son performing three acts of wisdom. The son overcomes the first problem, of his ignorance about the innkeeper's address, and twice in the course of two meals divides a bird in a way attesting to his sagacity. The two divisions entail riddles that the host cannot solve, and the man from Jerusalem is expected to provide answers showing proof of his keen mind. At the first meal, he divides five birds: one goes to the owner and his wife, one to the two sons, the two daughters receive one, and the guest himself two. The answer is that the number of diners and the number of birds consistently add up to three. At the second meal he divides one bird: the owner gets the head, the wife the stomach, the sons the legs, the daughters the wings, and for himself he takes the body. In this case the solution is symbolic: the owner is the head of the household, the wife carried the children inside her, the sons are the pillars of the house, and the daughters will fly away with their husbands, while the guest came by boat and will return by boat, which he seems to be comparing to the shape of the fowl.

In the fourth riddle tale in the sequence of eleven, children ask an Athenian a question. The Athenian seeks help from R. Yohannan b. Zakkai, to avoid having to give his clothes to the children in return for a solution. The riddle in this tale is identical to one of those that, according to a later midrashic tradition, the Queen of Sheba had posed to King Solomon.[10] The Jewish cultural context of this tale (with an allusion to circumcision), as well as its links with Hebrew texts (a verse about Samson from the biblical Book of Judges), may serve to explain the lack of any parallel versions of this riddling story, even in cultural settings close to Jewish culture.

∾

Of all the available parallel versions of the riddling tales included in *Lamentations Rabbah*, none precedes the Midrash.[11] India and Arabia are the two cultures where ancient texts of this type have survived. The story about the fastidious diners appears in an Indian anthology. In Arab tradition, stories about the diners and the story about the one-eyed slave are particularly prevalent, and the two tales are usually connected, resembling a link that is also found in Jewish sources in the manuscript version of TB Sanhedrin.[12] The slave story usually precedes the one about the diners, and both are usually joined together in one plot, as is the case in the Babylonian Talmud.

Let us first consider the Indian tradition, which is more distant, and its similarities and differences with the midrashic story. In the history of comparative research on folk literature, Indian folk narrative occupies a special place. Following the publication of the Indian *Panchatantra* by the German scholar Theodor Benfey in 1859, European folklorists proceeded to endorse a perception of India as the cradle of folk literature and, above all, as the birthplace of classic fictional genres, such as the folktale and the riddle. Even today, when scholars understand that this perception had emerged due to a dearth of written evidence about these genres in other cultures, Benfey's claim has remained with us as a general intuition. It is not a concern of this discussion, however, to establish criteria of time precedence regarding these stories.

The tale about the four diners appears in the Sanskrit anthology *Katha Sarit Sagara*, and is the eighth in the twenty-five tales of the Vetala.[13] These stories are a separate collection within a larger anthology. The frame narrative tells the story of a king who must carry back and forth a corpse entered by a Vetala, a kind of vampire or magic soul that nests in corpses, acts through them, and mainly speaks through them. The Vetala tells the king tales ending in riddles, which the king must solve. Questions are usually ambiguous, pointing to multiple ways of perceiving reality. The king's answers expose the limitations of human perception by sealing, with a clear-cut response, a question opening up toward infinity. The Vetala, therefore, releases the king from its presence only at the end of twenty-four stories, when the king's answer is a silence that actually conveys his knowledge, a knowledge which the king either cannot, or does not know how to convey in words.

The frame narrative unfolds in a magical, or perhaps demonic, world. No active mythical powers are present in this world, and no specific historical reality is reflected. Three sons of a Brahmin are all far too fastidious to bring to their father a turtle for sacrifice. The three sons are sensitive to food, women, and beds. The rice served to the first is indeed revealed to be, as he claims, a crop grown on a graveyard; the beautiful woman brought to the second was nursed on goat's milk; the one sensitive to beds sleeps on seven mattresses and discovers, when rising, a wound caused by a hair at the bottom of the mattress. Who is the most sensitive? asks the Vetala, and King Trivikramasena answers: the third, because the others could have attained information through someone, while the sensitivity of the third son is demonstratively that of his own body. This solution is paradoxical, anchored in the physical, in a story that is actually focused on the problematic of a soul seeking haven in a body.

Commenting on this story, Penzer draws a distinction between two main motifs: the motif of sensitivity and knowledge of the essence, and the motif of fastidiousness and overindulgence. In my view, this distinction does not follow from the Indian tale itself but from Penzer's acquaintance with stories from other cultures, and particularly with Arab ones. This Indian story, as well as another one close to it in the anthology—dealing with the exaggerated fastidiousness of the king's three wives, hurt by the fall of a flower, the rays of the moon, and the sound of physical work[14]—is not concerned with knowledge as an intellectual category. Instead, it deals with the perception of the world through the delicate and noble inwardness of the special individual. This sensibility, expressed in the turning of the individual's inner core toward the full variety of the world, is a frequent motif in the Indian anthology that includes our story. Without claiming that the Indian variant of this tale type is unique, we may say that Indian culture clearly abounds with stories resembling this one in genre, content, and style.

In his introduction to the French translation of the Vetala stories, Louis Renou hinted to the frequency, in ancient Veda literature, of riddling situations that people are asked to solve at their peril.[15] Elsewhere, he also pointed to the centrality of the enigma in Indian culture, a concept that seems to me broader than that of the riddle. The enigma is an instrument for the linguistic actualization of multiple meanings, a mechanism for semantic distinctions and their reorganization, which Renou considered specifically Indian.[16]

Whereas the parallel tales preserved in writing in the ancient Indian tradition are relatively few, Arab tradition offers many parallel versions, adaptations, and intimations of this tale. As in India, in Arabia too, this story has deep roots in oral tradition, and generally appears in two different contexts. One is that of the folktale, as in A Thousand Nights and A Night[17]; the other is the historical context, as in genealogies and ancestry stories about the prophet Muhammad, to which most of the versions that have reached us belong.[18] Arab tradition remains stable and consistent in most details, and it is only because of the shift to the folktale genre that some details differ in the story that appears in A Thousand Nights and A Night.

The Arab material, both in the folktales and in the genealogies, indicates more direct cultural contacts with the Lamentations Rabbah versions than with the Indian one. This is perfectly natural, given the geographical proximity between the Arabs and the authors of the Midrash.

The story, as it appears in the writings of the tenth-century historian Masoudi (d. 956), can be summed up as follows: Nazar Abu-Ayad Ibn-Muadda had four sons: Ayad, Anmar, Rabiah, and Muthir. The father left an enigmatic will, stating that each son's share in the legacy would be determined by a color code. He also ordered his sons to consult Af'a the Djourhami if they faced problems when dividing the inheritance. The sons set out on their way to the Djourhami, the ruler of Najran. On the way they meet a man who has lost his camel and the brothers, each one in turn, describe the camel's attributes: one eye, no tail, limps, wild. The camel's owner claims they are the robbers, and all proceed to be tried at the Djourhami's court. After the brothers explain how they deciphered the tracks, the camel's owner is sent on his way and they stay on as the Djourhami's guests. The host appoints a slave to listen to them. During dinner, the eldest son says the honey is the sweetest on earth because it had been in the body of a large animal (a rather clear allusion to Samson's riddle); the second praises the tenderness of the meat, because the kid had been nursed by a bitch; the third says the wine is the best and most aromatic, made from a vine that had grown on a grave(!); and the fourth says their host, although the best, is not his father's son. The Djourhami checks up on the information, and all the brothers had said turns out to be true. He helps them to divide the estate and they return home.[19]

The signs of cultural contacts are many. First, both the Hebrew and Arab story mention the practice of interpreting clues and tracks, widespread in nomadic Arab tribes, where members are famous for their scouting talents even today. The story also appears in the writings of the historian Tabari (d. 923), an older contemporary of Masoudi. In Zotenberg's edition of Tabari's chronicle, the identification of tracks in the desert is mentioned as a scientific pursuit, and considered a form of divination known as *Bab a-Tazkin*.[20] Authors of the Midrash also knew about the art of reading tracks, at which Arabs had excelled even before the texts so far cited had been written. This knowledge is reflected in the famous story about Rabbah bar bar Hana and the Arab who knows how to make out roads and distances in the desert by the quality of the dust (TB Bava Bathra 73b). The Arab in this story is called Taya, a name for Arabs elsewhere in rabbinic literature, as well as the name of a large tribe in the Arab peninsula (Al-Taya in Arabic) at the time. A similar motif appears in *Lamentations Rabbah* itself, in the tale about the birth of the Messiah who was swept away by *ruhin ve-al'olin* (winds and storms).[21] The Arab in that story knows how to decipher a code embodied in the behavior of animals, and interprets the lowing of the Jew's ox first as a warning about the destruction of the Temple, and then as the harbinger of the Messiah's birth. Unlike the story about the tracks, where the slave from Jerusalem is the one who deciphers the code, in the story about the birth of the Messiah it is the Jew who is unable to interpret the signs, while the Arab is the one who does.

Contrary to the Indian version of the diners' story in *Lamentations Rabbah*, the Arab texts deal with a concrete world, with decisions being made on the basis of tangible signs. The issue at stake is the partition of the estate and the division of authority, and even the camel that left the tracks becomes part of the negotiation in a civil trial. The world rests on signs and certainties, on tribal and patriarchal authority. The sons' knowledge of occult matters does not follow from their sensitivity or their subtlety, but from their expertise in the empirical study of the occult. The story ends with etiological details, which explain the names of the sons' children and the roles assigned to the representatives of all clans for generations to come on the basis of details from the narrative plot.

In later oral Arab tradition, the chronicle element linking this story to the history of Mecca and to the prophet Muhammad disappears. At the same time, the ordeal element of the trial that the heroes are expected to undergo so as to attain their inheritance, as well as the inheritance motif itself, become more prominent. The legendary character of the story as rooted in reality and even in historical circumstances is also thereby lost, making room for the novella, the folktale, and the fiction.

In a tale recorded in the spoken Arabic of Tunis, a father leaves a will stating that only two of his three sons will inherit his fortune. The genre of this story is close to that of the joke, and the kadi, who is the bastard host, proposes a solution. The third brother, who had discovered the host's dubious lineage, is not entitled to share in the inheritance as he is himself a bastard—"it takes one [a bastard] to know one."[22] In this version, as in *A Thousand Nights and A Night*, the motif of wine made from a vine growing on a grave does not appear. The ban of Islamic law on wine drinking may have precluded the inclusion of this motif, suited to a pre-Islamic background, in the more popular versions. The motif of the menstruating woman appears instead, either cooking food that turns out to be tasteless (in the Tunisian story), or baking a cake whose dough turns out to be lumpy (in *A Thousand Nights and A Night*).[23] In another story, from Iraqi oral tradition, the story of the camel is told without the sequel of the dining brothers. As in the Tunisian oral tale, here too the story is about three brothers, and the father's will leaving the estate to only two of them. In the Iraqi story, the last ordeal is made harder: the judge approaches each brother privately to tell him he will have no share in the inheritance and must marry the judge's sister. The youngest, and the only one to agree, is obviously the bastard, and thus ultimately not an heir.[24] The host in this version is a cook's son, who gives his guests only food. The story concludes with the saying: "Do not open your mouth if you're wise, because walls have ears!"[25]

Differences in the way various cultures shape identical motifs come to the fore in this story, particularly in the motif of determining the identity of the host and the heirs: in the midrashic story, the act of identification is translated mainly into existential dimensions; in Arab tradition, it is linked to a specific social reality; and in Indian tradition, to a symbolic perception of reality.

We have so far noted that the Midrash views Arabs as men who decode signs from nature and from animals' behavior, and particularly as interpreters of tracks. This motif is central in the riddling story appearing both in *Lamentations Rabbah* and in Arab tradition, but Arabs, or Taya, represent additional dimensions in rabbinic Midrashim. A binary opposition emerging from the narratives of *Lamentations Rabbah* is that between a thriving city and a destroyed city, which is then displaced further onto another close opposition, namely, that between a desert and an inhabited city. When this contrast is translated into concrete narrative terms, the Arabs represent the threat that the desert poses to the inhabited city, or the appeal of the inhabited city to desert dwellers.[26] The contrast between an inhabited city and the desert is also fundamental to many Arab texts.[27] The typological contrast between Arabs as desert dwellers and Jews as city dwellers is further amplified by explicit evidence about tension and hostility between Jews and Arabs in the Roman Empire.[28] More specifically, there is evidence, which is also found in *Lamentations Rabbah*, of hatred between Jews in the Galilee and the Arab inhabitants of Palmyra.[29]

In the context of cultural contacts between Arabs and the authors of Midrash, and particularly those authors who included the folk riddling tales, one could also envisage the possibility of literary contact between a very early, pre-Islamic Arabic tradition and *Lamentations Rabbah*. I am referring to a limited body of texts written in Syriac and also found in Greek, Coptic, and Roman translations, dealing with the destruction of the city of Najran in South Arabia. This is also the city mentioned in Masoudi's version of the riddle tale about the four diners, which was summarized above.[30]

Najran, an ancient city, was considered a fertile site. Among the tribes surrounding it, El-Af'a is mentioned, which is also the name of the governor in the mentioned Masoudi story about the four diners. The city was a stop on the caravan route from South Arabia to the Mediterranean shores and, according to one tradition, was destroyed by the Roman commander Gallus.[31]

In monastic texts describing the destruction of Najran, the city is said to have been razed by Joseph du-Nuwas, a Jewish king from the South Arabian Himyarite kingdom. The event was also recorded in Himyarite inscriptions.[32] We learn from later Arab traditions that du-Nuwas went out on a punitive expedition, which ended in the destruction of Najran, as a reaction to the murder of a Jew who had refused to convert to the Christian faith of the city's dwellers.[33] The texts on torture and suffering during the destruction of this city, as well as the religious persecutions, closely resemble in spirit and in details the martyrological elements in *Lamentations Rabbah*. Thus, for instance, the suffering and sacrifice of women are prominent motifs in both works.[34]

This literary kinship between *Lamentations Rabbah* and the Najran texts sheds new light on the appearance of parallels to the midrashic riddle tales speaking about the wisdom of the people of Jerusalem in the context of Arab genealogies. It also illuminates the mention of Najran, the destroyed city, in the Arabic parallels of the midrashic tale. Indeed, in the version of the story where the name of the city appears, it is not as the city of the wise riddle-solvers but as that of the wise judge, a character that is not found at all in the midrashic tale. The city of Najran, according to the Palestinian scholar Irfan Shahid, is "the Arabian martyropolis, a place for pilgrimage for the Peninsula Arabs, and its ideal, set by martyrdom."[35] The two cities, Jerusalem and Najran, are thus linked by the riddle tales and by the martyrological ideal.

Contrary to scholars who have sought to establish the direction of the story's transmission from Arabs to Jews or vice versa,[36] I will confine myself to a more general claim: the riddle tales found in *Lamentations Rabbah* and in the Babylonian Talmud, as well as in many Arab traditions over a very long period, are part of the communication between the two cultures. Stories may have moved back and forth many times, as is common in folk narratives, bearing, in both directions, the marks of this intercultural communication. Thus, whereas in Jewish culture the motifs of deciphering clues suggested associations with Arab culture, in Arab culture the name of Najran was linked to the Jews.

This discussion of the ties linking the riddle tales in *Lamentations Rabbah* to other cultures cannot be concluded without mentioning cultural contacts with Greece. We must remember that the stories speak of a confrontation between Athens and Jerusalem. Elimelech Halevy dealt briefly with the *Lamentations Rabbah* riddle tales that had international diffusion, pointing to possible parallel Greek material. He found the most persuasive resemblance in a line from Euripides, who says regarding the interpretation of a dream, "The pillar of a family is the son" (*Ifigenia in Tauris*, line 57). But it is questionable whether this parallel could point to actual links with the story about dividing the bird.[37]

However, the perception of Athens as a city of wisdom, which comes to the fore quite prominently in these stories, had been firmly established from early times. It was thus appropriate to contend with Athens' status as perceived by the world in general, and even by Jews in the Hellenistic world, by offering an alternative ideal of wisdom—the city of Jerusalem. The saying in *Lamentations Rabbah*: "Wherever a Jerusalemite would go, a chair of learning would be offered to him," reflects a self-perception similar to that of the Greek sage, who says about Athens, his city: "And our city has left the rest of humanity so far behind in respect of intellect and speech that her pupils have become the teachers of them all."[38] Indeed, it is questionable whether this self-image of the people of Jerusalem and of Judea as a beacon of wisdom to the surrounding cultures did strike roots in the consciousness of neighboring nations, and particularly Greece, although incipient signs of such recognition are discernible several centuries previously, at the outset of the Hellenistic period.[39] Athens, however, retained its role as a center of wisdom, despite several crises in the course of this period, until after the time our Midrash was written.[40]

Another type of link may be surmised from the study of the Finnish scholar Aarne on the riddle, where he mentions an ancient Greek practice of posing riddles at mealtimes, similar to that found in the story about the division of the fowl.[41] At a later period, it is also possible to point to a reverse vector of influence, from Jerusalem to Athens. In her study on the history of lamentations in Greece, Margaret Alexiou points to the influence of the biblical books of Job and Lamentations on poetry lamenting the destruction of cities, and particularly the razing of Antioch in 443 and 523.[42] Versions of the international tale types of the *Lamentations Rabbah* riddling tales are also found in contemporary anthologies recording Greek oral traditions.[43]

This concludes, but obviously does not complete, the study of folk-narrative traditions in cultures that may be assumed to have been in contact with Palestinian culture about the time that these Midrashim were written. I found in these cultures parallel versions of the stories that were the subject of this chapter's comparative research. It is hard to point to a direct line of transmission from the Indian stories to those in the Midrash, contrary to the view in Benfey's "Indian theory" noted above. As for cultural contacts between rabbinic Midrashim and Greece, it is apparently visible mainly in the sages' unilateral relationship toward Athens, but not vice versa. The study of contacts between Arab and Hebrew stories, however, points to a mutual cultural communication that was certainly not exhausted in this survey.

∽

Stories similar in genre to those included in the chain of eleven riddle tales in *Lamentations Rabbah* are thus found in other languages and other cultures, too. Two of them appear, in a more or less stable combination, in several cultural settings. Generally, it is hard to determine whether the transmission from place to place and from language to language was oral or written. But an inquiry into an interesting and important anthology of European texts points to a unique link with this sequence of midrashic tales. Discussing this anthology will take us from the time of Midrash and its place of writing to sixteenth-century Venice. We may assume that, despite the vast distances, this anthology from another culture and in another language, was acquainted with *Lamentations Rabbah* and took several riddle tales from it. In a discussion of the intercultural discourse that developed around these riddle tales, it is certainly interesting to explore this potential channel of communication. The anthology which, as noted, was printed in Venice in the sixteenth century, is known in European literature by the abridged name of *Peregrinaggio* (The Voyage). Its full name is *Peregrinaggio di Tre Giovani Figliuoli del re di Serendippo*.[44] This work appears to be a typical example of the standard transmission course followed by narrative anthologies of the time—from the Far East, through the Eastern Mediterranean, onto the shores of Southern Europe. The mediating role played by Jewish translators in this narrative-folkloristic chain of transmission has been acknowledged. At times, their mediation entailed mutual borrowing with the tradition of Hebrew narrative, namely, to and from Hebrew.[45]

Benfey, who translated the *Peregrinaggio* from Italian into German, was, as noted, one of the leaders of the school claiming that most European folk narratives, and particularly the genres of the folktale and the novella, come from India. Benfey also viewed in this light *The Voyage of Jaffar's Sons*, which is another name for the *Peregrinaggio*, and he pointed to Persian, Arab, and even Hebrew influences on the Italian anthology. The anthology has a complex frame narrative, with the beginning resembling the story about the inheritance and the fastidious diners in the various sources. For our purposes, what is most fascinating in this work is that it includes a relatively large number of stories from the sequence of *Lamentations Rabbah* riddle tales: four of the eleven tales making up the midrashic chain. As far as I know, no other works besides the *Peregrinaggio* and *Lamentations Rabbah* contain this combination. The translator, calling himself Cristoforo Armeno (apparently a fictitious name), who praises Christianity in his introduction and seeks to know it (Is he not a Christian? Is he perhaps a convert and new to Christianity?), may have been familiar with these midrashic stories, directly or indirectly. No information is available that would allow us to decide whether the transmission from the Midrash was direct or indirect, but the existence of a link seems to me quite probable.[46]

At the beginning of the *Peregrinaggio*, and after the frame narrative, the camel and the diners stories are introduced, more or less in the order known to us.[47] The one significant change is that the motif of the host king as a bastard is replaced by the motif of a scheming minister seeking to avenge the execution of his son, who had been killed by the king. Benfey remarks in his notes that a European hand is discernible in this change.[48] In my view, it seems that the main reason for introducing this modification was that the frame narrative could not allow the ancestry of King Baharam, the noble host of the brothers from Serendib, to be tarnished.

The diners' story is followed in the anthology by a story about a salt test, which the editors and translators claim has no paragon anywhere. The task that the brothers are assigned is to eat a roomful of salt in one day. The young man eats four grains of salt in the company of a friend and the problem is considered solved, but when viewed only within this context, the solution of the riddling test is not sufficiently clear. The editors attempted to settle this issue by invoking the sanctity of salt in the ancient world on the one hand and, on the other, by alluding to the Latin saying *cum granum salis* (grain of salt) that, metaphorically, implies the adoption of a detached and humorous perspective.[49] Against these options, the riddle tale of the salt in the midrashic sequence of stories might offer a more plausible solution:

> An Athenian went to Jerusalem and met a boy. He said: "Take this money and bring me enough food that I can eat and be satiated and have some left to take with me." He went and brought him salt. He said to him: "Did I tell you to bring me salt?" He said to him: "You told me that you wanted to eat and be satiated and have some left. By your life,

you have enough to eat, to be satiated, and to have left over to take with you."—*Lamentations Rabbah* 1:1

In both cases, concepts of quantity concerning salt are different from those concerning any other material, and even a little of it is a lot.

The next task assigned to the brothers is a division, not of fowl as in *Lamentations Rabbah*, but of eggs. (The question of what came first, the chicken or the egg, seems thus appropriate in this context . . .) As in the division in the first episode of the story about the son from Jerusalem, who also embarks on a trip on his father's orders (exactly like Jaffar's sons in the *Peregrinaggio*), the solution here also rests on a mathematical calculation. Instead of the family and the guest of the midrashic story, two men appear here, the prime minister and the boy undergoing the test, as well as the queen assigning the task, who is also the future bride.[50] The solution is simple, and fits the expressly erotic milieu typical of Baroque Venice. The five eggs are divided without breaking any, as required by the task: the woman receives three, and the men receive one each, to make up three together with the two in their pants.[51]

This cluster of four stories, per se, may suffice to presume that the Midrash was indeed a source used by the Italian text. Further support for this hypothesis may also be found in the fact that the "mirror of truth" motif, which appears in the *Peregrinaggio*, also features briefly in a Hebrew book, *The Itinerary of Benjamin of Tudela*, as the editors of the German version of the *Peregrinaggio* had already noted.[52] Furthermore, the editors cite only one parallel to the frame narrative about seven palaces (among which the king wanders daily to spend time with seven different women and hear stories by seven narrators from seven provinces in his kingdom), which also appears in a Jewish source.[53]

An additional argument supports the hypothesis about the direct or indirect influence of *Lamentations Rabbah* on the *Peregrinaggio*. Rather than a textual argument, as the ones adduced so far, this one is related to the sociocultural context at the time the Italian anthology was published. In the book he devoted to the Hebrew literary riddle, Dan Pagis described groups of Jewish intellectuals in Italy, whose cultural hallmark was the ability to switch freely between Italian and Hebrew.[54] They were not only capable of reading, but could also write, in both languages. Furthermore, the ambience and the pastimes of the period mentioned in Pagis's book, as well as the remarkable interest in riddles and their solutions, are also noted in the introduction to the translation of the *Peregrinaggio* as the background of this anthology:

> Between the forfeit games, the riddle competitions and the music, they would pass the time reading together and telling stories. . . . As far as possible, the story had to be new and unknown and, if known, the telling would make it look new. . . . Many anthologies of stories owe their printing to the parlor games of these groups of cultured aristocrats.[55]

Assuming that Jews in Northern Italy, because of their active bilingualism, were able to mingle in the literary salons of the period, it is possible that one of them supplied the need for exotic, new, and unknown material through the tales of *Lamentations Rabbah*.

☙

Folk literature is both written and oral. When studying ancient texts we can only be certain about the versions preserved in writing, but we must assume the existence of innumerable oral versions that have not reached us. This assumption relies both on what is reflected in the ancient written texts themselves, and on what we know about the dynamics of folk literature in our own times. Folk narratives included in the classic works of the rabbinic period, the Midrash and both Talmuds (and particularly their aggadic sections), are one of the main sources of folk literature orally transmitted by Jews in their various languages until this day.

The riddle tales in the *Lamentations Rabbah* sequence, which appear in other cultures as parallel versions of the same tale types, were also orally transmitted in various Jewish settings and traditions. The first fifteen thousand stories recorded at the Israel Folktale Archives at Haifa University (until the summer of 1986) reveal the following: all the stories collected since Dov Noy founded the Archives in 1955, belonging to the tale types relevant to our discussion, were recorded from Jewish narrators originating in Arab countries or in Persia, or from Israeli-Arab narrators.[56] The relevant tale types in the international catalogue are: No. 655, "The Wise Brothers" (AT 655 in the conventional research notation, which will be used henceforth);

AT 655A, "The Strayed Camel and the Clever Deductions"; and AT 1533, "The Wise Carving of the Fowl."[57] Concerning the first two types, the stories at the IFA point to an established narrative tradition, which usually links the two types together; there are versions, however, where each type exists independently.

Comparative international research, then, points to an oral tradition regarding these stories, particularly in Arab culture and to some extent in Indian culture. Jewish folk tradition, therefore, even if it relies on rabbinic sources, was strengthened by the presence of an oral tradition in the surrounding non-Jewish culture. Jews living in countries where the local folk traditions did not include versions of these tales were less inclined to tell them, despite their access to the classic rabbinic versions of these stories.

Two stories, told by an Iraqi-born narrator, Yehezkel Danos, are an exact repetition of the *Lamentations Rabbah* version of these tales (IFA 7438 and AT 1533; IFA 7349 and AT 655A). The narrator (or the recorder, Mukhtar Ezra), substituted Tunis for Athens in the midrashic story. It is unclear whether this is merely an error or perhaps an attempt at actualization in the context of the multicultural encounter taking place in Israeli society, as is sometimes the case.

These versions point to a close link with Arab narrative tradition: the link between the camel story and the diners story, which is well established in Arab narrative, continues in the Jewish stories, and particularly in those stories told by Jews of Iraqi extraction.[58] It should be noted here that the two tales from *Lamentations Rabbah* discussed in Chapter 3 are already united in one plot in the Babylonian Talmud, which is also a work born in Mesopotamia. Although claiming that this represents the continuation of an ethnic-geographic tradition typical of Babylonian-Iraqi Jews would be much too daring, it deserves mention. Stories told by Iraqi Jews obviously do not repeat the tribal genealogical traditions found in classical Arab sources. The genre of the story is thus also changed, shifting from a historical legend anchored in a specific historical context to a realistic novella. This course resembles that of folk narrative in Arab oral tradition, which was written up in *A Thousand Nights and A Night* and recorded by linguists and scholars of folk literature over the last hundred years.

The fictional world in the oral tradition of Iraqi Jews is often distinctly Arabic in character, as is clear from the names and from other stories mentioned in it.[59] Thus, one story ends in a phrase formulated as a saying:

"Muhammad will inherit, Muhammad will inherit and Muhammad will not inherit" (IFA 1938; IFA 6851), and another story mentions three sons named Ali (IFA 1730). The motif of the king's or the judge's illegitimate birth, because extreme, seems to have impressed itself on popular consciousness, and even appears on its own in several fragmented versions. One story, for instance, includes a contemporary topical detail claiming that the judge's mother was given "an injection" at his birth, and the judge is therefore not his father's son! (IFA 6851). In another story, the test that the sons must undergo as a condition, as it were, for the inheritance, is to take their father's head out of the grave. Obviously, only the bastard son is ready to do this, and is thereby exposed. This is the "blood test" motif, known from Jewish medieval folk literature as well as from international folk literature.[60] In another story, the judge, who is an illegitimate son, is also a Jew—in a Moslem family! (IFA 1477). Another includes an additional episode whereby the judge's daughter, who hears the wisdom of the three brothers, exposes the thief among them by telling a tale that, quite by chance (or perhaps not by chance), also appears in the *Katha Sarit Sagara* anthology, from which we quoted one of the Indian versions above.[61]

In some of the IFA stories, the story about the camel's tracks appears as a separate unit, unrelated to the story about the four diners. These tales originate mainly in Arab tradition, and were told by Israeli Druze and Arabs.[62]

These stories are apparently not widespread among North African Jews, although they do feature in the Arab folk traditions of the Maghreb. The tale types appear in several versions, and assume their Jewish form through the characters and the details of the surrounding reality. Changes have taken place in them according to the permutation and adaptation models characterizing Jewish folk literature in North Africa. These models differ from those prevalent in Jewish folk narratives in Iraq, which tend to structure two separate worlds—an "Arab world" and a "Jewish world." This separation also indicates that these stories draw inspiration from two separate and distinct bodies of sources: Arab wisdom literature, *Adab* and *Faraj*, as opposed to traditional Jewish literature, and mainly rabbinic literature. In the stories of Moroccan Jews, on the other hand, we find that reality is structured to bring these two worlds together, with the "Jewish world" at the center. In the folk literature of Moroccan Jews, therefore, it is more common for characters and other details to be "Judaized."[63] Thus, in a Jewish story from Morocco, R. Jacob Abi-Hatsira senses that his host's wife is menstruating even before he tastes the bread she has baked (IFA 8393, as told by Moshe Sharvit); three brothers sense they are about to be fed untithed wheat (IFA 5179, as told by Amram A'mar)[64]; R. Hayyim Pinto notices that the preacher to whom he had been listening is not a Jew (IFA 7192, as told by Avner Azulai). The mechanisms of reception and regulation in each tradition, and the encounter of each local culture with textual sources of influence, are the factors that determine the differences between traditions. Jewish folktales in Morocco, therefore, are poured into the generic mold of the saint legend, which is a dominant genre in this culture.[65] The appearance of rabbis and saints in Jewish Moroccan stories concurs with the centrality of saints in the beliefs and customs of this culture.

In other cultural settings, other characters are prominent. Thus, in an IFA story told by a Persian Jew, the hero is the famous Persian poet Sa'adi, who is described as wandering on the road between the cities of Shiraz and Yazd (IFA 5886, told by Moshe Nehmad). The story, in which Sa'adi wanders along the road, sees the signs, and interprets them, is strange in the logic of its plot—the interpretation of the signs precedes their appearance in reality, and the end of the story is skeptical and sophisticated. The hero, who is drawn into a brawl because of his discovery, ends up saying: "If they ever ask me, 'Have you seen a camel?' I will definitely answer 'I have not' and that's it."[66] The narrator carefully preserved in the Hebrew version the original rhymes of the admired poet. In the Archive of the Israeli Proverb Index at the Hebrew University there are many proverbs told by Iranian Jews quoting lines from Sa'adi (and from other poets), attesting to his popularity and to the close connection between written poetry and proverbs in Iranian culture.

Following this exploration of the relatively rich folk tradition of the camel story and the diners story, and particularly in versions based on combinations of the two, a brief comment is in order concerning the story about dividing the fowl, which is less widespread in oral tradition. In most IFA stories including versions of the tale about the fowl division (AT 1533), the division is part of a larger story pointing to moral and class distinctions between two brothers or two neighbors. The good brother divides the bird on the king's table correctly and is rewarded, while the other, who is driven by his own or his wife's jealousy, fails to impress the king with his wisdom, and is then punished and humiliated.[67]

This inquiry into the narrative tradition of the *Lamentations Rabbah* riddle tales, as they were recorded in the Israel Folktale Archives, reveals oral tradition as much richer and variegated than written tradition. Fixating the text in written form smoothes the edges and tones down the colors, as it were, tightening the structure and informing the work with stability and weight, even when formerly authored in oral style by oral narrators.

∾

This chapter adopted as its point of departure comparative folkloristic research, which examines a specific narrative text in the light of parallel versions in other cultures. We engaged in traditional comparative research as an auxiliary tool, in order to answer a new type of question. Through the comparative material, I was able to outline the contours of the intercultural discourse that had prevailed between Jewish culture and that of its neighbors, particularly Arab culture, throughout history.

Two main approaches become prominent through this comparison. One is a synchronic comparison between relevant types and motifs, in which Midrash is perceived as an evolving text, originating in a particular society and reflecting its cultural contacts. When considering the Indian material included in available anthologies, we found that the spiritual ambience, and even the narrative details, were considerably distant from those in the midrashic stories. Nevertheless, because of the general similarity between plot structures, the possibility of indirect contact cannot be ruled out. Indeed, we have no way of estimating the story's various transformations and the times at which these took place. The examination of links with Greek and Hellenistic culture suggested the possibility of Greek influence, conveyed by the general notion of Jerusalem as a city of wise people, but without any reciprocal influence of midrashic motifs and narrative types on contemporary Hellenistic literature.

The comparison with Arab culture resulted in a more complex picture. Although the midrashic text clearly precedes all Arab texts known to us, several narrative motifs found in the Midrash, such as the tracks motif, would seem to indicate that these stories constituted a fixed body in the intercultural discourse of Arabs and Jews at the time, and Arab narrative traditions may have been the original source of some of these motifs.

The second research direction compares midrashic riddle tales to parallel versions of the relevant tale types in a diachronic, historical sequence. The founders of the geographic-historical school had originally aimed to discover the *Urtypus*, namely, the form of the tale type as uttered by its first narrator, but this is not the aim of the present study. And yet, the probable influence of these midrashic tales on European tradition, through a very popular anthology of folk stories first printed during the Baroque period, cannot be ignored. On the other hand, the material collected at the Israel Folktale Archives reveals that the oral folk tradition of Jews (in this case, specifically Jews from Islamic countries) did not cling to the form that these stories had assumed in the Midrash, but was changed and enriched under the influence of surrounding oral traditions. Arab oral tradition influenced some of the stories in Jewish communities in the Middle East and North Africa. Every ethnic tradition, such as that of Jews in Iraq or in Morocco, preserves unique patterns, which are dictated by its characteristic cognitive and intellectual structures and in line with its own mechanisms of cultural adaptation.

The works of folk literature discussed in this chapter show yet again that, more than scholars in most other areas, scholars of folk literature remain invariably aware that the unknown far exceeds the known. Who might surmise the thousands of encounters where the story of dividing the fowl was told by a father to his son, by one woman to another, by a man to his neighbor, by a traveling merchant to the dwellers of a hamlet along his way, and more. Each one of these encounters is a link in the story's path, not only from one generation to another but also from one culture to another. Add to them the wanderings of the books where the story was printed and we face a network of boundlessly intricate links. Therefore, clarifications of the kind that have engaged us here, shedding light on new corners of this rich network, will lead us to admit that most of it has been and will remain hidden, sheltered in the darkness of years gone by.

5 THE FOLKLORISTIC CONTEXT OF FOLK NARRATIVES IN THE AGGADIC MIDRASH

TALES OF DREAM INTERPRETATION

FOLK NARRATIVES ARE a part of literature. A mutual relationship prevails between the written literature of a society and its folk literature, including its oral sources. Folk narratives in aggadic Midrash, and in rabbinic literature in general, display this kind of mutual relationship. Folk narratives, however, are also a part of a cultural creative phenomenon that extends beyond verbal creativity, namely, folklore.

Folklore refers to a range of creative modes performed through auditory, visual, and cognitive means. *Auditory folklore* is expressed in words and melodies, and includes all the genres of folk literature—stories, rhymes, proverbs, and riddles, as well as folk songs, including the music. Folk music without lyrics is also part of auditory folklore. *Visual folklore* includes various types of folk art and material culture: the buildings and clothes, as well as the shaping of the physical environment in general. *Cognitive folklore* is manifest in popular beliefs and their concrete expression in customs and rituals. Common to all forms of creativity in folklore as a cultural phenomenon is that they are traditional and collective.[1] Folklore emerges through a process, usually unfolding in groups where long-term relationships prevail (families, peer groups, professional associations, and the like).[2] Folklore is created in the course of performance[3] and is transmitted both vertically, across generations, and horizontally, across groups. Folklore spreads through multiple distribution, resulting in a wide spectrum of variants. Over time, folklore goes through a process of accepting, rejecting, and regulating folk creations. This process evolves through a mutual relationship between knowledge and praxis, in a mode that determines folklore as a special form of creativity.[4]

The realms of folklore, abstractly divided into auditory, visual, and cognitive, materialize in reality into configurations that integrate all three in varying degrees. Most modes of folkloristic creativity involve more than one form of expression. The art of folk narrators includes both visual and auditory aspects,[5] and this is also true of other forms of folkloristic creativity. Even modes of expression that are highly differentiated in their choice of channel maintain mutual relations with other modes. Narrating a folk *legend* about a holy figure will strengthen *belief* in its powers, and the narration often takes place within a *ritual* that is part of this belief's actual practices. This ritual may also include various expressions of *folk art* linked to the narrative and to the belief, such as pictures of the holy figure, or traditional objects used in the performance of various parts of the ritual.

As far as folk literature is concerned, and particularly folk literature in aggadic Midrash, the overall folkloristic context is, on the one hand, the context for performing the works of folk literature and, on the other, the repertoire of attitudes, contents, and forms included within it. The various realms of folklore, which are undifferentiated in reality, are varying representations of thought patterns, as well as of the locus and source of these thought patterns.[6] For the purpose of our analysis we isolate units, contents, forms, modes, genres, and so on, which are not available in this form in reality and in everyday life.[7]

In this chapter, the folk narrative will be presented in its general folkloristic context through a passage from *Lamentations Rabbah* dealing with the interpretation of dreams. On the one hand, this passage is a folk narrative describing events about dream interpretation; on the other, it sheds light on a characteristic folk practice, the endeavor of dream interpretation, providing us with detailed information about its participants, its underlying beliefs, and its spiritual assumptions.

Although all cultures known to us speak of the cultural phenomenon of dreaming, the structuring of, the understanding of, and the responses to dreaming are unquestionably specific to each culture.[8] In all cultures, dreaming is a phenomenon that takes place during sleep, which the dreamer remembers upon awakening. The dream has both visual and auditory aspects. The dreamer may report the dream, usually in words, but also through pictures and movements. Most cultures view the dream as a message to be interpreted and understood. In this respect, the dream resembles the riddle, and its interpretation the answer to the riddle. The interpretation of dreams, then, is largely an interactive cultural genre, whose participants are the *dreamer*, who narrates the *dreamtext*, and the *interpreter*, who provides the *explanation*, or the meaning, of the dream. Sometimes we are also told that the meaning was actually consummated in reality. The interpretation of dreams is thus a genre with a distinctive ritual dimension.[9] Note that the dreaming itself is not part of the ritual interaction described here, and the dreamer can only report it verbally, although visual dimensions are crucial to dreaming, in addition to words and other auditory aspects. Clearly, then, dreaming as such interacts with the cultural perceptions of this phenomenon, and dreamers react to the contents and the structures characteristic of their culture, even in this intimate activity.[10]

Bringing dreams to a more or less institutionalized interpreter points to their special place in the complex signification system of the culture. Of all activities that could be called cultural, dreaming appears to me as the sole one that can only take place in absolute seclusion. We may fantasize or hallucinate in company, but we can dream only alone. Dreamers remain the exclusive source of information about their dreams, and no outside corroboration is available, as yet. The interpretation of dreams thus takes place at the junction of the most private and public realms, as is emphasized in dreams quoted in the Bible, for instance, where the dreamers are leaders and public figures, and the dreams as well as their interpretation are significant to the group as a whole, or to the entire nation. The association of dreams with a specific physical state, and their inaccessibility except through the dreamer's report, indicate that the dream takes place at the crossroads between the physical and the spiritual. That they also communicate the junction between the past and the future is manifest both in the approach to the dream as a portent of what is to come, which is rather common in the ancient world and in traditional cultures to this day, as well as in the approach to the dream as a sign of hidden contents of consciousness, which is prevalent in all schools of modern psychology and is also found, as we will see, in midrashic discourse.

This distinction, which presents dreams and their interpretation as stretched between pivotal pairs of opposites—the private and the public, the physical and the spiritual, past and future—also attests to our view of the dream as pertaining to the twilight zones of life, as a glimpse into the unknown. The juncture of past and future highlights the dream (and its interpretation) as a means for conveying a unique model of time, namely, time as multidimensional rather than as linear and necessarily two-dimensional, moving from the past to the future. The dream is thus revealed as possessing a special link with death, and powerfully conveys the yearning to communicate with the dead.

The interpretation of dreams is a folk discourse formulated in surprisingly uniform and unvarying terms over thousands of years. Much of the European folk tradition of dream interpretation relies directly on the *Oneirocritica* by Artemidorus of Daldis, a pagan Greek of the second century c.e., the most famous and most widely copied work on dream interpretation of all time.[11] Nevertheless, as is true of many other manifestations of popular and religious culture in the Roman Empire at the time the book was written, Artemidorus's book must be viewed within the context of the ancient traditions then current in the area. Written evidence of these traditions can be found in the literature of Mesopotamia and of Egypt, which has been retrieved and researched.[12]

The Jewish tradition of dream interpretation, both written and oral, cannot be understood either unless placed within the context of classical Jewish culture, which culminated in the Talmudic and midrashic literature of the Babylonian and Palestinian *amoraim*. This tradition refers back to the interpretation of dreams as found in the Bible, and elaborates on it.

Dreams in the Bible are ambiguously construed. As in the ancient world in general, dreams may be messages from God, but also from evil, demonic forces deliberately attempting to mislead the dreamer. Patriarchs and leaders were favored with divine revelation through a dream, and the most celebrated were Jacob and Joseph. Their dreams exhibit two types of dream communication—Jacob's dreams are more direct, whereas Joseph's dreams are symbolic and require more complex interpretation. These two types of dreams parallel the central distinction between message dreams and symbol dreams in Artemidorus's book. In Joseph's story, the interpretation of dreams becomes a part of the hero's personality, an act that changes Joseph's fate several times. It is thus no wonder that, in rabbinic literature, Joseph serves as the positive archetype of the interpreter. The case of Daniel proves that even a man as wicked as Nebuchadnezzar may dream true dreams, and the man of God becomes a necessary mediator between the evildoer and the divine meaning of the dream. As in the ancient East in general, the dreams recorded in writing are usually those of kings and leaders, and most have public meanings (or their private meanings for the dreamer have further public implications).

In prophetic writings, the word "dream" is used differently, often denoting the fraudulent visions of false prophets, as opposed to the visions of God's true prophets: "I have heard what the prophets said, that prophesy lies in my name, saying, I have dreamed, I have dreamed" (Jeremiah 23:25); "The prophet that has a dream, let him tell a dream; and he that has my word, let him speak my word faithfully" (Jeremiah 23:28). Jeremiah also uses the term "dream" as parallel to magic and witchcraft (27:9; 29:8), as does Zechariah (10:2). In Isaiah 29:7–8, the "dream" is an illusion, a mirage, as it is in Psalms 73:20 and in Ecclesiastes 5:2.

Rabbinic literature reveals a different, less polarized, and more variegated attitude toward dreams, their source, and their interpretation. Not only public figures and "prophets" are privy to dreams, but also simple people. This human attitude toward dreaming might be linked to the dominant consciousness of the times concerning the cessation of prophecy.[13] The contrast between dreaming and prophecy is "mediated" in the conciliating final remarks of a long passage in the Babylonian Talmud dealing with dream interpretation: "A dream is one sixtieth part of prophecy" (Berakhot 57b; the passage begins on page 55a). The following equation also appears in this passage: "Sleep is one sixtieth part of death," adding a further, perhaps circumstantial dimension to the noted connection between dreams and death. A paramount example of the dream as a bridge between the living and the dead appears in a text in TB Moed Katan 28a, reported in the name of Babylonian *amoraim*:

> Rabbi Se'orim, Rabbah's brother, used to sit before Rabbah. He saw him napping [RaShI (the eleventh-century exegete): "dying"] and said to him: Tell him [the angel of death] that he should not hurt me. Said he: Are you not his companion? [i.e., honored and intimate with him in your own right]. Said he: Since my luck is no longer with me [the time of my death has been determined] he pays no attention to me. Said he: Show yourself to me [in a dream, after your death]. He appeared to him. Said he: Did you suffer pain? [at the time of death]. He said to him: Like the bloodletter's scratch. Rabbah used to sit

before Rabbi Nahman. He saw him napping [as above]. He said to him: Tell him [as above], that he should not hurt me. Said he: Are you not an important person? [enough to say so himself]. Said he: Who is important, who is safe, who is protected? [from the angel of death in general, and from the time one's death has been determined in particular]. He said to him: Show yourself to me [as above]. He appeared to him. He said to him: Did you suffer pain? [as above]. Said he: Like pulling a hair out of milk, and if the Holy One, blessed be He, should tell me, go to that world [namely, this world] in which you were, I would not want to, because the dread is great [the fear of death, as opposed to the pain of death, which he claims is negligible].—TB Mo'ed Katan 28a

According to this story, the appearance of the dead in a dream is within the realm of possibility, to the point that those who remain in this world can ask the dead to return to them in their dreams. The dream is described as the true liminal zone between the world of the living and the world of the dead, as the event where the living can obtain information about that which is most hidden from them, namely, what happens at the time of death. Nevertheless, it is worth noting that, however reassuring these two reports about the transition from this world to the next, the Talmud felt safer bringing two reports, thus suggesting that the subjective perspective is decisive. In other words, no personal testimony can guarantee anyone's fate.

Dreams appear in rabbinic literature in both stories and discussions.[14] Midrashic texts expounding biblical passages concerning dreams obviously include many references to dreaming, its nature, and its sources. An unusually rich instance are the homilies on dreams in the story of Joseph in *Genesis Rabbah*.

In the two Talmuds and in the aggadic Midrashim there are three central texts on dream interpretation: two are Palestinian and one is Babylonian. Of the three, the Babylonian text is the longest, most complex, and most influential on the later tradition. This is the only example in ancient Hebrew literature of something resembling a book on dream interpretation, such as the one by Artemidorus mentioned above. Even Hebrew medieval books on dream interpretation rely mainly on this Talmudic text, in different arrangements.[15] This text, however, is beyond the scope of the present discussion, which is concerned with the Palestinian aggadic Midrash. The Palestinian texts, one of them in the Palestinian Talmud (Ma'aser Sheni, end of chapter 4) and the other in *Lamentations Rabbah* 1, are closely similar in content and phrasing, but differ in their textual embedding.

In the Palestinian Talmud, the sequence on dream interpretation is within a distinctly halakhic context.[16] It concerns funds set aside by someone's father for the second tithe, to be consumed at a pilgrimage to Jerusalem. After his father's death, the son could not find the money or establish with any certainty what funds had been set aside for this purpose: "So he was distressed over his father's funds. His father appeared to him in a dream: The money is this much, and it is in such and such a place. When the matter was brought before the rabbis, they said that dreams are immaterial." The ensuing argument attempts to reconcile this radical statement with that of R. Judah Ha-Nasi, who allows easier arrangements than some of the other participants in the debate for the transfer of the second tithe from one person to another, even after the first person's death. Toward this end, a series of dreams and their interpretation as told by the rabbis is then presented, all showing that the interpretations later materialize in reality. Alternatively, they are presented so as to persuade us of the truth of the messages contained in the dreams, whether directly, as in the case of the first dream, or in more symbolic language, as in most of the other dreams cited.

The contents of the next dream in the discussion are very similar to the dream which sparked the halakhic debate:

> A man came to Rabbi Yose ben Halafta and said to him: I saw in my dream that I was being told: Go to Cappadocia, and you will find your father's holdings. He said to him: Did that man's father ever go to Cappadocia? He said to him: No. He said to him: Go count ten beams inside your house and you shall find your father's holdings. Ten beams.—PT Ma'aser Sheni, chap. 4

The interpreter requests crucial contextual information from the dreamer so as to decide whether he must interpret the dream as a direct message or through symbolic means. After the dreamer's reply clarifies to R. Yose ben Halafta that a direct interpretation is out of the question, he turns to the known aggadic hermeneutical rules for interpreting the Torah, such as *gematria* (the numerical value of letters) and *notarikon* (acronyms or the breakup of words). *Kappa* is the tenth letter in the Greek alphabet, which is evidently hinted at by the journey to this foreign city. *Docia* hints at the Greek word for construction beams (δοκος). The text in the Palestinian Talmud does not explain the interpretation of the dream, nor does it tell us whether this interpretation was corroborated by the ensuing events. In the parallel versions of this dream, both in *Lamentations Rabbah* and in the Babylonian Talmud, the story ends when the father's holdings are found in the place stipulated in R. Yose's interpretation.

In the Bible, the dead do not appear in dreams. This might be a mere coincidence, but it is consistent with the almost total absence of any reference to an afterlife in the Bible. Nevertheless, it is worth noting at this point that one of the most famous texts of Late Antiquity dealing with dreaming concerns the dream of the Roman general Scipio Africanus, as told by Macrobius, in which his dead father appears.[17] Macrobius interprets the dream in the terms of neo-Platonic philosophy, and its method is therefore different from that of Talmudic-midrashic texts. But the very transformation of the dream into a tool for communicating with the dead is part of the Hellenistic–Roman spiritual world, which does include a definite perception of life after death. The dead have indeed appeared in dreams from the dawn of Greek literature, such as the appearance of the slain Patroclus in the dream of his friend Achilles.[18] An approach assuming the existence of an afterworld paralleling ours was also prevalent among the rabbis, and the dead appear in dreams found in the Palestinian aggadic Midrash and in the Babylonian Talmud.

Following these dreams, the Palestinian Talmud cites more dreams interpreted symbolically by R. Yose ben Halafta, and then by R. Ishmael ben R. Yose. These dreams also appear in *Lamentations Rabbah*, and I will deal with them below. I wish to note here the following dream: "A man came to R. Ishmael b. R. Yose and said to him: I saw in my dream that I swallowed a star. Said he: May his spirit be taken! He has killed a Jew, as it is written, 'there shall come forth a star out of Jacob'" (Numbers 24:17). This is the only dream in this text of the Palestinian Talmud where the interpretation relies on a biblical verse. Another verse, which appears in the next passage to describe the relationship between the dream and its interpretation rather than to interpret a specific dream, is: "And it came to pass, as he interpreted to us, so it was" (Genesis 41:13, spoken by Pharaoh's chief butler), and it substantiates the principle that "the dream only follows its interpretation."

On the basis of the text in the Palestinian Talmud we may draw some

inferences about the folkloristic or ethnographic context of dream interpretation in Palestine, namely, that dream interpretation was a matter that
concerned scholars at the academy. Their discourse on dream interpretation
was connected to the dominant concern of their hermeneutical discourse,
which was to expound Scripture.[19] This explains the mode chosen to represent the folkloristic context of dream interpretation as it appears in *Lamentations Rabbah*. The passage devoted to dream interpretation follows immediately after the riddle stories discussed in Chapters 3 and 4, where the
overall narrative framework is the wisdom competition between Jerusalemites and Athenians. This passage, like the riddle stories, offers a homily on
the biblical verse "she that was great among the nations" (Lamentations 1:1):
"she that is great in knowledge" (the phrase "she that was great among the
nations," which is seemingly enhancing the meaning of a previous phrase in
the verse, "[she] that was full of people," relates to the additional meaning of
greater wisdom).

Stories about dream interpretation are set in a context of intergroup
relations resembling those in the riddle stories, while competition hinges on
the validity of dream interpretation. The last riddle, which ends in the
humiliation of the Athenian who came to Jerusalem to sell sandals to trick
the Jerusalemites, closes with the sentence: "From now on don't ever make
fun of the people of Jerusalem." The next story begins as follows: "A Cuthean
[a foreigner, usually a Samaritan] who pretended to be an interpreter of
dreams, used to make fun of people." In the sequence of stories on dream
interpretation in the Palestinian Talmud, which was partly described above,
in one instance a Cuthean confronts sages engaged in dream interpretation.
He does not interpret dreams, however, in order to mock people, but invents
a dream in order "to make fun of old Jews." The would-be dream, which he
relates, is made up of various grotesque and surrealistic images. The interpreter's name is not explicitly mentioned, but the context suggests it is R.
Ishmael ben R. Yose. He exposes the deceit of the Cuthean, who made up the
dream, and tells him that he will not go unpunished. He predicts a bitter end
for him, which is corroborated by events through the formula, "And thus it
happened to him." The next dream ends in the saying quoted above, that a
dream follows its interpretation; both, therefore, grant most of the power
latent in the dream to the interpreter rather than to the dreamer. The story
about the dream that was not really a dream, and the confrontation between

the Cuthean and R. Ishmael in the Palestinian Talmud, could be viewed as the narrative core, which the narrator or the author of *Lamentations Rabbah* adopted as the main narrative framework for the stories of dream interpretation he chose to present.

The first dreamer to approach the Cuthean, who pretends to be an interpreter of dreams, tells his dream: "In my dream I saw myself sprinkling an olive tree with oil. He said to him: The olive tree is light and the oil is light, light has come to light." The positive associations with light common in popular thought leave little doubt among readers or listeners that the Cuthean is promising the dreamer a bright future. From here onward, the confrontation begins, because R. Ishmael overhears the dialogue between the dreamer and the fraudulent interpreter and retorts: "May this man's spirit be taken—he has known his mother." The interpretation of R. Ishmael (as well as that in the Palestinian Talmud) is surprising in several respects. First, it does not hinge on the dreamer's future but on his past and, in this regard, it does not resemble the pattern of dream interpretation in the ancient world that is also prevalent in today's popular culture, but rather the method of dream interpretation presented by Sigmund Freud in his revolutionary and influential work, *The Interpretation of Dreams*.[20] Much has been written about Freud's Jewish cultural ancestry, and about the influence of Jewish textual criticism on his own interpretive endeavor.[21] As far as I know, Freud never mentioned the modes of dream interpretation described in the Midrashim and the Talmuds dealing with this subject. The similarities in method, however, are striking, not least due to the focus on language, the interpretation of texts, and the linguistic associations.[22]

R. Ishmael reminds us of his distant "descendant" not only in his turn to the past, but also in the content manifest in the interpretation. Like Freud, R. Ishmael assumes that the dream represents content that consciousness rejects and represses because it transgresses conventional moral restraints. As is true of Freud, the prohibitions breached in the dream, or the actual transgressions revealed by the dream, concern the most intimate family relations and become manifest in incest wishes, or even in actual incest. In my view, however, this midrashic text is ambiguous as to whether R. Ishmael is accusing the man of actual sexual intercourse with his mother or is simply attacking him for his incestuous wishes for his mother in the past, which could not be, or were not, realized.

The Cuthean carefully repeats the interpretation he gave concerning the first dream in all the other dreams he is asked to explain, and this very repetition makes him appear mechanical and unconvincing: "Another one came to him and said: In my dream I saw one eye swallowing the other. He said, your eye is light and the other is light, light has come to light." R. Ishmael also abides by his own method: "R. Ishmael ben R. Yose said: May that man's spirit be taken, [for] he has two children and they have 'blossomed' with each other."[23] The accusation of incest is not addressed at the dreamer himself but at his children (his son and daughter in both the Babylonian and the Palestinian Talmuds). Nonetheless, the dreamer, the father, is still considered guilty and deserving of R. Ishmael's condemnation.

The symbolic interpretation of the eyes as siblings is also found in other areas of culture, in a folk-literary genre that, as noted, is related to dream interpretation: the riddle. The following riddle appears in several European languages: "Two brothers (sometimes twins) who never see each other," and the answer is, "the eyes."

The use of the expression "that man" (*ha-hu gavra* in the original Aramaic), which fulfills several functions in rabbinic language, is worth noting.[24] It may be used to designate someone whose name the speaker finds too odious to mention, as in the case of Jesus in rabbinic literature, or the speaker may sometimes use it to speak about himself. The indefiniteness of this idiom strengthens the impression of this interpretation as ambiguous, particularly concerning the identity of the sinner exposed through the dream. It must be remembered that this interpretation is not created merely through the dreamer's words, but mainly through the language of the interpreter. Would it be too daring to suggest that this text implies that everyone, including R. Ishmael, is guilty of incestuous wishes?

A further matter arising from the impreciseness of this idiom is the actual openness and vagueness of the dream's meaning. In principle, a dream has multiple meanings, generally, and not just in this specific case. Unlike the riddle, therefore, it does not invite one single solution but a more complex interpretation. The authors of Midrash, as we will see below, held strong views concerning the limits of dream interpretation and its legitimate sources.

From here onward, R. Ishmael's interpretations shift to less titillating realms. He persists, however, in his method of exposing details from the dreamer's life, whereas the Cuthean automatically promises a bright future: "Another came to him and said: In my dream I saw that I had four ears. Said he: That man shall rise to greatness and the entire world listens to his words. R. Ishmael ben R. Yose said: May that man's spirit be taken! The man is a water-carrier, two [ears] are his, and two are the ears of the amphora." The curse "May that man's spirit be taken!" is more clearly targeted here against the fraudulent interpreter, for nothing in what is revealed about the dreamer justifies such condemnation. The associative link between this and the previous dream seems to be that both pertain to the paired sense organs, shifting from the eyes to the ears.

In a more general sense, the shift is from the intimacy of family relationships and sexuality to the intimacy of the body. At this point in the text in the Munich Ms. 229 version of this Midrash, a dream appears that creates a link between the previous dreams about eyes and ears, as follows: "Another came and said to him, in my dream I saw that I had three eyes, he [the Cuthean] said, that man will see much light. R. Ishmael said to him: May that man's spirit be taken! He is a baker and two [eyes] are his, one is the eye of the furnace." The following dream relates to the last one not through a picture in the dream image but through the interpretation, which also refers to the dreamer's occupation: "Another came to him and said: In my dream I saw everyone making way for me. He said to him: You shall rise to greatness. R. Ishmael ben R. Yose said: May that man's spirit be taken! He is a collector of thorns [for fire], and when he carries his load, everyone makes way for him." As noted, the interpretations are connected to the dreams through associations. In this passage, we can see that the linking of the dreams in this particular order reveals associative connections between successive dreams.

At this point in *Lamentations Rabbah* a dream is cited, which in the Palestinian Talmud is interpreted by reference to a verse in Numbers. Here, as well, a verse is cited: "Another came to him and said: In my dream I saw that I swallowed a star. He said to him: You are light and a star is light, there is light upon light, that man saw much light. R. Ishmael ben R. Yose said: May that man's spirit be taken! He has killed a Jewish man. On what grounds is he saying so? From this: 'And he brought him outside, and said: Look now toward heaven, and count the stars, if thou be able to number them: and he said to him, So shall thy seed be'" (Genesis 15:5). The dream hinting at the slaying of a Jew carries special significance in *Lamentations Rabbah*, a work dealing with the destruction of the Temple, where national confrontation is a central theme. The verse from Genesis cited here as the basis for this interpretation is more crucial to Jewish national definition than the verse from Numbers cited in the Jerusalem Talmud, although the Genesis context is not one of confrontation, as is the one in Numbers.

A sequence of dream interpretations follows, in which R. Ishmael ben R. Yose meets someone whose dreams the Cuthean had interpreted in positive and encouraging terms. R. Ishmael asks for payment to provide a second interpretation, which the dreamer refuses to give, claiming his dream has already been explained. It then turns out that R. Ishmael's interpretation, for which the man had refused to pay, stated that the dreamer's stockpile of wheat would rot. This did actually come true, and could have been avoided. The folk-narrative character of this text does not allow us to determine conclusively whether this story indeed reflects a practice of payment in exchange for dream-interpretation services. In TB Berakhot 56a we find a story about a Babylonian dream interpreter named Bar Hedya,[25] who interpreted positively the dreams of those who paid him, and negatively the dreams of those who did not. The Babylonian *amora* Abbaye paid him, and Bar Hedya gave him a positive interpretation. Rava, Abbaye's friend and contender, did not pay. Since the story illustrates the principle that the dream follows its interpretation, many disasters overtake Rava, the worst being the death of his wife. Bar Hedya is accused of her death and is sentenced to die by four-quartering.

Interpreters at different times and places did indeed request money for their services, as is also sometimes the case today.[26] The scheme of the Cuthean noted at the beginning of the story, "to make fun of people," may intimate his intention to extract money fraudulently for false and misleading interpretations.

The story cited above from the Palestinian Talmud about the Cuthean who invents a dream in order to cheat old Jews appears here as part of a direct confrontation with R. Ishmael ben R. Yose. As scholars have noted, the order of the images in the dream and the relationship between them is clearer here than in the PT version.

The passage in the Midrash staging the confrontation between the Cuthean and Rabbi Ishmael accounts for over half of the material on dream interpretation in *Lamentations Rabbah*. It ends with a pair of dreams that close the cycle with the same olive-tree motif that opened the passage:

Another came and said to him: In my dream I saw an olive tree being planted. He said to him: You see light. Another came and said to him: I saw olives being pounded. He said to him: Prepare yourself to receive lashings. Said he: To him you said so and so, and to me you said so and so. He said to him: To him at planting time, and to you at pounding time.—*Lamentations Rabbah* 1:1

This text is abridged and corrupt, so it is not clear to begin with whether the interpreter is R. Ishmael, pursuant to the previous dream, or perhaps the Cuthean, pursuant to the overall narrative framework. The phrase "You see light" could have led us to believe that the interpreter is the Cuthean, but, according to the second and more stringent interpretation, we understand it is R. Ishmael ben R. Yose. In this case, the explicit, clearer version appears in the Palestinian Talmud:

A man came to R. Yose ben Halafta and said to him: In my dream I saw [myself] dressed in an olive wreath. He said to him: [It means] that you will rise to greatness in the future. Another one came and said: In my dream I saw [myself] dressed in an olive wreath. He said to him: [It means] that you will be lashed. Said he: To that man you said—you will rise to greatness, and to me you said—you will be lashed. Said he: That one in growth, [you] in the pounding.—PT Ma'aser Sheni, end of chap. 4

The poignancy of this story is due to the two dreamers apparently reporting the same image but receiving different interpretations. The interpreter explains the difference between them by pointing to the contextual circumstances of the dreams—one had the dream at growth time, the other during the pounding season. In the Midrash version, the context of the dream is shifted unto the dream itself, and thus loses the element of surprise at the end of the story.

After the end of this story the text shifts inward, from the interethnic realm (between the Cuthean and the sage) to the academy, the shift resembling the change in the "realms" of dream interpretation in the Palestinian Talmud, but in the opposite direction. The dreams mostly parallel those in the Palestinian Talmud, although there are interesting differences in the identity of the interpreters and in the background descriptions:

A student once sat before R. Akiva [in the printed edition and in the Munich Ms., "Rabbi Yohannan"]. R. Akiva taught him but he failed to understand. He said to him: "What is the matter with you that you do not understand?" Said he: "In my dream I saw three harsh sayings." He asked: "What are they?" Said he: "I saw 'You will not see Nissan' [the seventh month in the Jewish calendar]; 'in Adar [the sixth month] you will die'; and 'sow and you will not harvest.'" Said he: "All three are good rather than bad. 'You will not see Nissan'—[this is a] test [*nisayion*]; 'in Adar you will die'—you will die resplendent [*mehudar*] in Torah; 'sow and you will not harvest'—what you beget you do not bury."—*Lamentations Rabbah* 1:1

The author of the Midrash is revealed here as highly sensitive to the mutual relationships between the context in which the interpretation of the dream takes place and the method of interpretation. The dreamer is unable to concentrate on his studies because his thoughts are occupied with another text, the text of the dream. This is indeed a verbal rather than a visual dream, as were all those discussed in the first part of the text. It thereby resembles the first in the sequence of dreams in the Palestinian Talmud, which is also interpreted in the academy. The method of interpretation is also suited to the educational context of the academy, and stresses the verbal associations, as is also true of two other dreams interpreted by R. Akiva:

Another student once studied with R. Akiva. R. Akiva taught him but he failed to learn. He said to him: "What is the matter with you?" Said he: "In my dream I saw a harsh saying." He asked: "What did you see?" Said he: "What did I see? That there was no *pshot* in my foot" [an obscure word, for which scholars have suggested "heel," "shoe," and more]. He said to him: "This is not bad either; the holidays will come and you will find fat meat." On what does R. Akiva rely for this? On "foot for foot" [Deuteronomy 19:21].[27]—*Lamentations Rabbah* 1:1

These dreams, like the ones from TB Mo'ed Katan cited above, highlight the connection between dream interpretation and textual interpretation, which is the dominant discursive practice of the rabbis.[28] The sequence of dream interpretations involving R. Akiva ends with the dream of the man that sees his father in his dream telling him that he should go to Cappadocia.

The interpretation is the same as in the PT version discussed above, but reached in a slightly different way. And the Midrash, as usual, is more detailed than the Palestinian Talmud in explaining the interpretation: "On what [authority] does R. Akiva learn this? *Kappa*—a beam[!], *deka*—ten [in Greek]" (but in the Munich Ms. in the printed edition, closer to the Palestinian Talmud, *kappa*—twenty, *doki*—beam).

This focus on language rather than on images brings the interpretation of the dream closer to the experience of study. Modern theories of dream interpretation, psychoanalytic as well as cognitive, increasingly emphasize language as the system that generates the "grammar of dreams" on the one hand, and provides the key to their interpretation on the other.[29] In the cultural context of Judaism, when biblical verses are employed as verbal signs in the endeavor of dream interpretation, the citing of texts is also an indication of the liminal status of dream interpretation: between the private and the public, between the momentary and the traditional. This liminal status characterizes folklore in general, as is also shown in ritual practices: when a boy eight days old is circumcised in a public ceremony, the parents externalize their private experience of childbirth and turn it into a socially significant event. The newborn is thus not only brought into the Covenant of Abraham, but into the social community that is home to his parents.

Another border trespassed in the interpretation of dreams is that between the conscious and the unconscious. Introducing verses into the interpretation of dreams, and in the Babylonian Talmud into the dreams themselves,[30] denotes a cultural effort to subordinate the unconscious to distinctively cultural contents. On the one hand, this opens up the biblical text to the personal, unconscious, and chaotic world manifest in dreams. On the other hand, the holy text of the culture becomes the mythological paradigmatic repertoire of personal dreams.[31] The biblical text is sometimes seen as the contents of the collective unconscious.[32]

The last sequence of dreams in this midrashic passage raises most poignantly the problem of the relationship between dreams and reality. The contact between dreams and reality transcends here the conceptual framework set up previously by the ethnic confrontation between Cuthean and Jew, and even the institutionalized framework of the academy. For the first time in the entire passage a woman appears, as a character and as a dreamer rather than as part of a dream or its interpretation, as subject rather than object. The endeavor of dream interpretation reaches the junction where the realm of Torah study and the realm of an all-encompassing social life come together. The full intensity of the existential potential latent in the dream is exposed here, and with it the enormous dangers attendant on the disclosure of a personal dream in public, and on dream interpretation in general:

> A woman once came to Rabbi Eleazar. She said to him: "In my dream I saw the beam of the house breaking." He said to her: "That woman [meaning the dreamer] will bear a male child." And so she did. She came at another time and did not find him [R. Eleazar] there, but found his students. She said to them: "Where is your Rabbi?" They said to her: "What do you want?" She said to them: "In my dream I saw the beam of the house breaking." They said to her: "That woman will bury her husband." When she left she heard that her husband was dead and she began to scream. R. Eleazar heard her voice and said to her: "What do you want?" His students said to him: "She came and asked us about a dream." Said he to them: "And what did you tell her?" Said they: "We told her that that woman would bury her husband." Said he: "You have lost a human being. Is it not written 'And it came to pass, as he interpreted to us, so it was'?" (Genesis 41:13).—*Lamentations Rabbah* 1:1

The two interpretations of the same dream image, which vary so widely, are not explained here in the context of the dreaming, as in the olive-wreath dream that appeared above. The differences here stem from the interpreters—the rabbi as opposed to his students. But the difference between the interpretations also points to another important matter: the visual materials of the dream represent a stratum of meaning that is presented, in a certain sense, as preceding the cultural structuring of basic human concepts. The interpretations clearly articulate the cultural construction of the meaning of dreams, in this case referring to sexuality, childbirth, and death. In R. Eleazar's interpretation, the dream image is interpreted symbolically as follows: The beam is the woman's body, which must be ruptured, broken, and torn for her to bear a child. In contrast, the students' interpretation identifies the beam with the man of the house: its undoing is his death.[33] R. Eleazar's maturity and his interpretive skills enable him not only to interpret the dream image in more sophisticated terms than those of a crude phallic symbol, but also to extract from the seemingly catastrophic image the growth latent in destruction. He is also able to expose, beneath an ostensibly masculine symbol, the femininity that is always part of a full masculinity, just as masculinity, including that of the child in her womb, is part of the dreamer's femininity. The students are incapable of this, and hence their tragic mistake.

The connection between dream interpretation and personal maturity on the one hand, and Torah knowledge on the other, suggests that, in many respects, they are one and the same. The text thus continues a trend, noted above, trespassing the border between learning and the soul of the individual. The Torah is the contents of the soul, the soul is conveyed through learning.

Dreams are texts of multiple meanings, the story tells us. As long as they have not been interpreted they contain everything between life and death or, in the words of the Babylonian *amora* R. Hisda: "A dream that is not interpreted is like a letter that is not read" (TB Berakhot 55a). The interpretation of dreams is thus an act of communication similar to that involving a letter. The letter may reach its destination or it may not; it may be read or it may not; and it may even be understood in different ways. Further on in the same text we read in the name of R. Bana'ah: "There were twenty-four interpreters of dreams in Jerusalem. Once I dreamt a dream and went round to all of them and they all gave different interpretations, and all were fulfilled" (TB Berakhot 55b).

An interpretation singles out one of all the possible meanings of the dream, and determines its fate to come true. The verses from Joseph's story are the vital textual basis for substantiating this daring claim by the rabbis: "And we told him, and he interpreted to us our dreams; to each man according to his dream he did interpret. And it came to pass, as he interpreted to us, so it was; me he restored unto mine office, and him he hanged" (Genesis 41:12–13). This quotation, from the King James version of the Bible, retains the ambiguity of the Hebrew original, leaving the subject's identity unclear. The informed reader obviously knows that only Pharaoh has the authority to carry out these acts, but the verses could also be suggesting that it was the interpretation per se that led to these results. The claim is a daring one because, if dreams are a communication from above, the opportunity granted to human beings to choose from the multiplicity of meanings the only one that will materialize entails a heady mixture of freedom and responsibility. The interpreter's language, so we learn, is no less powerful than God's language during Creation—God speaks and an event unfolds, and the interpreter has his say and something comes to pass. Life and death are in the power of the tongue, as the Hebrew proverb states. The interpretation of dreams in rabbinic culture is thus not a marginal social act, as it is generally in the modern world, but a highly consequential matter.

The rabbis remain equivocal about the importance and validity of dream contents, as well as about their ontological status. We read: "And Rabbi Yohannan said: A dream follows its interpretation"; but we also read: "Their Rabbi said to them: Dreams are immaterial."[34] Note that in reaction to this second, more skeptical contention, the sequence of dreams appears in the Ma'aser Sheni tractate in the Palestinian Talmud.

The discourse on dream interpretation in Talmudic and midrashic literature is a typical instance of the structure of discourse and the structure of thought characterizing this textual corpus in general. Contrary opinions appear side by side, and a positivistic perception of the dream as a verbal message of God's will is equal in standing to a text that is utterly dismissive of dream contents as sources of information. Together with the enormous power granted to the word, and to interpretive powers in particular, runs the probably endless debate over the human ability to understand, and interpret, not merely words but the secrets of life and death.

The interpretation of dreams is a powerful cultural tool that serves to regulate relationships between social forces. The rabbinic context privileges scholars in the academy as legitimate dream interpreters. These scholars thus play a central cognitive role in the (desperate?) attempt to map out the twilight zones of uncertainty surrounding human life.

The stories about dream interpretation cited above are not the only textual materials in this Midrash connecting it to the folkloristic context. A further instance is popular belief in the existence of demons and pernicious agents, such as Ketev Meriri, who rules during the dog days of summer, and especially during the difficult period between the seventeenth of Tammuz and the ninth of Av (dates connected with the historical narrative of the destruction of the Temple in Jerusalem). The interpretation of dreams is a cultural praxis that refers to the world of popular beliefs and translates it into custom, ritual, and text.

In general, we may agree with Dodd's view on the irrational elements in Greek culture when he argues that, on the one hand, dreams parallel reality but, on the other, they complement what is missing in the world.[35] Many rabbinic interpretations articulated in paradoxical terms support this view:

"If one dreams of a funeral oration, mercy will be bestowed on him from heaven and he will be redeemed" (TB Berakhot 57a). The formula suggesting that a dream is one-sixtieth part of prophecy (TB Berakhot 57b) characterizes the dream as an experience that, fundamentally, rests on the fragmentation of a world we experience as wanting. Nothing can equal a dream, which is entirely lost on awakening, to drive home the experience of recurring loss. As was pointed out by A. J. Festugière, a scholar of religions of Late Antiquity, the interpretation of dreams "is nothing other than the course from one probability to another."[36] A different, less optimistic, turn of phrase might approach the interpretation of dreams as a move from one uncertainty to another. It is not a mere coincidence that stories of dream interpretation, like riddle stories, have a central position in *Lamentations Rabbah*, a Midrash about the destruction of the Temple, for they are intimately connected with the fundamental experience of this text.

6 THE SOCIAL CONTEXT OF FOLK NARRATIVES IN THE AGGADIC MIDRASH

THE FEMININE POWER OF LAMENTS, TALES, AND LOVE

IN THIS CHAPTER, we read folk literature in *Lamentations Rabbah* in its social context. Scholars have tended to describe the context of folk literature at two levels: the *narrative context* or the performance, which is specific to every oral work, and a broader, *sociocultural context*.[1] Given the literary character of the text before us, as well as the huge time gap separating us from the performers of these stories, any examination of the actual narrative context of folk literature in the Midrash is hardly realistic. These works, however, do bear clear marks of the social context within which they were created and eventually included in the rabbinic corpus. The present discussion about the social context of folk literature in *Lamentations Rabbah* highlights the perspective of women, both as characters in the stories and as part of the society creating the folk literature. Unlike written literature, where the contribution of men was apparently major if not exclusive, folk literature was a creative realm where women's voices were also heard.

Generally, ancient texts reflect a social order pervaded by hierarchical values, mainly patriarchal ones. The aggadic Midrashim created by Palestinian *amoraim* in a process extending approximately between the second and fifth centuries C.E. are not exceptional on this score. Aggadic Midrashim originate in the learned context of the academy,[2] reflecting the critical, scholarly study of these texts, but also in the public context of sermons addressed to the synagogue congregation.[3] Out of thousands of scholarly and narrative rabbinic traditions, the ones ascribed to women constitute exceptions proving the rule.[4]

The apparently inevitable conclusion is, therefore, that female figures and female symbols, as they are presented in Midrashim, are merely reflections of male images of women and projections of male expectations from them.

Nevertheless, and contrary to this seemingly self-evident assumption, I will attempt to suggest options for "retrieving" from the midrashic texts messages that convey the female voice of the times. In this endeavor, I rely on several assumptions. The first, which is a leitmotif of this book, assumes that the entire corpus of Talmudic-midrashic literature bears a collective (as opposed to anonymous) hallmark, and consistently incorporates forms of discourse known to us from written and oral folk literature. In the current definitions of folklore as a unique form of expression, the collective criterion is one of the most prevalent[5]; folk literature is usually created orally and perceived by both its performers and its consumers as a collective endeavor, be it of the tribe, the community, the gender group, the professional association, or the people.

Midrash, including aggadic Midrash, was shaped within educational, intellectual, and spiritual establishments that were exclusively male. Narratives about isolated exceptions, such as the character of Beruriah, tend to highlight their uniqueness.[6] Folk literature, as present in these works, points to cracks in the establishment's armor, and to a fruitful verbal exchange between this establishment and its surroundings.[7]

Works of folk literature included in aggadic Midrashim—proverbs, historical legends, biographical legends, riddles, and jokes—bear messages attesting to the collective chain of transmission that had predated the final setting of these works in written form. Folk literature is the result of a living process engaging its authors in verbal and artistic negotiations with their social and cultural surroundings. Thus, folk-literary contents formally delivered only by male agents implicitly include their female partners in the creative dialogue described above.

An additional complex of assumptions, derived from feminist interpretation, deserves mention. Feminist theory did begin by focusing on distinctively "feminine" topics, but soon developed a comprehensive approach that was no longer confined to them. As a phenomenon, folk literature overlaps and interfaces with feminist theory, particularly in its stress on anti-hierarchical and anti-authoritarian elements. Feminist assumptions encourage two main types of critical reading, which also function as hermeneutic liberation mechanisms: on the one hand, exposing patriarchal trends in the text while pointing to the oppression and discrimination of women; on the other hand, pointing to anti-patriarchal elements within the text, as well as to women's voices and other subversive elements. One could say that these two basic alternatives in feminist hermeneutics point to the half-empty glass as opposed to the half-full glass.[8] The reading suggested here oscillates, to some extent, between these two options: by highlighting the concrete multi-vocality expressed in the consistent mode of quotation,[9] it presents the interaction between patriarchal attitudes and the female attempts at subverting them in the rabbinic discourse.

The perception of folk literature presented here is not synonymous with a naive simplicity placing childish and naive trust in the Creator, nor does it avoid relating to a complex spiritual problematic. Its creators, bearers, and consumers are not usually naive or "common folk," as they were usually thought of in romantic perceptions of folk literature.

Revealing the female voice in the literature of aggadic Midrash in contexts of folk literature emphasizes the horizontal axis of intergroup transmission, as opposed to the vertical axis of intergenerational transmission. In Talmudic-midrashic literature in general, the vertical axis is a more central and more prominent structuring principle than intergroup transmission. Statements are often formulated as "X said in the name of Y." The principle of intergroup transmission prevalent in folk literature articulates the cultural encounter between the discourse created within the academy and realms of discourse outside it—with children, women, converts, strangers, members of other religions, and even supernatural creatures. The focus on folk literature can thus reveal a facet of rabbinic literature that is less obvious and fails to receive equal emphasis in its own textual self-awareness.

As noted, a close relationship prevails between folk literature in general and women, and between folk literature in aggadic Midrash and the dialogue with groups other than the rabbis themselves. It is thus not surprising to see that, in stories emphasizing feminine elements, we find various forms of dialogue between the erudite culture of the rabbinic academy and other traditions, such as mystical ones—some of them probably created within the academy itself—as well as pagan and Christian traditions.

∽

At the experiential core of Talmudic-midrashic literature, and particularly in its Palestinian version, is the destruction of the Second Temple. The emotional and cognitive world that ensued with the destruction of the Temple, with the shattering of the cosmic frames of communication between human beings and God but also between God and the world, added fuel to the fire as far as the literary works considered here are concerned. This event was also the source of the perennial search for options of redemption and revelation driving homilists and narrators.

As the Midrash that focuses first and foremost on the biblical Book of Lamentations, *Lamentations Rabbah* stresses one aspect of womanhood— the mourning woman in the figures of the widow and the bereaved mother. This emphasis on the thematic level is also echoed at the level of generating the text, in referring directly to the traditional role of women as mourners. It may be assumed that the very centrality of the subject of mourning in this text is one of the reasons for the frequent appearance of female figures and symbols, due to the cultural and traditional link between lamentation as a genre and women as its performers.[10] This female role can be understood against the cultural perception of life as a cycle, between birth and death, between mother (and midwife) and lamenter. The traditional male roles, which are linked to leadership, combat, and various forms of control, including self-control, restrain the cultural license to express sensitivities and feelings with the heightened intensity of the lament.

Gender differentiation regarding mourning and lament is stressed in the following passage:

R. Simeon b. Lakish said: "[It may be likened] to a king who had two sons. He became enraged against the first, took a stick, and thrashed him so that he writhed in agony and died, and he began to mourn for him. He became enraged against the second, and he took the stick and thrashed him so that he writhed in agony and died. He said: 'No longer have I the strength to lament over them, so call for the mourning women and let them lament over them.' Similarly, when the ten tribes were exiled, He began to lament over them: 'Hear this word which I take up against you, a lamentation, O house of Israel' (Amos 5:1); when Judah and Benjamin were exiled the Holy One, blessed be He, said, if we dare say so, 'No longer have I the strength to lament over them,' saying: 'Thus says the Lord of hosts: "Consider, and call for the mourning women, that they may come: and send for the skillful women, that they may come: and let them make haste and take up a wailing for us, that our eyes may run down with tears, and our eyelids gush out with waters" ' " (Jeremiah 9:16–17).—*Lamentations Rabbah*, proem 2b

A parable is a literary genre that presents its message concisely,[11] and therefore, we do not know the background of the father's terrible rage, in a terseness that intensifies the impression of arbitrariness. The sense of almost inhuman alienation is made greater when the first killing ends with the lament of the father-murderer. But this reader's misunderstanding and resistance are replaced by an actual sense of revulsion when, after the killing of the second, and now only, son, the father says, "No longer have I the strength to lament over them, call for the mourning women." In one of the most famous parables in rabbinic literature (*Genesis Rabbah* 22:5), R. Simeon b. Yohai precedes the parable about two combating athletes, which deals with the moral responsibility for Abel's murder, with the remark "This is hard to understand, and we dare not even say it." This statement is immediately followed by a parable that, like the one cited here from *Lamentations Rabbah*, defies God with unconcealed anger. In other words, the approach prevalent in midrashic literature views the parable as a rhetorical device that, precisely because of its obliqueness, is qualified to bear contents of skepticism, accusations against God, and self-contradiction.[12]

The frequent appearance of a cruel father figure in the parables of *Lamentations Rabbah* indicates, so it seems to me, a comprehensive theological and emotional move attempting to break the dependence on a cruel father, and seeking a mother figure with a greater potential for compassion.[13] The father's behavior in this parable is, nevertheless, especially paradoxical.

Masculinity and femininity are confronted in this parable in complex ways. The father adopts a male, power-driven model in his behavior. The power drive becomes the sole and dominant feature of his figure, when the relationship between the father and the sons is translated into direct and brutal violence. The killing is not even preceded by a fight or by any type of relationship. When we reach the moral of the story, we infer that before us is a violent and frightening figure of God, jealous and vengeful. The broader historical context of the events described through the parable does not ease this impression either. The more or less agreed historiographic approach prevalent in midrashic literature, claiming that the kingdoms of Israel and

Judah, each one in turn, sinned and were punished in the measure of their sins, cannot soften the emotional impact of the phrase "took a stick, and thrashed him so that he writhed in agony and died." Paradoxically, the king who was first characterized by one sole feature—physical violence, which is related to strength—ends his first verbal appearance by complaining of his lack of strength to lament. Namely, he who uses his strength for violence has no strength left for creating a text, and the apparently unexplained violence of the father could be interpreted as an expression of frustration at his inability to develop a dialogue.[14]

The concept of strength undergoes a deep and awesome transformation in the text. Strength, which at the opening of the parable had spurred violent physical activity, is now revealed as a necessary spiritual resource in an activity conveying emotion: the lament. The use of physical force is no longer a sign of true strength; rather, it is what drained the king of his strength to bear the consequences of his actions, to face his bereavement. Strength is no longer merely a physical essence, whose possible consequences are registered in, or sensed through, the body. Strength may also be required for activities or aptitudes that are mainly psychical or spiritual. The man who exhausted his strength in a killing that, as far as we can judge, was humanly and personally senseless, lacks the strength required to express his own feelings of bereavement concerning the consequences of his action. At this moment, he can no longer avoid turning to those who have been entrusted by cultural tradition with the keys to the gates of tears, the lamenting women. He whose strength allowed him to become a murderer, is not strong enough to contend with the mourning, and shuns the confrontation with the cognitive and moral dimensions of his act.

From a feminist perspective, this text reverses the more familiar structural pattern: *women : men :: nature : culture.*[15] The analogy links the mourning women to the traditional cultural expression of mourning in the form of lament, while the man appears as the embodiment of natural, unbridled instinct.

The interpretation suggested here locates doubt and challenge at the very core of belief, inherent to its very essence. When doubt is viewed as a light beam illuminating the realm of belief, the attitude toward the enforcement of religious laws lacking any justification in human relationships must necessarily be projected against a wider frame of reference. It most certainly challenges laws entailing injury to others, whoever they may be. Considering the contradiction immanent in belief, let us mention that in medieval Hebrew texts as different as Maimonides and the Zohar, we find the saying "Whoever is angry is as one who worships idols."[16] How, then, should a raging God be considered?

The parable, as already noted, is a central genre in *Lamentations Rabbah*, from the thirty-six proems and continuing on to the five chapters that overlap the five chapters of the biblical Book of Lamentations. Six of the seven parables in which women appear in the parable itself (rather than only in the epimythium, as in the text discussed above[17]) are royal parables, the women being the wife or the divorcée of a king.[18] In the epimythium, the king is always God and the women figures are Israel or some symbolic representation of the people, such as Knesset Israel. The parables of the whole book create an integrated system that binds the midrashic text, which is non-linear by its very nature. Rather than because of the large number of parables in this text, this paradigm apparently emerges due to their distribution at the beginning and end of chapters, creating the impression of a dominant genre. Contributing to this perception is also the stylistic uniformity of this genre, which had already developed during the *tannaitic* period (first two centuries C.E.). The subgenre of royal parables gained ascendance because of the unique status of the Song of Songs as a hermeneutical key to the Bible, turning the royal couple into permanent symbols of God and Israel.[19] In the musical key of loss and mourning, the royal parables in *Lamentations Rabbah* echo the love of Song of Songs.

❧

Stories of martyrdom are not considered a prevalent genre in rabbinic literature. The theological status of suffering is problematic, and their presentation as an example worthy of emulation and admiration is fraught with tension and ambiguity.[20] In the story of the mother and her seven sons, one of the best-known tales of martyrdom in rabbinic literature, the tension focuses on the figure of the woman, the protagonist, and on her relationships with the male characters in the story.[21] A prominent feature in the Palestinian version of the story in *Lamentations Rabbah* is that the woman's heroism is not portrayed in the stereotypical pattern of the Spartan mother who sends her sons to die for the sanctity of an ideal, in this case martyrdom.

The dialogue between essentially different realms of discourse within the ostensibly simple text of a folk narrative adds to the story's literary and ideological complexity, as well as the thematic complexity suggested above.

> This is the story of Miriam bat Tanhum, who was taken captive with her seven sons. And what did the ruler do to her? He imprisoned each one separately, brought out the eldest and said to him: "Bow before the idol, as your brothers did." Said he: "Heaven forbid, my brothers have not bowed, nor will I." Said he: "Why?" "Because it is written: 'I am the Lord thy God'" (Exodus 20:2). He had him taken out and slain. He brought out the second . . .—*Lamentations Rabbah* 1:16

The story proceeds to repeat an almost identical dialogue between the emperor and each one of the other five brothers, with the main difference between the brief episodes being their use of different verses to justify the heroic act. The main ideological message, then, is delivered in a static and monotonic discourse. The confrontation is intensified when the seventh son, the youngest of the brothers, appears before the emperor:

> He had the seventh brought in, the youngest of them, and said to him: "Bow before the idol, as your brothers did." Said he: "Heaven forbid, my brothers have not bowed, nor will I." Said he: "Why?" [Said he]: "Because we have already sworn to our God that we will not exchange Him for any other, as it is said: 'Thou hast avouched this day the Lord to be thy God' (Deuteronomy 26:17), and as we have sworn to him so He has sworn to us not to exchange us for another nation, as it is said: 'And the Lord has avouched thee this day'" (Deuteronomy 26:18). Said he: "Then I will throw this ring before the idol, and you go bring it so that they will see and say—he has obeyed the emperor's command." Said he: "Woe unto you, emperor! Should I fear you, who are flesh and blood, and should I not fear the King of kings, the Holy One, blessed be He, who is the Lord of the universe?" Said he: "Is there a God in the universe then?" Said he: "Woe unto you, emperor! Do you believe you are seeing a world without a master?" Said he: "Does your God have a mouth then?" Said he: "Of your idolatry it is written, 'They have mouths, but they cannot speak' (Psalms 115:5), whereas of our God it is written, 'By the word of the Lord were the heavens made'" (Psalms

33:6). Said he: "Does your God have eyes then?" Said he: "Of your idolatry it is written, 'Eyes have they, but they cannot see' (Psalms 115:5), whereas of our God it is written, 'The eyes of the Lord thy God are always upon it' " (Deuteronomy 11:12).—*Lamentations Rabbah* 1:16

An amazing dialogue ensues from here onward, in which the emperor asks a series of questions (all relying on verses!) as to whether the boy's God has ears, a nose, hands, legs, and a throat, and the boy, quoting one verse after another, attempts to demonstrate that his God, although he does indeed have all these limbs, is not an idol! This discussion, staged, as it were, as a theological polemic, can be partly justified by claiming that the story illustrates a type of popular thinking not necessarily compatible with absolute monotheistic abstractions. One might also see here a satirical parody, whose distorted object is a type of mystical meditation found in contemporary sources and known under the general name of *Shiur Qomah*. This type of meditation was concerned, first and foremost, with the cosmic dimensions of a divinity construed in terms of—male!—bodily limbs. Research has shown that these texts were also known outside the esoteric circles that created them, as were the literary reactions to them.[22] The starting point for these meditative practices were verses in Song of Songs, in the passage partially quoted in the above story: " 'Does your God have a throat then?' Said he: 'Of your idolatry it is written, "Nor can they speak through their throat" (Psalms 115:7), whereas of our God it is written, "His mouth is most sweet and he is altogether lovely" ' " (Song of Songs 5:16).

The repertoire of images from *Shiur Qomah* resurfaces in the concept of "attributes" in the next answer of the young son to the emperor's question:

Said he: "If he is endowed with all these attributes, why did he not rescue you as He rescued Hananiah, Mishael, and Azariah?" Said he: "Hananiah, Mishael, and Azariah were blameless, and fell into the hands of a blameless king, but we are at fault, and we have fallen into the hands of a cruel and undeserving king so that he may seek our blood, because the Holy One, blessed be He, has many bears and tigers with which to hurt us, and the Holy One, blessed be He, has only delivered us to you so as to seek our blood from you in the future." He immediately ordered him to be slain.—*Lamentations Rabbah* 1:16

So far, it was the sons, and particularly the young son, who had borne the brunt of the ideal of heroism presented in the story. From here onward, this role is transferred to the mother:

> Said his mother: "By your life, emperor, give me my son that I may kiss him and embrace him." And they gave him to her, and she bared her breasts and nursed him to fulfill what is said, "Honey and milk are under thy tongue" (Song of Songs 4:11). Said his mother: "By your life, emperor, put a sword to my throat and his together." Said he [the emperor] to her: "Heaven forbid, I will not do such thing, as it is written in your Torah, 'You shall not kill it and its young both in one day'" (Leviticus 22:28). And the young boy said to him: "You wicked man, have you fulfilled all the commandments except for this one?" Immediately they took him away from her and killed him. His mother said to him: "My son, do not fear, you are going to your brothers and you are in the bosom of Abraham our father. Tell him in my name: 'You built one altar and did not sacrifice your son, but I built seven altars and sacrificed my sons on them. More than that, for you it was a test, and for me it was in earnest.'" After he was slain, the sages estimated the age of the boy and found him to be six and a half years and two hours. At that moment, all the nations of the world cried out: "What is it with their God? He does all this to them and they are all the time slain for His sake." They said that, after several days, the woman went out of her mind, climbed up to the roof and jumped to her death, and they said after her: "A joyful mother of children" (Psalms 113:9), and the Holy Spirit says: "For these things I weep" (Lamentations 1:16).—*Lamentations Rabbah* 1:16

From the outset, the story emphasizes the centrality of the mother, who is at the focus of the confrontation with the authorities: "And what did the ruler do *to her*? . . ." When actively entering the stage, her heroism is manifest, first and foremost, in the strength of her feeling, and in the courage to demand its expression at the ultimate frontier of her sons' lives. *She* does not quote biblical verses but simply asks to kiss and embrace her son and, in a somewhat surprising move, nurses him. The act of nursing returns the mother-son relationship to its primary level, when direct bodily orality replaces the orality shaped by culture, in the form of speeches and the quoting of verses. The mother is not mute, however. Quite the contrary, she and her young son, united in the act of nursing, are two figures capable of developing a true dialogue, his more intellectual, hers more emotional. The direct orality of nursing is a kind of precondition for a living dialogue, as opposed to the static act of quoting that characterizes the other figures.[23]

Here, as opposed to the parable analyzed above, the equation *women : men :: nature : culture* does indeed prevail. Along with the tinge of melodrama, the nursing scene creates a powerful emotional motivation within the plot, which enables the sharp transition from the sons' predicament of martyrdom, marked by signs of heroism, to a dismissal of the heroic ideal by the end of the story through the mother's words to Abraham and through her own suicide.

Contrary to the mother, who does not cite verses, the one who resorts to them, rather ironically, is the emperor, to justify his refusal to allow the mother to die with her sons. The story itself thus demonstrates the usually accurate claim that quoting verses can serve many and opposing causes, and sometimes even unjust ones.

The mother's encouraging words to her young son and the bitter greetings she sends to Abraham link this story with the most archetypal story of martyrdom in Jewish tradition, the sacrifice of Isaac. Miriam's standing, above that of Abraham, has ensured her a place of honor in Jewish traditions lasting hundreds of years and extending at least over three continents. As was intimated above, however, there is more here than a contrast between female and male heroism. The figure of the mother in the story implodes the very ideal of heroism and points to its fundamental inhumanity, when the emotional intensity ultimately overrides all other considerations, and the mother commits suicide in the madness that follows her bereavement.

In light of what was said about the ideal of heroism that emerges from the story, and female heroism in particular, it seems important to devote some discussion to its history. The story about the mother and her seven sons is, as noted, one of the most famous and widespread in Jewish tradition throughout its history and in its various languages. The story first appears in two versions in the Books of Maccabees (2 and 4), in which the mother is not identified by name and is not even the central figure in the story. In the rabbinic versions of this story, the mother has a more important role, and when her name is mentioned it is usually, as here, Miriam. The name of

Hannah, which entered later folk versions, was apparently given to her by the author of the book of *Josippon*, which is dated later than classical rabbinic literature.[24]

The story of Hannah was printed in many popular editions in anthologies or separate chapbooks in various Jewish languages, including Yiddish, Judeo-Arabic (both in North Africa and in Iraq), and Judeo-Spanish, where it assumed the form of a ballad known as *romance*, which is one of the dominant generic hallmarks of this tradition.[25] Furthermore, this tale became part of the Hebrew educational repertoire early in Zionist history, and was also performed as a play by an amateur group in Ottoman Jerusalem at the beginning of the twentieth century.[26] The place of the story about the mother and the seven sons has been fixed in Israeli imagination as specifically connected with the festival of Hanukkah because of one of its central motifs—individual heroism against an oppressive ruler. The story is perceived as a story of heroism, thematically focused on the relationship between mother and sons. In the context of the local, Israeli myth of heroism, it sheds a contradictory light on the sacrifice story intimated through it.

The story about the mother and the seven sons in *Lamentations Rabbah* ends in an ironical spirit of deep contradiction between a pair of quotations, a discursive mode that we have learned to approach with some suspicion in the course of this story: "a joyful mother of children," "and the Holy Spirit says 'for these things I weep.'" As it were, the mourning of the human mother is now the fate of the Holy Spirit, whereas the mother is now joyful to play the heroine in a plot of martyrdom. This last formulation is an editorial addition referring to the context of this story in *Lamentations Rabbah*, namely, a chain of martyrological stories cited one after another and all ending with the same quotation. All these stories share a multifaceted complexity, at times even full of contradictions, typical of the charged encounter between ideology, belief, and feelings within the concise poetics of aggadic rabbinic stories.[27]

Many of the following stories also feature women figures named Miriam, and share in common a plot best described as "from zenith to nadir." Although this formulation does not appear in this text, the Aramaic idiom *me-igra ram le-bira amiqta*, which bears this meaning, is quoted in TB Hagigah 5b as a homily by R. Judah ha-Nasi on the verse in Lamentations 2:1. At one end is the widow of Doeg ben Joseph who, when the Temple was still standing, would every year bring a sacrifice of gold equal to the weight of her youngest son, and in the famine at the time of the siege of Jerusalem killed the boy with her own hands and ate his flesh (*Lamentations Rabbah* 1). The verse in Lamentations quoted in the context of this dreadful deed is: "Shall the women eat their fruit, their cherished babes?" (Lamentations 2:20). Another fall is that of Martha (an Aramean name parallel to Miriam) bat Boethus, a rich daughter from a priestly family who used to step on carpets to go from her house to the Temple on the Day of Atonement. An eyewitness, R. Eleazar ben R. Zadok, describes her tied by her tresses to the tails of dragging Roman horses (*Lamentations Rabbah* 1).[28]

The same witness also tells us about Miriam bat Nakdimon, one of the wealthy women of Jerusalem, gleaning barley left over by the horses in Acre (*Lamentations Rabbah* 1). The explicit evidence provided by this eyewitness stresses the experiential aspect of the legend genre (here in a memorate, a legend with a first-person narrator).[29] Supporting the legend are quotes from verses pointing to the historiosophic framework of the Midrash, where events are woven into a divine plan that is conveyed through the verses of Scripture. The story about Martha bat Boethus is linked to the verse, "The tender and delicate woman among you, who would not venture to set the sole of her foot upon the ground . . ." (Deuteronomy 28:56), which is preceded by the verse, "And thou shalt eat the fruit of thy own body, the flesh of thy sons, and of thy daughters, which the Lord thy God has given thee, in the siege, and in the distress, with which thy enemy shall distress thee" (28:53), and after which it is said "and towards her children whom she shall bear: for she shall eat them for want of all things in secret; because of the siege and distress, wherewith thy enemy shall distress thee in thy gates" (28:57). The choice of the verse ascribed to R. Eleazar ben R. Zadok when witnessing the distress of Miriam bat Nakdimon is particularly ironic: "O thou fairest among women, go thy way forth by the footsteps of the flock and feed thy kids . . ." (Song of Songs 1:8). The verse is distorted to make it fit his interpretation: "Do not read *gediotayikh* [thy kids] but *geviotayikh* [thy corpses]."

As noted, the juxtaposition of verses from Song of Songs with verses from the Book of Lamentations dramatically symbolizes the transformation of Knesset Israel, the wife in the standard allegorical interpretation of Song of Songs, into Jerusalem, the widow that appears throughout the Book of Lamentations.

In the statements cited in the stories of R. Eleazar ben R. Zadok, the relationships between men and women are presented in a way known from other sources in literature and the arts: the woman is a victim of violence; the man telling the story focuses his inquiring gaze on her and reacts in words, in this case, in ready-made authoritative words—biblical verses.[30]

Framing the pained stories of women named Miriam are two stories about Miriam bat Tanhum. The opening story, which precedes the story about Doeg ben Joseph's widow, is the story about the mother and the seven sons. The story closing the sequence shifts the arena to Acre, which was also the scene of the preceding story about Nakdimon's daughter. In this story, Miriam bat Tanhum is imprisoned and ransomed, and her clothes are twice washed away by the sea (*Lamentations Rabbah* 1). When "she justifies the divine decree against her," God orders the sea to return her garments. The story does not quote any verses. As the only story introducing the notion of "justifying the divine decree" in the relatively trivial context of losing clothes, it sheds an ironical light on the very validity of this concept, given the other tragic narratives that precede it.

The story of Miriam bat Tanhum and her seven sons lends itself to yet another intertextual discussion, which further emphasizes the interweaving of rabbinic literature in the pluralistic narrative universe of Late Antiquity. The discussion that follows focuses once again on the Christian–Jewish narrative dialogue. The name Miriam may be seen as a general element shared by both communities or subcultures, and its popularity in Jewish literature could be explained as inspired by early uses, such as the name of Moses' sister or the names of Hasmonean princesses. Nevertheless, it is impossible to ignore that, at the time these narratives were being told, the rabbis and the communities from which they drew their stories must have been aware of the significance of this name to Christian narrative and to Christian religious imagination.

In contrast, the name of the Christian saint Perpetua, a young woman martyred in Carthage during the early years of the third century, cannot possibly have been known to the Jews of the time, and especially in Palestine. Perpetua's story, however, so strongly resembles that of Miriam bat Tanhum, that a serious reading of both tales cannot but infer the existence of a shared narrative tradition.

When she was about twenty, Perpetua was killed by the Roman ruler of her city for her refusal to offer the imperial sacrifice, the same transgression for which Miriam's seven sons were convicted and executed. This offense differs from that related in the earlier tradition of the Maccabean martyrs, who were punished for their refusal to break Jewish, mainly dietary, laws. In both the Jewish and Christian tales, the Roman official tries to thwart their decision, further testing the firmness of their convictions. Again, in both cases the martyrs are young, and their youth is highlighted in the narrative transmitted to later generations. In a recently published study dealing with the social and cultural aspects of Perpetua's life and death, Joyce E. Salisbury argued that both the youth and the gender of the martyred heroine are inspired by the tradition of Greek novels.[31] As Salisbury shows, Perpetua may have used these novels as models in her life and in the writing of her journal. In Miriam's story, the two characteristics are split up between the mother and her sons.

It should be stressed that, initially, the mother is not herself the martyr in the rabbinic tale. Neither is she the narrative focus in the earliest Jewish sources of the tale in Maccabees 2 and 4, and it is primarily her sons who are the martyrs. But whereas the mother's role in the Greek Jewish texts concentrates on her verbal interaction with her sons and with the enemy, in the plot of the rabbinic tale she engages in several dynamic activities, thus coming to resemble Perpetua much more closely. In fact, her two main activities in the tale, the nursing of her son and her suicide at the end, parallel central motifs in Perpetua's autobiographical rendering of the final stages of her life.

Salisbury elaborates in her study on the Phoenician and Punic traditions of human sacrifice, especially child sacrifice, as a cultural element that undergoes transformation in Roman imperial culture and assumes new form in the gladiatorial games. Although she does not claim so explicitly, her argument leads to the inference that human sacrifice, and even more so the idealization of ritual suicide in the Carthaginian tradition about Dido, the founder queen of the city in Virgil's *Aeneid*, are later transformed into the Christian martyrological ideal, particularly regarding women. The suicide in the Miriam bat Tanhum legend must have been problematic for the rabbis, and a number of the parallel versions indeed omit it. Nevertheless, its preservation in enough ancient, medieval, and modern versions, shows that this final act is inherent to the Miriam bat Tanhum (later Hannah) tradition. Suicide was shunned as a rule, but as a result of Stoic inspiration,[32] it may not have been completely taboo in extremely dire circumstances, such as the one described in this tale. Another martyrological legend tells of noble men and women from Jerusalem shipped to Rome as captives in three vessels, who jumped to their death to escape sexual abuse (*Lamentations Rabbah* 1). Similarly, a group of women whose husbands had been murdered by Roman soldiers, let themselves be slaughtered by the legionaries rather than surrender to sexual exploitation (ibid.).

The present discussion will not exhaust all the possible points of comparison between the tale of Perpetua and the tale of the mother and her seven sons in *Lamentations Rabbah*, which will be elaborated elsewhere. I confine myself here to a few instances, in order to substantiate the claim that their shared source in Maccabees 2 and 4, probably mainly Maccabees 2, is insufficient to explain the close similarities between these two narratives.[33] My interpretation of those similarities, based on the projection of a folk-narrative research perspective on these texts, is that the further development of the female martyrological legend in early Christian and rabbinic Jewish cultures occurs not only simultaneously but also in mutual communication, constituting a dialogue of narratives.[34] Salisbury recurrently mentions that Jewish–Christian communities provided the incentive for the emergence of the first Christian communities in North African cities, creating the background for the common narrative creativity underlying the female martyrological legends discussed here.

Visually, the most striking element is probably the nursing scene portrayed in Perpetua's tale and in that of the mother and the seven sons. In both tales, the impact of nursing in a context of violence is almost scandalizing, bordering on a kind of pornography of suffering, a "kitsch and death" version dating back to Late Antiquity.[35] The intimacy of the mother-infant relationship creates the starkest possible contrast with the torture and execution arena. The oppressive violence of the representative of earthly authority is the radical opposite of the physical devotion conveyed by the motherly body. God, however, spans the gap between the two opposites, encompassing both. These two aspects of the Creator are visibly present in the scene of martyrdom, although the cruel aspect seems indeed more evident. This is where the special force of the female martyrological narrative lies—it sharpens the experience of distinct human cruelty, as well as that of a divine force that requires such testimonies of its truth.[36] No tale about a male martyr could throw into such high relief the presence of birth as the absolute antithesis of death, albeit death as an ideal, as does the tale of a martyred woman, especially a nursing mother.

These tales specifically reflect the status of both religions at the time of their social and political powerlessness, while both were still being persecuted. Nevertheless, they render transparent the latent seeds of cruelty and destruction that would become manifest in later days, once their followers gained worldly power.

A less striking image common to both tales, although in quite different articulations, is the presence of wild animals. Christian martyrology speaks of concrete animals that attack the martyrs in the arena as a means of torture, as well as for the sake of entertainment. In the Jewish narrative, these animals appear as a metaphorical expression of God's action in the world, also violently turning against his own people. The parallel highlights the presence of God's will in the death of the martyr, which then requires the apologetic formulation of the Midrash—God directs the evildoer to do evil in order to retaliate at a later stage.

Both narratives refer, more or less directly, to a paradigmatic exemplar. In the Christian story of Perpetua, the martyr resembles Jesus, whereas in the Jewish tale of the mother and the seven sons, the mother compares herself with Abraham, thus creating a parallel between Isaac (himself a prefiguration of Jesus in many instances) and her sons. In both cases, the differences with the paradigmatic exemplar are significant: the martyrdom of Perpetua and her companions does not culminate in resurrection on the third day, nor are the seven brothers replaced by rams.

Later developments in the Christian and Jewish narrative traditions were superimposed on the versions of Late Antiquity in ways that dim their earlier, dialogic coexistence. Their relationship can be interpreted, at best, as a polemic exchange.[37] Some traditions still exist, however, one of them in the Georgian Church, which continue to preserve the spirit of narrative cooperation. According to Georgian legend, the Jews brought Christianity to Georgia on their return from a pilgrimage to Jerusalem.[38] This rendering of events reflects a reality similar to that portrayed by Salisbury, among others, who showed Christianity growing in the Jewish communities of North Africa. Although embedded in theologically separate universes of discourse, the perspective of folk literature reveals that these narratives of martyrdom have their roots in a shared communicative system, in a common folk-narrative tradition.

As has already been suggested, the stories about women in *Lamentations Rabbah* strongly emphasize the intertextual nature of the Midrash.[39] These stories reveal links with other, bordering realms of discourse, with which rabbinic literature maintains an ambiguous, tense, and sometimes even openly polemical relationship. Thus, we pointed to the option of a rather open parody of the texts of *Shiur Qomah* in the story about Miriam bat Tanhum and her seven sons. The Jewish–Christian connection is shown in yet another detail of the story. Although historical evidence indicates that the name Miriam was the most common female name in the relevant period,[40] its appearance as a recurrent motif in the chain of martyrological stories is particularly interesting in the cultural context of early Christianity in Palestine and its surroundings.

The place of the name Miriam in martyrological stories may draw from the phonological association between Miriam and *mar* (bitter), which is another meaning of the same root and is compatible, in symbolic terms, with the bitter fate of these heroines. But it could also express the power of these heroines, and the kernel of rebellion against religious authority latent in their stories. One should not forget that the name Miriam is an assonance of the Aramean word *Marah* (woman, lady, heroine), one of whose versions is "Martha."[41] Another associative link leads to the biblical heroine, Moses' sister, whose death is described in the Midrash (*Leviticus Rabbah* 20:12) as the death of a righteous woman, a death that atones for the sins of the community.

The comparison that Miriam bat Tanhum draws between herself and Abraham also evokes the Jewish–Christian dialogue, as the comparison clearly implies that her suffering is even greater than that of Mary, the mother of Jesus (the names are, of course, identical), who sacrificed "only" one son, unlike her seven.[42]

❧

In Jewish culture, the advent of redemption is linked to the appearance of a male figure, the Messiah. As is appropriate in a work devoted to the experience of destruction seeking comfort in a vision of redemption, the Midrash we are discussing includes a story about the birth of the Messiah. This story is unique in Jewish tradition, and concerns the birth of the Messiah Menahem in Beth Lehem in Judah (*Lamentations Rabbah* 1). In medieval Christian polemics against Jews, this story is cited to prove to the Jews that, even according to their own writings, the Messiah has already been born.[43] The plot elements do suggest a close affinity between this Midrash and that of

Jesus' birth in the Gospels of Matthew and Luke: the infant's mother is poor, natural signs appear pointing to the miraculous birth (a star in the New Testament, a lowing ox in *Lamentations Rabbah*), a stranger (from the East?) brings the infant a present, and the mother is the central figure while the father is absent or marginal. Yet, the name of the Messiah's mother in *Lamentations Rabbah* is not Miriam, despite the frequent appearance of this name in the work. Moreover, the mother in the birth story in *Lamentations Rabbah* reverses the figure of another mother linked to Beth Lehem, Rachel.[44] Rachel's love and faith will redeem her children; the mistrust and bitterness of the mother of the Messiah Menahem determine the story's frustrating conclusion, when Menahem is lifted into heaven in a whirlwind.

Rachel is indeed the most powerful female figure in *Lamentations Rabbah*, and latent in her appearance in this text is also the strongest redemptive potential in this work. The God mourning the loss of his people sends his mourning prophet Jeremiah, to whom tradition ascribes the authorship of the biblical Book of Lamentations, to call "Abraham, Isaac and Jacob and Moses from their graves, as they know how to cry" (*Lamentations Rabbah*, proem 24). They arrive, one after another, submit before the mourning God and the angels their great deeds and merits, and dismiss the indictment of the Torah and the personified twenty-two letters of the alphabet. The merits of the forefathers, however, cannot redirect the wheel of destruction and point it toward redemption:

> At once, Moses said to them: "My children, to return you now is impossible, as the divine decree has already been proclaimed, but God will soon bring you back." And he [Moses] left them. . . . And Moses spoke further before Him: "Lord of the Universe, You have written in your Torah, 'And whether it be cow or ewe, you shall not kill it and its young both in one day' (Leviticus 22:28),[45] and they have killed many, many mothers and their sons and you are silent." At that moment, Rachel leapt before the Holy One, blessed be He, and said: "Lord of the Universe, you know that Jacob your servant loved me exceedingly, and toiled for my father on my behalf for seven years. And at the end of the seven years, when the time of my marriage arrived, my father advised that my sister should replace me, and I suffered greatly because his counsel became known to me. And I informed my husband and I gave him a sign so that he might distinguish between my sister and me, and

my father would be unable to replace me. Later, I repented and suppressed my desire, and took pity on my sister so that she would not be shamed. In the evening, they substituted my sister for me with my husband, and I gave my sister all the signs I had agreed with my husband, so that he would believe she was Rachel. More than that, I went under the bed upon which he lay with my sister, and when he spoke to her and she remained silent, I made all the answers so that he would not recognize my sister's voice. I was gracious, I was not jealous, and spared her shame and dishonor. If I, only flesh and blood, dust and ashes, was not jealous of my rival and spared her shame and dishonor, why should you, the everlasting and compassionate King, be jealous of idolatry, which is insubstantial, and exile my children who were slain by the sword, and let their enemies do with them what they wish?" Forthwith, the mercy of the Holy One, blessed be He, was stirred, and he said: "For your sake, Rachel, I will restore Israel to their place." And so it was written: "Thus says the Lord: A voice was heard in Ramah, lamentation, and bitter weeping; Rachel weeping for her children; she refused to be comforted for her children, because they are not" (Jeremiah 31:14). And it is written: "Thus says the Lord: Keep thy voice from weeping, and thy eyes from tears: for thy work shall be rewarded, says the Lord" (Jeremiah 31:15). And it is written: "And there is hope for thy future, says the Lord, and thy children shall come back again to their own border" (Jeremiah 31:16).[46]—*Lamentations Rabbah*, proem 24

Despite the testimony of the patriarchs about their own sacrifices and efforts, particularly in their role as parents, the emotional intensity of their words cannot alter the divine decree. To begin with, Rachel is presented as their opposite, not only as a woman but also in regard to her behavior. They are brought by the prophet before God, while Rachel "leaps" on her own initiative to state her case. The teleological aspect of the text, which ensures Rachel's success in the redemption of her children, is obviously implied in the two verses from Jeremiah cited at the end of the passage, which give her written, indeed canonized assurance, that her children will be redeemed. Rachel does not speak of momentous national issues, such as those mentioned by the patriarchs, each one in his turn—the binding of Isaac, the wanderings in the desert with the children of Israel, and so forth. Her concerns are extremely personal and intimate. She is exclusively focused on the private sphere within the tent, the women's realm.[47] Her merit is her loyalty to her sister, for whose honor she renounced her yearning for her beloved for seven more years. This personal concern, together with the erotic energy of the love for her sister and her beloved that suffused Rachel's waiting, represent the strength required to shift the balance from condemnation to mercy. Love, in its most human and tender variation, rather than the zealous love of God expressed in the willingness to sacrifice a son, bears the power of redemption.

God, like a king exhausted by mourning, is also in need of additional powers in order to recuperate and redeem Israel. The extra strength supplied by the leaders of the nation proves insufficient, and further support from the female aspect is required. The story devoted to Rachel presents God's cosmic plan through the perspective of an erotic power of action. This is the most mythological text in *Lamentations Rabbah*, although not the only one. In his glosses as editor, Solomon Buber argued that this whole fragment entered the Midrash from a much later work, which he could not identify.[48] This is indeed an embryonic phase of the androgynous myth of the divinity, which will eventually be more fully developed in the Kabbala. This mythical motif, however, will not seem alien to *Lamentations Rabbah* when placed within the context of the marriage story between God and Knesset Israel related in the royal parables discussed above, which followed the allegorical tradition of interpretation of Song of Songs. Moreover, Gershom Scholem pointed out that the *almost* explicit expression of an anthropomorphized female figure of the *Shekhinah* appears, for the first time, in the same section of *Lamentations Rabbah* that includes the story about Rachel (the proems).[49] The feminine theme is thus a central axis of *Lamentations Rabbah*, a kind of semiotic and generative foundation of this text, also providing a crucial key for its interpretation. Together with the Rachel story, the *Shekhinah* figure suggests an additional extra-rabbinical intertextual realm, namely, the mythology of mysticism.[50]

Rachel, as presented above, is a symbolic female figure who returns us to the methodological question that opened this discussion: do female voices indeed speak in the Midrash, or are they only projections of femininity through male eyes? On the one hand, Rachel is driven by empathy and loyalty, features that male observers like to see in "good" women. In a distinctive act of self-sacrifice, bordering almost on self-effacement, she lends her voice to her sister. Whereas in the Genesis story about the house-hold idols Rachel lied when she put her love for her beloved above her love for her father, here she gives precedence to her love for her sister over her love for Jacob, and becomes a partner to deceit. But it is actually in this impressive picture of lovemaking through the voice (confirming, as it were, the Rabbinic saying that "a woman's voice is her sexual organ"), and seven years before her other limbs accomplish the same, that the female voice finds its typical avenue for self-expression in the midrashic text. This is not the loud voice of the textual establishment but a clandestine, concealed voice, finding expression in indirect and subversive paths, in the popular discourse of the tale and the lament.

A female figure is imputed to the Midrash on the Book of Lamentations by virtue of the first verse of the book, which describes Jerusalem as a widow sitting in mourning, as well as of many female images of the people and the city in the Bible.[51] This is a figure marked by endless images of loss and weakness but also embodying a possibility of turning the hidden voice toward a vertical power, directed upwards, like Rachel's voice under the bed, and like her voice, reaching God and bringing redemption. The strength of hidden weakness seems to be the key for unlocking the ancient Palestinian female voice, through an interpretation that relates to the midrashic text as including the concealed partners to the dialogue.

This chapter presented the social context, and gender relationships within society in particular, as a key for understanding the role of folk narratives in the midrashic text. Rather than presenting folk-narrative texts about women mainly as male projections of illegitimate male aspects, the feminine stories were presented in the social context of women as bearers of concrete folk-literary traditions, especially in the genre of the lament.

7 THE RELIGIOUS CONTEXT OF FOLK NARRATIVES IN THE AGGADIC MIDRASH

THE RHETORIC OF INTIMACY AS A RHETORIC OF THE SACRED

LIKE MOST RABBINICAL literature throughout the ages, *Lamentations Rabbah* focuses not only on the relationships between human beings, but also on the relationship between human beings and God. The relationship between human beings and God is rooted, first and foremost, in the sustained connection with the Bible as the text of God's revelation to the people of Israel.

Rabbinical Midrashim do not formulate a systematic religious doctrine or philosophy. Rather, they constitute a complex of more or less fixed associations, in which congruity is ensured through the links to the biblical text, established through frequent reference. Central experiences in the relationship between the people of Israel and God, as well as events linking God and Jewish individuals, take various forms in the Midrash which, constantly reilluminated, create a complex and multivalent system of meanings.

In *Lamentations Rabbah*, the traumatic story of devastation and exile is woven into an ideological and artistic design. Perhaps more than in other rabbinic Midrashim, tragic and painful events dominate in this work the discourse describing the relationship between human beings and God. Although this discourse deals with a collective traumatic experience, it strongly resembles the painful exchange evolving from individual trauma within the privacy of the analyst's room. Like analytic discourse, the Midrash too seeks to reconstruct the story behind the present distressing reality; in both cases, it is assumed that the key to the understanding of present suffering lies somewhere in the past. Like therapeutic discourse, the Midrash too focuses on intimate family relationships, on the fulfillment of forbidden wishes, on taboos like murder, incest, and cannibalism. Both entail an almost obsessive repetition of the narrative of aching separations.

Whereas the previous chapter was devoted to displays of femininity and female figures as the central interpretive key to *Lamentations Rabbah*, this chapter will point to the intimate close relationships emerging in this work between God and the people of Israel. This relationship, represented in the image of the son and the father, is, theologically, even more central in *Lamentations Rabbah* than the relationship between the spouses, which draws from the allegorical tradition of the Song of Songs.[1]

The father-son image, particularly in the more destructive aspects exposed in this Midrash, translates naturally in our times into the Freudian Oedipal model of interpretation. Freudian scholars, including Freud's disciples as well as his critics, have devoted foremost attention to the role of language as a central component of psychoanalytic theory and psychoanalytic interpretation.[2] *Lamentations Rabbah* clearly illustrates how language becomes the instrument for conveying powerful feelings, with modes of expression alternating between brief references, repetition, emphasis, and intensification. The language of Midrash often reflects primary, associative processes rather than causal or other logical links. Yet the closeness between midrashic and analytic discourse is not found primarily at the linguistic level, but in complex and multivalent contents, both emotional and cognitive: in the presence of ambivalent emotions without any imminent need for mediating or resolving inconsistencies; in contradictory attitudes toward the same phenomenon; in the lack of linear principles in the organization of materials; in a preference for associative rather than thematic associations; in repetitions; in the fulfillment of forbidden wishes concerning sexuality and aggression; in childish regressions.

When pointing to the interface between psychoanalytic concepts and midrashic modes of expression and creativity I am not thinking foremost of the Jewish sources of Freud's work.[3] Nor do I mean to argue that these are intercultural, universal modes of thought. Rather, by resorting to psychoanalytic terminology I mean to introduce into my study a mode of discourse that is central to the contemporary research and criticism of culture. Psychoanalytic terminology, including its various developments, expansions, and deviations, is crucial to any discourse of this kind.

The "psychoanalytic" character of the *Lamentations Rabbah* text is particularly visible in those sections that deviate bluntly from the typical pattern of exegetical Midrashim, which expound verses in their order. A prominent example of such a deviation in *Lamentations Rabbah* is the sequence of riddle tales and dreams expounding on a fragment of the verse "great among the nations."[4] Both in the riddle tales and in the dream stories we find two layers, a latent and a manifest one, which stimulate interpretation to reveal the concealed. In the riddle tales, the entire interpretive mechanism is indeed part of the traditional genre of riddling although, as I showed, "psychological motivations" are a crucial factor. In the tales on dream interpretation, the folkloristic-traditional context breaks through the textual framework and reveals in many places the personal, psychological moorings of the interpretation.

Already in the proems section of the Midrash, the relationship between God and the people of Israel is presented as a rather open metaphorical instance of the father-son relationship. Preceding the parable in proem 2b, which we discussed in the previous chapter, the section opens with the verse from Jeremiah 9:16, as follows:

"Thus says the Lord of hosts, Consider, and call for the mourning women, that they may come." R. Yohannan, and R. Simeon b. Lakish, and the Rabbis. R. Yohannan said: "God may be likened to a king who had two sons. He became enraged against the first, took a stick, thrashed him, drove him into banishment and exclaimed: 'Woe to him! From what comfort has he been banished!' He later became enraged against the second, took a stick, thrashed him, and drove him into banishment, and exclaimed: 'I am the one who brought them up badly.' Thus were the ten tribes banished, and the Holy One, blessed be He, began to repeat this verse to them: 'Woe to them! For they have fled from me' (Hosea 7:13), so that when Judah and Benjamin were banished, the Holy One, blessed be He, declared, if we dare say this: 'Woe is me for my hurt!'" (Jeremiah 10:19).—*Lamentations Rabbah*, proem 2b

An angry father appears in R. Yohannan's homily, thrashing his sons and banishing them one after another. As their mentor, the father first chooses to assume responsibility for his sons' improper behavior, thus establishing, for better or for worse, the inseparable link between father and sons. The homily leads to a verse in Jeremiah presenting the God-father in his sorrow, left without his sons. The irony of the father's deed, which has caused his own woe, is intimated but not developed until the second parable.

The father-God's reaction to the banishment of the first son is formulated almost in the very same words that the Midrash uses to describe Adam's plight after the expulsion from Eden: "From what comfort has he been banished" (*Genesis Rabbah* 22:2). The textual identity between these two expressions of loss echoes the associative link between Adam and the destruction of the Temple, which appears at the very beginning of *Lamentations Rabbah*, and is concisely summarized in the homograph *eikha–ayeka* which, as noted, is the unusual word form in which God looks for Adam in the Garden (Genesis 3:9).

The irony is stronger in the second passage of the proem, in the homily of R. Simeon ben Lakish (Resh Lakish) discussed in the previous chapter, stressing the female power of lament as opposed to the male inability to contend with mourning:

R. Simeon b. Lakish said: "[It may be likened] to a king who had two sons. He became enraged against the first, took a stick, and thrashed him so that he writhed in agony and died, and he began to mourn for him. He became enraged against the second, and he took the stick and thrashed him so that he writhed in agony and died. He said: 'No longer have I the strength to lament over them, so call for the mourning women and let them lament over them.' Similarly, when the ten tribes were exiled, He began to lament over them: 'Hear this word which I take up against you, a lamentation, O house of Israel' (Amos 5:1); when Judah and Benjamin were exiled the Holy One, blessed be He, said, if we dare say so, 'No longer have I the strength to lament over them,' saying: 'Thus says the Lord of hosts: Consider, and call for the mourning women . . . and let them make haste and take up a wailing for us' (Jeremiah 9:16–17). It does not say here, 'for them' but 'for us,' for me and for them. It does not say here, 'that their eyes may run down with tears' but 'our eyes,' mine and theirs; it does not say here 'their eyelids gush out with waters' but 'our eyelids,' mine and theirs."—*Lamentations Rabbah*, proem 2b

As in R. Yohannan's homily, a sharp confrontation emerges here from the perspective of the father-son relationship when, at the mourning stage, the borders between father and sons are encroached, and the conflict unfolds within the father himself. The meaning of the encroachment is twofold: first, the father physically destroys his sons by thrashing them, and then he denies their separate existence by turning his mourning for them into mourning for himself.

The third homily, that of the rabbis, is a weaker version of the previous ones, and its main rhetorical role is to shift the discourse from the private realm of the father and the two sons to the public realm of God and the twelve tribes of Israel, as befits the collective voice in which it is articulated:

> Our rabbis said: "God may be likened to a king who had twelve sons of whom two died. He began to console himself with ten. Two more died and he began to console himself with eight. Two more died and he began to console himself with six. Two more died and he began to console himself with four. Two more died and he began to console himself with two, and when all died he began to lament over them, 'How does the city sit solitary!' " (Lamentations 1:1).—*Lamentations Rabbah*, proem 2b

In this homily, the irony leans toward the grotesque in its wholesale attitude to the deaths of the sons, who are lost in pairs.

The figure of the father-God thus bears the full weight of the ambivalence of violence abiding at the core of love, in this case, parental love. According to the French philosopher Paul Ricoeur, ambivalence is also inherent in the symbols of the sacred, which are thereby linked to the symbols of evil: "The great symbols concerning the nature and origin of evil are not simply one set of symbols out of many, but are privileged symbols. . . . The symbols of evil teach us something decisive about the passage from a phenomenology of spirit to a phenomenology of the sacred."[5] Ricoeur thereby indicates that the experience of the sacred cannot be fully exhausted and understood as purely "spiritual," but has a concrete, sensuous, living dimension. In the text before us, and in the Midrash in general, which is alien to an abstract spirituality, the experience of the sacred is consistently shaped though symbols relating the realm of the intimate to the realm of the sacred. It is thus translated into the language of intimacy, in terms known to human beings from their own family and love relationships.

An additional instance of conveying the experience of the sacred through the ambivalent father-son relationship appears at the opening of *Lamentations Rabbah* 1, after the proems:

> "How does the city sit solitary [*badad*]!" (Lamentations 1:1). R. Berekhiah said in the name of R. Abdimi of Haifa: "It may be likened to a king who had a son. As long as he obeyed his father's will, he dressed him in fine garments, but whenever he made him angry, he dressed him in rags. So with Israel, as long as they obeyed the will of the Holy One, blessed be He, He dressed them in fine clothes, as it is written 'I clothed thee also with embroidered cloth . . .' (Ezekiel 16:10), and since they made him angry he dressed them in torn [*bedudim*] clothes."— *Lamentations Rabbah* 1:1

R. Berekhiah's homily points to the painful quality of a fatherly love contingent on unswerving compliance. A similar pain, mingled with a terrible frustration, emerges also from another homily:

> "Zion spreads out her hands" (Lamentations 1:17), as a man drowning in the river who spreads his hands seeking support. R. Joshua of Sachnin said in the name of R. Levi: "It may be likened to a king who was angry at his son, he would beat him and he would still stray, finally he spread his hands before him and said: 'He is all before you, beat him at your pleasure.' Thus 'Zion spreads her hands.' "—*Lamentations Rabbah* 1:18

The son is not guiltless either, as he admits to having disobeyed and strayed. The text thus preserves the option considered ideologically dominant in rabbinic literature, postulating a causal link between the sins of the Jews and their suffering. For Rubenstein, who considers the rabbinic historiosophy justifying the destruction of the Temple in these terms, rabbinic thought embodies a principle similar to Freud's, who views guilt as the cornerstone of restraint, sublimation, and culture.[6]

The opposite pole of ambivalence is represented in the figure of the mourning, bereaved father that appears, for instance, in proem 24.

At that time, the Holy One, blessed be He, weeps and says: "Woe is me, for my House! My children, where are you? My priests, where are you? My beloved ones, where are you? What will I do with you, I warned you, but you failed to repent!" The Holy One, blessed be He, said to Jeremiah: "I am now like a man who had an only son, and he set up a marriage canopy for him, and he died under it. Are you not pained for me and for my sons?"—*Lamentations Rabbah*, proem 24

The image of a son dying under the marriage canopy, to suggest a particularly harsh loss at a time of great joy, is not unusual in rabbinic parables. This picture points to a motif association between, on the one hand, the genre of the parable that is characterized as erudite, sophisticated, and always linked to verses from the text,[7] and on the other hand, folk narratives clearly drawing inspiration from non-scholarly sources. One of the more prominent folk narratives in *Leviticus Rabbah*, with many parallel versions in ancient Oriental literatures and in universal folk literature, does indeed describe the death of a son on his wedding night (*Leviticus Rabbah* 20:4). Although the *Leviticus Rabbah* story also represents a change from the usual folk plot structure in that it ends with the son's death, unlike the orally transmitted stories where the son is rescued, most of its motifs do remain close to the folk-narrative tradition.[8]

The anthropological perception of divinity, which is translated into intimate family relationships, is explicitly formulated at the beginning of chapter 1 of *Lamentations Rabbah*:

R. Nahman said: "The Holy One, blessed be He, asked the ministering angels: 'When a king of flesh and blood mourns, what does he do?' They replied: 'He hangs sackcloth over his door.' He said to them: 'I will do likewise, as it is said, "I clothe the heavens with blackness, and I make sackcloth their covering"' (Isaiah 50:3). And he asked further: 'When a king mourns, what does he do?' They replied: 'He dims the lamps.' He said to them: 'I will do likewise, as it is said, "The sun and the moon are darkened, and the stars withdraw their shining"' (Joel 4:15). And he asked further: 'When a king mourns, what does he do?' They replied: 'He overturns his couch.' He said to them: 'I will do likewise, as it is said, "As I looked, thrones were placed and an ancient of days did sit"' (Daniel 7:9). And he asked further: 'When a king mourns, what does he do?' They replied: 'He goes barefoot.' He said to them: 'I will do likewise, as it is said, "His way is in the tempest and in the storm, and the clouds are the dust of his feet"' (Nahum 1:3). 'Moreover,' they said, 'he rends his lavish robes.' He said to them: 'I will do likewise, as it is said, "The Lord has done that which he devised; he has fulfilled his word that he commanded in the days of old"' (Lamentations 2:17).[9] 'Moreover,' they said, 'he sits silent.' He said to them: 'I will do likewise, as it is said, "Let him sit alone and keep silence"' (Lamentations 3:28). 'Moreover,' they said, 'he weeps.' He said to them: 'I will do likewise, as it is said, "And on that day did the Lord God of hosts call to weeping, and to mourning"'" (Isaiah 22:12).—*Lamentations Rabbah* 1:1

The description of God as learning mourning practices from a king of flesh and blood reflects, in a mirror image, on the fact that the linguistic tools used to describe the divinity are usually taken from human, even everyday, life. The text itself thereby becomes an ethnographic account, describing the mourning practices prevalent at the time, or at least those pertaining to royalty.

The issue of gender differentiation communicated through mourning suffuses the next legend:

A woman living in the neighborhood of R. Gamaliel had a son, a young man[10] who died, and for whom she would weep at night. On hearing her, R. Gamaliel was reminded of the destruction of the Temple, and he wept until his lashes fell out. When his disciples noticed this, they removed her from his neighborhood.—*Lamentations Rabbah* 1:2

This story contrasts personal and collective grief—personal grief is represented by the bereaved mother, whereas the grief for the destruction of the Temple is personified by R. Gamaliel. A twofold message is suggested here, ideological as well as emotional. At the ideological level, the collective grief is so intense that his eyelashes fall off, and his compassionate disciples relieve him from the bereaved mother, who reminds him of the destruction of the Temple with her weeping. But the ideological message is strongly contradicted by the emotional message. At the emotional level, it is clear that the mother weeps at night because her grief constantly overcomes her, whereas Rabban Gamaliel weeps only when he "is reminded" of his grief. Furthermore, the private grief cannot be restrained but the collective one can be repressed by changing locations.

Once again we find that women bear their grief better than men do, since the weeping mother, unlike R. Gamaliel, suffers no physical damage from her tears. As in the parables about the father who kills and weeps, here too the young man's death is engulfed in the mourning of the older man. The reaction of R. Gamaliel's disciples, who move him to a new dwelling, seems somewhat cynical in light of the mother's inability to escape her own suffering. Nor is it entirely clear why the disciples should wish to prevent R. Gamaliel from mourning the destruction of the Temple.

The parallel between the mourning for a son and the mourning for God's Temple points to yet another dimension in the recourse of *Lamentations Rabbah* to the language of family intimacy concerning subjects that are distinctively theological. R. Gamaliel's injured eyes bring us back to the Oedipal theme (Oedipus was punished, or punished himself, with blindness), the Oedipal male guilt oscillating in this story between the loss of a son and the loss of the Temple. This motif is intensified in a homily where the sacrifice of children in the Valley of Hinnom appears as the direct reason for the punishment of the destruction (*Lamentations Rabbah* 1).

One of the most shocking stories in *Lamentations Rabbah*, and in midrashic literature in general, brings to a height the Oedipal theme in the context of destruction, transcending into the complexities of psychological problems hiding behind the Oedipal plight:

Hadrian, may his bones be smashed, set up three garrisons—one in Emmaus, and one in Beth Lehem, and one in Lekatia,[11] saying: "Whoever escapes from one will be captured at the other. . . ." He gathered them all in a valley and said to the commander of his army: "By the time I finish eating this slice of cake and this leg of fowl, they should be slaughtered until not one of them is standing on his feet." Those [Jews] in hiding would venture out at night and follow the stench of the corpses, and bring them back and eat them. Once a group was hiding in one of the caves and they said to one of them: "Bring us a body and we will eat it." On leaving, he found his dead father, buried him and marked the spot. He then returned and reported he had found nothing. Another one went out and followed the scent of the body, unearthed it, and brought it. As they were sitting and eating, the teeth of the youngster [*yanuka*] were blunted. He said: "Where did you find this body?" Said he: "In such and such a corner." He said: "What was the distinguishing mark on it?" He said: "Such and such a mark." Said he: "Woe to that boy [meaning himself, *talya* in the original] who has eaten his father's flesh, to fulfill what was said: 'Therefore the fathers shall eat the sons in the midst of thee, and the sons shall eat their fathers' (Ezekiel 5:10), and the Holy Spirit says: 'For these things I weep' " (Lamentations 1:16).—*Lamentations Rabbah* 1:16

This text is in the genre of the horror propaganda spread at times of catastrophe, which is partly based on scraps of information, possibly in this case as well.[12] The central theme of this rumor highlights intimate family images in the tragic saga of the Temple's destruction. As background, an introduction describes the relevant historical events in a manner typical of the historical legend, providing precise details: the name of the cruel ruler, Hadrian, whose name, like that of Titus, is usually accompanied by a forceful curse; names of places well known in the Palestine of the times; an exact description of the methods of oppression and physical extermination, as well as tactics of flight and survival. The specific episode at the focus of the legend, involving the hiding people in the cave, is spelled out in a concise language bearing multiple meanings.

In the introduction, Hadrian is described as eating cake and a leg of fowl while Jews are being slaughtered. This feasting picture creates a grotesque and infuriating antithesis with the concurrent slaughter, and with the description of the extreme starvation that followed. The text intensifies the actual bodily reality of the eating act by mentioning a leg of fowl and human feet in the same sentence. One need not be a vegetarian to sense here that eating a chicken is also, actually, eating a corpse, although here this is merely a preface to the true horror. This linkage joins a specific historical evil, perpetrated against Jews, to the existential roots of the evil entailed in the struggle for survival.

The story itself is prefaced by a statement of fact, namely, those in hiding used to eat human corpses. The brief and terse description is more effective than any expression of feelings, and actually precludes the option of presenting an emotional text that might be proportionate to the abomination. The most dreadful detail is their walk in the night following the stench. This would indeed appear to be a rational explanation, as one cannot rely on sight during the night and relying on scent is the only option, since the dead have no voice. But the description also intensifies the hopelessness of the plight, and portrays the food of those in hiding as most inhuman. The text is thus offering almost a structural scheme of the Lévi-Strauss variety—maximal food, Hadrian's food, and minimal food, the rotting corpses of the slain.[13] As opposed to the two "culture"-related modes of food preparation represented by Hadrian's dishes—baking and roasting (or cooking, or baking)—the Jews hiding in the cave are pushed beyond the borders of culture and forced to resort to a "natural" mode of food preparation, putrefaction, thereby losing their humanity.

The story itself opens with a genre sign, "once," which in rabbinic literature usually denotes various subgenres of the legend.[14] The story first presents a group of people hiding in a cave before exposing the individual who is the axis or theme of the story. The group hides in a cave, and this is probably their only realistic chance of survival, as we also learn from archaeological remnants of the period.[15] Hiding in a cave, however, also points to the psychological plight of those in hiding, who find themselves in the recesses of the earth in a situation closely resembling burial, as opposed to the slain who should have been buried but are exposed to the elements, to the birds, and to the animals. The closeness of those hiding in the cave to the plight of the dead sharpens the contrast between life and death because they, as opposed to the corpses, are nevertheless alive. A cave also represents a fetal situation, inside the womb, within the earth. I would not dwell on this symbolic issue if regression did not play an important role in the rest of the story.

This appalling breach of the taboo is lessened because responsibility is assumed by the group, but not for long. We soon realize that this is a story dealing with the individual in the most personal sense of the term, and the story turns to the protagonist, who is sent out to seek a corpse to eat and finds his slain father. The sense of intimacy overrides the hunger, and he buries his father's body and marks the place (the same verb is used in the original to describe the burial [tmareih] and the hiding in the cave [mitamrin]). At this stage, the hero acts like a civilized man—he renounces the satisfaction of a primary need, hunger, because of cultural inhibitions and intimate feelings, and protects the honor of his father's body. The breaking of the taboo thus seems to remain at the level of cannibalism (necrophagy, or eating the dead) without reaching the level of patriphagy (eating the father). This danger, however, is only temporarily avoided, as the next seeker, following the stench, naturally reaches the same corpse, implying that the son's burial was not sufficiently thorough.

Unavoidably, the story reaches the scene of the horrid feast and the son's teeth do indeed blunt. At this point, the son is called *yanuka* (literally, suckling), and satisfying his hunger is a suckling cannibalism that, as it were, releases him from the responsibility incumbent on a civilized adult. But, according to the story, the intimate relationship between a father and a son is not only cultural, and the physical reaction exposes its instinctual layer. Later, with a delay that might even seem objectionable, the son rushes to ask where did the other seeker find the corpse they are eating. Recognizing the sign, he understands that he has indeed eaten his father's body. Bemoaning his fate, the son calls himself *talya* (youngster), thus assuming a higher level of responsibility than that expected from a *yanuka*. (The printed version and the Munich Ms. do not include this play on words with the stages of the man's development, and refer to him as *barnash* [fellow] throughout the story.)

At the end, the awesome personal event is associated with a broader context of meaning, conveyed through the verse from Ezekiel's prophecy of wrath. The private case thus appears as part of a larger narrative. The question is what larger narrative, or larger narratives, unfold between father and son, emerging in this story as the ideological foundation of *Lamentations Rabbah*. One option is that the father is a threatening figure, capable even of killing (as in the above parables), and only by devouring him can the son overcome him and turn him into a part of himself and of his survival. Another option, less clear, is that the son eats his father in order to defeat him. The father punishes him violently, to death. The father loses his power and resorts to the lamenting women. The nonlinear, associative character of the Midrash obviously allows us to relate simultaneously to more than one narrative in the text.

An additional possible narrative is embodied in another verse from Ezekiel, which is not explicitly quoted here but is clearly alluded to in the son's physiological reaction: "The fathers have eaten sour grapes and the children's teeth are set on edge" (Ezekiel 18:2; also Jeremiah 31:29). For both biblical prophets, the situation described in the parable (and the saying) is one of unfairness. The story encapsulates the injustice conveyed in the parable, and Ezekiel therefore addresses a complaint of injustice toward Heaven.

The finale "and the Holy Spirit weeps . . ." is an editorial ending that creates an ironical, cosmic perspective—the omnipotent God cries for the destruction he brings upon his children, like the father who thrashes and kills his sons and then laments over them.

The breaking of taboos seems to reach a peak in this story, illustrating the extreme circumstances wrought by the destruction of the Temple. In the context of the relationships between father and son as a parable of the relationships between God and man, the story raises the issue of atavistic parricide as the basis for extant social relationships, on which Freud rested his view of religion in general, and of Judaism in particular.[16]

Freud discerned the double meaning of the concept *sacer*—"sacred," but also "guilty" and contemptible. Hence, he was aware of parallels in the ambivalence toward the sacred and toward intimate family relationships. These parallels are manifest in the language of images that are crucial in *Lamentations Rabbah*, where the God–man relationship assumes a literary form couched in terms of family relationships, particularly between father and son.

This approach to religion begs comparison with Paul Ricoeur's deliberation in his important book on Freud: "Why not link the destiny of faith with this fraternal conciliation, rather than with the perpetual repetition of the parricide?"[17] Freud's approach, although his knowledge of post-biblical Jewish texts was scanty at best, was closer to the spirit of Jewish texts like those, for instance, quoted in *Lamentations Rabbah*. In contrast, Ricoeur voices the Christian approach, which releases the generations after Jesus from the Oedipal struggle because of the death of the chosen, only Son. Whereas the Christian approach is close to the ritual of the scapegoat (Leviticus 16), releasing everyone from blame because of the suffering of the individual bearing the sins of the community, the Jewish approach resembles more closely the heroic and desperate continuation of the Oedipal struggle, acknowledging the cruel conditions of existence at the most intimate level.

It may not be a mere coincidence that the structure of *Lamentations Rabbah* is characterized by the repetition of some stories. On the other hand, this structure may actually reflect textual histories of which we are unaware.[18] The figure of the mourning God repeatedly appears in the shape of a king of flesh and blood (for instance, at the beginnings of chapter 1 and chapter 3 as well as in several proems); the story about Zekhariah's killing by his brethren is found in proem 5, proem 23, and chapter 4; the story about the birth and death of emperor Trajan's son appears in chapter 1 and chapter 4; the story about Doeg ben Yosef's wife eating the son she had dearly loved is found in chapter 1 and chapter 2.

This last story exposes an appalling contrast to the figure of the mourning, compassionate mother who, in this work, tends to represent a consoling antithesis to the cruel father figures, entailing a dreadful intensification of the story about eating the father's corpse: a son unintentionally eats his father, a mother deliberately eats her son, because of the total inhumanity of starvation.[19]

Parallel to the recurring stories, at the end of the Midrash there are also motifs negating or reversing others found at the beginning. Thus, contrary to the parable in the proem about the death of the innocent, guiltless son, the following parable appears:

> It is written: "A Psalm of Assaf: O God, heathen nations are come into thy inheritance" (Psalms 79:1). A psalm? Weeping was required! R. Eleazar said: "It may be likened to a king who erected a bridal canopy for his son, repaired his house, plastered, painted and adorned it. Once he [the son] made him angry, and he destroyed it. The son's teacher sat down to sing. Said the king: 'His house is destroyed and you sing?' Said he: 'That is why I sing, because he has poured out his wrath on his son's canopy and not on his son.' So it was said to Assaf: 'The Holy One, blessed be He, has destroyed his Temple, and you sit and sing?' And he said to them, 'I sing because the Holy One, blessed be He, has poured out his wrath on wood and stones and not on Israel, as it is written: "He has kindled his fire in Zion and it has devoured its foundations"'" (Lamentations 4:11).[20]—*Lamentations Rabbah* 4:11

The weak father who is unable to mourn (already known to us from the proem mentioned above) has a counterpart in the figure of R. Joshua ben Hananiah as the redeeming father who ransoms R. Ishmael from captivity:

> Once, R. Joshua b. Hananiah went to Rome and saw a handsome boy with beautiful eyes who was wickedly abused. He went past his door-

way to test him, and read him the verse: "Who gave Jacob for a spoil and Israel to the robbers?" (Isaiah 42:24), and the boy replied and said, "Did not the Lord, he against whom we have sinned and in whose ways they would not walk, and unto whose Torah they were not obedient?" (ibid.). When R. Joshua heard him, his eyes filled with tears and he said, "I call heaven and earth to witness that I will not move from here without ransoming him." And he paid a high price and released him, and they say he was from Jerusalem, to fulfill what is said "The precious sons of Zion" (Lamentations 4:2).—*Lamentations Rabbah* 4:2

Unlike the beating father, lacking strength even to lament, and unlike R. Gamaliel, who weeps for the destroyed Temple and loses his eyelashes, R. Joshua's weeping fosters the strength to ransom the captive boy. The Midrash thus presents once again a behavioral model where empathy is a source of redemption, as in the story about Rachel, Leah, and Jacob discussed in the previous chapter.

The following parable (*Lamentations Rabbah* 3) also reverses the motif of the raging, violent father:

R. Hiyya taught: "It may be likened to a king who went to Emmaus and took his children with him. Once they angered him and he swore never to take them again, and he would remember them and cry, saying: 'Would that my children were with me, even though they make me angry!' As it is written: 'O, that I were in the wilderness, in a lodging place of wayfaring men' (Jeremiah 9:1). Said the Holy One, blessed be He: 'Would that my children were with me, as they had been in the wilderness, even though they make me angry!' As it is also written: 'Son of man, when the house of Israel dwelt in their own land, they defiled it by their way and by their doings: their way was before me as the uncleanness of a menstruous woman' (Ezekiel 36:17). The Holy One, blessed be He, said: 'Would that my children were with me in the land of Israel, even though they defile it.'"—*Lamentations Rabbah* 3:20

The multivocality of the midrashic text is manifest both at the level of the plot and at the level of the structure. At the level of the plot, the multivocality is found in the ways feelings are shaped in the stories themselves, as in the extreme tale about eating the father's corpse, in which the clashing feelings of the hungry man, the loving son, and the civilized person cannot be reconciled. At the structural level, of the Midrash as a whole, different and even contradictory messages are manifest in the various sections of the text, oscillating between a killing father and a protecting, longing, and rescuing father.

∾

In this chapter I discussed folk discourse, and the interfacing parable discourse, in their religious-theological context. The theological problems unique to the midrashic text of *Lamentations Rabbah* stem from historical events following the destruction of the Temple and in the wake of Roman oppression, and they are structured to follow closely the text of the Book of Lamentations, in the typical pattern of an exegetical Midrash. The representation of the religious realm in human terms, and more particularly the consistent representation of God as father and king, enable the shaping of the religious experience in its historical context through narratives taken from the human world.

8 THE HISTORICAL CONTEXT OF FOLK NARRATIVES IN THE AGGADIC MIDRASH

THREE TALES ON MESSIANISM

THIS CONCLUDING CHAPTER is not meant as a summary of the theoretical issues discussed in previous ones. Rather, its purpose is to raise an additional theoretical question, touching on the historical context of folk narratives found within Palestinian aggadic Midrashim. Questions pointing to the tension between general, or might we say universal, categories, and their specific concretization in the Jewish culture of the time, have resonated throughout this work. Literature, folk-literary genres, motifs and narrative types, practices and beliefs, social relationships, religious concepts, all exist in every culture. Jewish culture in Late Antiquity crafted unique forms and modes of expression in every one of these dimensions. History, because it reflects the self-perception of a society over a time reaching back from the present to the past, is itself a conceptual and cultural category meaningfully present in folk narratives.[1]

The historical context of Palestinian aggadic Midrashim is reflected in them mainly as a plight of suffering, oppression, and loss. Folk narratives in this literature bear the same mark. The literature of the period, however, also contains elements of deliverance from the painful and humiliating historical present, a deliverance that may be characterized as utopian in its hints of a complete reversal of the course of history.[2] Utopian thought is also an intercultural category, which the sages shaped by drawing on contents and modes of expression found in their own culture.

As early as the dawn of the rabbinic period, in the first century C.E., the hope for a utopian reversal of history that would end anguish and persecution reaches classic narrative expression in the Messianic vision. By its very nature, the Jewish Messianic vision draws on well-known Messianic hints found in biblical and post-biblical literature. Its manifold elaboration in the rabbinic period interacts with materials drawn from the political and spiritual events of the time. The relationship between materials conceived as historical reality and the emergence of folk narratives situated at various angles of report, imitation, reshaping, and fiction, is an issue that has occupied both historians and scholars of folk literature. Historians have devoted increasing attention to it over the last two decades, following the heightened interest in the study of popular culture.[3]

In this chapter we will discuss the legend and the myth, two generic terms that were only briefly mentioned in the discussion in Chapter 3. Folk narratives referring to historical events usually belong to the genre that scholars of folk literature call "historical legends."[4] This is a subcategory of a more broadly defined genre, the "legend" (*Sage* in German). The legend, the historical as well as the biographical, is the most prevalent genre of folk literature in rabbinic writings.

A useful way of describing the genre of the legend is to compare it and contrast it with its counterpart, the folktale, which was described at length in Chapter 3. The distinction between folktale and legend is based mainly on the way each represents the world, which is manifest in differences of form, content, and style. The legend represents a possible world, in terms of the concepts and beliefs current in the narrating society.[5]

Almost everything that is true of the folktale is reversed in the legend, but a caveat is in order: genres, as ideal types or models in general, do not usually appear in "pure" form. Folk literature offers listeners and readers countless intermediate forms, and elements characteristic of the folktale may appear in legends, and vice versa.

The strong connection between the genre of the legend and the specific culture in which it emerges is particularly prominent. In contrast, the folktale is relatively independent of cultural context, and can thus wander more easily than the legend from one culture to another. Folktales, however, are transformed into versions characteristic of particular cultures and their unique ecology, known as ecotypes.[6]

Pervasive in the legend are signs linking the events described to a known reality. Thus, legends often begin with a description that situates the narrative plot at a particular time, that may even be specific to the date, and sometimes even alluding to a location familiar to the audience. Instead of the "never-never land" characterizing the folktale, the legend invariably takes place at a time and place perceived as part of the linear sequence reaching from the creation of the world to the narrator's present. The legend is also populated with characters familiar from the reality of the narrating society, and sometimes with historical characters identified by their name, or with supernatural figures, such as demons and spirits, which this society believes exist parallel to human beings.

The legend tends to be relatively brief, realistic, short on rhetorical and stylistic embellishments, and focusing on a specific episode. Narrators of legends mention numerous details linking the story to reality, such as natural formations (crevices in rocks, springs, burnt trees, or heaps of stones, for instance), which came into being as a result of the event narrated in the legend itself. The link between the legend and reality is thus reinforced, improving the legend's chances of imparting social norms and rules of behavior considered positive, and enhancing its capacity to warn against negative behaviors leading to disaster, failure, or punishment. Legends may end well or badly, all according to the protagonists' behavior: if the heroes abide by the norms endorsed in the story, they will see fortune, and if they break the rules, they will come to a bad ending. The legend, therefore, establishes itself as a meaningful element in the consciousness of the past and in the identity of the group narrating it and preserving it within its tradition.[7]

While discussing how consciousness of the past and a collective identity are structured by the legend, brief mention should be made of the legend's subgenres, which reflect these dimensions in unique modes. Subgenres of the legend include historical, local, and biographical legends, as well as legends about saintly figures (hagiography) and legends about demons (demonology), classified according to the dominant theme.[8] Some legends deal with various folk beliefs,[9] such as the belief in forces, neither of human origin nor of the one God, that are also active in the world. In Jewish texts, these legends attest to a possible multivocality within monotheistic faith. As a result, no consensus prevails concerning the actual relationship between those forces and reality. In legends dealing with beliefs, heroes meet devils, angels, and spirits. These encounters may prove helpful or harmful to the protagonists, depending on their skill in negotiating with these figures. The rules of this negotiation, and its potential results, comprise the system we call folk beliefs, which may shape up as legends about demons and reflect the culture's demonology.[10] Folk beliefs may also be embodied in biographical legends of saintly figures and link up with the accepted hagiography of the society narrating them.[11]

Legends dealing with beliefs need not always specify a time and a place, because the beliefs and the figures to which they allude may be a stable feature of the culture. Belief legends may, nevertheless, be very detailed regarding time and place, thus resembling more closely the other main subgenres of legends, which relate to places and events: local legends and historical legends.[12] Legends fulfill a unique role in shaping consciousness of the past as well as group identity, and in lending both a voice. In their capacity as central tools in the molding of these cognitive categories, historical legends interact with other types of discourse through which the past takes shape within a culture, including various textual modes—memoirs, autobiographies, biographies, letters, diaries, written documents, and so on. In addition, other, non-verbal modes of discourse, documentation, and expression, in the form of buildings, objects, or traces of natural phenomena, interact with these verbal modes to create the representation of the past. None of them, however, preserves the real past. Due to the time gaps between them and the historian, a mediating act of interpretation is always required between the types of discourse representing the past and the writing of history. In other words, there is no historical material at "degree zero," in the term coined by Roland Barthes concerning a (non-existent) mode of writing lacking any degrees of transformation, veiling, and mediation.[13]

In the self-reflection characteristic of modern history, the reciprocity between representations of the past and the process of collective memory has been highlighted.[14] Source criticism, which relates to each discursive and representative mode according to its specific nature—a building as a building, a legend as a legend, a private letter as a private letter—considerably improves the ability to interpret and discern the kind of information each one provides. Hence, in my view, no clear-cut contrast between true and legendary sources should be postulated.

In *The Hebrew Folktale*, Eli Yassif deals with the genre of the historical legend in various historical contexts, which he presents in a chronological sequence. I will refer to his specific interpretations below, in my own discussion of two stories that are also cited by Yassif. As for his general assumptions concerning the genre of the historical legend, I fully agree with his general conclusion that legends convey "truths" rather than "facts," and are an important source for mirroring historical processes shaped within collective consciousness.[15] I must nevertheless question Yassif's perception of the legend in particular, and of folk literature in general, as representing "the broad ranks of the people," whom he sets apart, in terms of class and education, from the "intellectual elite." Contrary to scholars of folk literature who adopt an orthodox Marxist perspective, I do not believe that creating a collective consciousness through oral means is a pursuit uniquely fit for the "masses," implying the poor, the weak, and the ignorant. We might wish this power were solely theirs, lacking as they are in other institutionalized modes of expression, whether written or artistic. We must admit, however, that sharing access to these means does not prevent intellectuals from taking an active part in the development of consciousness, including through legends. The sharp, bipolar division shown in textual analyses, although denied by Yassif in the programmatic introduction to his book, seems to perpetuate the division between "us" and "them," whereby "we" have a culture and "they" have "folklore." He thus grants the "masses" something he actually has no power to bestow: exclusive rights to the creation of folk literature. The multivocality characteristic of folk literature in general, and the unique ways in which rabbinic aggadic Midrashim interact with folk prose and other bodies of knowledge (such as Halakha and philosophical discourse), indicate that the authors of Midrash were highly sensitive to the broad range of sources nurturing cultural creativity. We might also say that, precisely because they understood that legends are created by women and men, rich and poor, they found any separation between their modes of expression inappropriate, since "these and these are the words of the living God."

The dichotomy between midrashic, rabbinical creativity, as opposed to popular creativity, is a basic assumption of Jonah Fraenkel's *The Methods of Aggadah and Midrash*, which presents the world of the intellectuals shielded in the house of study as separate and detached from the world of folk literature. Fraenkel points to Yitzhak Heinemann, author of *The Methods of Aggadah*,[16] as his main source of inspiration. But Fraenkel's description of rabbinic culture does not rhyme with Heinemann's perception of "organic thinking," which is wholly predicated on the notion that no barrier divides folk literature from learning, philosophy, and Halakha. The approach proposed throughout the present book, which also claims inspiration from Heinemann (as well as from Fraenkel in other matters), interprets organic thinking as an ethnographic Archimedean point, sustaining the creative mode so unique to Midrash. In the approach suggested here, organic thinking leaves room for opposing and contradictory voices. Given this totality, disharmonies will inevitably resonate in the system of thought and faith articulated by, and transmitted through, rabbinic literature.

Let us return to the genre of the historical legend, of which a number of examples will be at the focus of this chapter. This genre sharpens questions about the social basis of the text. In folktales, issues about credibility and links with reality—external reality according to historians relying on legendary sources, or spiritual-cultural reality according to the historians of *mentalité*—are minimized by the stylistic, formal, and content mechanisms of the genre itself. The features of the legend, as a genre, do not converge into a metonymy of the past (as positivist historians would choose to believe) but into a metaphor, often a very powerful one, of times gone by. As all readers of literature know, and particularly readers of poetry, a metaphor is a particularly profound and sophisticated tool for preserving meanings that escape direct representative discourse. The past, which is also elusive, cannot be represented except through metonymies, such as remnants of buildings or surviving documents, or through metaphors, such as legends told about events taking place in the spiritual or material reality. The very transformation of these events into a legend turns them into a palpable spiritual reality.

Contrary to the two main genres of folk prose, the legend and the folktale, I do not view myth as a genre but as a cognitive category that constitutes the necessary foundation for cultural creativity as a whole, whether folk, oral, written, artistic, or social. Mythical thought is characterized by a total, all-encompassing perception of being, and by an explanation of all details of existence through the narrative plot. Typically, expressions of mythical thinking emphasize antitheses between basic concepts in life and culture, such as life and death, culture and nature, femininity and masculinity.[17]

In different periods, and in varying cultural contexts, mythical expression appears in different cultural genres, such as epic poetry in the ancient East and Near East, or popular science, perhaps, in our own times. Mythical thought may appear in mythological motifs found in folk prose genres, including, as we will see below, both folktales and legends.[18] Given that the legend conveys the experience of the collective through the details of a known and plausible reality, the mythical motifs that may be woven into it suggest extreme, total possibilities, which test the very nature of reality. Legends affirm existence within a given reality, and convey a broad spectrum of relationships toward it, both positive and negative. But when myth bursts into the legend, the frame of reality collapses, either by retreating to the stage of its construction-creation, or by soaring way beyond it.

∾

Three historical legends, representing three different models of narrativization of the Messianic theme, will be discussed in this chapter. The interaction between the genre of the historical legend and the Messianic idea produces, on the one hand, mythological motifs projecting the future on the narrative level—eschatological motifs—and, on the other hand, associations with a utopian mode of thought. The mythological narrative and the utopian mode of thought clash concerning the timing of the event that will reverse the troubled historical present, with the former expecting it immediately and the latter at the end of history.[19]

The wide ideological and emotional spectrum covered by stories of the *amoraim* about the Messiah points to the various options available to creative popular imagination for dealing with Messianic hope and its inevitable frustration.

Two of the three stories we will be discussing have been the subject of much scholarly attention, particularly by historians. The story considered first, however, has been largely ignored, which is rather puzzling given its content and its message.[20]

The following story appears in two Palestinian sources, in *Lamentations Rabbah* and in the Palestinian Talmud. Following is the version from *Lamentations Rabbah* 1:16:

> Once upon a time a man was plowing. His ox lowed. An Arab passed by and asked: "What are you?" He answered, "I am a Jew." He said to him, "Unharness your ox and untie your plough." "Why?" he asked. "Because the Temple of the Jews is destroyed." Said he, "How do you know this?" He said, "I know it from the lowing of your ox." While he was talking to him, the ox lowed again. The Arab said to him: "Harness your ox and tie up your plough, because the redeemer of the Jews

is born." Said he, "What is his name?" He answered, "His name is Menahem" [Comforter]. "And his father, what is his name?" He answered, "Hezekiah" [In God is my strength]. "And where do they live?" He answered, "In Birat Ha-Aravah, in Bethlehem of Judah." The man sold his ox and plow and bought swathes [to wrap children]. He journeyed from hamlet to hamlet, and from town to town, until he arrived. All the villagers came to buy from him, but that woman, the infant's mother, bought nothing from him. He asked her: "Why do you not buy swathes?" She answered, "Because I fear hardships are in store for my child." [The text is difficult here; possibly also: "hardships from my child.] "Why?" he asked. Said she, "Because close to his coming the Temple was destroyed." Said he, "We trust the Master of the Universe that, as it was destroyed close to his coming, so close to his coming will it be rebuilt." He said, "Take from these swathes for your child." She said, "I have no money." Said he, "Do not worry, come buy them and after some days I will come to your house and collect the money." She took some and left. A few days later the man said, "I will go and see how the child is faring." He went to her and said: "That child, how is he?" She answered, "Did I not tell you that I feared hardships, . . . from that time, winds and whirlwinds came and lifted him away." Said he, "Did I not tell you it was destroyed at his coming, and at his coming it will be rebuilt?" R. Avin said, "Why should I learn this from an Arab? Is it not explicitly written, 'And Lebanon shall fall by a mighty one' (Isaiah 10:34), and afterwards it is written, 'And there shall come forth a rod out of the stem of Jesse, and a branch shall grow out of his roots'" (Isaiah 11:1).[21]—*Lamentations Rabbah* 1:16

A comparison between the PT version (Berakhot 2:4, 5a) and the one cited here reveals few but interesting differences. In the PT version, the Arab knows, without asking, that the tiller of the soil is a Jew; he also makes the more explicit claim that "The king Messiah has been born"; Bethlehem is called in this text *birat ha-melekh* (the royal fortress)[22]; the salesman identifies Menahem's mother because the other women call on her to come and buy, and mention her son's name, which the man has apparently identified as the Messiah's name; when approached by the salesman, the mother reacts in extreme terms: "I wish the enemies of Israel were strangled, because on the day he was born . . ." (or "I wish the enemy of Israel—the child—were strangled").

The Messiah's name, as it appears here, is also found in a long aggadic Messianic passage in the Babylonian Talmud: "And some say his name is Menahem, the son of Hezekiah" (Sanhedrin 98b). This tradition, however, is not ascribed to a particular sage but is a matter of common knowledge, unlike several homilies that precede it, where the name of the Messiah is derived, perhaps ironically, from the names of sages.[23]

Several important features characteristic of folk narratives, particularly of the historical legend genre, resonate in this story. The choice of the infant's name, and the name of his birthplace, rely on well-known traditions. Thus, Bethlehem is a natural choice according to a homily based on the well-known verse from Micha 5:1: "But thou, Bethlehem-Efrata, thou art little among the thousands of Judah, yet out of thee shall he come forth to me that is to be ruler in Israel and his goings out are from ancient time, from days of old." The verse echoes with the cyclic rhythm inherent in Messianism, and particularly Jewish Messianism, in which the coming of the Messiah is not a divine creation *ex nihilo*, but a return of the House of David to its previous glory. David's origins in Bethlehem are also intimated in this verse in the phrase "from ancient time, from days of old."

A similar exegesis on the verse from Micha appears in the birth stories in the Gospels of Matthew 1–2 and Luke 2, which the story about the birth of the Messiah Menahem closely resembles,[24] including in such details as the discovery of the Messiah by a man who had wandered toward him from far away in the Jewish narrative, the three wise men or the three magi of the New Testament, the gifts to mother and infant, and the mother's poverty in both traditions. These similarities, in details apparently lacking any theological significance, suggest that these are neither polemics nor imitations but parallels typical of folk narrative. Folk traditions were shared by those Jews who belonged to the majority and by others belonging to a minority group, who believed in Jesus as the Messiah and joined the early Christian Church, made up mostly of Jews.[25]

Oral folk tradition, which tends to preserve certain concrete details, may provide a reasonable explanation for the shared narrative motifs. Thus, for instance, it would seem that the name of the Messiah and the name of his father in this legend are not merely a coincidence but part of Messianic traditions prevalent at the time and even earlier. I noted above the name

Menahem son of Hezekiah in the Babylonian Talmud, although, in this case, the appearance of these names need not attest to oral transmission. However, the presence of these two names in a different set of family relationships in the writings of Josephus Flavius, the first-century C.E. Jewish historian who wrote in Greek for an educated Roman public, does lead us to ponder the presence of an oral tradition at the time of the events. Josephus Flavius himself operated in the Galilee, and when he writes about a family of rebels who also referred to Messianic images, with a father called Judah son of Hezekiah, and a son named Menahem,[26] we hear a different combination of the names from the *Lamentations Rabbah* story: Menahem son of Hezekiah from Bethlehem in Judah.

The story in *Lamentations Rabbah* resembles in many details, as noted, the story of Jesus' birth in the Gospels of Matthew 2:1–18 and Luke 2:1–16. The stranger represented in the Midrash by the Arab is paralleled in Matthew by the three magi, who are priests of the Persian religion, also often mentioned in rabbinic writings. The Jew who finds the infant Messiah in Bethlehem likewise reaches him after many wanderings from hamlet to hamlet and from town to town, as the magi arrive from far, "from the East." In the Luke story, the birth of the infant Messiah is announced to the shepherds who, like the Jew tilling the soil in the Midrash, are in the field when they hear the message. The shepherds are informed by the angels but, in Matthew, the magi follow a sign from nature, a star that announces or signals the birth of the Messiah. A sign from nature, in the shape of a lowing ox, also appears in the Midrash. In Matthew, the infant's life is threatened by Herod the King, who contrives to obtain information about the birth of the child announced by the magi, and then kill him. The magi save the child when they counsel his parents to escape, and Herod spends his wrath by slaying all infants in the Bethlehem area. In the Midrash, the threat to the infant is conveyed through the fears harbored by his mother regarding his future, and in the PT version, as noted, by her explicit desire to strangle the enemies of Israel or the child himself. The Jew selling swathes tries to save the infant by giving some of his merchandise on credit to the mother, and informs her he will return to visit, but to no avail. Swathes are also mentioned in the Christian story, in the annunciation to the shepherds in Luke: "Ye shall find the babe wrapped in swaddling clothes, lying in a manger" (2:12). This child is indeed swaddled but, due to his parents' poverty, resembling the mother's poverty in the Talmudic-midrashic story, the birth takes place in a manger.[27] A motif analogous to that of giving the swathes on credit appears in Matthew, in the lavish gifts brought by the magi from the East: gold, incense, and myrrh.[28]

The story about the Messiah's birth was thus a common tradition, a theme about which Jews in Palestine, beginning with the first century C.E., told stories in several versions. At another level, we may ponder about the perception of Messianism in a society that speaks of the Messiah as an infant born in dire poverty, whose life is threatened, and for whom the central, or even unique, figure in life is his mother.[29]

This question can hardly be answered unequivocally, but posing it sheds light on the issue of Messianism from several directions. First, the birth of the Messiah is told as the typical birth story of a "culture hero," constructing the biographical pattern of a sacred, important, and powerful figure.[30] The threat to the life of the newborn and his family's destitution are recurrent motifs in the birth stories of heroes. In the context of a story about the Messiah's birth, these motifs represent the sharp opposition between un-mitigated impotence and a vision of infinite might. The infant in distress personifies the Messianic dream of a positive reversal of history. From the parental perspective, the image of a newborn in his mother's bosom is the quintessential joining together of the might of childbirth and the impotence of the mother now charged with the task, which may become impossible, of caring for the survival of an infant whose life is in danger.

The Messianic idea, which entrusts a human individual, and in its Jewish formulation one who is not even a son of God, with the power to reverse the course of history, concretizes a yearning for power that could almost be called megalomanic. Subjecting the vision of the Messiah's redeeming power to the impotence of a swaddled infant shows a profound cultural under-standing of how narrow is the gap between hope and loss. This proximity emerges from two sources: a reality where pain and loss are pervasive begets the dream of a redeeming Messiah in human shape; at the same time, latent in the Messianic dream lie the seeds of its inevitable loss. The infant per-sonifies hope for the future, but the threat to him will end in a catastrophe that, at most, can merely be postponed.

The parallels between the motifs featuring in Jesus' birth story in the New Testament and the birth story of the Messiah Menahem in Bethlehem offer several possibilities for explaining the circumstances of Jewish folk narrative at the time. The preservation of this narrative tradition in the Palestinian

Talmud and in *Lamentations Rabbah* suggests that the inclusion of the story in the Christian corpus did not compel its eradication from the Jewish narrative tradition, despite developments within Christianity that distanced it from its Jewish sources. At the same time, it is again worth noting that the story is not necessarily formulated as a polemic against Christianity.[31] Folk narratives were shown to carry the weight of the intercultural dialogue between Jews and Arabs in Chapter 4. Similarly, an intercultural dialogue can be detected here too, first between Jews and Jewish Christians, and then between Jews and Christians in general. This dialogue between folk literatures shows how two historical perceptions may illuminate the same narrative motifs in various ways, creating local adaptations of folk motifs on a functional basis, when the same motif functions in different ideological contexts.[32]

Considering Messianic traditions from the perspective of folk literature enables us to take note of the possibility that some of the central themes formulated as dogmas by the Church from the beginning of the fourth century—the "dogmas" affirmed at the great ecclesiastical councils—have their roots in the Palestinian folk culture of the time. The Midrash deals with these motifs, which the Church articulated as dogmas, in its unique and totally non-dogmatic way.

The idea that the Messiah is born in the course of history was not alien, then, to the Jewish thought of the times. This idea, however, was rejected outright in the course of the renowned disputations between Jews and representatives of the Church in medieval Spain, when the rabbis resorted to disclaiming the historical validity of aggadic stories.[33]

In the sequence of the midrashic text, the story about the birth of the Messiah Menahem appears immediately after a number of stories about suffering women, all named Miriam, which I discussed in Chapter 6. The association with the name of Jesus' mother, as noted, is almost inevitable. The Midrash does not identify the Messiah's mother by name but, nevertheless, a phonological and topical association arises between the name of the child, Menahem, and the mother of the seven sons, Miriam the daughter of *Tanhum*. The root NHM, meaning comfort, which is found in the two Hebrew stories, and the name Miriam, meaning bitter, which is found in the Christian narrative and in one of the Hebrew stories, signal the process between consolation and grief that characterizes all three mothers.

Placing the story about the Messiah's birth in this sequence need not imply the meaning that Fraenkel ascribes to the story, namely, that the mother must understand it is her duty to continue raising the child despite the Temple's destruction on the day of his birth. Fraenkel, and others in his wake, assume that the mother had relinquished her son in her heart, and this is the reason for his disappearance.[34] The mother, holding in her bosom a living and breathing personification of boundless might coupled with endless impotence, represents a tragic plight taken to its radical extreme. The story thus singles her out, marking her with the tragic choice of motherhood to the Messiah. She is not, under any circumstances, a behavioral model for the Jewish "everywoman" of her time.

In his discussion of this story, Fraenkel argues that because the Jew actively engages in a search for the Messiah, he is punished with the delay of his coming. This interpretation seems to me completely tilted on the side of omnipotence, ascribing to an individual the power to determine the moment of the Messiah's advent, and thereby denying the presence of an opposite pole in the story. The infinite postponement in the coming of the Messiah is immanent to the very perception of the relationship between Messiah and history, as is indeed suggested by this midrashic text. The historical legend embodies the experiential dimensions of this insight.

The tension between the yearning for omnipotence and the acknowledgment of human weakness undergoes a narrative transformation into other concepts, which are superimposed on the characters. As in Chapter 6, which deals with the social context, might and weakness are personified by the woman and the man, and the woman is again the one who appears to be stronger.[35] She is the one who gave birth to the Messiah, and she is the one who knows how the story ends. The nebulous ending reflects our dependence, and that of the man in the story, on her willingness to tell the story in all its details, but the acknowledgment of loss as an expression of ultimate human weakness, the loss of the child Messiah, is wholly focused on her.

Further inquiry concerning the credibility of the narrative authority may lead to the question: Why is information about the destruction of the Temple, and even about the birth of the Messiah, transmitted by an Arab? The text in *Lamentations Rabbah* ascribes this question to R. Avin who, as an alternative source of information for the convergence of these two events— the destruction of the Temple and the birth of the Messiah—suggests the two verses from Isaiah: "And Lebanon shall fall by a mighty one" (Isaiah 10:34); "And there shall come forth a rod out of the stem of Jesse, and a branch shall grow out of his roots" (Isaiah 11:1).[36] And why does the Jew in the story rely on information from the Arab to launch his strenuous search?[37]

In rabbinic literature, Arabs appear mainly as a group characterized by ethnographic features rather than as a religious or national community. Their typical characteristics are nomadism and a close relationship with nature, particularly animals. In the context of rabbinic literature, which stresses the importance of interpretation, all interpretation, the exceptional exegetical skills of Arabs, touching mainly on the interpretation of signs and tracks in nature, are highly significant.[38] This aspect of Arab culture also appears in the riddle stories cited in Chapter 3, as I then showed in Chapter 4. There as well, the Arabs' intimacy with the desert provides them with important knowledge about the Israelite past, just as tracks in the sand, which are read in the light of the *Bab a-Tazkin* (the study of tracks), reflect someone's movement up to the point of arrival. Whoever knows how to interpret tracks, can transform a casual backward glance into an interpretive vision.

The definition of the other as the one who is closer to nature strengthens the definition of the narrators' membership group as owners of "culture."[39] In Talmudic-midrashic literature, this opposition is sharpened by placing "us," the interpreters of texts, against "them," the interpreters of signs from nature. The Arab becomes the mediator between nature and culture when he applies the cultural model of "interpretation" to nature. This mode of interpretation also refers to the multidimensional metaphor of the whole of creation as a divine text, a hypertext beyond all hypertexts.

The Arab plays a similar role in the series of classic folk narratives about Rabbah bar bar Hana.[40] The "tall tales" narrated by Rabbah bar bar Hana, a humorous genre, shift between the fantastic, the mythical, and the holy. The Arab, who is called Taya in those stories (and in various versions of the story about the Messiah's birth, as the name of a tribe in the Arab peninsula), shows Rabbah bar bar Hana the "dead of the desert" and Mount Sinai. About other sights, more fantastic and less mythical, Rabbah bar bar Hana hears mainly from sailors. The Talmudic text is built as a two-tiered dialogue, in which Rabbah bar bar Hana, in the context of "culture," tells the scholars at the academy the stories he has heard in the context of "nature." The Arab appears as the bearer of mythical knowledge, linked to the era when the Israelite nation was created in the desert, the place of nature, and of which the Arab is now (at the time of Rabbah bar bar Hana) the optimal interpreter. Knowledge of the mythical past is in the hands of the other. To reincorporate the past into the culture, it needs to be mediated through the dialogue between Rabbah bar bar Hana and the members of the academy.

The end of the midrashic tale on the birth of the Messiah touches on the connection between the historical legend and the mythical dimension of culture. When the man returns to Bethlehem, mainly to inquire after the child rather than to collect his money, the mother tells him that winds and storms have lifted the child away.[41] On this issue, Fraenkel's suggestion to turn to the Aramaic translation of the verse "and Elijah went up by a storm of wind into heaven" (Kings II, 2:11) is highly suggestive.[42] This translation uses the same rare word for a storm (al'ol) as that found in the story about the birth of the Messiah, intimating a link between the motifs of Elijah and the Messiah. This connection will eventually become the central tenor in Jewish Messianic narrative throughout history, as Elijah is traditionally cast as the harbinger of the Messiah's appearance (following the verse in Malakhi 4:5). Furthermore, the end of the story transposes Messianic hope onto a mythical plane, where it no longer has any real bearings in the time or space of concrete historical reality.

Messianism of the total kind intimated in the story about the birth of the infant Messiah, associated with the utopia of the young boy shepherding wild beasts in Isaiah's prophecy, is dismissed from Jewish historical discourse to the region of myth, borne by the storm. The impression left by this story on the repertoire of folk images about the Messiah concerns the infantile experience of impotence, from which redemption is sought through an omnipotent touch: a motherhood of might rather than a motherhood dreading harm as that of Menahem's mother, and a trustworthy fatherhood that only the good God can bestow, rather than the destructive God, or the wandering Jew, or the stranger interpreting signs, who are the only male characters in this story. And as myth was earlier described, it will structure much of later Jewish thought and behavior.

❧

Bar Kokhbah is the second Messianic character to which the Midrash in *Lamentations Rabbah* and in the Palestinian Talmud devotes a folk narrative. This tale, like the previous one, also offers a radical option for the narrative representation of the Messiah. But unlike the needy infant destined for disaster, a disaster perhaps caused by his own mother, Bar Kokhbah is a commander of legions. At the beginning of the story, his character emphasizes, in broad lines and sharp colors, the megalomanic dimension of the Messiah.

The story of the man known in the tradition as Bar Kokhbah, and in Palestinian sources as Ben Kozbah (*Lamentations Rabbah* 2 and, in a slightly different Hebrew spelling, in PT Ta'anit 4:5), also belongs to the genre of the historical legend:

> Said R. Yohannan: "Eighty thousand pairs of trumpeters besieged Bethar, each commanding several companies, and Ben Kozbah commanded two hundred thousand men with amputated fingers. The sages sent word to him: 'Till when will you go on mutilating the men of Israel?' Said he: 'How else shall I test them?' They answered: 'Do not enlist anyone who cannot pull up a cedar from Lebanon' [in the Munich Ms., "who cannot uproot a cedar from Lebanon," and in a fragment from the Cairo Genizah marked T.S.C. 2 (142) at the Cambridge Library, "Do not enroll in your army anyone who cannot ride a horse and uproot a cedar from Lebanon"]. He sent [word] that he had done so, and now had two hundred thousand men of one sort and two hundred thousand of the other. When going into battle, he said: 'Lord of the Universe, do not help us, and do not shame us either, as it is written: "Hast thou not rejected us, O God? So that thou goest not forth, O God, with our hosts"'" (Psalms 60:12).
>
> What was Ben Kozbah's strength? They said: "When going into battle, he caught the catapults with one of his knees and hurled them back, killing several people." Said R. Yohannan: "When R. Akiva looked at Ben Kozbah he said, 'There shall come a star out of Jacob' (Numbers 24:17). 'A star out of Jacob,' this refers to the king Messiah." R. Yohannan b. Tortha said: "Akiva, grass will grow on your cheeks, and still the son of David will not have come."
>
> For three and a half years, Hadrian besieged Bethar. And R. Eleazar of Modi'in sat wearing sackcloth and ashes and prayed: "Lord of the Universe, do not sit in judgment today, do not sit in judgment today!" As Hadrian could not conquer the city, he considered withdrawing. A Cuthean [Samaritan] was with him, and he said [to Hadrian]: "Be

patient today and I will help you subdue it. But as long as this hen sits on the hatchlings, on the sackcloth and on the ashes, you cannot conquer it."

After the apostate had said what he said, he entered the city. He found R. Eleazar standing and praying. He pretended to whisper in his ear, and R. Eleazar did not notice him. People went and told Ben Kozbah: "Your friend [another version: "uncle"] asked to surrender the city." He sent for the apostate and said to him: "What did you say to him?" He replied: "If I tell you, I divulge the king's secrets, and if I do not tell you, you will kill me. Better you should kill me than the king, and the king's secrets should not be known." Nevertheless, Ben Kozbah still believed that R. Eleazar had intended to surrender the city. When R. Eleazar finished praying, Ben Kozbah sent for him and asked: "What did the Cuthean say to you?" Said he: "I did not see the man." Ben Kozbah kicked him and killed him. A heavenly voice [bat-qol] then issued forth and declared: "Woe to my worthless shepherd, who forsakes the flock! The sword shall be upon his arm, and upon his right eye: his arm shall be dried up, and his right eye shall be darkened" (Zekhariah 11:17). Said the Holy One, blessed be He: "You have broken the arm of Israel and blinded its right eye; therefore, Ben Kozbah's arm will wither and his right eye will dim."

Forthwith, Bethar was conquered and Ben Kozbah was killed. His head was taken to Hadrian, who asked: "Who killed him?" "A soldier killed him," they replied. Hadrian did not believe them and ordered: "Go and bring his body [ptoma] to me." They went and brought his body, and found a snake curled on his knees. Said he: "Had his God not slain him, who could have beaten him? To fulfill the verse, 'unless their Rock had sold them, and the Lord had shut them up'" (Deuteronomy 32:30).—*Lamentations Rabbah* 2:2

The story, as cited here, describes the city's downfall and the death of the Messianic hero, without including all the narrative material dealing with the siege of Bethar. More details on the battle, and particularly on the cruel fate of those murdered in the carnage, appear further below in the PT version and in *Lamentations Rabbah*. Menahem, the infant Messiah, is represented in the Midrash through a standard opening episode in the cycle of biographical legends about culture heroes, with an account of his birth, and even of signs preceding birth. By comparison, Bar Kokhbah is represented through the closing link, the story of his death. In an article on the structure of the hero's biography in folk legends, Dov Noy pointed out that legends sometimes describe events that occurred after the hero's death and are linked to his heirs, his descendants, his grave, and his possessions.[43] In the rabbinic tradition about Bar Kokhbah there are no stories about objects or places connected to him after his death, but the event of his death is reported in great and intricate detail.

In my discussion of the story about the birth of the Messiah Menahem, I focused on the tension between history and eschatological myth, as this tension is conveyed through the shaping of the experiential world in the genre of the historical legend. The present story also refers mainly to the experiential dimension of the historical event known in collective memory as the Bar Kokhbah revolt.[44] An ancient description of the sequence of events that culminated in the Bar Kokhbah revolt appears in a book by the Roman historian Cassius Dio (150–235 C.E.), whose writings have reached us in the synopsis of an eleventh-century church historian.[45] The Church historian Eusebius (ca. 260–ca. 340) also provides details obtained from the writings of contemporary witnesses.[46] It is worth noting that historians writing in Greek and Latin called the hero Bar Kokhbah (in spellings and inflections typical of their own languages), whereas many of the Hebrew and Aramaic rabbinic texts referred to him in what was apparently his name, Ben Kozbah.[47]

In her book about Israeli collective memory in the Zionist era, Zerubavel explains why the Bar Kokhbah revolt belongs to the category of cultural materials that were, probably consciously, placed at the forefront of Zionist education when shaping our ritual culture, in stark contrast to their status in pre-Zionist Jewish historiography.[48] She shows how stories dealing with the end of the era of political independence, and particularly the stories of Bar Kokhbah and Massada (the latter is not discussed here because it does not appear in rabbinic texts), undergo symbolic and ritual adaptations in the new culture of Israel. The great interest evoked by these two stories was dramatically illustrated in the systematic exposure of their inscription on the land of Israel, namely, in the discovery of archaeological remnants attesting to them. Like historians, scholars of folk literature tend, quite naturally, to view archaeological findings as a more solid type of evidence, which contrasts with the vagueness of linguistic materials. Yet, one must remember that archaeological materials are one element in a broader hermeneutical system that also includes various texts, among them folk narratives, as crucial components.

Concerning the hero's name in our story, archaeology played a decisive role. Letters found in the Judean desert incontrovertibly prove that the name noted in the narrative texts of Palestinian *amoraim* was not a parodistic distortion denoting contempt and derived from the root KZB (deception), as had been claimed by Babylonian *amoraim* and many generations after them, but the man's name as he himself (or his scribe) had signed it.[49]

Jewish sources on the revolt differ strikingly from non-Jewish historical materials. Bar Kokhbah's revolt is a good example of the rabbis' total oblivion to historical occurrences "as they happened," and of their preference for approaches stressing experiential impressions of events and their historiosophical implications. It is for this reason that their historical narratives so readily invite folk-narrative study.

At the experiential level, the story about Ben Kozbah's death in *Lamentations Rabbah* poses a clear antithesis between physical and spiritual power represented, as is typical in folk literature, by two contrasting figures: Ben Kozbah and R. Eleazar of Modi'in. Historians feel it is important to indicate that this R. Eleazar may be the Eleazar Hacohen featuring in the coins minted by the military leader of the revolt, although some raise this hypothesis in order to reject it. The appearance of the Cuthean strolling between Hadrian's encampment and the city of Bethar is also related to an issue that historians have considered from a critical perspective: What was the role of the Samaritans in Bar Kokhbah's revolt? Did they support the Jewish rebels? Did they support the Romans? Did they stay away?[50]

The folk narrative does not provide any information that might help to clarify these historiographical issues. It does, however, reveal a great deal about the spiritual, and particularly the emotional, attitudes toward the question of independence on the one hand, and the status of the sages as well as their perception of Messianism on the other. Ben Kozbah is presented as a military leader resorting to tough means to choose his soldiers, including the candidates' self-mutilation.[51]

The discussion that follows touches on the dynamics, within the range noted above, between the genres of folktale and legend. Motifs of supernatural power are known in folk literature, and are also widespread in the folktale genre, including "strong man uproots tree and uses it as weapon"

(F 614.2 in the international index),[52] or "strong man's labor contract: anger bargain" (F 613.3). These motifs, which are typical of the folktale genre and appear in the story we are discussing here, strengthen the impression that this tale is removed from objective historical reality. Furthermore, they ensure that the story will have a powerful grip on the subjective realm of imaginary wishes, which are an acknowledged mechanism for coping with a harsh reality. Although Ben Kozbah's supernatural, or at least unusual, power is eventually defeated at the plot level, the very existence of a physical hero of this type in the Jewish repertoire of folk images nourishes the imagination and directs thinking toward more suppressive and megalomanic aspects of the Messianic idea. The ways in which this option comes to the fore in present Israeli reality are the concern of Zerubavel's book.[53]

Ben Kozbah's arrogance toward God under the garb of erudition, as it were, evident in his quoting a verse from Psalms, somehow resembles the arrogance of Titus, who drew his sword in the Holy of Holies but was defeated by a mosquito on God's mission, as narrated in the famous historical legend.[54] Here too, arrogance will lead to defeat through a reptile on God's mission, the snake. The use of a snake in a punitive mission is undoubtedly a more common motif in rabbinic writings than punishment by a mosquito, as the snake had served as an "emissary" since Genesis.[55]

The homily on the verse from Balaam's prophecy—"there shall come a star out of Jacob"—quoted by R. Yohannan in the name of R. Akiva, introduces another dimension of Ben Kozbah's role into the story, which had so far been shaped by concrete, mainly authoritarian and anti-spiritual motifs. It is worth noting that this verse inspired the cosmic sign of Jesus' birth in the Gospel of Matthew, as the magi follow a star to Bethlehem. The absence of the star in the story about Menahem's birth is thus significant. In contrast, the verse "There shall come a star out of Jacob" is quoted in this story by R. Akiva in order to anoint Ben Kozbah as the King Messiah. Notably, the use of the title is uniquely limited here to the terrestrial rule of the King Messiah, as one leading the people in a national revolt, and has no bearing on the spiritual, metaphysical Messianic perception.[56] R. Akiva formulates his political support for Ben Kozbah as the leader of the revolt in a rhetoric that is highly typical of him, the homily of a verse. R. Yohannan b. Tortha, who holds the opposite view, also formulates it in political terms—the leader you are supporting is not a worthy leader. The two sages do not seem to be at odds on the question of whether the era of universal redemption has arrived;

rather, they disagree on whether the talented military leader capable of releasing the people of Israel from the yoke of the Roman conqueror has indeed risen. The use of the word King Messiah in this story greatly lessens the utopian dimension of the Messianic idea, and highlights its historical aspect.[57]

After the introduction, the gist of the story follows. The link between the two parts of the story—the megalomanic description of Ben Kozbah at the beginning and then the move that leads to his downfall—is strengthened, probably by the editor, through the repetition of Ben Kozbah's arrogant address to God, "Lord of the Universe," in the expiatory prayer of R. Eleazar of Modi'in. This editorial selection is unique to the text of *Lamentations Rabbah*, since the formulations in the Palestinian Talmud, although very similar, are not identical.

In any event, R. Eleazar of Modi'in sitting in sackcloth and ashes is an ominous sign. Indeed, a literal reading obviously interprets it as an ascetic act meant to evoke divine pity. But the double entendre in the words of the praying sage informs his words with unique urgency, even in the PT version of the story. The Cuthean who, from a Jewish point of view, is only half a stranger, as opposed to the Roman, who is a total stranger, plays a complex role in the story. On the one hand, he knows the location of the power protecting the city from the besieging emperor; on the other hand, he will eventually use this knowledge to bring about the city's destruction.

The image that the Cuthean uses to describe R. Eleazar's activity highlights an ideological and emotional dimension that constitutes an important hermeneutical focus of the folk literature included in *Lamentations Rabbah*: womanhood as opposed to manhood. To describe R. Eleazar's protective action, the Cuthean takes an image from the realm of motherhood, a brooding hen. This inward-oriented activity, leading the sage to be oblivious to his surroundings, is a perfect antithesis to Ben Kozbah's aggressive belligerence, and represents, above all, the opposite view regarding God's involvement in the city's distress. As opposed to the megalomanic pole of a forceful hero, R. Eleazar represents the power latent in motherly warmth, while still appealing to God out of the impotence of humanity. In his motherly approach, R. Eleazar could be a spouse to the male God and bring about redemption, as Rachel did in the text of proem 24 in *Lamentations Rabbah*, presented in Chapter 6. Ben Kozbah's overt male attitude rules him out for this role.

The idiom of a couple as a conceptual model of the relationship between

God and the people of Israel is a metaphorical paradigm that is also used in parables about kings where, as noted, the people of Israel feature either as the king's wife or as the king's divorcée. Here, too, as in the proem to the verse "Call for the mourning women, that they may come" (Jeremiah 9:16), discussed in Chapter 6, the ability to mourn that culture traditionally assigns to women may be revealed as the true redemptive power, were it not destroyed by male violence.[58]

In proem 20 of *Lamentations Rabbah*, God is likened to a mother bird in a homily on Psalms 102:8: " 'I watch, and am like a lonely sparrow upon the house top': as this sparrow, when you take away its young, sits solitary, so said the Holy One, blessed be He, I burnt my house, and destroyed my city, and exiled my children among the nations, and I sit solitary, how I sit solitary." The Psalms chapter serving as the basis of the parable would have been an appropriate prayer for R. Eleazar to bring before God in the situation described in the story. The chapter in Psalms opens with the verse "A prayer of the afflicted, when he faints, and pours out his complaint before the Lord," includes pleas for the city of Jerusalem and its dwellers, and ends in an optimistic mood: "The children of thy servants shall continue, and their seed shall be established before thee."[59]

The image of the bird, particularly when relating to God, is also a clear opposite of the snake, the other animal featured in the story and representing the punitive, lethal aspect of God. Thus, R. Eleazar can be seen as the embodiment of God's motherly compassion, and as long as this feeling is alive within the city, there is hope. Ben Kozbah, who seeks to win by force, invalidates the power of divine compassion represented by the praying sage.[60]

Mechanisms common in the folk-narrative genre of the swindler novellae come to the fore at the plot level that concerns us here, although this story still belongs mainly to the genre of the historical legend: the Cuthean plays the role of the trickster.[61] His success reverses the possibility of redemptive change, a change with potential Messianic implications in the historical context, at least in military and political terms. The concept of the king's secrets, to which the Cuthean claims to be privy, becomes a multivalent sign when one kingdom faces another, the kingdom of Caesar against the kingdom of God. Ostensibly, the plot ends with the victory of God's kingdom, but the emperor is the one who provides the interpretation that renders God victorious. In the concluding scene, too, which reveals the truth about Ben

Kozbah's death, an important role is assigned to a stranger, in the figure of the soldier who kills the hero.[62]

Ben Kozbah's behavior toward R. Eleazar reveals the destructive might of the force that had been described in such overstated terms. His knees, as we are told at the opening, are the source of his strength, and catapult back the enemy stones. They then become an instrument of naked power, when Ben Kozbah reacts to R. Eleazar's introversion and his detachment from external events with a senseless kick. Ben Kozbah's action functions exactly like the moral flaw (*hamartia*) of the tragic hero,[63] and precisely at the point where he feels strongest, he fails in a tragic mistake that leads to his downfall. But Ben Kozbah is not a tragic hero, because at no point in the story does he realize his mistake. Paradoxically, the tragic hero is Hadrian who, like Titus in the above-mentioned story about his own punishment, becomes aware of the divine power ruling the world. In this story, Hadrian is the one who interprets the event in the moral-religious perspective fitting the text's broader system of norms. The interpretation of the event's religious meaning by a non-Jew resembles the Arab's interpretation of the cow's lowing in the story about the Messiah's birth, discussed at the opening of this chapter.

The element of the double interpretation, the additional voice, appears in the presentation of Ben Kozbah's body. On the one hand, Bar Kokhbah's death resembles that of Goliath, whose head was brought to the victor, here the Roman emperor rather than David. The Messianic plot undergoes an ironic, almost grotesque inversion in this case. He who was supposed to represent the House of David ends his life in a manner similar to the man David defeated. The decapitated head of the vanquished enemy, a fixed feature in many battle stories, is also a somewhat gross sign of the man's lack of wisdom. His fury led to his own downfall, to the downfall of the city he was defending, and, in the broader historical context, to the final eclipse, for many years to come, of Jewish political independence. On the other hand, the tortured body of the defeated victim, who cruelly embodies the crushed, tormented fate of his people, allows us for the first time to view Ben Kozbah as an object of potential identification. The beheading turns him, for the first time in the story, into the representative of the people for whose freedom he was struggling. In splitting off the warrior's knees from the supplicant's lips, the story transfoms the complete social body into a *ptoma* (a torso that is only a part of the body).[64] The experience of loss represented by a headless body amplifies the image of the failed political Messianism entailed by Bar Kokhbah's leadership. R. Akiva's cruel death at the hands of the Romans, as one of the Ten Martyrs, further stresses the harsh spiritual implications of the military failure.[65]

In the story about the infant Messiah Menahem, knowledge about the Messiah's moment of birth is ascribed to the stranger, the other, the Arab passing by the Jew tilling his field. In the story about Bar Kokhbah's death, the stranger (who is even an enemy, Hadrian) is the one who draws the lesson from the story. Something in the mechanism bringing together Jewish awareness and the Messianic phenomenon is revealed in these two legends as painfully flawed; the story about the infant Messiah sent Messianic hope soaring into the mythical realm, whereas the story about Bar Kokhbah returns it to a maimed, beheaded despair.

A reading of this story from a folk-narrative perspective highlights the voices of characters considered "other." These are the voices of women, such as the Messiah's mother, strangers such as the Cuthean, Hadrian, and the Arab, and even the androgynous voice conveyed here by R. Eleazar.

∾

Another story bearing on the issue discussed in this chapter is the story about the blood of Zekhariah ben Yehoyada, who was stoned in the Temple by the people. I will not consider this story in detail. Its core is an event mentioned in Chronicles 2, 24:20–22, during the reign of Joash king of Judea, the murder of the priest Zekhariah ben Yehoyada. According to the Midrash, Zekhariah's seething blood led Nebuzardan to murder many Jews: 80,000 novice priests according to the more modest version, and up to 210,000 (including the Great and Small Sanhedrins, youths, virgins, and schoolchildren) in other versions, until the blood of the murdered touched Zekhariah's blood and stopped it from seething. The story is cited four times in *Lamentations Rabbah* and in PT Ta'anit 4:5, in *Pesikta de-Rav Kahana* (which is also a Palestinian *amoraic* Midrash),[66] and in TB Gittin 57a–b. Proem 5 in *Lamentations Rabbah* includes an abridged version, essentially close to the PT version, whereas proem 23 cites a longer version, close to the one in the Babylonian Talmud; *Lamentations Rabbah* 2:2 contains a very short quotation, while in *Lamentations Rabbah* 4:3, the whole story is included.

Research has dealt with the story from the perspective of the Jewish–

Christian dialogue in the first centuries C.E.[67] This dialogue does indeed resonate in many *Lamentations Rabbah* stories, as many of the previous discussions indicate. Nevertheless, the versions of the story about Zekhariah's blood found in the Talmuds and the Midrash seem to include fewer allusions to this dialogue than might have been expected. The homiletical question of who is the Zekhariah in question—the Zekhariah ben Yehoyada mentioned above, Zekhariah ben Berakhyahu, son of the prophet Ido, or Zekhariah ben Yeverekhyahu (mentioned in Isaiah 8:2 together with Uriah the priest)—was a matter of concern to Christian, but not to Jewish, homilists. Although the murder victim is alternatively called priest, prophet, and judge, the character in this story is unquestionably the priest from Chronicles. It is puzzling to see that in the Palestinian Talmud, in *Pesikta de-Rav Kahana*, and in *Lamentations Rabbah*, this tale is tied to stories about the destruction of the Second Temple (the tie in the Babylonian Talmud follows from the Palestinian sources and is secondary).

The prominence of this story in the Jewish consciousness of the time may stem from its use in Christian texts, and first and foremost in its explicit mention in Matthew 23:35, where the Jewish dwellers of Jerusalem are blamed for the death of innocent prophets and apostles from Abel to Zekhariah.[68] Jean-Daniel Dubois suggested that this story should be understood in the parallel Jewish and Christian traditions as a concretization of the name Zekhariah, namely, as dealing with memory (from the Hebrew root ZKR). To Jews, says Dubois, the memory concretized in the story is the sacrifice ritual of the Temple, while for Christians it embodies the memory of their Messiah's sacrifice.

My interpretation is close to that suggested by Dubois, with the added perspective of a folk-narrative viewpoint. The story may have survived this long because of its generic features as a historical legend anchored in a typical local tradition connected with Jerusalem. This tradition is linked to the location of the Temple and, in this sense, it erects the lost sanctuary in memory, creating "a place of memory" linked to a real place.[69] Christian tradition has preserved the testimony of the "pilgrim from Bordeaux," who described the place in the Temple where traces of Zekhariah's blood had been preserved until his time, together with traces of his murderers' boots.[70] In *Lamentations Rabbah* 4:14, on the biblical verse "They wandered blind through the streets, polluted with blood," we read: "The blind, what would they say? Who will show us Zekhariah's blood? And the lame, what would they say? Who will show us the place where Zekhariah was killed, and we'll embrace it and kiss it." The homilist relates here to the verse following the one used in the homily on Zekhariah's blood, and attaches to it a local tradition ascribing to the place of the murder healing powers for such afflictions as blindness and lameness. Local traditions of this type are often the reason for the continued vitality of earlier traditions.[71] Compared with the Messianic perspective, this story is actually translating redemption into the concrete terms of physical health, and transposing it to the private realm of the individual's body.

Allusions to the human body in a story, even if only in passing, as is the case here, often intimate that this is a text from folk literature. The power of body symbols in literary texts is well known in the study of texts dating from Late Antiquity.[72] In folk stories, beside the general meaning of body symbols, it must be noted that these stories were originally told to a listening public that was physically present, by a narrator performing with his/her body.[73] The actual physical presence of folk narrators in the oral telling of the story comes to the fore in various ways, such as voices and pointing to limbs, but also in the adaptation of signs found in the text, such as physical descriptions of the protagonists and, as is the case here, in the allusion to healing powers mentioned at the end of the story on Zekhariah's blood in *Lamentations Rabbah* 4.

∾

The last story to be considered in this chapter has also concerned historians, perhaps even more than the tale of Bar Kokhbah's death. This is the story of R. Yohannan b. Zakkai's exit from Jerusalem in a coffin while Vespasian was besieging the city.[74] This story appears in numerous versions in several sources: in addition to *Lamentations Rabbah* 1, it also appears in *Avot de-Rabbi Nathan*, version A, chapter 4; *Avot de-Rabbi Nathan*, version B, chapter 6; TB Gittin 56a–b; and *Midrash Mishle* 15, in a version almost exactly like the one in *Avot de-Rabbi Nathan*, version B.[75]

Following is the *Lamentations Rabbah* version:

Another interpretation [of the verse], "Her adversaries have become the chief" (Lamentations 1:5), this refers to Vespasian; "her enemies prosper" (ibid.), this refers to Trajan. Vespasian spent three and a half years in Jerusalem, and four dukes were there with him: the duke of Arabia, the duke of Phoenicia, the duke of Sebatini [apparently Sebastia in Samaria], the duke of Alexandria. The duke of Arabia, what was his name? Two *amoraim* differed, one said his name was Ilam and the other said his name was Abgar.

In Jerusalem there were three wealthy men, each of whom could have supported the city for five years: Ben Tsitsit Hakkeset, Ben Kalba Savua, and Nakdimon ben Gurion. And why was his name Nakdimon ben Gurion? Because the sun shone through [*naqdah*] for him; Ben Kalba Savua, because whoever entered his house hungry as a dog [*kalba*] came out sated [*savua*]; Ben Tsitsit Hakesset, because his ritual fringes [*tsitsit*] brushed against pillows and cushions [*kesset*]. One said, I can support Jerusalem for ten years on wheat and barley; one said on wine and oil, and one said on burning wood. And the sages praised the wood above all.

And Ben Batiah was there [in some of the manuscripts: "ben Avtiah," but in the Munich Ms., and in the first printed edition, as here], the son of R. Yohannan b. Zakkai's sister, who was in charge of the storehouses and burnt them all. R. Yohannan ben Zakkai heard this and said, "woe." They went and told Ben Batiah: "Your uncle [or friend] said 'woe.'" He sent for him and said: "Why did you say 'woe'?" Said he: "I only said 'wow.'" Said he: "As long as the storehouses were here, the people would not go into battle and would not pursue the enemy." Between "woe" and "wow," R. Yohannan b. Zakkai was saved. And of him [the verse] said: "The excellency of knowledge is that wisdom gives life to those who have it" (Ecclesiastes 7:12). Three days later, R. Yohannan b. Zakkai went for a walk in the market and saw people boiling straw and drinking its water. He said: "Can people who boil straw and drink its water confront Vespasian's armies? The remedy is for me to depart." R. Yohannan sent for Ben Batiah in secret and asked him: "How long will you persist on starving everyone to death?" Said he: "What can I do? If I say anything to them, they will kill me." Said he: "Show me how to get out, maybe there will be rescue from above." He said: "I will not let you out of here, except in the guise of a dead man [in a coffin]." Said he: "So let me out in the guise of a dead man!" He feigned himself dead and placed himself in a coffin. R. Eliezer carried him by the head, R. Joshua by the feet, and Ben

Batiah walked before them in rent garments [as a sign of mourning].
When they approached the city gates, the guards wanted to stab him
with lances fearing he might be deceiving them, but Ben Batiah did
not let them and said: "Do you wish the enemies to say, they did not
pity even the greatest among them, their rabbi?" They carried him
out, placed him in a cemetery, and returned to the city.

After they left, R. Yohannan b. Zakkai walked to the armies of Vespasian. He said to them: "Where is the king?" They said: "Why?" Said
he: "Because I wish to salute him." They went and told him: "There is a
Jew who wishes to salute him [the king]." Said he: "Bring him to me."
He came and began lauding him: "Long live the king." Said he [the
king]: "You have killed me." Said he: "Why?" "Because you saluted me
as a king and I am not a king, and when the king hears he will put me
to death." He said: "If you are not the king, you will one day be the
king, because this house will not be destroyed by an ordinary man but
by a king, as this is the house of the Lord of the Universe, and no ordinary man could vanquish it, as it is said: 'And Lebanon shall fall by a
mighty one' " (Isaiah 10:34). What did they do to R. Yohannan b.
Zakkai? They placed him in the innermost of seven chambers and
lit candles by day and by night. And they would ask him what hour
of the day it was and he would tell them, and what hour of the night it
was and he would tell them. And how did R. Yohannan b. Zakkai
know? From his study. After three days, Vespasian went to the bath in
Gophna.[76] After he had bathed, dressed and put on one of his shoes,
letters arrived from Rome announcing that the emperor had died and
the Romans had made him king. He wished to put on the other shoe
but could not fit in his foot, and he said: "Go and bring me the Jew."
They went and brought him. He said to him: "Why did I wear these
shoes all these days and now, when I put on one and wanted to put on
the other, I could not fit in my foot?" He answered: "You have heard
good news and made yourself fat,[77] as is written: 'A good report makes
the bones fat' " (Proverbs 15:30). He asked: "What shall we do to get my
foot in?" He said: "Do you have an enemy or a debtor? Let him pass in
front of you, you will languish, and your bone will shrink, as it is written, 'A broken spirit dries the bones' " (Proverbs 17:22). He did so and
put on his other shoe. He said: "If I am a king, why did you not come
to me before?" Said he, "The guards that are here would not let me."

The dukes then began to speak to him in parables: "If a snake nests in a tower, what is to be done with it?" R. Yohannan said: "Bring a sword and kill the snake." Said Abgar: "Quite the contrary, smash the tower and kill the snake." "If a snake nests in a cask, what is to be done with it?" R. Yohannan said: "Bring a sword and kill the snake, and save the cask." Said Amgar [variant spelling in original]: "Kill the snake and break the cask." R. Yohannan b. Zakkai said to him: "Instead of putting in a plea for our defense, you argue against us." Said he: "By your life, I speak in your favor, for as long as this house exists, the kingdom will grieve you." Said R. Yohannan b. Zakkai: "The heart knows whether it is for *aqel* or *aqalqalon* [for gain or loss]."[78]

When Vespasian was about to conquer the city, he said to R. Yohannan b. Zakkai: "Make me a request and I will grant it." Said he: "I demand that you withdraw from the city and leave." Said he: "The Romans made me king solely for this affair of state [namely, to conquer Jerusalem] and you tell me leave the city and go?" Said he: "Then I demand that you leave the Western gate leading to Lydda open until the third hour. Whoever passes through it shall be spared." When he went out to conquer the city, [Vespasian] said: "If you have a relative, send for him." He sent for all the rabbis and brought them out. He sought out R. Zadok and his son but could not find them. He sent R. Eliezer and R. Joshua to bring out R. Zadok and his son. They looked for them, very carefully, for three days, but could not find them. After three [days] they found them at one of the city gates. They brought them to R. Yohannan b. Zakkai. When he saw R. Zadok, he stood up before him. Said Vespasian: "You stand before this emaciated old man?" Said he: "Had there been one like him in the city, you would never have taken it." He asked: "What is his strength?" Said he: "That on one dish of beans he studies one hundred chapters." Said he: "Why is he so gaunt?" Said he: "Because of his fasts and his abstinence." Vespasian sent for doctors and said to them: "Cover his bones with flesh." They fed him bit by bit, until he recovered his soul. His son, R. Eleazar, said to him: "Father, give the doctors their reward so that they will have no share in the world to come." And he gave them a large scale and a finger counter.[79] Said R. Eleazar, son of R. Zadok: "May I see consolation [an oath wording] because, although father lived for many years after the destruction of the Temple, his flesh did not recover as in the days when the Temple had stood intact, to fulfill what is written 'their skin is shriveled upon their bones; it is withered, it is become like a stick' " (Lamentations 4:8).

After Jerusalem was conquered, he [Vespasian] assigned the four ramparts of the city to the four dukes. The Western rampart to Amgar. And it had been decreed by Heaven that the Western Wall would never be destroyed, and the three dukes demolished their sections, and Amgar did not destroy his. Vespasian sent for him and said: "Why did the others destroy their sections and you did not destroy yours?" Said he: "If I had demolished my section as they did theirs, the kingdoms that will come after you would never have known the mighty glory you have destroyed." Said he: "By your life, you have spoken well, but now that you have disobeyed the king's order [since his part of the wall was not destroyed], we order you to ascend to the top of the tower and throw yourself on the earth; if you survive, you will live, and if you die, you shall die." He did so. He ascended to the top of the tower and he threw himself and fell and died, and was struck by R. Yohannan b. Zakkai's curse.—*Lamentations Rabbah* 1:5

This is a complex story, both concerning the number of characters and their traits, and also concerning the plot. Actually, we are dealing here with two stories woven together. The story about the four dukes is a frame narrative to the story about R. Yohannan b. Zakkai, and the two are connected at the end.

As in the story about the death of Bar Kokhbah and the fall of Bethar, the length of the siege is denoted here too through a formulaic number, three and a half years. The introduction of formulaic numbers makes the description appear less realistic. The four dukes increase the sense of the siege as a massive endeavor, but the formulaic element is overriding in this case, too, when only the Arab duke is mentioned by name. Immediately after the mention of the four dukes, the story mentions the three wealthy men of Jerusalem who could sustain the city. Details about the food they could provide, as well as the rabbis' judgment that the wood for burning was the main issue, thicken the description and make the story more concrete. This description, however, is in fact a preface to the core narrative, which is the story of R. Yohannan b. Zakkai leaving Jerusalem during the siege disguised as a corpse in a coffin.

Similarities with the motifs in the story about the downfall of Bethar continue in greater detail. In both stories, the spiritual hero and the leader face each other, intimacy between them is suggested, and someone incites the secular leader against the rabbi. I am carefully refraining from suggesting that the opposition is necessarily between the military commander and the spiritual leader because Ben Batiah, according to the version of the story in the Buber edition of *Lamentations Rabbah*, is not necessarily the leader of the zealots (as is the case in other versions, for instance, in TB Gittin), but rather in charge of the storehouses. As such, he certainly exerts a great deal of influence on the forces fighting in the city, as is also manifest at the end of the story: when the guards heed the command of Ben Batiah as the administrator of the storehouses, he decides, apparently on his own (according to his part in the second dialogue with R. Yohannan), to burn everything so as to bring the situation to a head, spurring the city's inhabitants to engage in battle with Vespasian's besieging legions.

The incitement against R. Yohannan ben Zakkai is translated into an accusation, apparently justified (according to the sequel), that he had objected to the burning of the storehouses. The wording of the incitement is also very similar to that in the Bar Kokhbah story and, in both cases, stress is placed on the intimacy between the leader and the slandered rabbi. The slanderers use these hints of intimacy to compel the leader to restrain the sage's independent activity. In the story about the fall of Bethar we read, "Your friend [uncle] asked to surrender the city," and here, "Your uncle [friend] said 'woe.'" In this story, the opposition between the two figures is less extreme than that between the typical power hero and R. Eleazar of Modi'in, who emerges as much more passive than R. Yohannan ben Zakkai. A different chain of events then ensues, where R. Yohannan b. Zakkai does not fall prey to the brutal violence of the character facing him, as does R. Eleazar in the previous story. Death appears here only as a powerful symbolic representation, in the shape of a coffin used to smuggle the sage out of the besieged city. Ben Batiah is a less extreme character than Bar Kozbah, and his inner conflict is more exposed in the story. The negotiation between Ben Batiah and R. Yohannan is also more sophisticated than the dialogue between Bar Kozbah and R. Eleazar. The description in the Bar Kozbah story gives a heavier and more oppressive sense of the surrounding circumstances, with the tragic end of the city's downfall looming even closer.

In the story about the fall of Bethar the protagonist, albeit not a hero who evokes sympathy, is most certainly Bar Kozbah, whereas R. Eleazar, who is favored by the narrator, is a secondary character. Although Bar Kozbah's death is perceived as a punishment for the killing of R. Eleazar, the death of the commander denotes the fall of the city he had been charged with defending. In the story we are now discussing, the hero is unquestionably R. Yohannan, and Ben Batiah serves as an antagonist. The set of roles is thus parallel, but the balance between them is reversed.

The initial short negotiation between R. Yohannan and Ben Batiah ends in a sentence that could be characterized as a proverb: "Between 'woe' and 'wow,' R. Yohannan b. Zakkai was saved." The word "woe" [*vai*] as an expression of sorrow is known to us from many sources, whereas the fact that "wow" [*vah*] indicates joy is less well known.[80] As a researcher of proverbs, I can only regret that none of the examined manuscripts includes the formula "between 'wow' and 'woe,' " which would have created a rhyme (*vai-Zakkai*) that characterizes proverbs of this type. Sentences of this type often serve as concise allusions to a well-known legend, and belong to the category of proverbs that are unintelligible to those unaware of the legend.[81] As is true of all proverbs, I suggest that this sentence too might be used in more general and metaphoric terms, to mean that "a small difference may lead to a big difference in the results."

Note that Ben Batiah, the antagonist, is altogether missing from the text in both versions of *Avot de-Rabbi Nathan*. Instead, R. Yohannan confronts the people of Jerusalem, thereby restricting the personal, experiential dimensions of the story and blurring the dramatic tension. In the TB Gittin version, the figure confronting R. Yohannan b. Zakkai is given the typological name of Bar-Siqra ("dagger-man"), which also occurs in several Palestinian versions of the story apparently influenced by the Babylonian Talmud.[82] This name reflects the ideological portrayal of the character as totally identified with the values of violence and belligerence it represents. The preference for an ideological over an experiential and emotional perspective is discernible in several TB versions of stories about the destruction of the Temple that we have examined in the Palestinian Midrash. The classic example is the tale about the two children of the High Priest, which I discussed in Chapter 2. The present narrative in the Babylonian Talmud, and certainly that in both versions of *Avot de-Rabbi Nathan*, includes no preliminaries, in the shape of the "woe–wow" story, to the tale about the smuggling out of R. Yohannan b. Zakkai in the guise of a corpse.

At this stage of the story, R. Yohannan b. Zakkai's decision to leave the city is prompted by his observation of the simple facts of life rather than by a strategic military analysis. The picture of boiling straw to drink its water brings the story closer to the physical human plight, to the bodily facts ensuing from the siege. Indeed, R. Yohannan b. Zakkai's activity in this story focuses attention on the body as a narrative element, and particularly on the living as opposed to the dead body. Those boiling straw represent a dangerous liminal situation between actual life and death, a liminal situation that R. Yohannan b. Zakkai escapes when he passes, symbolically, through absolute death onto full life.

The balance of power between R. Yohannan b. Zakkai and Ben Batiah begins to change at this point in the narrative. Whereas Ben Batiah had summoned R. Yohannan after hearing the latter's reaction to the burning of the storehouses, it is now R. Yohannan who summons his nephew, probably younger and certainly less learned, to come to him. R. Yohannan's self-reliance when he addresses Ben Batiah contrasts with his behavior at the previous encounter between them, when R. Yohannan had felt a need to explain, and even to dispel, the rumor that had been spread regarding his condemnation of the burning.

The only explanation for this change in the balance of power is that R. Yohannan felt that his impression that the city's defenders were demoralized had been justified, and the sight of hungry people in the market had also undermined Ben Batiah's self-confidence.[83]

R. Yohannan b. Zakkai's strong appeal to Ben Batiah relates to a central existential question, which had been resonating in the story and is now raised explicitly: this is a life-and-death issue. As in rabbinic stories about the destruction of the Temple in general, and in the Palestinian Midrash in particular, collective fate and the fate of the city of Jerusalem are embodied in the personal fate of the legends' protagonists. R. Yohannan b. Zakkai accuses Ben Batiah of starving Jerusalem's inhabitants to death, and the latter defends himself by claiming he was protecting his own life, a claim that is incompatible with his previous actions but may reflect his present impotence. In response to Ben Batiah's admission of weakness, R. Yohannan asks for his assistance in bringing some relief to the present situation by helping him leave the city. Ben Batiah's response shifts the discussion of the life-and-death issues from the theoretical to the symbolic-concrete level: R. Yohannan may not leave the city unless he pretends to be dead, namely, in a coffin.

R. Yohannan accepts this proposal and agrees to leave the city in the guise of a corpse.

The description of the sham funeral points to the public character and to the collective meaning of the act when R. Eliezer and R. Joshua, R. Yohannan's senior disciples, carry the bier. They themselves are also the teachers of R. Akiva, who will eventually be Bar Kozbah's enthusiastic supporter and, in the story about Bethar's downfall, plays a role parallel to that of Ben Batiah. In the fake funeral procession, Ben Batiah plays his role as a relative of the "deceased" when he rends his garment in an act of mourning. The detail concluding this part of the story is the threat of the city guards to stab R. Yohannan, which Ben Batiah manages to deflect with his clever words. Ben Batiah addresses the guards, who are here called *biriyonim* (a term that has also acquired negative connotations such as "outlaws"), and appeals to their national honor as Jews and as residents of Jerusalem bound to respect Torah scholars. The risk that the besieging enemy might detect signs of stabbing on the corpse (which *we* know is a fake but the guards do not) constitutes a sufficient argument to forestall the scrutiny that would have disclosed the hoax.

By taking the risks entailed in deceiving the city guards, Ben Batiah is perhaps presented as atoning for the burning of the storehouses and for his fatal contribution to the speedier fall of Jerusalem. Another latent assumption could be that Ben Batiah has accepted ben Zakkai's view that, with the city's downfall, the leadership is charged with saving whatever is possible.

Saving a persecuted individual by having him feign death is an international folk-literary motif, as is the motif of hiding the leader in order to save the community. The Jewish legend about the fall of Jerusalem thus joins the general tradition of folk narrative and is adapted to oral folk communication. This is how scattered Jerusalemites, and lovers of Jerusalem everywhere, will tell the story about their city's last days.[84]

As will be shown below, however, the story about the fall of Jerusalem is also the story about the creation of a new communal-cultural entity. Undoubtedly, life and death as the central motif of the story do not only represent a historically concrete experience, but also beliefs and outlooks about life and death and the relationship between them at the time the story was created. In the first centuries C.E., Jewish culture was deeply interested in the question of death and the posthumous fate of the soul, with the belief in an afterworld and in the resurrection of the body featuring as part of this concern.[85] Scholars have argued that this concern is also reflected in the burial practices common in this period among Palestinian Jews.[86] The carrying of the deceased from place to place, for various reasons, as well as the use of wooden coffins, which would allow the successful concealment of the "deceased," were common practice in this period, and their mention serves to enhance the realistic dimension of the legend.

Belief in the resurrection of the dead was a crucial element in the world picture that provided the context for a unique interpretation of the historical situation, in this case the destruction of Jerusalem and its loss as a ritual and political center. This world picture, rooted in a belief in an afterworld and in the resurrection of the dead, is based on the cyclic nature of existence, with the end of one chapter in the cycle heralding the beginning of the next. The description of R. Yohannan's exit in a coffin informs the story with a sense of a transition from one life to another, in a concrete, visual form. The optimistic note of a new beginning sown in the midst of a devastating collapse is only possible within a world-view that includes a grain of utopia, even if we take into account that the description conveys a later perspective.

But the uniqueness of the utopian thinking conveyed here becomes clear later in the story. This is a utopia acted out by its bearers. In the case of R. Yohannan b. Zakkai, the acting out of the utopia builds on a chain of transmission known to us from the beginning of the first *mishnah* in *Avot*: "Moses received the Torah from Sinai, and transmitted it to Joshua, Joshua to the elders, the elders to the prophets, and the prophets transmitted it to the men of the Great Assembly." After the men of the Great Assembly, the chain of generations continues through pairs of sages that preceded the *tannaim*, until the last pair, Hillel and Shammai, from the beginning to the middle of the first century C.E., and from them to the leaders of the *tannaim* generations. In the second chapter of *Avot* we read: "R. Yohannan ben Zakkai received from Hillel and Shammai. He used to say: 'If you have learned much Torah, do not claim merit for yourself, because it is for this purpose that you were created.' R. Yohannan ben Zakkai had five disciples: R. Eliezer b. Hyrcanus, R. Joshua b. Hananyah, R. Yose Hacohen, R. Simeon b. Netanel, and R. Eleazar b. Arakh" (*Avot* 2:8). Unlike other sages cited in *Avot*, all the sayings of R. Yohannan b. Zakkai relate to his disciples, all of whom he praises for their learning. In these sayings, too, he ascribes great importance to the transmission chain from teachers to students.

From the sayings in the Mishnah, we learn that R. Yohannan b. Zakkai is identified through his sayings about Torah study as the aim of existence, which create an equation between life and study. Having seen the citizens of Jerusalem boiling straw might have led him to conclude not only that, "If there is no meal, there is no Torah," but also that, "If there is no Torah, there is no meal," as in the two subsequent sayings by R. Eleazar ben Azariah (*Avot* 3:17).

After the mourners leave R. Yohannan at the cemetery, he walks over to Vespasian's camp, just as he had walked through the market of Jerusalem in a previous section of the story. R. Yohannan acts like someone who knows what he wants and asks to see the king. When reaching Vespasian, R. Yohannan opens with words of praise and adulation, as is proper in the circumstances. Vespasian reacts curtly, in words that link the present situation to the life-and-death motif central to the chain of stories, by saying "You have killed me." His explanation tempers this statement, however, when he clarifies that he might have been killed as a result of R. Yohannan's praise, because he is not entitled to be called king. The death motif appears once again in the story, not as an ending but in the transition from one situation to another, in this case Vespasian's rise from his status as commander of the Roman army besieging Jerusalem to that of Roman emperor. R. Yohannan b. Zakkai relies on the verse "And Lebanon shall fall by a mighty one." In the context of a story about someone for whom life and Torah are one, a biblical verse is the appropriate perspective for examining a situation.[87]

Another episode is introduced at this point in the story, unique and without paragon in the parallel sources, as was the "woe–wow" episode. The passage opens with a rhetorical question characteristic of folk narrative: "What did they do . . . ?" The tests R. Yohannan must now undergo follow naturally from the wisdom he had previously displayed in his interpretation of the verse, where he had predicted the appointment of Vespasian. When a hero shows signs of this type of mysterious, almost supernatural, wisdom, it is only natural that the ruler or the judge will wish to test the sources of his wisdom. An accepted way is to impose tasks to test the hero anew, often including his isolation so as to preclude access to outside sources of potential assistance.[88]

The pattern of the relationship between Vespasian and R. Yohannan ben Zakkai reminds us of hundreds of Jewish folktales about a Jewish minister or a Jewish sage responsible for saving his afflicted community, standing before a non-Jewish ruler. This tale type has roots in biblical stories (Joseph, Mordechai, Daniel) and is an "ecotype," an international tale type known as "the King and the Abbot" in a specifically Jewish articulation.[89]

R. Yohannan b. Zakkai is placed "in the innermost of seven chambers" (seven is a well-known formulaic number), namely, a room separated from natural light by seven walls and illuminated by candlelight day and night. Like heroes of legends and folktales who pass tests of this kind, R. Yohannan b. Zakkai also passes the recurring test by relying once again on the same source of wisdom—the study of Torah that had served him when he predicted Vespasian's appointment. R. Yohannan b. Zakkai's success emphasizes that Torah study is a source of inner wisdom, totally independent from external information. This passage in the story hints to two main cyclical constructions for reckoning time in culture—one is day and night, and the second is the week (seven days). In Jewish culture, these two time constructions are related to the mythological phase of Creation in Genesis.

The letter nominating Vespasian as emperor is carried by an emissary from Rome, and arrives after three days, again a formulaic number. It is not clear, however, whether the count began after R. Yohannan b. Zakkai had predicted the impending appointment according to the verse, or after the test of distinguishing night from day (especially since that had supposedly taken at least a week). Vespasian, in any event, is bathing in Gophna when the letter arrives. The Romans' passion for bathing was apparently well known to storytellers in Palestine. Thus, for instance, Titus, who is Vespasian's son, is placed in a bathhouse in a story dealing with his return to Rome from the conquest of Jerusalem and Palestine (*Leviticus Rabbah* 22:3; TB Gittin 56b). And in the story about Nakdimon Ben-Gurion, for whom the sun shone through, the Roman ruler goes to the bathhouse when Nakdimon is deep in prayer in the house of study or in the Temple (*Avot de-Rabbi Nathan*, version A, chapter 6; TB Ta'anit 19b–20a). As Titus immediately knew that the mosquito in his brain causing him headaches had been sent by the god of the Jews whose temple he had destroyed, so does Vespasian understand that the Jewish sage who had envisioned his appointment even before the news had arrived from Rome may solve the riddle of his shoe, which has suddenly become too narrow.

In this passage of the story, too, emphasis is again placed on the body, which becomes almost a text. The biblical verse "A good report makes the bones fat" materializes in Vespasian's body. Similarly, the solution to the problem, namely, bringing the foot down to its normal size, is attained by implementing another verse from Proverbs, "A broken spirit dries the bones." One cannot but be reminded of Cinderella's sisters vainly trying on the slipper that may turn them into princesses, if only their foot fitted.[90]

Trying on the shoe, therefore, is a folk motif related to the rise from humble origins, as is the case with the folktale Cinderella, and as will eventually be true of both Vespasian and R. Yohannan ben Zakkai. Trying on the shoe on a swollen foot is also a topos in the legendary historiography of the period. Israel Yuval points this out when discussing this story as a parallel to the leprosy legend of the emperor Constantine, who was healed when baptized by Bishop Sylvester. In a later version of the legend, cited in a text that was written around 1000 C.E. by Landolfus Sagax, it is told that when the news from Rome that his father had been made emperor reached Titus, he was so overjoyed that his right foot swelled up and he could not fit his shoe. His foot was returned to shape when he heeded the advice of Josephus, "the duke of the Jews," who told him to have someone he hates pass before him.[91] This motif appears, in the context of the same story, in the thirteenth-century work *Legenda Aurea* (The Golden Legends), by Jacobus de Voragine. The term "duke" that appears in this text creates a further link with the story in *Lamentations Rabbah*, where the dukes of the lands appear. The character of Josephus as the Jewish sage who solves the problem links this story, as well as the story in the Midrash we are discussing, to Josephus's prophecy. Josephus had told Vespasian that he would become emperor in an attempt to avoid his being sent to Rome to be judged by Nero.[92]

At this point, the story in *Lamentations Rabbah* returns to the frame narrative about the foreign dukes besieging Jerusalem with Vespasian's legions. The frame narrative now joins the main story, which describes R. Yohannan's exit from the beleaguered city. After putting on the shoe, and in his new capacity, Vespasian turns to R. Yohannan b. Zakkai and teases him by asking him why had he not come to pay his respects if he knew that Vespasian would become king. R. Yohannan's answer shifts the story from the limited frame of the dialogue between two leaders representing their nations, back to the harsh collective reality from which he speaks as a Jew.

This concluding passage takes the form of a confrontation between R. Yohannan as a Jewish minister and Abgar as an Arab minister, while Vespasian becomes a neutral figure. This structure is also known in forms of the Jewish "ecotype" of "the King and the Abbot," in numerous stories of confrontations in Jewish communities. The archetypal formulation is the confrontation between Mordechai and Haman in the Book of Esther.[93] Unlike folk narratives of this type, this story ends tragically; its basic structure as a folktale, however, ensures it will be imbued with the optimism typical of the genre, which includes a happy ending as one of its permanent features. In the broader historical context, this is indeed a catastrophe of cosmic proportions, and the destruction of the Temple is often described in Midrash literature as a cosmic disaster. In the separate plot of the folktale, however, which creates an autonomous world, and within its own terms, this is a happy ending: R. Yohannan defeats the Arab duke facing him, and receives the three formulaic gifts. The story, then, although anchored in a reality of suffering and loss, serves as a powerful expression of the "principle of hope" (in the phrase of Ernst Bloch), bearing within this historical legend the implicit utopian message.[94]

I wish to stress once again that the story about R. Yohannan b. Zakkai is obviously a historical legend and certainly not a folktale. The fact that many historians such as Alon, Baer, Schalit, and others were concerned with this story is relevant to the clarification of its relationship to the historical reality it describes, on the one hand, and the one from which it grew, on the other. Like many legends including a folktale structure as subtext, this story too reveals a strong tension between the perception of the narration as reality and the element of the fantastic. One might say that the utopia, the collective dream of a historical reversal, assumes here the form of a folktale. It thus introduces the wish dimension into a legend that, in principle, is shaped in close resemblance to reality. Because of the folktale's deep connection with human experience, a legend that includes folktale elements can bear further implications than those conveyed by a direct historical description.

The folk elements in this text, in the episode of the confrontation with the dukes, are many and varied. When engaging in his dialogue with Abgar, R. Yohannan b. Zakkai complains to him that, in his answers to the allegorical riddles, Abgar is actually advising the destruction of Jerusalem. According to Abgar, the Temple is the very reason for the empire's wish to defeat the Jews and, therefore, the existence of the Temple brings the Jews more harm than good. In the context of the story, this exchange turns into a complex and interesting use of the voice of the other as expressing less legitimate aspects of the self. On the one hand, in the central episode of the story,

R. Yohannan b. Zakkai is determined to abandon Jerusalem when he understands that the inhabitants, led by the zealots, obstruct the effective defense of the city. On the other hand, in the present episode that, as noted, is structured as a folktale of confrontation, R. Yohannan b. Zakkai is presented as one who is trying to save the city in exchange for stabbing the dragon (the zealots?). R. Yohannan's character is shaped by the complex structure of the story and by a series of dialogues with various interlocutors—Jews, Romans, and others—as someone harboring incompatible pieces of knowledge. The knowledge that Jerusalem symbolizes everything the Romans want to destroy is hard to reconcile with the idea that Jerusalem does not, at the same time, exhaust the meaning of the nation's existence. This approach, which R. Yohannan b. Zakkai implements by actually leaving the city, is ascribed here to the one who sounds like the prosecution rather than the defense, the Arab minister. At the confrontation level, however, according to the folktale structure discussed above, we expect that R. Yohannan's rival, "the other," will be defeated by "our" representative.[95]

R. Yohannan b. Zakkai, whom we have already met above as a character in a proverb, utters at this point a proverb that, in its ambiguous formulation, acts almost as an oracle: "The heart knows whether it is for *aqel*[96] or *aqalqalon*." This proverb is built on an agricultural metaphor, wherein "*aqel*" is a bale for collecting olives and grapes.[97] In what is probably the original agricultural context (PT Shevi'it 4:1, 35a), it is not totally clear whether the "*aqel*" serves to collect edible fruit or perhaps refuse. The biblical associations of the word *aqalqalon* (crooked) (or *aqalqalot* as in some versions, including the PT)—"crooked byways" (Judges 5:6); "turn aside to their crooked ways" (Psalms 125:5); "crooked serpent" (Isaiah 27:1)— point to a possibly causal link between the two similar words. The form "*aqalqalon*" denotes a blending of both biblical forms. The meaning of the word in the verse from Isaiah links the proverb to the allegorical riddles about the serpent that appear in the text. Since the proverb is quoted by R. Yohannan, the positive hero in the story with whom both the narrator and the readers identify, this saying is certain to come true in the future, proving that "the curse of the sage will be fulfilled."[98]

This whole episode fully acquits R. Yohannan from any suspicion that he harbors feelings of revenge toward the zealots. In this spirit, when allowed one request before the destruction of the city, he first asks Vespasian to relent, namely, to save the city and go away.[99] Vespasian says he cannot grant this. R. Yohannan, like Abraham when negotiating with God for Sodom, secures a partial achievement—the city gate that opens toward Lydda is to be left open during the battle, so that the refugees can be saved. The mention of Lydda places on the map another Palestinian Torah center, besides Yavneh (Jabneh, Jamnia), which is the one usually identified with R. Yohannan's endeavor. The story, then, ascribes to R. Yohannan a claim not only to the center in Yavneh but actually to Torah study in Palestine as a whole (or at least in the South as distinguished from the Galilee) toward the end of the first century C.E.

As the story continues, Vespasian remains a generous figure, and deep concern is attributed to R. Yohannan for the communal welfare: when the Roman allows the Jewish sage to enter the city to save his relative, he asks to save all the sages.[100] But he cannot find R. Zadok and his son, so he sends a message to R. Eliezer and R. Joshua—the disciples who carried him out in a coffin—that they should save R. Zadok and his son and take them out of the city. Their three-day search (how else!) fails at first, but then proves successful when the two are found hiding in one of the city's gates. This location points to their stay in a liminal zone between the inside and outside of the city, as R. Yohannan himself had been when led out in a coffin: between Jews and Romans, between the living and the dead, between Jerusalem and other Torah centers. Whereas the power of R. Eleazar of Modi'in had been in his prayer and his motherly brooding, R. Zadok preserved the city through his study of Torah and his asceticism. He saved the starving city in what emerges as almost a form of sympathetic magic, healing an affliction through something that resembles it—in this case, prolonged fasts.

R. Yohannan b. Zakkai is once again involved in a double-aimed act because, as he said to the emperor, R. Zadok's presence saved Jerusalem from devastation. When he insisted on rescuing him from the city, he probably knew that he was thereby hastening its final destruction.

Vespasian brings a doctor for R. Zadok, who slowly regains his health and puts on flesh. This is another case of a quasi-return from the world of death, turning a skeleton into a fleshed-out body. Paradoxically, the call to the doctors resembles the course of events in the story about the punishment of Titus that was mentioned above, when Titus's redemption from the suffering caused by the mosquito brings about his death. The similarity continues when R. Zadok is given a *kristiona* (large scale)[101] and an abacus, in order to calculate the doctors' wages. Titus's story also ends with scales on which his soul, which has already been swallowed by the mosquito and is now the size of a fledgling, is to be weighed, symbolizing the "measure for measure" punishment meted out by God: God enters his head as he had entered the Holy of Holies.[102] Through the picture of the scales, then, the story may be raising the option of punishing Vespasian, the destroyer of Jerusalem, although the punishment itself is not carried out in the story.

The words of R. Zadok's son appear in the text at the point when the contrast (the "cognitive dissonance") between Vespasian's evil as the destroyer of Jerusalem and the favors he grants R. Yohannan, and particularly R. Zadok, threatens to explode the story's credibility. R. Eleazar, who is R. Zadok's son, seeks to prevent the doctors brought by the Roman from being rewarded for the healing of his father in the world to come, by paying their wages in this world.[103] The concern of the story with life and death and with various dimensions of life after death is thus expanded further, to reward and punishment after death. R. Zadok's son settles a further contradiction, between his father's physical decay from starvation inside Jerusalem and his healing outside it, by reconciling his father's state with the verse "their skin is shriveled upon their bones," claiming that his father had not returned to his original health even after the doctors' treatment.

At the end the story again returns to the four dukes, who are each given control over one of the city's ramparts. Three dukes destroy the rampart they have been given, but the Arab duke cannot do so because of a divine decree that the Western Wall would stand forever. As in the Zekhariah story quoted above, the historical story includes a local piece of wisdom about the Wall's continued existence, and gives it an etiology, a narrative motif explaining the existence of something observed in reality. Abgar justifies his inability to destroy the wall by claiming that this had been his original intention, aiming to leave traces of the city's glory and thus show the greatness of the emperor who had destroyed it. As is true of many stories confronting Jewish and Gentile ministers, however, Abgar's end is also unfortunate. He dies as a result of a "divine ordeal" ordered by Vespasian. Although it was expected, as noted, that R. Yohannan's curse "for *aqel* or *aqalqalon*" would hurt Abgar too, it is still puzzling that Abgar's death is ascribed to the curse, as his chances of surviving a jump from the tower were slight to begin with.

The narrator may wish to imply that the emperor's very order to submit him to this jumping test followed from the curse of the Jewish sage.[104]

Ending the story with the success of R. Yohannan's curse preserves the bizarre ambiguity of discussing the destruction of Jerusalem together with the triumph of R. Yohannan b. Zakkai. The complex mechanism involved in the shaping of a historical legend comes to the fore in this story, in the blending of elements that draw us toward reality (such as historical figures and place names), together with typical folktale elements bordering at times on the fantastic.

The story of the exit from the city as a rescue reflects, as do the other stories I discussed in this chapter, traditions common to Jewish folk narratives in rabbinic texts, on the one hand, and folk narratives of Jewish groups that were marginal to the culture embodied in these texts, on the other. According to later testimonies, a story was told in the early Christian Church of Jerusalem about its remnants leaving the city at the time of the Temple's destruction and escaping to the city of Pella in Transjordan.[105] In both cases, the story about leaving the city was meant to grant the necessary legitimation for the creation of a religious center outside Jerusalem after the city was destroyed.

In addition to the quasi-historical information common to the rescue stories told within both groups, the story about R. Yohannan b. Zakkai's exit from Jerusalem relates to a motif that is much more essential in Christian mythology, namely, the hero's resurrection three days after his death, a recurring numerical formula in the story about R. Yohannan's exit from Jerusalem.[106]

The story about R. Yohannan's exit appears in many versions in rabbinic literature and is often cited by scholars, particularly historians, because in the consciousness of later generations it was perceived as the cornerstone of the Jewish culture that developed after the destruction of the Temple and the loss of political independence. The consensus was that this story was important because it outlined an alternative cultural plan, which enabled the growth and vitality of the spirituality and scholarship so unique to rabbinical creativity. Through the preceding analysis, I have sought to show that this story gripped the imagination and the memory of the narrators and their audiences mainly because it mobilized powerful cultural symbols. Furthermore, the narrative text was skillfully branded with the central experience of the nation's life, then and many times since, an experience that is often critical in individual lives: standing on the awesome, although sometimes unavoidable, line that divides life from death.

The status of Jerusalem in Jewish thinking throughout history undergoes a transformation by way of this story, which could be defined in the folk-literary terms discussed earlier in this chapter. In addition to its legendary dimensions, preserved in historical and local legends about the city, Jerusalem may become the Shangri-La of folktale plots. Above all, it becomes a mythical essence described in modes that remove it further and further from the real city, crystallizing into the picture of "heavenly Jerusalem."[107]

❧

The folk narratives discussed in this last chapter clearly convey the central assumption of this book in general, namely, that folk narratives in the literature of Palestinian *amoraim* are literary works devoted to the central issues concerning scholars and their society at the time. Their shaping within *Lamentations Rabbah*, which was at the focus of this discussion, developed through a continuous relationship to the literary context of the Palestinian aggadic Midrash. They are told within the generic context of folk literature, which includes the legend and the folktale as its main forms of prose, and they embody the dialectical interaction between those generic poles in the actual text. The comparative context of folk literature points to the links of these stories to the folk literatures of other contemporary cultural and ideological groups, on the one hand, and to types of stories found in other cultures and in other periods, on the other. The folkloristic context of the stories links them to cultural practices, beliefs, and concepts current at the time. The social context shapes the perception of the individual, the woman, the man, and their concrete and symbolic roles in the stories. The religious context bestows on the stories their existential and spiritual dimension, and raises questions dealing with God and the individual, as well as God and the people. The historical context of the stories weaves the strong ties between folk narratives and the events experienced by the narrators in the reality of their own lives.

Rabbinical stories have been the subject of extensive research dealing, in one way or another, with all these contexts. In this work, I have sought to turn the readers' eyes and hearts to the unique aspects of stories in Palestinian aggadic Midrash that stem from their nature as folk narratives. This book cannot hope to exhaust this topic. Nevertheless, I hope a method has been suggested here, allowing us to deepen and expand our acquaintance with rabbinic literature. Indeed, folk narratives are the weft of Midrash literature—they are woven as a beautiful tapestry, rich and colorful, creating the web of life in its body and soul.

EPILOGUE

RABBI JOSHUA'S ODYSSEY

Ithaca gave you the marvelous journey.
Without her you wouldn't have set out.
She has nothing left to give you now.
—CONSTANTINE CAVAFY

IN HIS LAST BOOK, published a few months before his untimely death, poet and scholar Dan Pagis explored the various meanings of the concept of the riddle and pointed out three prevalent usages: "*literally*, the term 'riddle' refers to a specific literary genre in which the subject of the cryptic formulation remains hidden . . . [its function] a challenging question demanding to be answered. *A slightly metaphorical meaning* . . . refers to genres that are indeed cryptic but do not function as proper riddles, such as allegories and prophesies . . . *a more distant metaphorical meaning* . . . is a general concept for unintelligible modes of discourse, some evoking wonder and demanding explanation: visions, dreams, cosmic riddles, the enigma of human existence."[1]

Pagis needed a precise definition to delimit the parameters of the textual basis he had used as the foundation of his historical study on the Hebrew riddle in Italy and Holland. The texts he considered had pointed to a unique and continuous phenomenon in a given cultural context, which is revived in the pages of his book. Given the importance of Pagis's distinctions, then, we need to draw a line between the "true riddle" and other meanings of the term "riddle," and I have therefore chosen, in this discussion, to rely on the broader concept of "enigma."

According to Pagis's definition, which is based on literary and folkloristic criteria, "true riddles" have hardly been found so far in ancient Hebrew literature. The most famous riddle in this corpus, which is posed by Samson, is, as he states, a "neck-riddle."[2] A neck riddle can only be solved through recourse to the private experience of the riddler, which is inaccessible to the riddlee. Hence, it does not preserve the necessary balance between encoding elements, which hinder riddlees from reaching a solution, and decoding elements, which assist them in the search for it. As far as I know, aggadic rabbinic literature includes only one true riddle, to which I will return, and Pagis rightfully rejected all attempts to reconstruct riddles through what appear to be their solutions.[3] Many aggadic narratives are nevertheless re-vealed as enigmatic, characterized by the playfulness typical of true riddles while also articulating the enigma present in these texts, which is generically expressed in the riddle, and itself remains unresolved even after the riddle has been decoded.

The concentration of riddle tales in *Lamentations Rabbah* is explained through their connection with the many meanings of the anaphoric lament question, *Eikha?* Three series of narratives appear in sequence in *Lamentations Rabbah* 1, all enigmatic.[4] All are part of homilies on the second half of the first verse in the biblical Book of Lamentations, "great among the nations," and all praise the wisdom of the inhabitants of Jerusalem, especially its youngsters. The series include the eleven riddle tales and the stories about dream interpretation discussed earlier, followed by a shorter cycle of stories on R. Joshua[5]:

R. Joshua was once walking along a path when a man met him who was also walking along. He said to him: "What are you doing?" Said he: "I am walking along a path." He retorted: "You have well said that you are walking along a path, as it has been trodden by robbers like you" [Ms.: "others more than you"]. He went further and met a child sitting at the crossroad. He asked: "Which is the nearest road to the city?" [Ms.: "approaches the city"]. He told him: "This one is near and far, and that one is far and near." R. Joshua took the one that was near and far. As he approached the city [Ms.: "close to the wall"] he found

[Ms.: "there were"] gardens and orchards surrounding the wall, [Ms.: "and he could not enter the city"] so he returned to the child and told him: "My son, is that one, then, the nearest road to the city?" [Ms: "Did you not tell me that that road was near and far?"]. Said he: "Rabbi, you are a sage in Israel [Ms.: "you are the greatest sage of Israel"]. Did I not tell you that this one is far and near, and that one is near and far?" Thereupon R. Joshua said: "Blessed be you, Oh Israel, for you are all wise, from your oldest to your youngest" [Ms.: "Blessed are they, Oh Israel, for they are all wise, from their youngest to their oldest"].

[Ms.: "The next two stories in reverse order."] He left [Ms: "further away"] and met a child carrying a covered dish in his hand. He said: "What is in your hand covered by that dish?" [Ms.: "What do you carry?"]. Said he: "Had my mother wanted you to know what I have [Ms.: "carry"] she would not have told me to cover it."

He went further away from there [Ms.: "from here"] and met a child. He said: "What is the water like in this city?" He said: "Why worry? [Ms.: "Be not afraid"], garlic and onions are plentiful." As he entered the city he met a girl standing and filling water from the spring [Ms.: "from the well"]. He told her: "Give me some [Ms.: "a little"] water." She said: "Both for you and your donkey" [Ms.: "and your beast"]. When he had drunk and was turning to go away [Ms.: "and she had given water to him and his beast"], he said to her: "My child, you have acted like Rebecca did." [Ms.: "Said she"], "I acted like Rebecca but you did not act like Eliezer."

It has been taught: We leave *peah* [gleanings, border of the field left for the poor] from food prepared in a *qederah* [boiling pot] but not in an *ilpas* [a tightly covered stew pot] [Ms.: "and we need not even say in pots"]. Once R. Joshua visited a widow. The first day she brought him a dish and he ate it, and left no *peah*. The second day she brought him a dish and he ate it and left no *peah*. The third day [Ms.: "what did she do?"] she spoiled the dish of grits with salt. When R. Joshua tasted it he put it aside [Ms.: "and began to eat his bread empty"]. She told him: "Why did you put away the grits?" [Ms.: "Why did you eat so little of these grits?"]. Said he: "I had already eaten earlier in the day." She said: "If you had already eaten earlier in the day, why did you not put aside the bread as you put aside these grits?" [Ms.: "Were you perhaps leaving some *peah* from these two dishes?"]. Then and there R. Joshua said: "No one has ever defeated me but this widow, and a girl, and those boys [Ms.: "but those boys, and that girl, and this widow"], to fulfill what has been said: 'Great among the nations— great in wisdom.' "[6]—*Lamentations Rabbah* 1:1

The text focuses on R. Joshua, who travels from story to story, from one encounter to another. This is the journey of the self as a constantly evolving subject, engaged in a complex negotiation with others as well as with the powers in his unknown inner being, with his destiny. The journey of the evolving self oscillates between the need to reach integration and stability and forces threatening disintegration.

R. Joshua's story is implicitly set within a particular historical context, confronting the Temple's destruction and its reverberations, as well as the presence of an all-encompassing and multifaceted textual universe. The enigma in this narrative, which is an expression of unknown elements from both inside and outside, never crystallizes into a generic riddle configuration. Instead, the story articulates the transformative process of the self as a vague and metonymic enigmatic presence and, unlike the generic riddle, unable to reach decisive resolution. The true riddle, which is balanced and capable of solution, conveys the possibility of reaching stability and integration, even if temporarily. The enigmatic elements, by failing to evolve into an "active" generic configuration, articulate the processes of deconstruction, which are also the processes that enable dynamic development.

It is not only the identity of the individual self and its existence as a subject that are continually tested by the enigma, however, but also society as an ethnic, cultural, and national framework constantly evolving and breaking apart, facing a dialectic of construction and disintegration at work from within and from without.

Aggadic narratives in the Midrash tend to present single-stranded plots, with episodes conglomerating at the editorial stage. Some editing has most probably taken place here as well, since the parallel version of these stories in TB Eruvin 53b presents them in reverse order, in a slightly different formulation, and with one episode completely missing.

Solutions to the enigmatic dialogues are delayed. In the first episode, R. Joshua, who represents the wandering self, is attacked by a man who challenges the root image of the journey itself, the road.[7] As early as the second episode, however, the road emerges as an assured and communicative entity, in the shape of a crossroads. The embodiment of the enigma here is a city without easy access.

The self's desire for quick gratification is hindered by the child's enigmatic reply. The enigmatic design of the city draws on the fantastic materials of the folktale: it is surrounded by impenetrable vegetation, just as the castle of Briar-rose, better known as Sleeping Beauty. But in R. Joshua's tales of wandering there is no fairy-tale happy ending, and nowhere are the intimations of harmonious sexual consummation actually realized. In the absence of a well-defined subject, then, the erotic puzzle remains incomplete. In an association with the historical situation, the city itself may, at the symbolic level, function as an enchanted princess expecting the awakening kiss of her lover and liberator. I prefer to read the following two episodes in the order in which they appear in the Ms. version, although the hermeneutical implications of this change should not be exaggerated. Encountering the second child (who does not feature in the Babylonian Talmud version), R. Joshua asks about the water situation in the city, seemingly anticipating the words of the exiled Hebrew poet, "I thirst for thy waters, Jerusalem."[8] The child's enigmatic reply delays immediate gratification even further, by sending R. Joshua to two especially pungent vegetables, garlic and onions, as if to say: Whoever cannot reach the city and its waters will be filled with thirst and longing.

After introducing the first primary need—thirst, which was not quenched—the second primary need is intimated—hunger. The covered vessel could obviously be empty. The mention of the mother, the most primary source of nourishment, as the one who forbids its exposure, reminds us that she is the one who can satisfy the hunger but also prevent this satisfaction at the initial developmental stages of the evolving self.

The image of the covered vessel, whose contents are invisible and must be guessed, powerfully conveys the notion of an enigma that cannot be solved through fair means of encoding and decoding but rather by leaving everything to fate or to a wild guess, not unlike the three caskets in *The Merchant of Venice*.[9] The subject seeking to establish his presence stands before a blank mirror, and yet another attempt to construct the self through its reflection in the other miscarries.

The pattern of delayed solutions is repeated when R. Joshua manages to enter the city and drink its water. After the frustrating experience with the boys, it would appear that the encounter with the girl leads him to an integration of the self, which compensates for its imperfections by bonding with the other sex. The dialogic self, opening up toward the girl, covers up its own vulnerability by resorting to the cultural discourse. He quotes a biblical verse to flatter her by comparing her to Rebecca. She, however, because of her vulnerable dependence on his help to accomplish her own bonding, exposes his inability to identify himself as an active subject in the biblical plot he knows only intellectually.

From here onward, the enigma assumes an erotic guise that brings the text closer to the generic riddle. The generic riddle is erotic both in its structure—teasing as in a courtship and reaching the temporary climax of a solution—and in its social function, in the wedding banquets of Samson in the Bible, Solomon and the Queen of Sheba in the Midrash, up to and including the many weddings of Italian and Dutch Jews mentioned in Pagis's book.[10]

A great deal of effort is invested in the last stage of the self's journey, which is embodied in the move inward—from the road, to the city wall, to the well, and up to the widow's house, herself a somewhat paradoxical transformation of the folktale princess asleep in the city shrouded in gardens. She is indeed an appropriate transformation as an object of desire for the male Jewish self at a time when a city "that was full of people . . . [has] become like a widow" (Lamentations 1:1).

The stay in the widow's home and the meals she serves create a sense of comfort and an atmosphere of intimacy, suggesting that the self could attain integration at the end of a journey involving confrontations with various forms of otherness. To begin with, the primary need of hunger intimated earlier will now reach delayed and temporary gratification. The tests in the three meals confirm the folktale association, raising expectations of an ending where the hero solves the riddle, which is the riddle of his own self. Of all the tests, R. Joshua would seem best equipped to deal with the last one, for he is a sage and the test concerns a halakhic issue.[11] Indeed, the term *peah* occurs here with a reference that is slightly different from its standard meaning in the Bible and in rabbinical literature, namely, as leftovers of a dish rather than as the margins of a field. In this context, the term *peah* may also be hinting to the destruction of the Temple, as in the quotation: "This represents the kingdom of Media, which turned Israel into *peah* and lawlessness, to annihilate, to kill, and to destroy."[12] Mainly, however, it serves to create an association between R. Joshua's failure, as a personal subject, to face the tests posed by the widow, and his failure to meet the norms of communal responsibility underlying the commandment of *peah*.[13]

In the various stations of R. Joshua's quest, the enigma is translated into an enigmatic form of interpersonal communication, thereby presenting the self with a range of options for establishing relationships with the other. The integration of the subject is repeatedly undermined because of the enigma entailed in the very encounter with the other—boy, girl, woman—and because, in the narrative text, these others also represent the inchoate, unintelligible, total, and annihilating forces of the inner space and of destiny.[14]

The power and wisdom of weak, young figures overriding adult authority suggest a potential for social criticism of the leadership. Note that R. Joshua was the man sent by the sages of Usha to a gathering in the Beit Rimon Valley to quell a budding insurrection by Galilean Jews. At this mission, at which he was certainly more successful than in the dialogues quoted in these narratives, he told his audience the fable about the long-beaked Egyptian heron extracting a bone stuck in the lion's throat and emerging unscathed.[15]

In the present stories, the entanglement in enigmatic situations is accompanied by the absence of a generic riddle, in which encoding and decoding elements are sufficiently balanced to enable the riddlee a fair chance. As rays of light unable to converge into a coherent image, the encoding and decoding elements remain threateningly dazzling and diffuse, almost as if something at the very core of the seeing, creative, deciphering subject had been fatally injured. As is true of many texts in *Lamentations Rabbah*, the injury is also sensed as a process of creation and destruction affecting the most universal metaphysical subject, God.

The most poignant instance of the enigma hovering above this chain of stories is the destruction of the Temple, which is never explicitly mentioned. The enigma itself is God's presence in a world that human understanding experiences as utterly devoid of meaning. Translating the enigma into the language of myth does not help to clarify it; instead, it blurs the borders between physical and metaphysical, historical and ahistorical in the narrative plot. Although the city is not mentioned by name, it is symbolically associated with Jerusalem, which is closed to Jews in one way or another and, after the destruction of the Temple, undergoes a transformation from a concrete into a spiritual entity. There is no shortcut to the city and R. Joshua, who is seeking one, finds there is no simple answer to the riddle posed by the boy, as there is no answer to the lament's typical question, *"Eikha?"*

The only true riddle known to me in classical rabbinic literature appears in the sequence of riddle tales in *Lamentations Rabbah* preceding the dream narratives before R. Joshua's journey: "What is this thing, nine go out and eight are complete, and twenty four serve, and two pour, and one drinks?" (*Lamentations Rabbah* 1).[16] Schoolchildren in Jerusalem pose this riddle to an Athenian, who manages to solve it only after requesting help from R. Yohannan ben Zakkai. The answer, "nine months of pregnancy, eight days before circumcision, two nipples, the infant and the twenty-four months of nursing," portrays the stage before the self separates from the mother to become a separate subject, before the rise of the enigma with which the primary layers will threaten the evolving subject, but also before the self turns into an entity growing toward independence, painful separations, and maturity.

The generic riddle is an unadulterated form of discourse temporarily released from the enigma. R. Joshua comes closest to unraveling the enigma when he reaches the understanding, formulated as a proverb: "No one has ever defeated me but this widow, and a girl, and those boys." Note that the man from the first encounter is not mentioned in the summary (and the stories in the Babylonian Talmud were made to conform with this summary and omitted the episode), perhaps because he is more R. Joshua's double than a confronting "other."[17]

The unique linguistic articulation of R. Joshua's understanding through the use of the verb form "defeated me" (*nitshuni*), found only a few times in rabbinical literature, links its meaning to myth as the cognitive correlation of the enigma. In its two other additional appearances in rabbinic literature, this linguistic form is ascribed to God. At the end of a story about a dispute between R. Eliezer and all the other sages, led by R. Joshua, we read: "R. Nathan met Elijah and asked him: 'What did the Holy One, blessed be He, do at that moment?' He replied: 'He smiled, saying: "My sons have defeated me, my sons have defeated me"'" (TB Bava Metsia 59b). In another text, this form is cited together with the theme of the destruction of the Temple: "I defeated Jeremiah, but did I not lose in destroying my house and banishing my children? But with the golden calf, Moses defeated me and thus I won. It is therefore my wish that you should defeat me" (*Pesikta*

Rabbati, 40). The divine subject, much as the human subject, is presented as dynamic and dialogical.

Self-knowledge resulting from experience includes the tragic notion that the enigma remains hermetically sealed. Solutions are delayed, so that, regarding most important issues, experience becomes hindsight, but also continues to drive the quest. The enigma also represents the possibility, at once anxiety-ridden and playful, of release from the boundaries of subjectivity. Returning to Cavafy, with a slight change:

> The enigma gave you the marvelous journey.
> Without her you wouldn't have set out.
> She has nothing left to give you now.

∽

I have sought in this book to demonstrate that each narrative unit can be examined separately, according to the various contextual criteria outlined in the chapters of this book. The texts chosen for discussion were meant to focus on the specific aspects stressed in each chapter rather than to cover them exhaustively, as I tried to show by illuminating them from various contextual perspectives.

The first folk narrative I presented at the end of Chapter 1 was the last story in *Lamentations Rabbah*. It therefore seems appropriate that the last story in this book should be the first folk narrative in the body of the Midrash (as opposed to the proems, which do not include proper folk narratives):

R. Eleazar said: "Once a merchant was traveling with a caravan of three hundred camels laden with pepper. He came to Tyre and met a tailor who sat at the city gate. He said to him: 'What do you sell?' Said he: 'Pepper.' He said: 'Do you not sell piecemeal?' Said he: 'No, only the entire stock.' He said: 'You will only sell it in a city of Jews [in Judea].' He went to a city of Jews and met another tailor who sat at the city gate. He said: 'What do your camels carry?' Said he: 'Stick to your cutting.' He repeated his question: 'What do you sell?' Said he: 'Stick to your sewing.' He said: 'Tell me what you carry and if I can I shall purchase it and, if not, I shall bring you someone who will.' Said he:

'Pepper.' He [the tailor] took him to his house, [the merchant] unloaded and then fixed a price. He [the tailor] took him into the house, showed him a pile of *dinars*, and said: 'See if this money is current in your country.' He [the merchant] took his leave and went for a walk in the market, where he met one of his friends. He asked him: 'What did you bring here?' He said: 'Pepper.' He said: 'If you have any left, bring me for one hundred *dinars* worth, I'm having a feast.' Said he: 'I've already sold it to a tailor, but I shall tell him and he will give you.' So he went to him and said: 'Do you still have any of that pepper left?' He said: 'By your life, it's already been sold. In the first floor, some bought one ounce, and some bought an ounce and a half; in the second floor, some bought and some did not; in the third floor I did not even notice them, to fulfill what is written: "a city that was full of people." ' "— *Lamentations Rabbah* 1:1

In the printed version of *Lamentations Rabbah* it is explicitly noted that the caravan is on its way to Jerusalem. We do not know the exact purpose of the journey, whether sacred or secular, bringing offerings, a business trip, or perhaps some combination of both. In the present version, translated from the Buber edition, the journey to the city of Jews—possibly Jerusalem, but not for sure—is the result of a commercial failure in Tyre. In contrast, in the printed version, it is clear that the purpose of the journey is to reach Jerusalem, and the stopover in Tyre is incidental.

The style and the contents of this story are those typical of folk narratives in *Lamentations Rabbah* and other Palestinian aggadic Midrashim: the use of the formulaic number three; a dialogue full of tension and movement; a moving caravan; the character of the tailor; a festive meal described through its Greek name, *ariston*; a pile of coins known by their Roman name, *moneta*; a Latin name for a weight unit, *uncia*; wise Jews; and wanderings. I have chosen to end with this story because, of all the stories in *Lamentations Rabbah*, it is the one I understand least. Perhaps it joins the riddle tales in describing Jerusalem as a bustling, lively city, in line with the explicit homiletic-explanatory link to the verse "a city that was full of people." It cites two sentences reminiscent of proverbs known in other languages: "Tailor, stick to your cutting, stick to your sewing," like "shoemaker, stick to your last," namely, know thy place. Nevertheless, it is not clear to me why the merchant is carrying pepper to Jerusalem, unless the pepper is hinting to its complement, salt—"with pepper and with a grain of salt" (M. Shabbat 6:5), salt being the grain sown on the ruins of destroyed cities. And the tailors sitting at the gates of both cities—could they be intimating the mourners of Zion eventually rending their clothes? The story's opacity serves to remind us that, when we study folk narratives, particularly from ancient literature, relatively little of what was told orally appears in writing. This loss results from an inherent fragmentation rather than from an unfortunate sequence of technical mishaps. Generally, the unknown surpasses the known, and the unfathomable is greater than the obvious. The voices captured in the folk-tales echo the many voices of ancient culture. The folktales of *Lamentations Rabbah* allow us a glimpse into the ragged scraps of the web of life.

NOTES

---

1. In recent times, the study of the languages and versions of aggadic literature has concerned, among others, the following scholars: Saul Lieberman, Eliezer Shimshon Rosenthal, Louis Finkelstein, David Weiss Halivni, Chaim Dimitrovsky, Yaakov Sussman, Daniel Sperber, Jacob Neusner, Shamma Friedman, Steven Fraade, Menahem Kahana. On beliefs and thought in aggadic literature, see the work of Jacob Lauterbach, Yitzhak Heinemann, Abraham J. Heschel, Ephraim E. Urbach, Daniel Boyarin, and Marc G. (Menahem) Hirshman. On aggadic literary forms, see Joseph Heinemann, Judah Goldin, Jonah Fraenkel, Yaakov Elbaum, Ofra Meir, David Stern, and Avigdor Shinan. This is not, by any means, an exhaustive listing of this rich scholarly endeavor, and a detailed account of these studies is beyond the scope of this work. The division into research fields, as presented here, is also necessarily schematic.

2. This list might also include Max Kadushin and Yitzhak Heinemann. Both dealt specifically with rabbinic thought, and with the way in which it excels at the organic integration of scholarly and popular thinking. Some of the other scholars mentioned above have devoted specific studies to folk literature, among them Yaakov Elbaum, Avigdor Shinan, and, more recently, Joshua Levinson and Dina Stein. Eli Yassif's comprehensive book, *The Hebrew Folktale: History, Genre, Meaning* (in Hebrew) (Jerusalem: Bialik Institute, 1994), translated into English by Jacqueline S. Teitelbaum (Bloomington: Indiana University Press, 1999), traces the course of the Hebrew folk narrative throughout its history. My page references are to the Hebrew edition.

3. See Clifford Geertz, *The Interpretation of Cultures* (New York: Basic Books, 1973), particularly the first chapter.

4. Louis Ginzberg, *On Jewish Law and Lore* (Philadelphia: Jewish Publication Society, 1955), 61.

5. Eli Yassif, "Folklore Research and Jewish Studies" (in Hebrew), parts 1 and 2, *World Union of Jewish Studies Newsletter* 27 (1987): 3–26; 28 (1988): 3–26.

6. See Hayyim N. Bialik, *Collected Works* (in Hebrew) (Tel Aviv: Dvir, 1983), 232–39, 242–44, and particularly his monumental popularizing compilation, *Sefer Ha-Aggadah*, which he edited and translated together with Yehoshua Hana Ravnitzky, *The Book of Legends—Sefer Ha-Aggadah: Legends from the Talmud and Midrash*, translated by William G. Braude, introduction by David Stern (New York: Schocken Books, 1992); also Louis Ginzberg, *The Legends of the Jews*.

7. Unlike Bialik, Berdyczewski worked mainly, but not exclusively, in German, and was later translated into Hebrew by his son Immanuel Bin-Gorion in *Mi-Mekor Israel* and other anthologies. For an English version, see Micha Josef Bin-Gorion, *Mi-Mekor Israel: Classical Jewish Folktales*, translated by I. M. Lask; prepared, with an Introduction and Headnotes, by Dan Ben-Amos (Bloomington: Indiana University Press, 1990).

8. Israël Lévi, *Le Ravissement du Messie a sa Naissance et Outre Essais*, ed. Evelyn Patlagean (Paris: Peeters, 1994).

9. See Bernhard Heller, "Das hebräische und arabische Märchen," in *Anmerkungen zu den Kinder und Hausmärchen der Brüder Grimm*, ed. Bolte and Polívka; also Patai, Utley, and Noy, eds., *Studies in Biblical and Jewish Folklore*.

10. Roland Barthes, *Mythologies* (London: Paladin, 1973).

11. Jonah Fraenkel, *The Methods of Aggadah and Midrash* (in Hebrew), 2 vols. (Givatayyim: Yad la-Talmud, 1991).

12. See Dov Noy, "Folklore" (in Hebrew), in *Encyclopedia of Social Sciences* (Merhavia: Sifriat Hapoalim, 1968), 4:597–613. A different, updated version appeared as "Folklore: Definition and Boundaries" (in Hebrew), in *"Forever After . . .": On the Art of the Folk Narrator*, edited by Tamar Alexander (Ramat Gan: Tag, 1993), 17–38. See also Francis Lee Utley, "Folk Literature: An Operational Definition," in *The Study of Folklore*, edited by Alan Dundes (Englewood Cliffs, N.J.: Prentice Hall, 1965), 7–24; Dan Ben-Amos, "Toward a Definition of Folklore in Context," *Journal of American Folklore* 84 (1971): 3–15; Richard Bauman, "Conceptions of Folklore in the Development of Literary Semiotics," *Semiotica* 39 (1982): 1–20; and idem, "Folklore," in *Folklore, Cultural Performances, and Popular Entertainments*, ed. Richard Bauman (New York: Oxford University Press, 1992), 29–40.

13. Dan Ben-Amos, "'Context' in Context," *Western Folklore* 52 (1993), 209–26; Richard Bauman, "Performance," in *International Encyclopedia of Communications*, ed. Erik Barnouw (New York: Oxford University Press, 1989), 3:262–66. Reprinted in Bauman, *Folklore, Cultural Performances, and Popular Entertainments*, ed. Richard Bauman (New York: Oxford University Press, 1992), 41–49.

14. The concept of "everyday life" as a research category was developed in various

directions. Michel de Certau, *The Practice of Everyday Life*, translated by Steven Rendall (Berkeley and Los Angeles: University of California Press, 1988), offers a version unique in its attention to the voices of people leading their daily lives, contrasting with several anthological approaches to the subject that relate mainly to objects and to the environment.

15. See, for instance, Menahem Kister, *Studies in Avot de-Rabbi Nathan: Studies in Text, Redaction, and Interpretation* (in Hebrew) (Jerusalem: The Hebrew University, Department of Talmud, and Yad Izhak Ben-Zvi, The Institute for Research of Eretz Israel, Dissertation Series, 1998).

16. The history of this work and its reception in early medieval Jewish literature are related in Solomon Buber's introduction to his edition of *Eikha Rabbah* (Vilna: Press of Widow and Brothers Romm, 1893), 1–77; see also Pinhas Mandel, "The Tale in Midrash Lamentations Rabbah: Version and Style" (master's thesis, Hebrew University of Jerusalem, 1983); idem, "Midrash Lamentations Rabbati: Prolegomenon, and a Critical Edition to the Third Parasha" (in Hebrew) (Ph.D. diss., Hebrew University of Jerusalem, 1997); and Alexander Marx, "Midrasch Eicha Rabbati," *Orientalistische Literatur Zeitung* 5 (1902): 293–95.

17. Fraenkel, *Methods of Aggadah and Midrash*, 2:552.

18. Walter J. Ong, *Orality and Literacy: The Technologizing of the Word* (London: Methuen, 1982); Jack Goody, *The Interface Between the Written and the Oral* (Cambridge: Cambridge University Press, 1987).

19. The theoretical approaches informing the methodologies of this work are further clarified in the separate chapters of the book. I will only point out here that, generally, the main sources of inspiration were structural, semiotic, and hermeneutical approaches.

20. See Daniel Boyarin, *Intertextuality and the Reading of the Midrash* (Bloomington: Indiana University Press, 1990), which is specifically concerned with the *Mekhilta of Rabbi Ishmael*. See also David Stern, *Parables in Midrash: Narrative and Exegesis in Rabbinic Literature* (Cambridge, Mass.: Harvard University Press, 1991), which, like the present work, focuses mainly on *Lamentations Rabbah*. And see Steven Fraade, *From Tradition to Commentary: Torah and its Interpretation in the Midrash Sifre to Deuteronomy* (Albany: State University of New York Press, 1991); as the title indicates, this work deals mainly with the *Sifre* to Deuteronomy. Alan Mintz, in *Hurban: Responses to Catastrophe in Hebrew Literature* (New York: Columbia University Press, 1984), adopts the opposite course and presents a cross section on the topic of catastrophe in Hebrew literature, from the Bible to the present; a chapter in Mintz's book (see part 1, chap. 2, 49–83) is devoted to *Lamentations Rabbah*. Finally, see Anat Yisraeli-Taran, *The Legends of the Destruction* (in Hebrew) (Tel Aviv: Hakibbutz Hameuhad, 1997).

21. Buber, introduction to *Eikha Rabbah*; Mandel, "The Tale in Midrash Lamentations Rabbah"; Mandel, "Midrash Lamentations Rabbati."

22. The proem form received special attention in a study emphasizing the origins of midrashic literature in the synagogue (see Joseph Heinemann, *Public Sermons in the Talmudic Era* [in Hebrew] [Jerusalem: Bialik Institute, 1970]). Minor inexactitudes in the game created by the numerical value of the word and the number of the proems are not discussed here.

23. Haim Schwarzbaum, "The Jewish and Moslem Versions of Some Theodicy Legends," *Fabula* 3 (1959): 119–69; idem, "The Prophet Elijah and R. Joshua b. Levi" (in Hebrew), in *Roots and Landscapes: Studies in Folklore*, edited by Eli Yassif (Beer Sheva: Ben Gurion University Press, 1993), 33–44.

CHAPTER 2: THE LITERARY CONTEXT OF FOLK NARRATIVES IN THE AGGADIC MIDRASH

1. Bialik and Ravnitsky, preface to *Sefer Ha-Aggadah*. The English translation does not include the authors' original preface. An early version of the following discussion appeared in my article "Ideological and Psychological Messages in 'The Tale about the Two Children of Zadok the Priest': Toward an Interpretation of Aggadic Midrash" (in Hebrew), *Jerusalem Studies in Hebrew Literature* 3 (1983): 122–39.

2. Elizabeth Fine, *The Folklore Text* (Bloomington: Indiana University Press, 1984), describes systematically and in great detail the process of transcribing an oral account.

3. Phenomenological scholars of literature share this perception of the work as a series of levels working in unison. The *locus classicus* is Roman Ingarden, *The Literary Work of Art*, trans. George G. Grabowic (Evanston: Northwestern University Press, 1973). This work appeared originally in German as *Das Literarische Kunstwerk* (Tübingen: M. Niemeyer, 1930). For further development, see Benjamin Hrushovski, "Segmentation and Motivation in the Text Continuum of Literary Prose," in vol. 5 of *Papers on Poetics and Semiotics*, ed. Benjamin Hrushovski and Itamar Even-Zohar (Tel Aviv: Tel Aviv University Press, 1976).

4. Roland Barthes, *S/Z*, trans. Richard Miller (New York: Hill and Wang, 1974), 20–21. Barthes relates to the various levels of organization in the work as codes. In literary criticism, the meaning of the term code was established in the classic article by Roman Jakobson, "Concluding Statement: Linguistics and Poetics," in *Style in Language*, ed. Thomas Sebeok (Cambridge, Mass.: MIT Press, 1960), 350–77.

5. See *Greek in Jewish Palestine: Studies in the Life and Manners of Jewish Palestine in the II–IV Centuries* c.e. (New York: Jewish Theological Seminary, 1942), and *Hellenism in Jewish Palestine: Studies in the Literary Transmission, Beliefs, and Manners of Palestine in the I Century* b.c.e.*–IV Century* c.e. (New York: Jewish Theological Seminary, 1950).

6. Fraade, *From Tradition to Commentary*.

7. Jonah Fraenkel, "Hermeneutic Problems in the Study of the Aggadic Narrative" (in Hebrew), *Tarbiz* 47 (1978): 140 (reprinted in *The Aggadic Literature: A Reader*, ed. Avigdor Shinan [Jerusalem: Magnes Press, 1983], 325–58).

8. Emilio Betti, "Hermeneutics as the General Methodology of the Geisteswissenschaften," in *Contemporary Hermeneutics: Hermeneutics as Method, Philosophy, and Critique*, ed. Josef Bleicher (London: Routledge and Kegan Paul, 1980).

9. Hans Georg Gadamer, *Wahrheit und Methode* (Tübingen: J. C. B. Mohr, 1975).

10. Claude Lévi-Strauss, *Structural Anthropology*, trans. Claire Jacobson and Brooke Grundfest Schoepf (New York: Doubleday, 1967), 202–28.

11. Jürgen Habermas, *Knowledge and Human Interests*, trans. Jeremy J. Shapiro (London: Heinemann, 1972), 309.

12. Among numerous works, see, e.g., Paul Rabinov, "Representations are Social Facts: Modernity and Post-Modernity in Anthropology," in *Writing Culture: The Poetics and Politics of Ethnography*, ed. James Clifford and George E. Marcus (Berkeley and Los Angeles: University of California Press, 1986), 234–61.

13. Paul Ricoeur, "The Hermeneutical Function of Distanciation," *Philosophy Today* 17 (1973): 129–41.

14. Paul Ricoeur, *Freud and Philosophy: An Essay in Interpretation*, trans. Denis Savage (New Haven: Yale University Press, 1970).

15. On these terms, see Ricoeur, "Hermeneutical Function of Distanciation."

16. The philological analysis shows that textual variants of this particular narrative are relatively insignificant, although they do occur. Thanks to Pinhas Mandel, who placed at my disposal the versions of the story he found in the manuscripts and printed versions of *Lamentations Rabbah*. Throughout my work, I also used the various versions of the stories in Munich manuscript 229 (dated 1295), which is almost identical to the first printed version (Pesaro 1520). See Zvi M. Rabinowitz, "Fragments of Midrash Echa Rabba from the Geniza" (in Hebrew), in *Bar-Ilan: Annual of Bar-Ilan University*, ed. Menachem Zevi Kaddari, Nathaniel Katzburg, and Daniel Sperber (Ramat Gan: Bar Ilan University, 1973), 69–80; and idem, "Geniza Fragments of Midrash Ekha Rabba" (in Hebrew), in *Proceedings of the Sixth World Congress of Jewish Studies* (Jerusalem: World Union of Jewish Studies, 1977), 3:437–39.

17. Yassif, *Hebrew Folktale*, 238–39, 246–47.

18. Benjamin Hrushovski, "Do Sounds Have Meaning? The Problem of Expressiveness of Sound Patterns in Poetry" (in Hebrew), *Ha-Sifrut* 1 (1968–1969), 410–20 (and particularly 419–20).

19. Jonah Fraenkel, "Paranomasia in Aggadic Narratives," *Scripta Hierosolymitana* 27 (1978): 27–51.

20. Axel Olrik, "Epic Laws of Folk Narrative," in *The Study of Folklore*, ed. Alan Dundes (Englewood Cliffs, N.J.: Prentice Hall, 1965), 129–41.

21. The computerized database of the Historical Dictionary of the Academy of Hebrew Language has a tentative statistical analysis, which confirms these claims. For

further details on the language of the text, readers may consult the Hebrew edition of the present book (33–35).

22. Shlomith Rimmon-Kenan, *Narrative Fiction: Contemporary Poetics* (London: Routledge, 1980), 52–53.

23. Gedalyah Alon, *The Jews in their Land in the Talmudic Age (70–640 C.E.)*, trans. and ed. Gershon Levi (Jerusalem: Magnes Press, 1980; Cambridge, Mass.: Harvard University Press, 1989), 1:101–3, 254–58 (particularly n. 8).

24. The perception of the Temple as *axis mundi* appears in many legends and parallels similar perceptions of holy places, particularly mountaintops, in many other cultures. See s.v. "Axis Mundi," *The Encyclopedia of Religion*, vol. 2 (New York: MacMillan, 1987); Mircea Eliade, *Patterns in Comparative Religion* (Cleveland: World Publishing, 1968), 265–303, 367–87. See also David Shulman, *Tamil Temple Myths* (Princeton: Princeton University Press, 1980).

25. *The Fathers According to R. Nathan: Version A,* trans. Judah Goldin (New Haven: Yale University Press, 1955), chap. 16.

26. Aaron Hyman, *Toldoth Ha-Tannaim Ve-Ha-Amoraim* (in Hebrew) (Jerusalem: Boys Town, 1964); Mordechai Margaliot, *Encyclopedia of Talmudic and Geonic Literature* (in Hebrew) (Tel Aviv: Chechik, 1940), under their names. Neither concordances to rabbinic language nor biographical lexicons shed any light on the identity of a R. Yehozadak. On the other hand, there is one mention of R. Ishmael b. Yehozadak (which was corrected in the Talmudic glosses known as *Masoret Ha-Shas* to Simeon b. Yehozadak). This could be an interesting detail, given that in the version of this story in the Babylonian Talmud, and also in the derived version of Moses Gaster, *The Exempla of the Rabbis* (1924; reprint, New York: Ktav, 1968), the father's name is Ishmael. On R. Zadok, see also Fraenkel, "Hermeneutic Problems in the Study of the Aggadic Narrative."

27. Boyarin, *Intertextuality and the Reading of the Midrash*, especially pp. 28–29, wherein he refers to Galit Hasan-Rokem, *Proverbs in Israeli Folk Narratives: A Structural Semantic Analysis*, Folklore Fellows Communications, no. 232 (Helsinki: Academia Scientiarum Fennica, 1982), 55–56, omitting to mention, however, that the discussion on pp. 57–64 is actually devoted to biblical texts.

28. Avigdor Shinan, "A Tale of a Dog and Ten Kids" (in Hebrew), *Sinai* 85 (1979): 138–64.

29. The beauty of the youngsters as the motivation for the harlot's initiative is not mentioned in any of the groups of manuscripts of *Lamentations Rabbah*, and we learn about it only from the parallel version in the Babylonian Talmud, as well as from other versions inspired by it.

30. C. W. Keyes, "Half-Sister Marriage in New Comedy and the Epidicus," *Transactions of the American Philological Association* 71 (1940): 217–29. Keyes mentions in his article six other Greek plays on the same topic, reconstructed from Roman comedies, and clarifies the legal and historical background for the rise and fall of this

motif. On the topic of incest in literature in general, see Otto Rank, *The Incest Theme in Literature and Legend: Fundamentals of a Psychology of Literary Creation*, trans. Gregory C. Richter (Baltimore: Johns Hopkins University Press, 1992); originally published as *Das Inzest-Motif in Dichtung und Sage* (Leipzig: F. Deuticke, 1912). See Joshua Levinson, "The Tragedy of Romance: A Case of Literary Exile," *Harvard Theological Review* 89 [1996]: 227–44. For a Christian parallel, see Averil Cameron, *Christianity and the Rhetoric of Empire* (Berkeley: University of California Press, 1994), 182.

31. Aeschylus, *The Libation Bearers*, trans. Herbert Weir Smyth (Cambridge, Mass.: Harvard University Press, 1983), pp. 179–87, lines 207–77. Electra first recognizes her brother's footsteps as similar to her own. Orestes reinforces this identification by pointing to the location where the hair, in a display of overwhelming sorrow, was cut and then kept by his sister. As in our story, here too identification is made through bodily signs.

32. See Fraenkel, "Paranomasia in Aggadic Narratives."

33. On "the knowledge of the body," see Elaine Scarry, *The Body in Pain: The Making and Unmaking of the World* (New York: Oxford University Press, 1985).

34. Homer, *The Odyssey*, trans. A. T. Murray and George E. Dimock (Cambridge, Mass.: Harvard University Press, 1995), bk. 19, p. 263, line 390.

35. Marc G. (Menahem) Hirshman, "Shifting Sacred Loci: Honi and His Grandchildren" (in Hebrew), *Tura* 1 (1989): 109–18.

• 36. Galit Hasan-Rokem, "Within Limits and Beyond: History and Body in Midrashic Texts," *International Folklore Review* 9 (1993): 5–12. More about the identification of Jerusalem and the Temple with the female body appears in Chapter 6 of the present volume.

37. Antti Aarne and Stith Thompson, *The Types of the Folktale: A Classification and Bibliography*, Folklore Fellows Communications, no. 184 (Helsinki: Academia Scientiarum Fennica, 1973), 325–35, AT nos. 930–49.

38. Aristotle, *Poetics*, trans. Stephen Halliwell (Cambridge, Mass.: Harvard University Press, 1995), 83–87.

39. Rimmon-Kenan, *Narrative Fiction*, chap. 6.

40. In a discussion with the author that took place in Jerusalem in 1997, Shlomo Naeh remarked that the singular verb form is puzzling not only at the logical level, but also syntactically as inserted in a structure that conveys mutuality.

41. There are other parallel versions of this story: *Midrash Ha-Gadol*, Ki Tavo; Gaster, *Exempla of the Rabbis* (no. 59, as well as other versions mentioned there). The form of the parallel renditions is influenced by the Babylonian Talmud version as quoted here in the text. *Piyyutim* (liturgical poems) have also been written on this subject, and some can be found at the Geniza Research Institute for Hebrew Poetry of the Israel Academy of Science, located in the Jewish National and University Library in Jerusalem. In the catalogue of the Geniza Research Institute, these *piy-*

yutim, which also follow the Babylonian Talmud form, are recorded under "story of R. Ishmael's children." Three versions open with "How, my city, have I sinned against Heaven," a wording representative of the collective guilt mentioned above. This opening also appears in Daniel Goldsmith, ed., *Seder Ha-Kinot le-Tish'a be-Av According to the Ashkenazi Ritual* (Jerusalem: Mossad Ha-Rav Kook, 1977), no. 24, pp. 88–90: "And against my city I have sinned"; as well as in Ladino in *Kinot Tish'a be-Av* (no date in the book, but annotated in the Jerusalem National Library as Salonika 1890), pp. 8–9. Three additional *piyyutim* mention the story at various lengths, and in the catalogue of the Geniza Research Institute they appear under such titles as "The story of R. Ishmael's daughter" and "The daughter of Ishmael the High Priest and her story." As noted, all these *piyyutim* were inspired by the TB version of the story. Ezra Fleischer was most helpful in locating some of these sources, and I thank him.

42. Aristotle, *Poetics*, chap. 13. Moreover, note that the ending of the story evokes awe and compassion, as in Aristotle's definition of "catharsis."

43. The story also appears in several editions of *Lamentations Rabbah*. Mandel, however, argues that this story was copied from the Babylonian Talmud and is definitely not part of the Midrash.

44. This view on the story about R. Yohannan b. Zakkai emerges from Alon's discussion in Gedalyah Alon, *Jews, Judaism, and the Classical World* (Jerusalem: Magnes Press, 1977), 269–313. This story is extensively discussed in Chapter 8 of the present volume.

45. Ricoeur, *Freud and Philosophy*, 292 (emphasis in original).

46. Richard L. Rubenstein, *The Religious Imagination: A Study in Psychoanalysis and Jewish Theology* (Boston: Beacon Press, 1971), 35.

CHAPTER 3: THE GENRE CONTEXT OF FOLK NARRATIVES IN THE AGGADIC MIDRASH

1. Dan Ben-Amos, "Analytical Categories and Ethnic Genres," *Genre* 3 (1969): 275–301.

2. Giuseppe Cocchiara, *The History of Folklore in Europe*, trans. John McDaniel (Philadelphia: Institute for the Study of Human Issues, 1981); Rosemary Levy-Zumwalt, *American Folklore Scholarship: A Dialogue of Dissent* (Bloomington: Indiana University Press, 1988).

3. Ofra Meir, "'A Garden in Eden': On the Redaction of Genesis Rabba" (in Hebrew), *Dappim: Research in Literature* 5–6 (months? 1989): 309–30; Ofra Meir, "The Continuity of Editing as the Shaping of a World View" (in Hebrew), in *Rabbinic Thought: Proceedings of the First Conference on 'Makhshevet Hazal'*, ed. Marc G. (Menahem) Hirshman and Tsvi Groner (Haifa: University of Haifa, 1989), 85–110; Yassif, *Hebrew Folktale*, chap. 5.

4. Richard Bauman, *Story, Performance, Event: Contextual Studies of Oral Narrative* (Cambridge: Cambridge University Press, 1986).

5. Max Lüthi, *The Fairytale as Art Form and Portrait of Man* (Bloomington: Indiana University Press, 1984).

6. On this question, see the studies by Claude Lévi-Strauss on the mythical structure of human thought as manifest in narrative works. Lévi-Strauss does not follow the threefold genre division pointed out above. See, for instance, *Structural Anthropology*, 202–28; *L'origine des maniéres de table*, vol. 3 (Paris: Plon, 1968); *The Raw and the Cooked*, trans. John Weightman and Doreen Weightman (New York: Harper and Row, 1969); *From Honey to Ashes*, trans. John Weightman and Doreen Weightman (New York: Harper and Row, 1973); and *The Naked Man*, trans. John Weightman and Doreen Weightman (New York: Harper and Row, 1981).

7. Lüthi, *The Fairytale as Art Form and Portrait of Man*. See also Tzvetan Todorov, *The Fantastic: A Structural Approach to Literary Genre*, trans. Richard Howard (Ithaca, N.Y.: Cornell University Press, 1971).

8. Carl Gustav Jung, with Marie L. von Franz, Joseph L. Henderson, Jolande Jacobi, and Aniela Jaffé, *Man and His Symbols* (London: Picador, 1964); Bruno Bettelheim, *The Uses of Enchantment: The Meaning and Importance of Fairytales* (New York: Vintage Books, 1977).

9. Bettelheim, *Uses of Enchantment*.

10. Stith Thompson, *The Folktale* (New York: Dryden Press, 1946); Hermann Bausinger, "Märchen," in *Formen der Volkpoesie* (Berlin: Eschmidt, 1980), 169–72.

11. Aliza Shenhar-Alroy, *Stories of Yore: Children's Folktales* (in Hebrew) (Haifa: University of Haifa, 1986).

12. Heda Jason, *Genre: An Essay in Oral Literature* (Tel Aviv: Tel Aviv University Press, 1972); Aesopus, *Fables of Aesop*, trans. S. A. Handford (Harmondsworth, Middlesex: Penguin Books, 1979); Stern, *Parables in Midrash*.

13. Volker Klotz, *Das Europäische Kunstmärchen* (Stuttgart: J. B. Metzler, 1985).

14. André Jolles, *Einfache Formen* (Halle [Saale]: Niemeyer, 1956).

15. *The Mishnah of R. Eliezer* (in Hebrew), 2 vols., ed. Hyman G. Enelow (New York: Bloch, 1934).

16. Lieberman, *Greek in Jewish Palestine*, 144–60.

17. Donald W. Winnicott, *Playing and Reality* (Middlesex: Pelican Books, 1985).

18. The link between *"Eikha?"* and *"Ayeka?"* more than hints to the Christian idea of "original sin," and its relationship with the doctrine of retribution prevalent in rabbinic literature is extremely problematic.

19. James Kugel, *The Idea of Biblical Poetry: Parallelism and its History* (New Haven: Yale University Press, 1981). The passage discussed here is in chapter 1 of *Lamentations Rabbah*. The following translations are according to the Buber edition. According to Mandel, all the tales discussed here exist in all the manuscripts of the Midrash and are indeed an integral part of the work.

20. Wilhelm Bacher, "Alter jüdisher Volkswitz in der muhammedanischer Litera-tur," *Monatsschrift für Geschichte und Wissenschaft des Judentums* 19 (1870): 68–72; Josef Perles, "Rabbinische Agadas in 1001 Nacht: Ein beitrag zur Geschichte der Wanderung Orientalischen Märchen," *Monatsschrift für Geschichte und Wissenschaft des Judentums* 22 (1873): 61–85; Israël Lévi, "Contes Juifs," *Revue des Études Juives* 40 (1885): 209–23; Sigmund Fraenkel, "Die Scharfsinnsproben," *Zeitschrift für vergleich-ende Literaturgeschichte und Renaissance-Literatur* 3 (1890): 220–35; Haim Schwarz-baum, *Studies in Jewish and World Folklore* (Berlin: Walter de Gruyter, 1968), 204–21. Schwarzbaum's note contains additional bibliographical material. "Athenians will be worsted by Galileans," quoted in Cameron, *Christianity and the Rhetorics of Empire*, 190.

21. Roger D. Abrahams, *Between the Living and the Dead*, Folklore Fellows Com-munications, no. 225 (Helsinki: Academia Scientiarum Fennica, 1980), 22–23; Galit Hasan-Rokem, "Spinning Threads of Sand: Riddles as Images of Loss in the Midrash on Lamentations," in *Untying the Knot: On Riddles and Other Enigmatic Modes*, ed. Galit Hasan-Rokem and David Shulman (New York: Oxford University Press, 1996), 109–24, which is an earlier version of this chapter.

22. Arnaldo Momigliano, *Alien Wisdom: The Limits of Hellenization* (Cambridge: Cambridge University Press, 1975), 92.

23. Abrahams, *Between the Living and the Dead*, 22. See also Don Handelman, "Traps of Trans-formation: Theoretical Convergences," in Hasan-Rokem and Shul-man, *Untying the Knot*, 37–61.

24. Thomas A. Green, "Riddle," in *Folklore, Cultural Performances, and Popu-lar Entertainments: A Communications-Centered Handbook*, ed. Richard Bauman (New York: Oxford University Press, 1992), 134–38. See also Annikki Kaivola Bre-genhøj, "Riddles and Their Use," in Hasan-Rokem and Shulman, *Untying the Knot*, 10–36.

25. Dan Pagis, *A Secret Sealed: Hebrew Baroque Emblem-Riddles from Italy and Holland* (in Hebrew) (Jerusalem: Magnes Press, 1986), particularly 34–61 and 89–90. On the theoretical aspects of this subject, see Dan Pagis, "Toward a Theory of the Literary Riddle," in Hasan-Rokem and Shulman, *Untying the Knot*, 81.

26. Pagis, *A Secret Sealed*, 37.   27. Pagis, "Toward a Theory," 82.

28. Pagis, *A Secret Sealed*, 35.   29. Pagis, "Toward a Theory," 82.

30. Ibid., 82, 94–95.   31. Ibid., 95.

32. Norman Mosley Penzer, ed., *The Ocean of Story: Somadeva's Katha-Sarit Sagara*, vols. 6–7, trans. C. H. Tawney (London: Sawyer, 1926); Somadeva, *Tales from the Kathasaritsagara*, trans. Arshia Sattar (Delhi: Penguin Books, 1994), 190–234. The story relevant for our purpose, named "The Three Fastidious Brahmins," appears in Somadeva, 225–28. See also Louis Renou, ed. and trans., *Contes du Vampire* (Paris: Gallimard, 1963).

33. Abrahams, *Between the Living and the Dead*, 8–9; Pagis, *A Secret Sealed*, 36.

34. Aarne and Thompson, *The Types of the Folktale*, 167–68; *The Complete Grimm's Fairy Tales*, trans. Margaret Hunt and James Stern (New York: Pantheon Books, 1972).

35. Aristotle, *Poetics*, 83–87.

36. In Aarne and Thompson, *The Types of the Folktale*, 328, AT 930. Freddie Rokem, "One Voice and Many Legs: Oedipus and the Riddle of the Sphinx," in Hasan-Rokem and Shulman, *Untying the Knot*, 255–70.

37. Leea Virtanen, "On the Function of Riddles," in *Finnish Riddles*, ed. Leea Virtanen, Annikki Kaivola-Bregenhøj, and Aarre Nyman (Helsinki-Pieksämaki: Finnish Literature Society Publications, 1977).

38. Dov Noy, "Riddles at a Wedding-Banquet" (in Hebrew), *Mahanayim* 83 (1963): 64–71. See also Dina Stein, "A King, a Queen, and the Riddle Between: Riddles and Interpretation in a Late Midrashic Text," in Hasan-Rokem and Shulman, *Untying the Knot*, 125–50.

39. It is possible that the encounter between Jerusalemites and Athenians involves Jews, namely, Jerusalem Jews and Athenian Jews, pointing to the tension between center and periphery.

40. David Shulman, "The Yaksa's Questions," in Hasan-Rokem and Shulman, *Untying the Knot*, 151–67.

41. Abrahams, *Between the Living and the Dead*, 19.

42. Jason, *Genre*.

43. For this distinction, see Hasan-Rokem, *Proverbs in Israeli Folk Narratives*, 27. The concept, as used here, was developed by Dina Stein, "The Queen of Sheba vs. Solomon: Riddles and Interpretation in Midrash Mishlei A" (in Hebrew), *Jerusalem Studies in Jewish Folklore* 15 (1993): 7–35 (on the issue discussed here, see particularly p. 11).

44. Aaron Oppenheimer, "The Reconstruction of Jewish Settlement in the Galilee" (in Hebrew), in *Eretz Israel from the Destruction of the Second Temple to the Muslim Conquest*, ed. Zvi Baras, Shmuel Safrai, Menahem Stern, and Yoram Tsafrir (Jerusalem: Yad Izhak Ben-Zvi, 1982), 1:75–92.

45. A textual problem seems to emerge here. In the printed version of *Lamentations Rabbah*, the phrase is *'m' dtbyr qdl* (a broken-necked people). *qšh qdl* is the idiom found in Aramaic translations of the biblical verses about the golden calf (see L. Smolar and M. Aberbach, "The Golden Calf Episode in Post-Biblical Literature," *Hebrew Union College Annual* 39 [1970]: 91–116).

46. Saul Lieberman, *Studies in Palestinian Talmudic Literature* (in Hebrew), ed. David Rosenthal (Jerusalem: Magnes Press, 1991), 516–20, shows that stiff-necked and broken-necked are both derogatory expressions referring to Israel. See Dov Noy, "The Jewish Versions of the 'Animal Languages' Folktale (AT 670): A Typological-Structural Study," *Scripta Hierosolymitana* 22 (1971): 171–208, on tales evolving around the verse, "Cast thy bread upon the waters" (Ecclesiastes 11:1).

47. Ms. Karlsruhe, Reuchlin 2 (S 11340 at the Institute of Microfilmed Hebrew Manuscripts at the Jewish National and University Library in Jerusalem), lacks the second story, as does the printed version of the Babylonian Talmud. The same is true of the Yemenite manuscript of Tractate Sanhedrin located at the Rabbi Herzog Institute for the Complete Israeli Talmud (sometimes called Rav Maimon Ms.). Note in this manuscript the special care of the scribe, who set aside a special place for the Lamentations stories in the Talmud by marking the word *Eikha* in large and ornamented letters. On the quality of this manuscript, see Yehiel Kara, *The Yemenite Manuscripts of the Babylonian Talmud: Studies in their Aramaic Language* (in Hebrew) (Jerusalem: Hebrew University of Jerusalem, Institute of Jewish Studies, 1984). Kara calls this manuscript Ms. M (8–9). Although the two stories are not linked in the Yemenite manuscript, this linking does appear in a Yemenite Midrash on Lamentations from the year 1510, *The Book of Lamentations with Translations and Interpretations from Ancient Manuscripts* (in Hebrew), arranged, edited, and with glosses by Yosef D. Kafah (Jerusalem: Ha-Agudah le-Hatzalat Ginzei Yehudei Teiman, 1962), 330 (the story is on 356). The versions of the stories in this Midrash are generally close to those in the Babylonian Talmud. Parallel versions of the story in the Babylonian Talmud also appear in the following works: *Eikha Zuta* (in Solomon Buber, ed., *Midrash Zuta* [Berlin: Mekizei Nirdamim, 1894], 60); *Yalkut Shimoni, Eikha* no. 1004 (quoted in Buber's edition of *Midrash Zuta*, 154); and Isaac Aboab, *Menorath ha-Ma'or*, ed. Yehudah Horev and M. J. Katzenelnbogen (Jerusalem: Mossad Harav Kook, 1961), no. 305, 659–60. There is no room here for a discussion of the different textual variants, interesting in and of themselves. The two stories, however, are linked in a manuscript fragment taken from a book binding now at the Gratz University Library, no. 1703 (at the Institute of Microfilmed Hebrew Manuscripts at the Jewish National and University Library in Jerusalem, Ms. S 30369, and also PA 404/13). This version is very close to the Munich Ms. of the Babylonian Talmud. For further details on commentaries by the *geonim*, Ba'al he-Arukh and Rashi, see Galit Hasan-Rokem, "Eikha? . . . Ayeka?: On Riddles in the Stories of Midrash Eikha Rabba" (in Hebrew), *Jerusalem Studies in Hebrew Literature: Essays in Memory of Dan Pagis* 11 (1988): 531–47, and n. 24.

48. Fraenkel, "Die Scharfsinnsproben," 222, also claims that the Palestinian version is better. Nevertheless, he also rightly points out that this in itself does not prove this version is older. Schwarzbaum, *Studies in Jewish and World Folklore*, 212, agrees with Fraenkel's view.

49. In the Gratz manuscript noted above: "When she went into bed." The word "bed" was inserted with another pen and in another script, apparently over an erasure. This could be an allusion to the *Jus Primae Noctis* custom, practiced mainly by rulers during feudal times (Raphael Patai, "Jus Primae Noctis," *Folklore Research Center Studies* 4 [1974]: 177–80). The text in the Gratz manuscript is preferable on several counts, although the text there is fragmented because of the cut made to

recycle it as a bookbinding, and I have therefore brought the Munich manuscript version *in extenso* (see my study, "Eikha? . . . Ayeka?," n. 26).

50. Fraenkel, "Die Scharfsinnsproben," 222, argues that these are two separate, independent sources.

51. Noy, "Riddles at a Wedding-Banquet," and Stein, "The Queen of Sheba vs. Solomon."

52. Pagis, "Toward a Theory," 84.

53. Ibid., 97.

54. Mieke Bal, "The Rape of Narrative and the Narrative of Rape: Speech Acts and Body Language in Judges," in *Literature and the Body: Essays on Populations and Persons*, ed. Elaine Scarry (Baltimore: Johns Hopkins University Press, 1986), 1–32. On the relationship between riddle and incest, see also Claude Lévi-Strauss, *The Scope of Anthropology*, trans. Sherry O. Paul and Robert A. Paul (London: Jonathan Cape, 1967), 36–37.

55. Noy, "Riddles at a Wedding-Banquet," and Stein, "The Queen of Sheba vs. Solomon."

56. Galit Hasan-Rokem, "Cognition in the Folktale: Aesthetic Judgements and Symbolic Structures," *Scripta Hierosolymitana* 27 (1978): 192–204.

CHAPTER 4: THE COMPARATIVE CONTEXT OF FOLK NARRATIVES IN THE AGGADIC MIDRASH

1. Galit Hasan-Rokem, "Between Unity and Plurality: Dov Noy's Studies of Folklore in Talmudic-Midrashic Literature" (in Hebrew), *Jerusalem Studies in Jewish Folkore: For Dov Noy* 13–14 (1992): 18–29. See also, Chapter 1, this volume.

2. Kaarle Krohn, *Folklore Methodology*, trans. Roger L. Welch (Austin: The University of Texas Press, 1971). The German original appeared in 1926.

3. Vladimir Propp, *The Morphology of the Folktale*, trans. Laurence Scott, rev. and ed. Louis A. Wagner (Austin: The University of Texas Press, 1977); originally published as *Morfologija skazki* (Leningrad: Academia, 1928).

4. William R. Bascom, "Four Functions of Folklore," in *The Study of Folklore*, ed. Alan Dundes (Englewood Cliffs, N.J.: Prentice Hall, 1965), 279–99.

5. Claude Lévi-Strauss, "The Story of Asdiwal," in *The Structural Study of Myth and Totemism*, ed. Edmund Leach (London: Tavistock, 1967), 1–47.

6. Noy, "The Jewish Versions of the 'Animal Languages' Folktale (AT 670)."

7. See also Galit Hasan-Rokem, "The Study of Processes of Change in the Folk Narrative" (in Hebrew), *Jerusalem Studies in Jewish Folklore* 3 (1982): 129–37; Galit Hasan-Rokem, "The Snake at the Wedding: Semiotic Reconsideration of the Comparative Method of Folk Narrative Research," *ARV: Scandinavian Yearbook of Folklore* 43 (1987): 73–87.

8. Albert Wesselski, a scholar of medieval literature, argued that books rather

than oral traditions are the most important instrument for the transmission of folk literature (see Emma Emily Kiefer, *Albert Wesselski and Recent Folktale Theories* [Bloomington: Indiana University Press, 1945]). In his study of Jewish folklore, Haim Schwarzbaum upheld the same view, and so does Eli Yassif to some extent (see Eli Yassif, "The Chapbook—Folklore or Popular Culture?" [in Hebrew], *Jerusalem Studies in Jewish Folklore* 1 [1981]: 127–33); see also Yehuda Yudel Rosenberg, *The Golem of Prague and Other Tales of Wonder* (in Hebrew), selected and edited, with an introduction and notes, by Eli Yassif (Jerusalem: Bialik Institute, 1991), 7–27.

9. This terminology is based on the method suggested by Pagis, *A Secret Sealed*, 37. In Chapter 3, I suggested that this category includes riddling tales, where the riddler is a character in the story, and riddle tales, where the riddler is the narrator.

10. The first of the four riddles in *Midrash Mishle*, ed. Solomon Buber (Vilna: Press of Widow and Brothers Romm, 1893), 40. See also Buber's note in *Lamentations Rabbah ad locum*, now also in *Midrash Mishle: A Critical Edition based on Vatican MS. Ebr. 44* (in Hebrew), ed. Burton L. Visotzky (New York: Jewish Theological Seminary of America, 1990), 4. In the latter, too, the riddle is portrayed as representing the wisdom of Jerusalem, known throughout the world, as opposed to foreign wisdom. Stein, "The Queen of Sheba vs. Solomon," focuses her discussion on sexual, religious, and national problems of identity.

With slight variations, all the riddle tales are found in the Lamentations Midrash in Oxford Ms. 2792 in the Neubauer Catalogue (207a–210a), which is part of an anthology from the Yerahmiel school. The story about the division of the fowl also appears, with more significant linguistic changes, in the anthology in Oxford Ms. OR. 135 (16385 at the Institute of Microfilmed Hebrew Manuscripts in the National Library—301a). For a description of this manuscript, see Malachi Beth Arié, "Ms. Oxford, Bodleian Library, Bodl. Or. 135" (in Hebrew), *Tarbiz* 54 (1985): 631–34. On the origins of the Hebrew folk narrative in this period, see Eli Yassif, "Theory and Practice in the Creation of the Hebrew Narrative in the Middle Ages" (in Hebrew), *Kiryat Sefer* 62 (1988–1989): 887–905. A later adaptation of the riddles is also found in Joseph Ben Meir Zabara, *The Book of Delight*, trans. Moses Hadas (New York: Columbia University Press, 1932), 100–110.

11. Aarne and Thompson, *The Types of the Folktale*, AT nos. 655, 655A, 1533. For bibliographical material on the story in *A Thousand Nights and a Night*, see Victor Chauvin, *Bibliographie des ouvrages arabes* (Liège: H. Vaillant-Carmanne and Leipzig: Otto Harrassowitz, 1901), 7:158–61, no. 438. See also the comment by Penzer, *The Ocean of Story*, 285–94; and Somadeva, *Tales from the Kathasaritsagara*, 225–28.

12. See Chapter 3, this volume.

13. In Tawney's English translation of *The Ocean of Story*, 4:217–21, no. 26; in Sattar's English translation, 190–234; and in the separate French translation, *Contes du Vampire*, no. 8.

14. In Tawney's English translation, 7:10–12, no. 11; *Contes du Vampire*, 894–96, no. 11.

15. *Contes du Vampire*, 19. Renou, the translator and editor, also suggests that the king's quest has a spiritual content (12). Renou assumes that an oral or semi-oral series of stories was the background of the Vetala tales. The original of the famous Kashmiri version of the Somadeva in the Penzer edition dates from the second half of the eleventh century, but scholarship assumes that these stories rely on much earlier sources (*Contes du Vampire*, 9).

16. Louis Renou, "L'enigme," *L'Inde Fondamentale*, ed. Charles Malamoud (Paris: Hermann, 1978), 11–20.

17. Richard Burton, ed., *The Book of a Thousand Nights and a Night*, vol. 10 (London: H. S. Nichols, 1897); Richard Burton, *Supplemental Nights in The Book of a Thousand Nights and a Night* (London: H. S. Nichols, 1897), 3:351–59. For further material related to *A Thousand Nights and A Night*, see Chauvin, *Bibliographie des ouvrages arabes*, vol. 7 (Beirut: Khayats, 1964).

18. According to a legendary tradition, the grandfather of the four heroes, Muadda Abu Nazar, is a cousin of Nebuchadnezzar(!). Ferdinand Wüstenfeld, ed., *Die Chroniken der Stadt Mekka* (Leipzig: F. A. Brockhaus, 1861), 4:20.

19. Masoudi [al Masudi], *Les prairies d'or*, ed. and trans. C. Barbier de Meynard and Pavet de Courteille (Paris: Societé Asiatique, 1917), 3:228–36. Masoudi was familiar with the stories of *A Thousand Nights and a Night*, although not in the form known to us today. On the link between the motif of sweet honey in the body of an animal and Samson's riddle, see Fraenkel, "Die Scharfsinnsproben," 234.

20. *Chronique de Tabari*, trans. M. Hermann Zotenberg (Paris: Besson et Chantemerle, 1958), 2:356–62. See also his note on following tracks (359). The story also appears in a book by Ibn al-Athir, *Kitab al-Kamil fi-l Tarikh* (oral communication by Meir J. Kister and Hava Lazarus-Yafeh). For a more detailed comparison and further details on this issue, see Galit Hasan-Rokem, "Perspectives of Comparative Research of Folk Narratives in Aggadic Midrashim: Enigmatic Tales in *Lamentations Rabba* 1" (in Hebrew), *Tarbiz* 59 (1990): 109–31, particularly 118, n. 21.

21. *Lamentations Rabbah* 1, on the verse "because the comforter who should relieve my soul is far from me" (Lamentations 1:16); PT Berakhot 2:4; and TB Sanhedrin 98b. See a discussion of this story in Chapter 8, this volume.

22. Hans Stumme, *Tunisische Märchen und Gedichte*, (Leipzig: J. C. Hinrichs, 1893), 1:73–75, 2:123–26.

23. The substitution of the wine motif by the menstruating cook sheds an interesting light on the links between Arab and Jewish traditions. See Meir J. Kister and Menahem Kister, "On the Jews of Arabia: Some Notes" (in Hebrew), *Tarbiz* 48 (1979): 241–42; Hava Lazarus-Yafeh, "Some Halakhic Differences between Judaism and Islam" (in Hebrew), *Tarbiz* 51 (1982): 207–25, particularly 216–18. See also my article, "Perspectives of Comparative Research," 118, n. 23.

24. Bruno Meissner, *Neuarabische Geschichten aus dem Iraq* (Leipzig: J. C. Hinrichs, 1903), 307–9.

25. The expression "Walls have ears" is well known in rabbinic literature, for example: *Leviticus Rabbah*, ch. 32.

26. On the expression of this opposition in the actions of nomadic marauders, see Brent D. Shaw, "Bandits in the Roman Empire," *Past and Present* 105 (1984): 3–52, particularly 25, 42–43; Benjamin Isaac, "Bandits in Judea and Arabia," *Harvard Studies in Classical Philology* 88 (1984): 171–203, particularly 173, 181, 189, 198, and 202.

27. For this and other useful comments on this chapter, I am grateful to the late Hava Lazarus-Yafeh. Thanks are also due to Meir J. Kister, Matti Huss, and Oded Irshai.

28. S. Krauss, "Talmudische Nachricthen über Arabien," *Zeitschrift der Deutschen Morgenländischen Gesellschaft* 70 (1916), 321–53. At p. 327, he quotes both Tacitus and Josephus Flavius on the appearance of Arabs as cruel auxiliary forces in the Roman occupying army during the Great Revolt and in Bar Kokhbah's times. Krauss also quotes from *Lamentations Rabbah*. He identifies Beth Garem, the place assumed to be paradise in Arabia according to TB Eruvin 19a, with the dwelling place of the Djurhami tribe, mentioned in the text of the story quoted by Masoudi.

29. "Happy is he who beheld the downfall of Palmyra," *Lamentations Rabbah* 2. For further details on Palmyra's dwellers as mediating between the desert and the inhabited areas, see my article, "Perspectives of Comparative Research," 119, n. 26.

30. J. Halévy, "Examen critique de sources relatives a la persécution des chrétiens de Nedjran par le roi juif des Himyarites," *Revue des Études Juives* 18 (1889): 16–42, 161–78; J. Halévy, "Remarque sur un point contesté touchant la persécution de Nedjaran," *Revue des Études Juives* 21 (1890): 73–79; Axel Moberg, *The Book of Himyarites: A Hitherto Unknown Syriac Work on the Himyarite Martyrs* (Lund: Gleerup, 1921); Irfan Shahid, *The Martyrs of Najran: New Document* (Bruxelles: Societé des Bollandistes, 1971); Irfan Shahid, " 'The Martyrs of Najran': Miscellaneous Reflections," *Le Muséon* 9 (1980): 149–61; and Lucas van Rompay, "The Martyrs of Najran: Some Remarks on the Nature of the Sources," *Orientalia Lovaniensia Analecta* 1 (1982): 301–9. Whereas Moberg and Shahid relate to the texts under discussion as historical documents for all intents and purposes, the textual criticism of Halévy and van Rompay rules out this possibility. Thanks to Muin Haloun.

31. It seems improbable that this is the Gallus who destroyed Tiberias and Sepphoris in 351 C.E. See Joseph Geiger, "The Revolt (in Gallus' Times), and Building the Temple (in Julian's Times)" (in Hebrew), in *Eretz Israel from the Destruction of the Second Temple to the Muslim Conquest*, ed. Zvi Baras, Shmuel Safrai, Menahem Stern, and Yoram Tsafrir (Jerusalem: Yad Izhak Ben-Zvi, 1982), 1:202–17.

32. On the ancient South Arabian inscriptions, on the whole affair, and on the special place of Tiberias's Jews and its priests in South Arabian traditions, see

Haim Z. Hirschberg, "Joseph, King of Himyar, and the Coming of Mar Zutra to Tiberias" (in Hebrew), in *All the Land of Naphtali*, ed. Hirschberg (Jerusalem: Israel Exploration Society, 1978), 139–46. Hirschberg cites the primary sources on the subject from the articles by Jacques Reikmans (1953, 1956) and E. G. Lundin (1961). See also Yaron Dan, *The City in Eretz Israel During the Late Roman and Byzantine Periods* (in Hebrew) (Jerusalem: Yad Izhak Ben-Zvi, 1984), 43, 49–50 (particularly n. 74).

33. *Chronique de Tabari*, 2:175–79.

34. Sebastian P. Brock and Susan Ashbrook Harvey, eds. and trans., "Women Martyrs of Najran," chap. 4 in *Holy Women of the Christian Orient*, 2d updated ed. (Berkeley and Los Angeles: University of California Press, 1998).

35. Shahid, *The Martyrs of Najran*, 11. On lamentations regarding cities, see Margaret Alexiou, *Ritual Lament in Greek Tradition* (Cambridge: Cambridge University Press, 1974). On destroyed cities, see pp. 84–86 in particular. On eulogies of cities in Arab poetry and their recourse to Greek models, as well as on further bibliographical information on Arab attitudes to Jewish traditions, see my article, "Perspectives of Comparative Research," 121, n. 33.

36. Fraenkel, "Die Scharfsinnsproben," 223–24. Fraenkel is obviously referring here to the well-known story from TB Bava Bathra 73b, where the Arab shows Rabbah bar bar Hana the place of the "dead of the desert" and Mount Sinai. Both versions of the riddle tales, in *Lamentations Rabbah* and in TB Sanhedrin, draw on two separate Arab sources, according to Fraenkel. In his view, the *Lamentations Rabbah* adaptation is looser. Quite surprisingly, Fraenkel concludes his article by stating the contrary view, namely, that it was the Arabs who took the story from the Midrash (229), thus supporting Bacher's view in "Alter jüdisher Volkswitz in der muhammedanischer Literatur," 70. The treatment of this topic is characterized by confusion because of the dearth of information on cultural relationships between Jews and Arabs at this time. Schwarzbaum, *Studies in Jewish and World Folklore*, 204–21, accepted the claim about the precedence of Jewish versions that, in his view as well, had influenced Arab tradition. In contrast, Noy presents Jews in the role of mediators between East and West and relies, among others, on Heller's article, "Das hebräische und arabische Märchen," in Bolte and Polívka, *Handwörterbuch des deutschen Märchens*, 1:99.

37. Elimelech Halevy, *The Historical-Biographical Legend: From the Great Knesset until R. Judah Hanasi in Light of Greek and Latin Sources* (in Hebrew) (Tel Aviv: n.p., 1975), 205–9. David Grene and Richard Lattimore, eds., *Greek Tragedies* (Chicago: University of Chicago Press, 1960), 117, line 56. The puzzling sentence at the end of the story, "in a ship I came . . . ," which appears in all versions (according to Buber's notes to his edition of *Lamentations Rabbah* and according to Pinhas Mandel, who has studied the manuscripts of this work), hints at a play on the Greek words *fowl* and *ship*, two words that include the consonants π and λ: πέλεια and πλοίου.

Archaeological findings from the Roman and Byzantine period point to the close contacts that had prevailed between Jewish and Hellenistic cultures in Palestine in Late Antiquity. See, for instance, Zeev Weiss and Ehud Netser, *Promise and Redemption: A Synagogue Mosaic from Sepphoris* (Jerusalem: The Israel Museum, 1996).

38. Isocrates in *Panegyricos* (fourth century B.C.E.), quoted in Werner Jaeger, *Early Christianity and Greek Paideia* (Cambridge, Mass.: Harvard University Press, 1961), 134, n. 34. Jaeger (75) points out that in the fourth century C.E., classic culture and the Greek *paideia* undergo a renaissance and a redefinition within Christianity, rather than in opposition to it.

39. Momigliano, *Alien Wisdom*, 92. On this issue, see Menahem Stern's seminal article, "Jerusalem, Incomparably Famous Among Cities of the East" (in Hebrew), in *Studies in Jewish History in the Second Temple Period*, ed. Moshe Amit, Isaiah Gafni, and Moshe David Herr (Jerusalem: Yad Izhak Ben-Zvi, 1991), 518–30. See also Moshe Amit's comments on Momigliano's book, "Worlds That Did Not Meet" (in Hebrew), in *The Jews in the Hellenistic Roman World: Studies in Memory of Menahem Stern*, ed. Isaiah M. Gafni, Aaron Oppenheimer, and Daniel R. Schwartz (Jerusalem: Zalman Shazar Center for Jewish History, 1996), 251–71, particularly 270. See also Martin Hengel, in collaboration with Christoph Markschies, *The "Hellenization" of Judea in the First Century after Christ* (London: SCM Press; Philadelphia: Trinity Press International, 1989). "In an epigraph Meleager praises the city [Gadara] as the 'Athens of Syria,' and an epitaph from Hippo calls it χρηστομουσία, 'an excellent abode of learning' " (p. 20). And, "It was at this early period, presumably in Jerusalem and on the basis of a Jewish initiative, that the legend came into being of the primal affinity between Jews and Spartans through Abraham. The Graecizing of Jerusalem as Ἱεροσόλυμα is along the same lines; the designation first identified the city as a Hellenistic holy temple city, 'the holy Solyma' (ἱερόμολις: Philo, *Leg. Gai.* 225, 281, etc.), and secondly associated it with the 'canonical' primal document of the Greeks, the *Iliad*, in which the 'glorious Solymi' appear (96.184), while according to the *Odyssey* 5.283 the Solymi mountains are near to Ethiopia. Such interpretations were to exalt the significance of the city and the Jewish people in the eyes of the Greeks" (p. 22). About the Megarians admitting Athenians to their homes, see Anthony R. Birley, *Hadrian the Restless Emperor* (New York: Routledge, 1997), 178.

40. Henry J. Blumenthal, "529 and its Sequel: What Happened to the Academy?" *Byzantion* 48 (1978): 369–85. Blumenthal discusses the continued intellectual primacy of the classical legacy, even after the ascendancy of Christianity in the fourth century. See also Dan, *The City in Eretz Israel*, 157–68.

41. Antti Aarne, *Vergleichende Rätselforschungen*, Folklore Fellows Communications, no. 26 (Helsinki: Academia Scientiarum Fennica, 1918), 10.

42. Alexiou, *Ritual Lament in Greek Tradition*, 86.

43. "Contes populaires grecs, recueillis à Smyrne en 1875, et traduits par Emile Legrand," *Revue de l'Histoire des Religions* 10 (1884): 72–93. Four stories are included

in this article, and the third, "Le marchand et ses trois fils" (79–85), is relevant for our purposes. On further links between the Greek and Jewish traditions in later periods, see my article, "Perspectives of Comparative Research," 123, n. 40.

44. Richard Fick and Alfons Hilka, eds., *Die Reise der drei Söhne des Königs von Serendippo*, trans. Theodor Benfey, Folklore Fellows Communications, no. 98 (Helsinki: Academia Scientiarum Fennica, 1932). The book was first printed in 1557, and the author was reportedly Cristoforo Armeno. The original work, *Peregrinaggio di Tre Giovani Figliuoli del Re di Serendippo*, was printed in Venice by Michele Tramezzino (according to the bibliographical work by Marino Parenti, *Prime Edizioni Italiane* [Milano, 1948], 39). All further mentions of this work will refer to the German translation as the *Peregrinaggio*. For additional material about the Italian printings of this book, see my article, "Perspectives of Comparative Research," 123, n. 41. Thanks to Robert Bonfil.

45. Israel Zinberg, *A History of Jewish Literature*, trans. and ed. Bernard Martin (Cleveland: Press of Case Western Reserve University, 1972), 1:185. Moritz Steinschneider, *Die hebräischen Übersetzungen des Mittelalters und die Juden als Dolmetscher* (Berlin: Kommissionsverlag des Bibliographischer Bureaus, 1893).

46. In his learned article about the *Peregrinaggio*, "Christopher the Armenian and the Three Princes of Serendip," *Comparative Literature Studies* 4 (1967), 229–58, Schuyler V. R. Cammann has forcefully argued for a Persian original. Cammann's article makes no mention of the Midrash or any other Hebrew material. On the other hand, he toys with the idea that Christopher the Armenian (who Cammann firmly believes was a real person and very active in creating the book) came into contact with Jews from Spain or the Arab world.

47. *Peregrinaggio*, 36–51.

48. *Peregrinaggio*, 50. The editors of the German edition refute this claim, and so does Georg Huth (see "Die Reisen der drei Söhne des Königs von Serendippo: Ein Beitrag zur vergleichender Märchenkunde," *Zeitschrift für Vergleichende Litteraturgeshichte und Renaissance-Litteratur*, Neue Folge, 2 [1889]: 404–14). It is probably not a coincidence that in the anthology by R. Nissim of Kairuan, *An Elegant Composition for Relief After Adversity*, trans. William Z. Brinner (New Haven: Yale University Press, 1977), 168–72, a story involving mainly a riddling situation mentions Serendib. Nahum of Gimzo demonstrates the wisdom of the Jews, while the riddlers are sixty philosophers from Serendib, in the court of the Persian king! Hirschberg says: "Serendib is Ceylon, which Arab legend believes to be Adam's place of exile after his expulsion from Paradise" (n. 1). The story is based on the riddles in TB Bekhorot 8b–9a, and Hayim Hirschberg, the translator and editor of the Hebrew edition of the *Composition*, draws a comparison (63, n. 5). On Adam's evolvement in Moslem tradition after his expulsion from Paradise, see: Meir J. Kister, "Adam: A Study of Some Legends in Tafsir and Hadith Literature," *Israel Oriental Studies* 13 (1993): 113–74, particularly 164 and 169; and idem, "Legends in Tafsir and Hadith Literature:

Creation of Adam and Related Stories," in *Approaches to the History of the Interpretation of the Qur'an* (Oxford: Clarendon Press, 1988), 82–114.

49. *Peregrinaggio*, 66. For the full story of the salt, see 64–66.

50. On the convergence of the two roles—the bride and the task assigner—see Propp, *The Morphology of the Folktale*, 79–83.

51. *Peregrinaggio*, 66–67. In several Mediterranean languages, Semitic as well as Indo-European, testicles are popularly called "eggs." Captain Bartolomeo Colleoni was one of the greatest Venetian condottieri. He was active in the mid–fifteenth century (and immortalized in the capella at Bergamo, his native city, and in an equestrian statue by Verrocchio), and is mentioned as someone who displayed testicles (*coglioni*) on his shield. See *A Concise Encyclopedia of the Italian Renaissance* (London: Thames and Hudson, 1981), under "Colleoni," 91–92. According to an oral tradition I heard from Maria Modena, Colleoni had three testicles, evidence of his impressive virility. For further information on biographical literature and on the legends that grew around Colleoni's figure, see my article, "Perspectives of Comparative Research," 126, n. 47.

52. *Peregrinaggio*, 51–54. Huth, "Die Reise der drei Söhne," 308, n. 64; *The Itinerary of Benjamin of Tudela*, ed. and trans. Adolf Asher (London: Hakesheth, 1840), 104–6, and in the volume of notes, 214. Another version of this book was edited by Marcus Nathan Adler (London: P. Feldheim, 1964). *The Itinerary of Benjamin of Tudela* was printed in Ferrara in 1556 (see David Werner Amram, *The Makers of Hebrew Books in Italy* [Philadelphia: Julius H. Greenstone, 1909], 303).

53. The editors of the *Peregrinaggio*, on p. 71, make an inaccurate reference to M. J. Bin-Gorion, which should read: Micha Josef Bin-Gorion, *Die Sagen der Juden* (Frankfurt am Main: Kütten & Loening, 1913–1927), 4:245–251, 5:359–360. Other motifs found in Jewish literature could be added, such as that of the treacherous minister usurping the place of the king who had left his body, not only his palace, and is exposed by the king's wife, who notices the difference in their lovemaking (*Peregrinaggio*, 81). This motif resembles the unmasking of Asmodeus (Ashmedai), who took the place of King Solomon and was exposed by the King's wives (TB Gittin 68b). It is worth noting that, in Italian novellae in general, there are almost no motifs parallel to those found in Midrash riddle tales. See Dominic Peter Rotunda, *Motif Index of the Italian Novella in Prose* (Bloomington: Indiana University Press, 1942), J 601; J 1661.1; J. 1661.12; J 1661.5; J 1661.1.5.1; J 1661.1.8*; and J 1661.2.1.

54. Pagis, *A Secret Sealed*.

55. *Peregrinaggio*, 8–9.

56. Galit Hasan-Rokem, "Textualizing the Tales of the People of the Book: Folk Narrative Anthologies and National Identity in Modern Israel," *Prooftexts* 19 (1999): 69–80; and idem, "The Birth of Scholarship out of the Spirit of Oral Tradition: Folk Narrative Publications and National Identity in Modern Israel," *Fabula* 39 (1998): 277–90.

57. Aarne and Thompson, *The Types of the Folktale*. I thank Edna Heichal, administrative director of Israel Folktale Archives (henceforth notated IFA), for her generous assistance.

58. IFA 1477 (recorded by Sarah Bashari, as told by Shalom Bashari, Yemen); IFA 1790 (recorded by Mukhtar Ezra, as told by Menahem Abadi, Iraq); IFA 1938 (recorded by Rachel Heller, as told by Yitzhak Yitzhak, Iraq); IFA 5515 (recorded by Yitzhak Weksler as told by Samuel Tako, Iraqi Kurdistan); and IFA 6851 (recorded by David Eyni, Iraq).

59. Galit Hasan-Rokem, "Sources of Iraqi-Jewish Folk Narratives: Proverbs in Folk Narrative" (in Hebrew), in *Studies in the History and the Culture of the Jews of Iraq*, ed. Shmuel Moreh (Or Yehudah: Babylonian Jewry Heritage Center, 1981), 187–96. The scope of the Jewish–Iraqi folk narrative, alternatively "Arab" or "Jewish," is compared in this article to the Jewish–Moroccan folk narrative, which is usually "Judaized" to some extent or, at least, points to a mixed and pluralistic culture, as opposed to the more monolithic culture reflected in the stories of Iraqi Jews.

60. Stith Thompson, *Motif Index of Folk Literature* (Copenhagen: Rosenkilde and Bagger, 1961), H 486. On the appearance of this motif in Hebrew narrative, see Tamar Alexander-Frizer, *The Pious Sinner: Ethics and Aesthetics in the Medieval Hassidic Narrative*, ed. Maurice-Ruben Hayoun, Ivan G. Marcus, and Peter Schäfer (Tübingen: J. C. B. Mohr, 1992), 47–52.

61. *Katha Sarit Sagara*, 7:5–9, no. 10. There is no mention of the thief's exposure in the Indian story. See Aarne and Thompson, *The Types of the Folktale*, types 976 and 976a. See also my article, "Perspectives of Comparative Research," 123, n. 40.

62. IFA 1507 (recorded by Sarah Bashari, as told by Saliman Jabber, an Israeli Druze); IFA 8047 (recorded by Na'im Gil'adi, as told by Abu Daud, Iraq); IFA 9432 (recorded by Zevulun Kort, as told by Yitzhak Siman Tov, Afghanistan); and IFA 9494 (recorded by Issa Diyab Shibli, an Israeli Bedouin, as told by the elders of his tribe), the latter printed in the anthology, *A Tale for Every Month* (in Hebrew), ed. Dov Noy (Haifa: IFA, 1973), story no. 12. See also the appropriate note at the end of the book.

63. Hasan-Rokem, "Sources of Iraqi-Jewish Folk Narratives."

64. We might detect an allusion to R. Pinhas ben Yair's she-ass (PT Demai 1, 3), who also refused to eat grain that had not been tithed (see Ofra Meir, *The Poetics of Rabbinic Stories* [in Hebrew] [Tel Aviv: Sifriat Hapoalim, 1993], 35–55).

65. On the theoretical aspects of the cultural adaptation of tradition, see Lauri Honko, "Four Forms of Adaptation to Tradition," *Studia Fennica* 26 (1981): 19–33. See also Galit Hasan-Rokem, s.v. "Ökotyp," in *Enzyklopädie des Märchens* (Berlin: Walter de Gruyter, in press). The appearance of rabbis and saints in Jewish Moroccan stories accords with the centrality of saints in the folk thought of this culture. See also Issachar ben-Ami, *Saint Veneration among the Jews in Morocco* (Detroit: Wayne State University Press, 1998); Yoram Bilu, *Without Bounds: The Life and Death of R. Ya'acov*

Wazana (in Hebrew) (Jerusalem: Magnes Press, 1993), forthcoming in English from Wayne State University Press.

66. Cf. the saying "You saw a donkey, neither black nor white." Eli Yassif, *The Tales of Ben Sira in the Middle Ages* (in Hebrew) (Jerusalem: Magnes Press, 1985), 267–68. In Jewish–Spanish oral tradition, see also Tamar Alexander and Galit Hasan-Rokem, "The Multivalent Construction of Ethos in the Proverbs of a Sephardic Woman" (in Hebrew), *Jerusalem Studies in Jewish Folklore* 17 (1995): 69, 78.

67. This construct is typical of the well-known story in *A Thousand Nights and A Night* known as "Open Sesame," an international tale type (see Aarne and Thompson, *The Types of the Folktale*, AT 676). The combination appears in the following IFA stories: IFA 1714 (recorded by Mordechai Haimowitz, as told by David Eliyahu, Iraq); IFA 5692 (recorded by Efraim Hanukka, as told by his mother Miriam, Iraqi Kurdistan), and printed in the anthology *Min Ha-Mabua* (From the fountainhead), ed. Eliezer Marcus (Haifa: Israel Folktale Archives, 1966), no. 22; IFA 7025 (recorded by Mazal Eini, as told by her father David Eini, Iraq); IFA 7432 (recorded by Rachel Seri, as told by Ziona Cohen, Iraqi Kurdistan); and IFA 8155 (recorded by Yifrah Haviv, as told by Zion Zinni, Morocco). The two Arab–Israeli versions of AT 1533 in IFA are highly similar, and may suggest a common written or oral source: in both stories (IFA 822—handwritten record by Tuviah Ashkenazi, as told by an unidentified Israeli Bedouin; and IFA 3534, recorded by Menahem ben Arieh, as told by his father Moshe ben Arieh, who had heard this story from a Bedouin of the Arab-al-Hib tribe, in the vicinity of Rosh Pinah), the divided fowl is a goose. On this issue, there is also a non-typical Jewish Iranian story, IFA 4839 (recorded by Jonathan Danieli, as told by his mother), where the division of the fowl blends with a story mainly concerned with the "pound of flesh" (AT 820); this story was printed in Marcus, *Min Ha-Mabua*, no. 14.

CHAPTER 5: THE FOLKLORISTIC CONTEXT OF FOLK NARRATIVES IN THE AGGADIC MIDRASH

1. Bauman, "Folklore."
2. Ben-Amos, "Toward a Definition of Folklore in Context."
3. Bauman, "Performance."
4. Petr Bogatyrev and Roman Jakobson, "Folklore as a Special Form of Creativity," in Peter Steiner, *The Prague School: Selected Writings, 1929–1946* (Austin: University of Texas Press, 1982); translated from a revised version which appeared in Roman Jakobson, *Selected Writings* (The Hague: Mouton, 1966), 6:1–15.
5. Galit Hasan-Rokem, " 'To See the Voices': A Functional, Semiotic, and Hermeneutic Approach to Folk-Narrating" (in Hebrew), *Jerusalem Studies in Jewish Folklore* 10 (1988): 20–31.
6. Lévi-Strauss, "The Story of Asdiwal." The concept of "modes of articulation"

was coined and developed by Hagar Salamon (see *The Hyena People: Ethiopian Jews in Christian Ethiopia* [Berkeley and Los Angeles: University of California Press, 1999], 117–24).

7. de Certeau, *Practice of Everyday Life*, 20, 26, 62–63. See also Daniel Sperber, *Magic and Folklore in Rabbinic Literature* (Ramat Gan: Bar-Ilan University Press, 1994); the focus of this work is philological. See also Yassif, *Hebrew Folktale*, 269–83.

8. Gustave E. von Gruenebaum and Roger Caillois, *The Dream and Human Societies* (Berkeley: University of California Press, 1966); Barbara Tedlock, *Dreaming: Anthropological and Psychological Interpretations* (Cambridge: Cambridge University Press, 1987); David Shulman and Guy Stroumsa, *Dream Cultures: Toward a Comparative History of Dreaming* (New York: Oxford University Press, 1999).

9. Galit Hasan-Rokem, "'A Dream Amounts to the Sixtieth Part of Prophecy': On Interaction between Textual Establishment and Popular Context in Dream Interpretation by the Jewish Sages" (in Hebrew), in *Studies in the History of Popular Culture*, ed. Benjamin Z. Kedar (Jerusalem: Zalman Shazar Center for Jewish History, 1996), 45–54.

10. Vincent Crapanzano, *Hermes' Dilemma and Hamlet's Desire: On the Epistemology of Interpretation* (Cambridge, Mass.: Harvard University Press, 1992), 239–59; Yoram Bilu, "Dreams and the Wishes of the Saint," in *Judaism Viewed from Within and from Without: Anthropological Studies*, ed. Harvey Goldberg (Albany: State University of New York Press, 1986), 285–313; Eric R. Dodds, *The Greeks and the Irrational* (Berkeley: University of California Press, 1951), 110–16; Nathaniel Bland, *On the Muhammedan Science of Tabir, or Interpretation of Dreams* (London: Harrison and Sons, St. Martin's Lane, 1856); Meir J. Kister, "The Interpretation of Dreams: An Unknown Manuscript of Ibn Qutayba's 'Ibarat al-Ru'ya,'" *Israel Oriental Studies* 4 (1974): 67–103; Wendy Doniger O'Flaherty, *Dreams, Illusions, and Other Realities* (Chicago: University of Chicago Press, 1984).

11. Roger Pack, "Artemidorus and His Waking World," *Transactions and Proceedings of the American Philological Association* 86 (1955): 280–90; Patricia Cox Miller, *Dreams in Late Antiquity: Studies in the Imagination of a Culture* (Princeton: Princeton University Press, 1994), 77–91. For a comparison between Artemidorus and rabbinic literature, see Hans Lewy, "Zu dem Traumbuche des Artemidoros," *Rheinische Museum für Philologie*, Neue Folge, 48 (1893): 398–419.

12. A. Leo Oppenheim, "The Interpretation of Dreams in the Ancient Near East with a Translation of an Assyrian Dreambook," *Transactions of the American Philosophical Society* 46 (1956): 179–373; Hans Lewy, *Chaldean Oracles and Theurgy: Mysticism, Magic, and Platonism in the Later Roman Empire* (Paris: Études Augustiniennes, 1978).

13. Ephraim E. Urbach, "When Did Prophecy Cease?" (in Hebrew), *Tarbiz* 17 (1946): 1–11; reprinted in Urbach, *The World of the Sages: Collected Studies* (in Hebrew) (Jerusalem: Magnes Press, 1988).

14. Alexander Kristianpoller, *Traum und Traumdeutung*, vol. 4: *Monumenta Talmudica* (Wien: Benjamin Harz, 1923); Brigitte Stemberger, "Der Traum in der Rabbinischen Literatur," *Kairos* 18 (1976): 1–42. Maren Niehoff, "A Dream Which Is Not Interpreted Is Like a Letter Which Is Not Read," *Journal of Jewish Studies* 43 (1992): 58–84, compares rabbinic dream interpretation to the technique of *petirah*, drawing inspiration from the Dead Sea sect.

15. Shlomo Almoli (1490–1542), a refugee from Christian Spain who was active in Salonika, apparently published his *Pitron Halomot* ca. 1515. The Jewish National and University Library in Jerusalem holds the Venice 1623 edition. The book was and still is very popular. A Yiddish translation was published in Amsterdam in 1694, and reprints in Hebrew appear in Israel regularly. The latest was included in the *Pitron Halomot ha-Shalem* (Jerusalem: Bakal, 1997). For another branch of tradition, see Joseph Dan, "On the Dream Theory of Ashkenaz Pietists" (in Hebrew), *Sinai* 68 (1971): 288–93; and Monford Harris, "Dreams in Sefer Hasidim," *Proceedings of the American Academy for Jewish Research* 31 (1963): 51–80. See also Joshua Trachtenberg, *Jewish Magic and Superstition: A Study in Folk Religion* (New York: Atheneum, 1974), 230–49.

16. In addition to the printed version of the Palestinian Talmud cited in the text, I have checked the following printed manuscripts: PT, Vatican Ms. No. 1970 (Jerusalem: Maqor, 1976), 282; PT, Leiden Ms. Cod. Scal. 3 (Jerusalem: Qedem, 1971), 259; Levi Ginzburg, *Yerushalmi Fragments from the Genizah* (in Hebrew) (New York: Jewish Theological Seminary of America, 1908; reprint, Jerusalem: Maqor, 1969).

17. Ambrosius Macrobius, *Commentary on the Dream of Scipio*, trans. W. H. Stahl (New York: Columbia University Press, 1952).

18. Homer, *The Iliad* (Penguin Books, 1966), bk. 23, 413–15.

19. In *Hellenism in Jewish Palestine*, 71–77, Lieberman draws a comparison between techniques of dream interpretation as opposed to Jewish and Greek hermeneutical techniques; James Kugel, "Two Introductions to Midrash," in *Midrash and Literature*, ed. Geoffrey H. Hartman and Sanford Budick (New Haven: Yale University Press, 1986), 77–103, and particularly 100–101, n. 7, makes a reference to the similarity between the exegetical techniques of the rabbis and the Dead Sea sect on the one hand, and dream interpretation on the other.

20. Sigmund Freud, *The Interpretation of Dreams*, trans. James Strachey (New York: Basic Books, 1953); originally published as *Die Traumdeutung* (1900; Strachey's translation is based on the 8th enl. and rev. ed. [Leipzig and Vienna: Franz Deuticke, 1930]).

21. David Bakan, *Sigmund Freud and the Jewish Mystical Tradition* (Boston: Beacon Press, 1975); Yoram Bilu, "Sigmund Freud and Rabbi Yehudah: On a Jewish Mystical Tradition of 'Psychoanalytic' Dream Interpretation," *The Journal of Psychological Anthropology* 2 (1979): 443–63; Justin Miller, "Interpretations of Freud's Jewishness, 1924–1974," *Journal of the History of Behavioral Sciences* 17 (1981): 357–74; Ken

Frieden, *Freud's Dream of Interpretation* (Albany: State University of New York Press, 1990).

22. Ricoeur, *Freud and Philosophy*, 3–56.

23. Michael Sokoloff, *A Dictionary of Jewish Palestinian Aramaic* (Ramat Gan: Bar Ilan University Press, 1990), 276. The text from *Lamentations Rabbah* is his sole example.

24. Gustaf Dalman, *Die Worte Jesu* (Leipzig, 1930), according to Sokoloff, *Dictionary of Jewish Palestinian Aramaic*.

25. I suggest that Bar Hedya be considered a name for the profession of dream interpreter, according to the denotation of *hedya* (clarity), and *be-hedya* (clearly), as in TB Shabbat 133b: "R. Ashi demurred: 'It is clearly [*be-hedya*] stated' "; Shabbat 27a: "Of *kilayim* [cloth that is a mixture of wool and flax] it is clearly [*be-hedya*] stated"; Shabbat 27b: "Of fringes [required in wool and linen garments] it is clearly [*be-hedya*] stated." Hence Bar Hedya, namely, one who clarifies obscure matters by interpreting dreams.

26. As reported in field work by students from the Jewish and Comparative Folklore Program at the Hebrew University at a seminar on dream interpretation in 1994.

27. Unlike his usual practice, Buber gives no reference for this verse but rather interprets it as a simple homonym—*regel*, meaning both "foot" and "one of the three holidays of pilgrimage."

28. Niehoff, "A Dream Which Is Not Interpreted," follows the course of the relationship between these two practices from the biblical period, through the exegeses of the Dead Sea sect, up to the rabbinic period.

29. Harry Hunt, *The Multiplicity of Dreams: Memory, Imagination, and Consciousness* (New Haven: Yale University Press, 1989).

30. TB Berakhot 56a.

31. Dorothy Eggan, "The Personal Use of Myth in Dreams," *Journal of American Folklore* 68 (1955): 445–63.

32. Michael Fishbein suggested this terminology at a discussion at the Institute for Advanced Study at the Hebrew University in 1988. Manifestations of the collective unconscious in individual dreams are discussed in Carl G. Jung, *Dreams*, trans. R. F. C. Hull, Bollingen Series (Princeton: Princeton University Press, 1974).

33. The beam plays a central role in Penelope's famous dream in *The Odyssey*, bk. 19, 273. For an extensive discussion, see Galit Hasan-Rokem, "Communication with the Dead in Jewish Dream Culture," in *Dream Cultures: Toward a Comparative History of Dreaming*, ed. David Shulman and Guy Stroumsa (New York: Oxford University Press, 1999), 213–32. Both Homer and the Midrash may have highlighted beams in dreams due to the phonetic similarity between beam (δόκος) and vision (δοκή). A word play with the Greek for childbearer, Τόκος, may also be assumed.

34. In the TB Berakhot passage, the contradiction is solved by referring to the

ancient belief in distinct divine or demonic sources of dreams. See also Oppenheim, "Interpretation of Dreams in the Ancient Near East."

35. Dodds, *Greeks and the Irrational.*

36. A. J. Festugière, *Personal Religion Among the Greeks* (Berkeley: University of California Press, 1960), 101.

CHAPTER 6: THE SOCIAL CONTEXT OF FOLK NARRATIVES IN THE AGGADIC MIDRASH

1. On various meanings of the concept of context in the study of folklore see Ben-Amos, " 'Context' in Context." For narratives in particular, see Annikki Kaivola-Bregenhøj, *Narrative and Narrating: Variation in Juha Oksanen's Storytelling,* Folklore Fellows Communications, no. 261 (Helsinki: Academia Scientiarum Fennica, 1996), 52–54.

2. Fraenkel, *Methods of Aggadah and Midrash.*

3. Heinemann, *Public Sermons in the Talmudic Era.*

4. Tal Ilan, *Jewish Women in Greco Roman Palestine* (Tübingen: J. C. B. Mohr [Paul Siebeck], 1995), 195; David Goodblatt, "The Beruriah Traditions," *Journal of Jewish Studies* 26 (1975): 83.

5. Utley, "Folk Literature."

6. Goodblatt, "Beruriah Traditions"; Daniel Boyarin, *Carnal Israel: Reading Sex in Talmudic Culture* (Berkeley and Los Angeles: University of California Press, 1993), 181–96.

7. Dov Noy, "The Daughters of Zelophehad and the Daughters of Jerusalem" (in Hebrew), *Mahanayim* 48 (1960): 20–25.

8. Phyllis Trible, *God and the Rhetorics of Sexuality* (Philadelphia: Fortress Press, 1978); Carol Meyers, *Discovering Eve: Ancient Israelite Women in Context* (New York: Oxford University Press, 1988); Ilana Pardes, *Countertraditions in the Bible: A Feminist Approach* (Cambridge, Mass.: Harvard University Press, 1992). On non-feminist approaches to women in rabbinic literature, see Yaakov Elbaum, "Female Characters in Rabbinic Legends: A Model for Emulation" (in Hebrew), in *Hagut: The Woman in Jewish Sources* (Jerusalem: The Ministry of Education, 1983), 13–26; Shulamit Valler, *Women and Womanhood in the Stories of the Babylonian Talmud* (in Hebrew) (Tel Aviv: Hakibbutz Hameuhad, 1993).

9. Multivocality is an even more explicit feature of folk literature than of the novel, as characterized by Bakhtin. See Mikhail Bakhtin, *Problems of Dostoevsky's Poetics,* trans. C. Emerson (Minneapolis: University of Minnesota Press, 1984). See also Shirley Kaufman, Galit Hasan-Rokem, and Tamar Hess, eds., *The Defiant Muse: Hebrew Feminist Poems from Antiquity to the Present* (New York: The Feminist Press at CUNY, 1999), introduction, especially 1–29, and chaps. 1–5.

10. Alexiou, *Ritual Lament in Greek Tradition*; Aili Nenola-Kallio, *Studies in Ingrian Laments*, Folklore Fellows Communications, no. 234 (Helsinki: Academia Scientiarum Fennica, 1982), 97–111.

11. Fraenkel, *Methods of Aggadah and Midrash*, 1:323–93.

12. Stern, *Parables in Midrash*, 161–62.

13. Galit Hasan-Rokem, "The Rhetoric of Intimacy, the Rhetoric of the Sacred," *Temenos* 23 (1987): 45–57. This issue is also discussed in Chapter 7 of this volume.

14. Verbal communication from Dina Stein.

15. The contrast between nature and culture is fundamental to the works of Claude Lévi-Strauss. See, for instance, "The Story of Asdiwal."

16. See Zohar, Genesis 27b; *Ra'aya Meheimana*, Numbers 179a; *Ra'aya Meheimana*, Numbers 234b; Code of Maimonides, *Hilkhot De'ot* (Laws of ethical conduct) 2:3.

17. Stern prefers to use the Hebrew terminology *mashal* and *nimshal* for parable and epimythium, for the reasons he discusses in *Parables in Midrash*, 9–19.

18. Ignaz Ziegler, *Die Königsgleichnisse in der Midrash* (Breslau: Schlesische Verlags-Anstalt, 1903).

19. Boyarin, *Intertextuality and the Reading of the Midrash*, 105–16.

20. Ephraim E. Urbach, *The Sages: Their Concepts and Beliefs*, trans. Israel Abrahams (Jerusalem: Magnes Press, 1975), 444–48; Aaron Oppenheimer, "Sanctity of Life and Martyrdom Following the Bar Kokhba Revolt" (in Hebrew), in *Sanctity of Life and Martyrdom: Studies in Memory of Amir Yekutiel*, ed. Isaiah M. Gafni and Aviezer Ravitzky (Jerusalem: Zalman Shazar Center for Jewish History, 1992).

21. Joshua Gutmann, "The Mother and Her Seven Sons in the Aggadah and in the Book of the Maccabees 2 and 4" (in Hebrew), in *In Memoriam: Johannis Lewy (1901–1945)*, ed. Menahem Schwabe and Joshua Gutmann (Jerusalem: Magnes Press, 1949), 25–32; Gershon D. Cohen, "The Story of Hannah and Her Seven Sons in Hebrew Literature" (in Hebrew), in *Mordecai M. Kaplan Jubilee Volume: On the Occasion of His Seventieth Birthday*, ed. Moshe Davis (New York: Jewish Theological Seminary, 1953), 109–22. The earliest known version is apparently that found in the Second Book of Maccabees, chapter 7, which does not mention the mother's name. Nor is the name mentioned in TB Gittin 56b, or in some other versions of the story.

Miriam is also the mother's name in the version in *Pesikta Rabbati*, trans. William G. Braude (New Haven: Yale University Press, 1968), 760–61. This version, incidentally, may have led to the mother's new name, Hannah, which spread and became well known due to the parallel version of this story in *The Jossipon (Josephus Gorionides)* (in Hebrew), ed. David Flusser (Jerusalem: Bialik Institute, 1978), 1:70–75. See, in particular, Flusser's note to line 1 of the tale's version in *The Jossipon*, which mentions that *Pesikta Rabbati* cites the stories of three barren women—Sarah, Yokheved, and Hannah—close to the story about Miriam bat Tanhum. Hannah is the common name in later versions in various Jewish languages, and in contemporary educational folklore in Israel. Possibly, the phonological association between Hannah and Hanukkah, beside the link of the story with the festival of Hanukkah because of its appearance in the Book of Maccabees, has strengthened this tradition.

22. The youngest son includes many verses from the central meditation passage in *Shiur Qomah*, namely, Song of Songs 5:9–16. The order of the verses is different from that in the mystical tradition, as is obviously the tone, although the youngster's final verse is the same as the concluding verse in the Song of Songs passage. See Gershom Scholem, *On the Mystical Shape of the Godhead: Basic Concepts in the Kabbalah*, trans. Joachim Neugroschel (New York: Schocken, 1991), 15–55; and Martin S. Cohen, *The Shiur Qomah: Liturgy and Theurgy in Pre-Kabbalistic Jewish Mysticism* (Lanham, Md.: University Press of America, 1983), on the specific order of the verses, 58; on the order of naming the limbs, 214; on literary reactions to *Shiur Qomah*, 60. Cohen argues that these texts were well known outside the esoteric circle of their authors at the time of the Palestinian poet Eleazar Kallir, roughly the same as the date assumed for the compilation of *Lamentations Rabbah*. See Gershom Scholem, *Jewish Gnosticism and Merkabah Mysticism and Talmudic Tradition* (New York: Jewish Theological Seminary, 1965), 37.

23. Dina Stein, "Types of Discourse: The Interweaving of Different Types of Discourse in a Riddling Tale" (in Hebrew), (master's thesis, Hebrew University, Jerusalem, 1992). Stein deals with the riddles that the Queen of Sheba posed to King Solomon, among them only one with an early parallel version, in *Lamentations Rabbah*. See Chapters 3 and 4, and the Epilogue in this volume. The answer to this ancient riddle is: pregnancy, birth, and nursing. Stein, following French feminist theories, points out that the role of this riddle is to mark the breakdown of the opposition between the self and the other, between subject and object (87). See also Stein, "The Queen of Sheba vs. Solomon."

24. See *The Jossipon*, 70–75.

25. Moshe Attias, *Romancero Sefaradi* (in Hebrew), (Jerusalem: Machon Ben Tsvi, 1961), song no. 87, "Hannah's Seven Sons," 194–95.

26. Freddie Rokem, "The Beginning of the Hebrew Theater in Erez Israel: An Analysis of the Repertoire Between the Years 1890–1914" (in Hebrew), *Ha-Sifrut* 29 (1979): 76–81.

27. Hasan-Rokem, "Ideological and Psychological Messages in 'The Tale about the Two Children of Zadok the Priest.'" For further elaboration, see Chapter 2 in this volume.

28. Burton L. Visotzky, "Most Tender and Fairest of Women: A Study in the Transmission of Aggada," *Harvard Theological Review* 76 (1983): 403–18. Visotzky deals with the appearance of the same verse in another story about Martha b. Boethus. See also Naomi Cohen, "The Theological Stratum of the Martha b. Boethus

Tradition: An Explication of the Text in Gittin 56a," *Harvard Theological Review* 69 (1976): 187–95. Cohen compares the story from Josephus about the mother eating her child with Martha b. Boethus rather than with the widow of Doeg b. Joseph, which seems the more obvious parallel.

29. See Linda Dégh and André Vazsonyi, "Legend and Belief," in *Folklore Genres*, ed. Dan Ben-Amos (Austin: University of Texas Press, 1976), 93–123; and Tekla Dö-mötör, "Some Questions Concerning Belief Legend as a Genre," *Studia Fennica* 26 (1981): 11–27.

30. Freddie Rokem, "The Erotic, the Scientific, and the Aesthetic Gazes in the Theatre," *Assaph: Studies in the Theatre* 7 (1991): 61–73.

31. Joyce E. Salisbury, *Perpetua's Passion: The Death and Memory of a Young Roman Woman* (New York: Routledge, 1997). Her study is the main basis for the present discussion concerning Perpetua. See also Brent D. Shaw, "The Passion of Perpetua," *Past and Present* 139 (1993): 3–45; and my "Nursing in the Teeth of Death: Shared Narrative Traditions of Jewish and Christian Martyrdom" (in manuscript).

32. Marc G. (Menahem) Hirshman, *A Rivalry of Genius: Jewish and Christian Biblical Interpretation*, trans. Batya Stein (Albany: State University of New York Press, 1996).

33. For a most extensive and thorough study of those sources, see Jan Willem van Henten, *The Maccabean Martyrs as Saviours of the Jewish People—A Study of 2 and 4 Maccabees* (Leiden: Brill, 1997).

34. Galit Hasan-Rokem, "Narratives in Dialogue: A Folk Literary Perspective on Interreligious Contacts in the Holy Land in Rabbinic Literature of Late Antiquity," in *Sharing the Sacred: Religious Contacts and Conflicts in the Holy Land—First–Fifteenth Centuries C.E.*, ed. Arieh Kofsky and Guy G. Stroumsa (Jerusalem: Yad Izhak Ben-Zvi, 1998), 109–29. For a Christian parallel in Syriac, see Witold Witakowski, "Mart(y) Shmuni, the Mother of the Maccabean Martyrs in Syriac Tradition," in René Lave-nant, ed., VI Symposium Syriacum, *Orientalia Christiana Analecta* 247 (1994): 153–68.

35. Saul Friedländer, *Reflections on Nazism: An Essay on Kitsch and Death* (New York: Harper and Row, 1984).

36. Israel J. Yuval, " 'The Lord Will Take Vengeance, Vengeance for His Temple': Historia Sine Ira et Studio" (in Hebrew), *Zion* 59 (1994): 351–414.

37. There was also a significant number of women among the Pagan martyrs mentioned in the literature. See *The Acts of the Pagan Martyrs: Acta Alexandrinorum*, ed. with commentary by Herbert A. Musurillo (Oxford: Clarendon Press, 1954), 243–46.

38. Galit Hasan-Rokem, *Adam le-Adam Gesher: The Proverbs of Georgian Jews in Israel* (in Hebrew) (Jerusalem: Ben-Zvi Institute, 1993), 23.

39. Boyarin's earlier work concentrates on inner rabbinic intertextuality. He has since introduced strong cases of Jewish–Christian intertextualities. See, especially,

his *Dying for God: Martyrdom and the Making of Christianity and Judaism* (Stanford, Calif.: Stanford University Press, 1999). Intercultural dialogue as an element in stories is discussed in Chapters 4 and 8 in this volume. See also my articles, "Within Limits and Beyond," and "Narratives in Dialogue."

40. Tal Ilan points out the dominance of the names Miriam or Shalom/Shlom-zion, inspired by Hasmonean influences. Naomi G. Cohen, "The Greek and Latin Transliterations *Mariam* and *Maria*: Their Sociological Significance" (in Hebrew), *Leshonenu* 38 (1974): 170–80, deals with the influence of Roman culture on the transliterations of the name Maria among Hellenistic Jews and among non-Jews.

41. For other hypotheses, some rather extravagant, relating to the meaning of the name Miriam and its cultural role, see Alan Dundes, "The Hero Pattern and the Life of Jesus," in *Interpreting Folklore*, ed. Alan Dundes (Bloomington: Indiana University Press, 1980), 223–61.

42. A direct and clearer connection between the story of Jesus' birth and *Lamentations Rabbah* is discussed in Chapter 8 of this volume.

43. See Chapter 8, this volume.

44. On Beth Lehem as a cultic location of women honoring Rachel and Mary, see Susan Starr Sered, "Rachel's Tomb and the Milk Grotto of the Virgin Mary: Two Women's Shrines in Beth Lehem," *Journal of Feminist Studies in Religion* 2 (1986): 7–22; and idem, "A Tale of Three Rachels, Or: The Cultural *Her*story of a Symbol," *Nashim—A Journal of Jewish Women's Studies and Gender Issues* 1 (1998): 5–41.

45. In the story about the mother and the seven sons, the emperor cites this verse.

46. This passage, in Shirley Kaufman's translation, is included in Kaufman, Hasan-Rokem, and Hess, *The Defiant Muse*, 62–63.

47. Pierre Bourdieu, "The Structure of the Kabyle House," in *Algeria 1960* (Cambridge: Cambridge University Press, 1979), 133–53; Tamar Alexander and Galit Hasan-Rokem, "Spatial Elements in the Proverbs of the Jews of Turkey" (in Hebrew), *Pe'amim* 41 (1990): 112–32, particularly 131.

48. Pinhas Mandel has reinforced this view in an oral communication and has promised to publish an article on the textological aspects of the passage, so I will not discuss the variant versions he placed at my disposal. For an argument against my interpretation of the text, see David Stern, *Midrash and Theory: Ancient Jewish Exegesis and Contemporary Literary Studies* (Evanston, Ill.: Northwestern University Press, 1996), 85, 114 n. 36.

49. Scholem, *The Mystical Shape of the Godhead*, 140–96; *Lamentations Rabbah*, proem 25.

50. Moshe Idel, "La concubine de Dieu," *Revue de l'Histoire de Religions* (forthcoming).

51. On the representation of Jerusalem as a woman in contexts of destruction, see my article, "Within Limits and Beyond."

1. Stern, *Parables in Midrash*; Alon Goshen-Gottstein, "God and Israel as Father and Son in Tannaitic Literature" (in Hebrew) (Ph.D. diss., Hebrew University, Jerusalem, 1986); Hasan-Rokem, "Rhetoric of Intimacy—Rhetoric of the Sacred." On the marital relationship, see Chapter 6 in this volume, and Boyarin, *Intertextuality and the Reading of the Midrash*, 105–16.

2. Ricoeur, *Freud and Philosophy*, 6.

3. The literature on this subject is growing: see Bakan, *Sigmund Freud and the Jewish Mystical Tradition*; Bilu, "Sigmund Freud and Rabbi Yehudah"; Frieden, *Freud's Dream of Interpretation*; Miller, "Interpretation of Freud's Jewishness"; and Susan A. Handelman, *The Slayers of Moses: The Emergence of Rabbinic Interpretation in Modern Literary Theory* (Albany: State University of New York Press, 1982).

4. See Chapters 3, 4, and 5 in this volume.

5. Ricoeur, *Freud and Philosophy*, 527.

6. Rubenstein, *Religious Imagination*, 35. For full reference and discussion of this point, see Chapter 2 in this volume.

7. Stern, *Parables in Midrash*, 160–66.

8. Hasan-Rokem, "Snake at the Wedding."

9. The homilist relied here on a play of words on a Hebrew expression that means both " 'fulfilled his word'," as used in the verse, and "rended his hem."

10. The Hebrew expression is *ben tishhoret*, pointing to someone whose hair was still black (*shahor*) at his death, usually suggesting death in young manhood.

11. Possibly Likya or Lagin-Legio, where Roman troops were concentrated. On Hadrian in Palestine, see Birley, *Hadrian the Restless Emperor*, 229–34, 268–78.

12. On horror propaganda as the nucleus of historical legends in the Midrash, see also my article on Titus and the mosquito, "Within Limits and Beyond." See data on corroborating historical details in, for instance, Aaron Oppenheimer, "The Bar Kokhva Revolt," in *Eretz Israel from the Destruction of the Second Temple to the Muslim Conquest*, ed. Zvi Baras, Shmuel Safrai, Menahem Stern, and Yoram Tsafrir (Jerusalem: Yad Izhak Ben-Zvi, 1982), 1:67, 72. See also Aaron Oppenheimer, *Galilee in the Mishnaic Period* (Jerusalem: Zalman Shazar Center for Jewish History, 1991), 40. On Hadrian's royal meals, see Birley, *Hadrian*, 246.

13. The terminology follows Lévi-Strauss, "The Story of Asdiwal." See also Lévi-Strauss, *The Raw and the Cooked*.

14. Dan Ben-Amos, "Generic Distinctions in the Aggadah," in *Studies in Jewish Folklore*, ed. Frank Talmage (Cambridge, Mass.: Association for Jewish Studies, 1980), 45–71.

15. Yohannan Aharoni, "Expedition B: 'Cave of Horror' " (in Hebrew), in *The*

Judean Desert Caves 1961 (Jerusalem: Israel Exploration Society, 1962), 172–73. See also Amos Kloner, "Hideout Complexes from the Period of Bar Kokhva in the Judean Plain" (in Hebrew), in *The Bar Kokhba Revolt: A New Approach*, ed. Aaron Oppenheimer and Uriel Rapaport (Jerusalem: Yad Izhak Ben-Zvi, 1984), 153–71.

16. Sigmund Freud, *Totem and Taboo: Resemblances Between the Psychic Lives of Savages and Neurotics*, trans. A. A. Brill (Middlesex: Pelican Books, 1938); and idem, *Moses and Monotheism*, trans. Katherine Jones (New York: Vintage Books, 1955).

17. Ricoeur, *Freud and Philosophy*, 535.

18. Mandel, "The Tale in Midrash Lamentations Rabbah"; and idem, "Midrash Lamentations Rabbati."

19. Avigdor Shinan, "The Unfolding of a Rabbinical Legend: The Story of Doeg ben Yosef's Son," *Mahanayim* 7 (1994): 70–75; Garney, *Food and Society*, 37.

20. Joshua Gutmann, *The Parable in the Tannaitic Era* (in Hebrew) (Jerusalem: n.p., 1940), shows that this parable was already known in the first two centuries C.E.

CHAPTER 8: THE HISTORICAL CONTEXT OF FOLK NARRATIVES IN THE AGGADIC MIDRASH

1. On the influence of the German Jewish philosopher Herman Cohen on Bakhtin's conception of history, by which I am here informed, see Dimitri Segal's preface to the Hebrew translation of Mikhail Bakhtin, *Slovo V Romane (Voprosy Literatury I Estetiki)*, trans. Ari Avneri (Tel Aviv: Sifriat Poalim, 1989).

2. Frank E. Manuel and Fritzie P. Manuel, *Utopian Thought in the Western World* (Oxford: Basil Blackwell, 1979); Gershom Scholem, "The Messianic Idea in Judaism," in *The Messianic Idea in Judaism and Other Essays in Jewish Spirituality* (New York: Schocken Books, 1972). On the idea in the Bible, see Sigmund Movinckel, *He That Cometh*, trans. G. W. Anderson (Oxford: Basil Blackwell, 1954); Ronald Ernest Clements, "The Messianic Hope in the Old Testament," *Journal for the Study of the Old Testament* 43 (1989): 3–19. In the literature of the Second Temple, see Devorah Dimant, "Election and Laws of History in Apocalyptic Literature" (in Hebrew), in *Chosen People, Elect Nation, and Universal Mission: Collected Essays* (in Hebrew), ed. Shmuel Almog and Michael Heyd (Jerusalem: Zalman Shazar Center for Jewish History, 1991), 59–69. In Jewish folklore, see Dov Noy, "The Messiah as Folk Hero" (in Hebrew), *Mahanayim* 124 (1970): 114–25; Haim Schwarzbaum, "The Messiah in Folklore" (in Hebrew), in *Roots and Landscapes: Studies in Folklore*, ed. Eli Yassif (Beer Sheva: Ben Gurion University Press, 1993), 96–111.

3. Robert Darnton, *The Great Cat Massacre and Other Episodes in French Cultural History* (New York: Basic Books, 1984); Aaron Gurevitch, *Medieval Popular Culture: Problems of Belief and Perception*, trans. Janos M. Bak and Paul Hollingsworth (Cambridge: Cambridge University Press, 1988); idem, *Historical Anthropology of the Middle Ages* (Chicago: University of Chicago Press, 1993); and many others.

4. Bausinger, *Formen der Volkpoesie*, "Sage," 179–95.

5. Dégh and Vazsonyi, "Legend and Belief"; Tamar Alexander, "A Sephardic Version of a Blood-Libel Story in Jerusalem," *International Folklore Review* 6 (1986): 131–52. For further material on the distinction between the folktale and legend genres in the analysis of a tale type, see Hasan-Rokem, *Proverbs in Israeli Folk Narratives*, 73–74; and Sara Zfatman, *The Jewish Tale in the Middle Ages: Between Ashkenaz and Sefarad* (in Hebrew) (Jerusalem: Magnes Press, 1993), chap. 5 and also 103–4 ff.

6. Honko, "Four Forms of Adaptation to Tradition."

7. Zfatman, *Jewish Tale in the Middle Ages*; Yassif, *Hebrew Folktale*, chap. 4.

8. Bausinger, *Formen der Volkpoesie*, "Sage," 179–95; "Legende," 195–210. See also *Enzyklopädie des Märchens*, s.vv. "Sage" and "Legende." For subgenres, see, for instance, on the hagiographical legend, Dov Noy, "Rabbi Shalem Shabazi in the Folktales of the Jews of Yemen" (in Hebrew), in *Boi Teman [Come thou south]: Studies and Documents Concerning the Culture of the Yemenite Jews*, ed. Jehuda Ratzaby (Tel Aviv: Afikim, 1967); and idem, "The Death of Rabbi Shalem Shabazi in the Yemenite Folk Legend" (in Hebrew), in *Legacy of the Jews of Yemen: Studies and Researches*, ed. Yosef Tobi (Jerusalem: Boi Teiman, 1976), 132–49. On the historical and local legend, see Heda Jason, "Concerning the 'Historical' and the 'Local' Legends and Their Relatives," *Journal of American Folklore* 84 (1971): 134–44; reprinted in Heda Jason, *Studies in Jewish Ethnopoetry* (Taipei: Chinese Association for Folklore, 1975), 37–49. On demonological legends, see Tamar Alexander, "The Woman Demon in Jewish Customs and Folktales" (in Hebrew), *Dappim: Research in Literature* 8 (1992): 203–19.

9. Linda Dégh, *Narratives in Society: A Performer-Centered Study of Narration*, Folkore Fellows Communications, no. 255 (Helsinki: Academia Scientiarum Fennica, 1995), 226–35.

10. Yassif, *Hebrew Folktale*, 161–85; Alexander, "The Woman Demon in Jewish Customs and Folktales"; Yosef Dan, *The Hebrew Narrative in the Middle Ages* (in Hebrew) (Jerusalem: Keter, 1974), 170–76; Sara Zfatman, *The Marriage of a Mortal Man and a She-Demon: The Transformation of a Motif in the Folk Narrative of Ashkenazi Jewry in the Sixteenth–Nineteenth Centuries* (in Hebrew) (Jerusalem: Magnes Press, 1987); Bilu, *Without Bounds*, especially chaps. 7, 8, and 13.

11. Tamar Alexander, "A 'Saint' and a 'Sage': Ha-Ari and Maimonides in Jewish Folktales" (in Hebrew), *Jerusalem Studies in Hebrew Literature* 13 (1992): 29–64. The *locus classicus* on this issue is Hippolyte Delehaye, *The Legends of the Saints: An Introduction to Hagiography*, trans. V. M. Crawford (Norwood, Pa.: Norwood Editions, 1962); Allison Goddard Elliot, *Roads to Paradise: Reading the Lives of the Early Saints* (Hanover: University Press of New England, 1987); Thomas J. Heffernan, *Sacred Biography: Saints and Their Biographers in the Middle Ages* (New York: Oxford University Press, 1988).

12. Alexander, "Sephardic Version of a Blood-Libel Story in Jerusalem"; Yassif,

Hebrew Folktale, 52–57; 148–61; 325–49; Jason, "Concerning the 'Historical' and the 'Local' Legends and their Relatives"; Hasan-Rokem, "Within Limits and Beyond."

13. Roland Barthes, *Writing Degree Zero*, trans. Annette Lavers and Colin Smith (New York: Hill and Wang, 1968); Hayden White, *Metahistory* (Baltimore: Johns Hopkins University Press, 1973); and idem, *Tropics of Discourse* (Baltimore: Johns Hopkins University Press, 1978).

14. Pierre Nora, *Realms of Memory: Rethinking the French Past*, trans. Arthur Goldhammer, 2 vols. (New York: Columbia University Press, 1996–1998); Yael Zerubavel, *Recovered Roots: Collective Memory and the Making of Israeli National Tradition* (Chicago: University of Chicago Press, 1995).

15. Yassif, *Hebrew Folktale*, 325–49. Another important contribution to the understanding of folktales as historical records of cultural processes is Zfatman, *Jewish Tale in the Middle Ages*.

16. Yitzhak Heinemann, *The Methods of Aggadah* (in Hebrew) (Givatayyim: Magnes Press and Massada, 1970).

17. Claude Lévi-Strauss, *The Savage Mind* (Chicago: University of Chicago Press, 1978); originally published as *La Pensée Sauvage* (Paris: Plon, 1962); and idem, "The Story of Asdiwal." Over the last few years, many scholars have shown awareness of the central role of myth in midrashic rabbinic creativity, contrary to the traditional perception of research as seeking to "expurgate" biblical tradition from its mythical foundations. See Michael Fishbane, " 'The Holy One Sits and Roars': Mythopoesis and the Midrashic Imagination," *Jewish Thought and Philosophy* 1 (1991): 1–21; and Yehuda Liebes, "*De Natura Dei*: On the Development of the Jewish Myth," in *Studies in Jewish Myth and Jewish Messianism*, trans. Batya Stein (Albany: State University of New York Press, 1993). Both these authors refrain from relating to the contemporary theoretical discourse on myth—the former explicitly so, and the latter as can be inferred from the fact that his only theoretical reference is to the late-nineteenth-century author Max Müller.

18. On mythological elements as potential components of folktales, see E. Meletinskii, S. Nekludov, E. Novik, and D. Segal, "Problems of the Structural Analysis of Fairytales," in *Soviet Structural Folkloristics*, ed. Pierre Maranda (The Hague: Mouton, 1974), 73–139.

19. Scholem, "The Messianic Idea in Judaism." Urbach, *The Sages*, chap. 17, "On Redemption" (649–92), opens with a description of the broad spectrum of rabbinic views on the issue of redemption and the end of days. I believe that Urbach's critique (990, n. 3) of Scholem's excessive emphasis on the catastrophic aspects of the Messianic era in "The Messianic Idea" is justified. So is his critique of Yizhak Baer, who had argued against the tendency of medieval commentators to separate trends that, in Baer's view, had been united in rabbinic thought (991, n. 8).

20. Urbach, *The Sages*, mentions the story briefly when dealing with the names of the Messiah, and refers to the plot only incidentally (1006, n. 13). In contrast, an

analysis of the PT version of the story appears in Jonah Fraenkel, *Studies on the Spiritual World of the Aggadic Story* (in Hebrew) (Tel Aviv: Ha-Kibbutz Ha-Meuhad, 1981), 159–63.

21. Translated from the Buber edition, 1:89–90.

22. Contrary to Fraenkel (*Studies on the Spiritual World*, 161), I do not think this name is unrealistic. Fraenkel assumes that the reference to *birat ha-melekh* must reflect the location's situation in the present of the narrative, but this is not necessarily the case. Names of places often reflect memories of past events.

23. Such as Shiloh from Shila, Yinnon from Yannai, Hanina from Hanania, all based on specific verses.

24. Obviously, it is implicit that I am not inclined to accept the view suggested by Fraenkel (*Studies on the Spiritual World*, 161, n. 15), who argues that the narrator could tell this story because he was unaware of the Christian interpretation of this verse, or was not "afraid" of it. Particularly the earlier scholars, in many of their discussions about Jewish-Christian relationships in this period, seem to assume a reality more familiar to us from the situation of Jews in medieval and modern Christian Europe. This reality, however, differs from the cultural relationships between Jews and Christians, and particularly between Jews and Jewish-Christians in Palestine in Late Antiquity, especially before Constantine proclaimed Christianity the official religion of the Roman empire.

25. The most comprehensive research on this field so far is found in David Flusser, *Jewish Sources in Early Christianity: Studies and Essays* (in Hebrew) (Jerusalem: Sifriat Hapoalim, 1979). On the mutual cultural relationships between Jews and Christians, and particularly between Jews and Jewish-Christians, see Oded Irshai, "Historical Aspects of the Christian-Jewish Polemic Concerning the Church of Jerusalem in the Fourth Century (In The Light of Patristic and Rabbinic Literature)" (in Hebrew) (Ph.D. diss., The Hebrew University of Jerusalem, 1993). See also the article by Israel J. Yuval, "'The Lord Will Take Vengeance, Vengeance for His Temple,'" particularly the section answering Ezra Fleischer's critique of Yuval's previous article, where Yuval expands the scope of his discussion beyond the period following 1000 C.E. to include Late Antiquity (see Israel J. Yuval, "Vengeance and Damnation, Blood and Defamation: From Jewish Martyrdom to Blood Libel Accusations," *Zion* 58 [1993]: 33–90, and Fleischer's rejoinder, "Christian-Jewish Relations in the Middle Ages Distorted," *Zion* 59 [1994]: 267–316). In *A Rivalry of Genius*, Hirshman deals with contacts between Christians and Jews in the rabbinic period but focuses on the intellectual leadership, without addressing mutual relationships at the folk level. A recent important contribution to this discussion was made by Elchanan Reiner, "From Joshua to Jesus: The Transformation of a Biblical Story to a Local Myth: A Chapter in the Religious Life of the Galilean Jew," in *Sharing the Sacred: Religious Contacts in the Holy Land*, ed. Arieh Kofsky and Guy G. Stroumsa (Jerusalem: Yad Izhak Ben-Zvi, 1998), 223–71.

26. On the importance of a rebel family originating in the Galil and the Golan where these names were common, see Menahem Stern, s.v. "Zealots," *Encyclopaedia Judaica Yearbook* (1973), 135–52, and particularly 135–38.

27. The term in Luke, ἐσπαργάνωμένος (wrapped in swaddling clothes or swathes), also connotes the term σπάργανον, which in classical Greek has explicitly taken over the secondary meaning of "tokens by which a person is identified" (Liddell and Scott's *Greek–English Lexicon* [Oxford: Clarendon Press, 1986], s.vv. σπάργανον and σπαργανόω), a motif occurring in the birth episodes of many biographical legends on folk heroes.

28. Lévi, *Le Ravissement du Messie*, 228–41. Lévi concludes from another New Testament parallel—*Apocalypse of John*, chap. 12, especially verse 5—that the folk narrative is a simplified version of the apocalyptic traditions in which the woman is Israel. As is clear from my reasoning, I take a different view.

29. Raymond E. Brown, *The Birth of the Messiah: A Commentary on the Infancy Narratives in Matthew and Luke* (New York: Doubleday, 1993). Brown relates directly to the Midrash in *Lamentations Rabbah* at 513–15; at 169, he cites an ancient tradition claiming that the sages from the East who had come to worship Jesus were Arabs, like the character of the stranger in this story; at 558, Brown refers to the influence of midrashic literature on Matthew and Luke in general; at 393, he mentions the swathes motif (swaddling clothes) that is also found in the story about the birth of the Messiah Menahem; at 399, the author links the appearance of asses and oxen in the story about Jesus' birth to the verse in Isaiah 1:3: "The ox knows his owner, and the ass his master's crib."

30. Otto Rank, *The Myth of the Birth of the Hero and Other Writings* (1914; New York: Vintage, 1964); Lord Raglan, *The Hero: A Study in Tradition, Myth, and Drama* (1936; reprint, New York: Vintage, 1956); Archer Taylor, "The Biographical Pattern in Traditional Narrative," *Journal of the Folklore Institute* 1 (1964): 114–29; Joseph Campbell, *The Hero with a Thousand Faces* (London: Abacus, 1975); Dundes, "The Hero Pattern and the Life of Jesus"; Noy, "Rabbi Shalem Shabazi in the Folktales of the Jews of Yemen" and "The Death of Rabbi Shalem Shabazi in the Yemenite Folk Legend"; Alexander, "The 'Saint' and the 'Sage.'"

31. The widespread use of the term "polemic" to denote the main mode of intergroup communication between Jews and Christians seems to me narrow, and perhaps even incorrect, as it misses dialogical modes that are not necessarily polemical. On the writing of history as polemics, see Amos Funkenstein, "History, Counterhistory, and Narrative" (in Hebrew), *Alpayim* 4 (1991): 206–23.

32. Honko refers to these processes as functional adaptation in the context of creating "ecotypes" (see Honko, "Four Forms of Adaptation to Tradition"). See also Carl Wilhelm von Sydow, "Geography and Folktale Oicotypes," in *Selected Papers on Folklore* (Copenhagen: Rosenkilde and Bagger, 1948), 44–59; first published in *Bealoideas* 4 (1934): 344–55. And see also Hasan-Rokem, "Ökotyp."

33. On the rabbinical legend about the Messiah's birth, see Urbach, *The Sages*, 684–85; Yehuda Liebes, "Mazmiah Qeren Yeshu'ah" (Who causes the glory of salvation to sprout), *Jerusalem Studies in Jewish Thought* 3 (1984): 336. This legend occupied a central role in medieval Jewish-Christian theological disputations, since it enabled the Christian contender to prove that the Messiah had actually been born. When specifically confronted with this challenge, Jewish contenders claimed that aggadic tales were not to be believed. See Hyam Maccoby, ed. and trans., *Judaism on Trial: Jewish-Christian disputations in the Middle Ages* (East Brunswick, N.J.: Associated University Presses, 1982). Mentions of this legend appear in the Hebrew account of the Tortosa disputation (translated by Maccoby from Solomon ibn Verga's *Shevet Yehudah*), which explicitly mentions *Lamentations Rabbah* (179), and in the Christian account of the Tortosa disputation, translated from the Latin protocols, which cites only the Palestinian Talmud version (199). In his public disputation with Pablo Christiani (111), Nahmanides claimed that this tale proved that Jesus could not be the Messiah, since Jesus had been born before the destruction of the Temple. Referring to Nahmanides' plight, Yizhak Abarbanel suggests that his reply may have been dictated by tactical considerations, and also that aggadic tales are preferably interpreted allegorically (Yizhak Abarbanel, *Sefer Yeshu'ot Meshiho* [Benei Berak: Makhon Meorei Sefarad, 1993], 102–3). On the eschatological aspects of the Jewish political struggle against the Romans from the first century onward, see Stern, "Zealots."

34. Fraenkel, *Studies on the Spiritual World*, 162.

35. Compare to the strength of the woman, revealed in lament and mourning, Chapter 6, this volume.

36. The first of these two verses fulfills an interesting function in the third story analyzed in this chapter, about R. Yohannan b. Zakkai's exit from Jerusalem in a coffin; the second verse is hinted in New Testament Christological interpretations.

37. I thank Ariel Rokem for suggesting a clear and sharp formulation of this question.

38. Hasan-Rokem, "Narratives in Dialogue," especially 122–26.

39. Meletinskii et al., "Problems of the Structural Analysis of Fairytales"; Lévi-Strauss, *The Savage Mind*.

40. Bava Bathra 73a–74b. See Yassif, *Hebrew Folktale*, 206–9; Dan Ben-Amos, "Talmudic Tall-Tales," in *Folklore Today: A Festschrift for Richard M. Dorson*, ed. Linda Dégh, Henry Glassie, and Felix J. Oinas (Bloomington: Research Center for Language and Semiotic Studies at Indiana University, 1976), 25–43; Dina Stein, "Believing Is Seeing: A Reading of Baba Bathra 73a–75b" (in Hebrew), *Jerusalem Studies in Hebrew Literature* 17 (1999): 9–32.

41. At a conference on Hebrew Literature in Jerusalem in 1990, Joshua Levinson suggested the possibility that the mother may have murdered the child, and was now concocting this fantastic story as a cover for his disappearance.

42. Fraenkel, *Studies on the Spiritual World*, 163, n. 19.

43. See Noy, "Rabbi Shalem Shabazi in the Folktales of the Jews of Yemen," and "The Death of Rabbi Shalem Shabazi in the Yemenite Folk Legend."

44. Joshua Efron, "Bar Kokhbah in the Light of the Palestinian and Babylonian Talmudic Traditions" (in Hebrew), in *The Bar Kokhba Revolt: A New Approach*, ed. Aaron Oppenheimer and Uriel Rapaport (Jerusalem: Yad Izhak Ben-Zvi, 1984), 105–47; Aaron Oppenheimer and Benjamin Isaac, "Research History of the Bar Kokhba War" (in Hebrew), *Hiding Complexes in Judean Shephelah*, ed. Amos Kloner and Yigal Tepper (Tel Aviv: Hakibbutz Hameuhad and Israel Exploration Society, 1987), 405–428; Peter Schäfer, *Der Bar-Kokhba Aufstand* (Tübingen: J. C. B. Mohr, 1981).

45. Benjamin Isaac, "The Revolt of Bar Kokhba as Described by Cassius Dio and Other Revolts Against the Romans in Greek and Latin Literature" (in Hebrew), in *The Bar Kokhba Revolt: A New Approach*, ed. Aaron Oppenheimer and Uriel Rapaport (Jerusalem: Yad Izhak Ben-Zvi, 1984), 106–12.

46. Gedalyah Alon, "The Bar Kokhba War," in *The Jews in Their Land in the Talmudic Age (70–640 C.E.)*, ed. and trans. Gershon Levi (Jerusalem: Magnes Press, 1984), 2:593.

47. Pierre Benoit, Jozef Tadeusz Milik, and Roland de Vaux, "Hebrew and Aramean Texts in the Caves of Murabba ât" (in Hebrew), in *The Bar Kokhba Revolt*, ed. Aaron Oppenheimer (Jerusalem: Zalman Shazar Center for Jewish History, 1980), 129–48; Yigael Yadin, "Bar Kokhba's Letters (From Camp D)," in *The Bar Kokhba Revolt*, ed. Aaron Oppenheimer (Jerusalem: Zalman Shazar Center for Jewish History, 1980), 149–58; Efron, "Bar Kokhba in the Light of the Palestinian and Babylonian Talmudic Traditions," 55.

48. Zerubavel, *Recovered Roots*, chap. 4.

49. See Cotton, Cockle, and Millar, "The Papyrology."

50. Efron, "Bar Kokhba in the Light of the Palestinian and Babylonian Talmudic Traditions," at p. 61, quotes Arieh Kindler, "Coins from Bar Kokhba's War" (in Hebrew), in *The Bar Kokhba Revolt*, ed. Aaron Oppenheimer (Jerusalem: Zalman Shazar Center for Jewish History, 1980), 175. Alon, "The Bar Kokhba War," 2:593–95; Abraham (Adolf) Büchler, "The Samaritans' Share in the Bar Kokhba Revolt" (in Hebrew), in *The Bar Kokhba Revolt*, ed. Aaron Oppenheimer (Jerusalem: Zalman Shazar Center for Jewish History, 1980), 115–21; and Menachem Mor, *The Bar-Kochba Revolt: Its Extent and Effect* (Jerusalem: Yad Izhak Ben-Zvi, 1991).

51. Samuel Krauss, "The Armies of Bar Kokhba" (in Hebrew), in *Alexander Marx Jubilee Volume*, ed. Saul Lieberman (New York: Jewish Theological Seminary, 1950), 391–99.

52. Thompson, *Motif Index of Folk Literature*. On the recurrence of the name "Simeon" among charismatic military leaders at the time, see Menahem Stern, "The Leadership in Freedom Fighters Groups at the End of the Second Temple" (in Hebrew), in *Studies in Jewish History in the Second Temple Period*, ed. Moshe Amit, Isaiah Gafni, and Moshe David Herr (Jerusalem: Yad Izhak Ben-Zvi, 1991), 307.

53. Zerubavel, *Recovered Roots*.

54. *Leviticus Rabbah* 22:3; Hasan-Rokem, "Within Limits and Beyond."

55. Hasan-Rokem, "Snake at the Wedding," 32.

56. In contrast, Urbach, *The Sages*, 672–74, argues that R. Akiva's faith in Bar Kokhbah as a Messiah included an eschatological element as well. This is also implied in Stern, "Zealots." See also Mor, *Bar-Kochba Revolt*, 218–23.

57. Stern, "Zealots."

58. It seems redundant to point out the phallic character of the kick. The word "leg" is sometimes used in rabbinic literature as a euphemism for the male organ.

59. The phenomenon of verses that are not cited but are close to a verse quoted in full and used as a basis for understanding the meaning of the story is also described by Fraenkel in *Methods of Aggadah and Midrash*, 1:247–48, when dealing with R. Joshuah, who ransomed a Jewish slave in Rome. Fraenkel analyzes the PT Horayot version of the story. This story appears in *Lamentations Rabbah* 4, and is also mentioned in the discussion in Chapter 7 of this volume. On the same issue, see Cohen, "The Theological Stratum of the Martha b. Boethus Tradition," 187–95, and especially the bibliography contained in n. 6.

60. Urbach, *The Sages*, 690–92, quotes a homily by R. Eleazar of Modi'in from *Song of Songs Rabbah*—also a Palestinian aggadic Midrash—where he rules out any role for the personal Messiah in the eschatological endeavor, which is compatible with his behavior in the present story. See also Mor, *Bar-Kochba Revolt*, 211–18.

61. Jason, *Genre*.

62. Efron, "Bar Kokhba in the Light of the Palestinian and Babylonian Talmudic Traditions," 62, n. 74, wavers between *gunthai* or *gundai* (meaning soldier in Arabic) and *Gothai* (Gothic), hinting to the possible presence of Gothic mercenaries in Vespasian's legions. Samuel Krauss, *Griechische und lateinische Lehnwörter in Talmud, Midrash, und Targum* (Berlin: S. Calvary, 1899), 2:70. See also Sperber, *Magic and Folklore in Rabbinic Literature*, 137–38 and the bibliography. On the death of the Roman emperor Julian the Apostate, a widespread Christian legend claimed that he was killed as a divine punishment for his apostasy (*Pauly's Real-Encyclopaedie der classischen Altertumswissenschaft* [Stuttgart: J. B. Metzlersche, 1918], s.v. "Julianus Apostata," 19:62; and Averil Cameron, *The Later Roman Empire—A.D. 284–430* [Cambridge, Mass.: Harvard University Press, 1993], 98). Thanks to Doron Mendels and Oded Irshai for these references.

63. Aristotle, *Poetics*, chap. 13, pp. 69–73.

64. See Sokoloff, *Dictionary of Jewish Palestinian Aramaic*, who quotes Lieberman to point out the Greek origin of *ptoma*. See also *protoma*.

65. Michael Higger, ed., *Semahot* 8:9 (in Hebrew) (Tel Aviv: Ha-Oved Ha-Dati, 1949), 154–55; Urbach, *The Sages*, 443–44.

66. *Pesikta de-Rav Kahana*, trans. and ed. William J. Braude and Israel Kapstein (Philadelphia: Jewish Publications Society, 1978).

67. Sheldon H. Blank, "The Death of Zechariah in Rabbinic Literature," *Hebrew Union College Annual* 12–13 (1937–1938): 327–46; Jean-Daniel Dubois, "La mort de Zacharie: mémoire juive et mémoire chrétienne," *Revue des Études Augustiniennes* 40 (1994): 23–38. On the similarity in the motifs included in the story of Jacob's martyrdom and the story about the killing of the prophet Zekhariah (priest and prophet, in the Temple area—the bloodthirsty mob, the function of Jerusalem's centrality in the tradition), see Irshai, *Historical Aspects of the Christian-Jewish Polemic*, 8–12.

68. Note the linguistic similarity: Abel is the son of Adam, God refers to Ezekiel as "son of Adam," and this is also one of the names of Jesus in the New Testament (Son of Man).

69. Nora, *Realms of Memory*.

70. Blank, "The Death of Zechariah," 337–38, n. 16; Dubois, "La mort de Zacharie," 37.

71. Honko, "Four Forms of Adaptation to Tradition."

72. Peter Brown, *The Body and Society: Men, Women, and Sexual Renunciation in Early Christianity* (New York: Columbia University Press, 1988). Brown's book emphasizes sexual aspects of the body and, in his wake, Boyarin, *Carnal Israel*. See also Hasan-Rokem, "Within Limits and Beyond." On the symbolic dimensions of the body in a cultural context at a later period, see, for instance, Richard Bauman, *Let Your Words Be Few: Symbolism of Speaking and Silence Among Seventeenth-Century Quakers* (Cambridge: Cambridge University Press, 1983).

73. On Zekhariah's murder in the folk tradition of the Jews of Ashkenaz, see the story "The Man Who Killed The Prophet Zekhariah" (in Hebrew), in Pinhas Sadeh, ed., *The Book of Fantasies of the Jews* (Tel Aviv: Schocken, 1983), 162–64. Sadeh took the story from a booklet entitled *Sipurim Nifla'im* (Wondrous stories), which he claims originates in the book *Notser Hesed*, where the story is ascribed to the Baal-Shem Tov (389).

74. Following is a list of the most important studies on the story. This review points to the central questions that have concerned scholars, namely, the historical time of the story, the dating of its composition, its links with other texts, and particularly with Josephus Flavius. Some of these scholars, among them Aaron Kaminka, Jacob Neusner, Yizhak Baer, and recently Israel Yuval, consider, in passing, the possibility of folk traditions, but fail to draw from this any methodological or hermeneutical conclusions.

Gedalyah Alon, "R. Johanan B. Zakkai's Removal to Jabneh," in *Jews and Judaism and the Classical World: Studies in Jewish History in the Times of the Second Temple and Talmud*, trans. Israel Abrahams (Jerusalem: Magnes Press, 1977), 269–313. Alon points to the originality of Palestinian traditions as opposed to Babylonian ones, and explains the story against its Palestinian historical background. In his view, Gophnah and Jabneh, the two cities outside Jerusalem mentioned in the story, were prepared by Vespasian to serve Jewish refugees, at first from besieged Jerusalem and later from the destroyed city. Alon's ideological interpretation is exposed in his perception of R. Yohannan b. Zakkai's move as a banishment rather than as an escape. Alon's view has remained the most radical claim for this text as a reflection of historical events. This article was written and published in several versions, and Alon began dealing with this topic during the 1930s.

Aaron Kaminka, *Studies in Bible, Talmud, and Rabbinical Literature* (in Hebrew) (Tel Aviv: Devir, 1951), 99, unequivocally states that the story is a "legend," namely, that it has no links to historical events. He also points to parallel versions, particularly of the escape motif: "The ploy of carrying fugitives in a coffin is a legend that recurs in the East, at various times."

Jacob Neusner, *A Life of Yohanan ben Zakkai* (Leiden: E. J. Brill, 1970). Neusner is interested in the transformations of the various narrative versions and seeks to limit their historical validity by pointing to two main versions, one in *Avot de-Rabbi Nathan* (both versions), and the other in the Babylonian Talmud and in *Lamentations Rabbah* (157–63). Contrary to Alon, Neusner considers the text appearing in *Lamentations Rabbah* as the latest version. On the other hand, he dates the events related in the legend precisely to the spring of 68 C.E. (151). His historical perception contradicts Baer's, and Neusner claims that the legend reflects the attitudes of those who created Jewish culture while cooperating, to some extent, with the Roman establishment (171).

Jacob Neusner, *The Development of a Legend: Studies on the Tradition Concerning Yohanan ben Zakkai* (Leiden: E. J. Brill, 1970). Neusner analyzes the tradition in greater detail in this work, but rules out any plausible spiritual or ideological function for this story in the *amoraic* period (228). He assumes the existence of (oral?) traditions, and argues that the various sources of the legend were not necessarily mutually dependent (233). Neusner offers a theory about the creation of legends from partial traditions, somewhat similar to Jolles's theory (297). For greater detail, see Jolles, *Einfache Formen*, s.v. "Legende," 19–49; s.v. "Sage," 50–74.

Yizhak Baer, "Jerusalem in the Times of the Great Revolt" (in Hebrew), *Zion* 36 (1971): 127–90. Baer thought that the legend was a later product, developed by the sages from Greek and Latin sources, among them Josephus, Suetonius, and Sulpicius Severus, as well as from Christian texts, both Eastern (the Abgar story) and Western (the story about the healing of the swollen leg). Baer's ideological approach is revealed in his claim that this is not a historical story, because a leader like R. Yohannan b. Zakkai could not have engaged in such a despicable act!

Jonah Fraenkel, "Bible Verses Quoted in the Tales of the Sages," *Scripta Hierosolymitana* 22 (1971): 80–99. Fraenkel completely divorces the literary dimension from the historical questions, and mentions only Alon's article and Neusner's earlier book.

Abraham Schalit, "The Prophecies of Josephus and of R. Yohannan ben Zakkai on the Ascent of Vespasian to the Throne" (in Hebrew), in *Salo Wittmeyer Baron Jubilee*

Volume, ed. Saul Lieberman (Jerusalem: American Academy for Jewish Research, 1975), 3:397–432. Schalit demonstrates the centrality of prophecies about emperors, and particularly Vespasian, in Roman sources.

Anthony J. Saldarini, "Johanan ben Zakkai's Escape from Jerusalem," *Journal for the Study of Judaism* 6 (1975): 189–204. Saldarini seeks to establish which one was the "original" version of the story by drawing a distinction, unlike Alon and close to Neusner, between the *Avot de-Rabbi Nathan* version on the one hand, and the one in the Babylonian Talmud and *Lamentations Rabbah* on the other. He dates the creation of the story to the time between the destruction of the Temple and the suppression of Bar Kokhbah's revolt. His remark that the story was meant to establish the legitimacy of the Yavneh center "in official and 'secular' circles and to a limited extent in the popular Jewish consciousness" (194) is extremely puzzling. The details focusing on the fall of Jerusalem, such as the story about the dukes, are, in his view, a later addition.

Peter Schaefer, "Zur Geschichtsauffassung des rabbinischen Judentums," *Journal for the Study of Judaism* 6 (1975): 167–88; and idem, "Die Flucht Johanan b. Zakkais aus Jerusalem und die Gründung 'Lehrhauses' in Jabne," *Aufstieg und Niedergang der römischen Welt* 2 (1979): 43–101. Schaefer suggests reading the story against the background of a rabbinic religious world-view, as opposed, for instance, to that of the authors of the *Hekhalot* literature. This reading illuminates the story from a perspective of creation and redemption, as I sought to do in the present study. Schaefer too reads the story as conveying this generation's *experience* of history, "die gegenwartige erlebte Geschichte," although he anchors this experience mainly in theological concepts.

Jacob Neusner, *Beyond Historicism, After Structuralism: Story as History in Ancient Judaism*, The Harry Spindel Memorial Lecture (Brunswick, Me.: Bowdoin College, 1980); Shaye J. D. Cohen, "Parallel Historical Tradition in Josephus and Rabbinic Literature," *Proceedings of the Ninth World Congress of Jewish Studies* (Jerusalem: World Union of Jewish Studies, 1986), vol. 1, division B, 7–14. Cohen claims that Josephus's writings contain more parallel versions of rabbinic texts than any other textual corpus. In response to a review that Horst R. Moehring wrote on Abraham Schalit, Daniel Schwartz touches on this story (see Daniel R. Schwartz, "On Abraham Schalit, Herod, Josephus, the Holocaust, Horst R. Moehring, and the Study of Ancient Jewish History," *Jewish History* 2 [1987]: 9–28, particularly 16–19). Schwartz's comments, as well as his quotations from Moehring, indicate the intense ideological implications of this story, even for contemporary authors.

Jonathan J. Price, *Jerusalem Under Siege: The Collapse of the Jewish State 66–70 C.E.* (Leiden: E. J. Brill, 1992). Price devotes a special supplement to the story (264–70), including an exhaustive critical review of most of the literature. His views seem close to Schaefer's, although he appropriately shows that Schaefer left open the issue of historical validity. Price states that this story may be the sole exception to the rule that Josephus had no influence whatsoever on the sages (200), and claims that the first part of the story on the escape from the city is "possible," unlike the meeting with Vespasian. Nevertheless, he claims it is methodologically impossible to test the historical validity of rabbinic statements unsupported by an external source.

David Flusser, "The Dead of Massada in the Eyes of Their Contemporaries" (in Hebrew), in *Jews and Judaism in the Second Temple, Mishna, and Talmud Period: Studies in Honor of Shmuel Safrai*, ed. Isaiah Gafni, Aaron Oppenheimer, and Menahem Stern (Jerusalem: Yad Izhak Ben-Zvi, 1993). On the dispute between R. Yohannan ben Zakkai and the zealots, see pp. 121–22; on the eschatological aspects, see pp. 127–28.

Israel J. Yuval, "Jews and Christians in the Middle Ages: Shared Myths, Common Language," in *Demonizing the Other: Antisemitism, Racism, and Xenophobia*, ed. Robert S. Wistrich (Amsterdam: Harwood Academic Publishers, 1999), 88–107. Yuval compares "Constantinus' gift" to Silvester, the bishop of Rome, to Vespasian's gift of Yavneh to R. Yohannan b. Zakkai, and points to many shared motifs. Yuval interprets the story as part of the cultural dialogue between Jews and Christians, in terms similar to the view I have offered here, although, in my assessment, he overemphasizes the element of polemics and communication between elites.

Also, Menahem Kister, "Legends on the Destruction of the Second Temple in Avot de-Rabbi Natan," *Tarbiz* 67 (1998): 483–529.

It is worth noting that the Palestinian Talmud contains no version of this story.

75. *The Fathers According to R. Nathan: Version A*, trans. Judah Goldin (New Haven: Yale University Press, 1955); *The Fathers According to R. Nathan: Version B*, trans. Anthony J. Saldarini (Leiden: E. J. Brill, 1975); *Midrash Mishle* (Visotzky edition), 125–26.

76. See Alon, "R. Johanan B. Zakkai's Removal to Jabneh," as well as the various glosses on the word in Solomon Buber's notes to the text "under a vineplant" or "in a river named Gophna" (according to the traditional exegete *Matnot Kehunah*); also, "feet tub, a wash bowl" (according to the eleventh-century dictionary *Arukh*, from the Arabic) as well as "a city next to Bira, near Jerusalem." The last denotation is the one most scholars have accepted as the only option.

77. The expression in the Hebrew version remains ambiguous: *etsem* (bone) or *atsmekha* (yourself). The Munich Ms. contains an interesting play on words here, between *besorah* (good news) and *basar* (flesh).

78. According to Jastrow's *Dictionary of Talmud, Bible, Yerushalmi, Midrashic Literature, and Targumim*, s.vv. *eqel* or *iqal*, p. 1106. Jastrow translates the phrase as follows: "the heart knows whether is close for *'ekel* (a legitimate purpose) or for *'akalkaloth* (perverseness)."

79. This could be referring to an abacus.

80. Sokoloff, *Dictionary of Jewish Palestinian Aramaic*, does not distinguish between "woe" (*vai*) and "wow" (*vah*), and defines both as "shouts of joy or woe," although he brings no example of "wow" as an expression of sorrow.

81. Examples can be found, for instance, in: Galit Hasan-Rokem, "The Cobbler of Jerusalem in Finnish Folklore," in *The Wandering Jew: Interpretations of a Christian Legend*, ed. Galit Hasan-Rokem and Alan Dundes (Bloomington: Indiana University Press, 1986); Nigel Barley, " 'The Proverb' and Related Problems of Genre-Definition," *Proverbium* 23 (1974): 880–84.

82. *Siqra* as a term for dagger, borrowed from the Latin (*sica*), is quite rare in Palestinian Aramaic. According to Sokoloff's dictionary , the term *sicarii* as a name for the zealots is not found in Palestinian sources. See also Urbach, *The Sages*, 597, n. 40; and Stern, "Zealots," 136–37.

83. A phonological link could be assumed between the name Ben Batiah and the word *bitahon* (safety, security), which in this story undergoes a transformation, from a designation related to his role to secure food for Jerusalem's inhabitants, into an ironic designation (although he is the one who ensured R. Yohannan's safe exit).

84. On international motifs: disguised as a corpse and the escape of a disguised leader, see Thompson, *Motif Index of Folk Literature*, K629, K1861, K1864.

85. Urbach, *The Sages*, chap. 17, particularly the beginning of the chapter.

86. Rachel Hachlili, "Changes in Burial Practices in the Late Second Temple Period: The Evidence from Jericho" (in Hebrew), in *Graves and Burial Practices in Israel in the Ancient Period*, ed. Itamar Singer (Jerusalem: Yad Izhak Ben-Zvi and the Israel Exploration Society, 1994), 173–89, particularly 187–88; and Joseph Patrich, "Graves and Burial Practices in Talmudic Sources" (in Hebrew), in *Graves and Burial Practices in Israel in the Ancient Period*, ed. Itamar Singer (Jerusalem: Yad Izhak Ben-Zvi and the Israel Exploration Society, 1994), 190–211, particularly 205.

87. As Fraenkel has shown, this use of a verse is a plot device often used by the rabbis (see Fraenkel, "Bible Verses Quoted in the Tales of the Sages," 80–87).

88. Tests of wisdom of this type appear in several folktales, as in international narrative type AT 875 (Aarne and Thompson, *The Types of the Folktale*, 293–95). See also Ofra Meir, "The Jewish Versions of AT 875" (in Hebrew), *Yeda-Am* 19 (1979): 55–61.

89. International tale type AT 922 (Aarne and Thompson, *The Types of the Folktale*, 320–21); see also Walter Anderson, *Kaiser und Abt: Die Geschichte eines Schwanks*, Folklore Fellows Communications, no. 42 (Helsinki: Academia Scientiarum Fennica, 1923).

90. On the sexual symbolism of the foot squeezing into the shoe, see Bruno Bettleheim's analysis of Cinderella (see Bettelheim, *The Uses of Enchantment*, 236–77). In Jewish tradition, see Jacob Nacht, *Der Fuss, Eine Folkloristische Studie* (Wien: 1923), which is an offprint from *Jahrbuch für Jüdische Volkskunde* (1923). An English version appeared in "The Symbolism of the Shoe with Special Reference to Jewish Sources," *Jewish Quarterly Review*, New Series, 6 (1915–1916): 1–22. Herbert W. Benario, *A Commentary on the Vita Hadriani in the Historia Augusta* (Missoula, Mont.: Scholars Press, 1980), p. 109 quotes Suetonius about Titus's public bathing, unusual for emperors.

91. Yuval, " 'The Lord Will Take Vengeance, Vengeance for His Temple'," 366.

92. Josephus Flavius, *The Jewish War*, in *Collected Works*, trans. H. St. J. Thackeray (Cambridge, Mass.: Harvard University Press, Loeb Classical Library; London: Heinemann, 1976), vol. 2, bk. 3, pp. 399–408, 689–91. See also Schalit ("The Prophecies of Josephus and of R. Yohannan ben Zakkai on the Ascent of Vespasian to the Throne") and Baer ("Jerusalem in the Times of the Great Revolt"), each of whom is writing from an opposite vantage point. In light of Baer's studies (on which Yuval relies heavily) and Price's cautious qualification in *Jerusalem Under Siege*, Yuval's statement that the authors of the Midrash could not possibly be following Josephus or his sources seems to me unnecessarily definitive. In any event, in the context of the communication processes within folk literature, this option cannot rule out the cultural negotiation between Jews and Christians, which certainly extended beyond the level of polemics.

93. Eliezer Marcus, "The Confrontation Between Jews and Non-Jews In Folktales of the Jews of Islamic Countries" (in Hebrew) (Ph.D. diss., The Hebrew University of Jerusalem, 1978).

94. Ernst Bloch, *The Principle of Hope*, trans. Neville Plaice, Stephen Plaice, and Paul Knight (Cambridge, Mass.: MIT Press, 1986), particularly 1:441–47, chap. 32, "Happy End, Seen Through and Yet Still Defended," and 3:1183–1312, chap. 53, "Growing Human Commitment to Religious Mystery, to Astral Myth, Exodus, Kingdom: Atheism and the Utopia of the Kingdom."

95. Meletinskii et al., "Problems of the Structural Analysis of Fairytales."

96. Jastrow includes *iqal* as a variant reading.

97. Sokoloff, *Dictionary of Jewish Palestinian Aramaic*, s.v. " '*ql*."

98. Hasan-Rokem, *Proverbs in Israeli Folk Narratives*, 65–69.

99. This is not the case in all versions of the story.

100. Cf. Yaffa Eliach, ed., *Hasidic Tales of the Holocaust* (New York: Oxford University Press, 1982), where only the rabbis are rescued.

101. Sokoloff, *Dictionary of Jewish Palestinian Aramaic*, s.v. "*krstywn*" (χαραστίων), or "*qrtstywn*'" in the printed version of *Lamentations Rabbah*.

102. Hasan-Rokem, "Within Limits and Beyond."

103. See also *Sifra, Behuqotai* 2: "Israel ask God for their reward in this world, and the nations of the world ask God for their reward. And God says to Israel: 'My children, I will turn to you; the nations of the world performed a small chore for me, and I give them a small reward, but with you, I will balance a large account in the future,' and hence it is written, 'I will turn myself to you' (Leviticus 26:9)." In *Deuteronomy Rabbah* (Saul Lieberman edition), *Eqev*, 74: "Another interpretation of 'Wherefore it shall come to pass' (Deuteronomy 7:12): As it is written above 'and repays them that hate him' (Deuteronomy 7:10), the Holy One, blessed be He, said: All the minor commandments that the nations of the world observe, I repay them in this world so that they may lose [the world] to come." See also Alon Goshen-Gottstein, "Mitzva

Kalla (A Lenient Commandment)" (in Hebrew), in *'Alei Shefer: Studies in the Litera-ture of Jewish Thought Presented to Alexander Safran*, ed. Moshe Halamish (Ramat Gan: Bar Ilan University Press, 1990), 51–65, and 59–60 in particular.

104. Abgar was the name of the king of Edessa, a Mesopotamian kingdom that converted to Christianity at the end of the second or beginning of the third century C.E. Many legends surrounded the conversion of Abgar's dynasty to Christianity (see Robin Lane Fox, *Pagans and Christians* [Penguin, 1988], 279–80).

105. Gerd Lüdemann, "The Successors of the Jerusalem Christianity: A Critical Evaluation of the Pella Tradition," in *Jewish and Christian Self-Definition*, ed. P. Sanders (London: SCM Press, 1980), 161–73; Jozef Verheyden, "The Flight of the Christians to Pella," *Ephemerides Theologicae Lovanienses* 66 (1990): 368–84. On the exit to Pella, see also Irshai, *Historical Aspects of the Christian-Jewish Polemic*, 13–19. According to Nodet and Taylor, the return of the Jerusalem Christians from Pella was an important milestone in their separation from Jewish customs (Étienne Nodet and Justin Taylor, *The Origins of Christianity: An Exploration* [Collegeville, Minn.: The Liturgical Press, 1998], 230). See also Boyarin, *Dying for God*, 136, n. 19; and Oded Irshai, "The Church of Jerusalem: From 'The Church of the Circumcision' to 'The Church from the Gentiles,'" in *The History of Jerusalem: The Roman and Byzantine Periods (to 638 C.E.)*, ed. Yoram Tsafrir and Shmuel Safrai (Jerusalem: Yad Izhak Ben-Zvi, 1999), 74–77.

106. Dundes, "The Hero Pattern and the Life of Jesus."

107. Avigdor Aptowizer, "The Heavenly Temple in the Aggada" (in Hebrew), *Tarbiz* 2 (1931): 137–57, 257–87; reprinted in Avigdor Shinan, ed., *The Aggadic Litera-ture: A Reader* (in Hebrew) (Jerusalem: Magnes Press, 1983), 51–98. On Jerusalem's unique role in Jewish folktale, see Hasan-Rokem, "Cognition in the Folktale."

EPILOGUE: RABBI JOSHUA'S ODYSSEY

1. Pagis, *A Secret Sealed*, 35 (emphasis added). See also Pagis, "Toward a Theory."

2. Abrahams, *Between the Living and the Dead*, 52–54.

3. For instance, Georg Nador, *Jüdische Rätsel aus Talmud und Midrasch* (Köln: J. Hegner, 1967).

4. See Chapters 3 and 4, this volume.

5. Eli Yassif, "The Narrative Chain in Rabbinic Literature" (in Hebrew), *Jeru-salem Studies in Hebrew Literature* 12 (1990): 103–45, further elaborated in his *Hebrew Folktale*, chap. 4, sec. 11.

6. *Lamentations Rabbah* 1:1, printed edition and Munich Ms., and some of the alternative Ms. versions according to Buber's edition, 55–56.

7. Fraenkel, "Hermeneutic Problems in the Study of the Aggadic Narrative." Fraenkel analyzes the version found in the Babylonian Talmud (140–42), and ignores the parallel versions of this story. In line with the central concern of his article, he

quotes some early commentators. In his discussion of the wordplay on the root KBš, he clarifies that this word is never used in rabbinic literature in the sense of paving a road (*kevish*), but only in the sense of pickling fruit and vegetables, and in the sense of conquest (*kibbush*). There is room for exploring the association with the notion of covering, as in the combination *kavash panav*, which appears in rabbinic literature, and in other contexts. Also worth considering is the term *kevesh*, implying the ramp to the altar in the Temple, as well as the meaning of squashing with a heavy weight, pressing. See also s.v. KBš in Sokoloff, *Dictionary of Jewish Palestinian Aramaic*, 249–50.

8. Avraham Ben-David, "Amallel Shir" (bilingual Hebrew-Arabic poem), in *Diwan Amallel Shir: Yemenite Poems Anthology*, eds. Yosef Tobi and Shalom Seri (Ramat-Gan: E'eleh Be-Tamar, 1988), 107, line 7.

9. Sigmund Freud, "The Theme of the Three Caskets," in *Art and Literature* (Middlesex: Pelican Freud Library, 1985), 233–47.

10. Pagis, *A Secret Sealed*. See also Chapter 3, this volume.

11. Ilan's characterization of the exchange as "a woman defeated him in a halakhic debate with matters connected with the kitchen" disregards the literary context, but points out the issue of Halakha (Ilan, *Jewish Women in Greco-Roman Palestine*, 195–96).

12. *Midrash Tanhuma*, printed edition, *Shemini*, 8, "Zot ha-haya."

13. "These are things beyond measure: *peah*, first fruits, pilgrimage, deeds of lovingkindness, and the study of Torah. These are things the fruits of which a man enjoys in this world and the principal remains for him in the world to come: the honoring of one's father and mother, and deeds of lovingkindness and making peace between a man and his fellow, and the study of Torah outweighs them all" (M. Peah 1:1).

The status of this sentence in the story, formulated as a halakhic ruling, is problematic. The medieval commentators known as Tosafists pointed out the contradictions between various versions: "Rabenu Hananel says, 'You leave *peah* in a *qeara* but not in an *ilpas*.' In the Ben-Azzai chapter [TB *Derekh Eretz*, one of the so-called minor tractates, chap. 6] we read: 'You leave *peah* in a dish cooked in a *qederah* but not in an *ilpas*, means that if he fails to leave *peah* from a *qederah* he will seem greedy, but he will not seem greedy if he does not leave from an *ilpas*. You leave *peah* in a dish cooked in an *ilpas* but not in a *qederah*, means that if he fails to leave *peah* from an *ilpas* he will seem greedy, but he will not seem greedy if he does not leave from a *qederah*.' According to R. Solomon Luria, R. Hananel's ruling was, 'You leave *peah* in an *ilpas* but not in a *qeara*. And it is simple.'" Rashi supported the opposite view, which was also endorsed by Fraenkel in his discussion in "Hermeneutic Problems in the Study of the Aggadic Narrative," 141, n. 4.

I am grateful to Yaakov Sussman for our conversations on *peah* and other matters, in which he shared with me his illuminating thoughts on rabbinical literature as entirely oral. This perception sheds light on folk literature within rabbinic texts, strengthening the view that there is no separation between lower and higher forms, and pointing to folk literature as an important creative channel for the authors of Midrash. According to Sussman's assumptions, written textual works date from the post-*amoraic* period. Orality completely dominates Halakha, whereas in Aggadah, even in ancient times, some exceptions can be found.

14. These forces—the "semiotic" in Julia Kristeva's terminology—parallel the emotional sphere that Melanie Klein termed pre-Oedipal, which precedes the dialogical and dynamic emergence of the subject, and thus also the ability to discern the other. Aspects in the text inspired by the semiotic are characterized by primary process adaptations, notably condensation and displacement, which could be discerned in the delayed solutions. In contrast, the mechanism through which the subject is defined in relationship to a given social system is represented in the texts by what Kristeva, following Lacan, has called the "symbolic," namely, by the development of a split between the self and the other, which allows for mutual communication. The semiotic level, which is a precondition for the actual existence of the symbolic level, is also a force that destroys the symbolic. But subject-object relations, such as hatred and attraction, can only develop at the symbolic level, as opposed to their absence in the undifferentiated condition of the semiotic. See Julia Kristeva, "Revolution in Poetic Language," in *The Kristeva Reader*, ed. Toril Moi (Oxford: Blackwell, 1986), 89–136.

15. *Midrash Rabbah, Genesis*, trans. H. Freedman (London: Soncino Press, 1951), 580.

16. See Chapters 3 and 4, this volume.

17. In a discussion with my students at the University of Pennsylvania Philadelphia in spring 2000, many of them suggested that the first question was posed by Rabbi Joshua to the other man, contrary to my interpretation. The implications are interesting and may explain the omission of the man from Rabbi Joshua's proverbial summary of his experience.

BIBLIOGRAPHY

Aarne, Antti. *Vergleichende Rätselforschungen*. Folklore Fellows Communications, no. 26. Helsinki: Academia Scientiarum Fennica, 1918.

Aarne, Antti, and Stith Thompson. *The Types of the Folktale: A Classification and Bibliography*. Folklore Fellows Communications, no. 184. Helsinki: Academia Scientiarum Fennica, 1973.

Abarbanel, Yitzhak. *Sefer Yeshu'ot Meshiho*. Benei Berak: Makhon Meorei Sefarad, 1993.

Aboab, Isaac. *Menorath ha-Ma'or*. Edited by Yehudah Horev and M. J. Katzeneln-bogen. Jerusalem: Mossad Harav Kook, 1961.

Abrahams, Roger D. *Between the Living and the Dead*. Folklore Fellows Communications, no. 225. Helsinki: Academia Scientiarum Fennica, 1980.

Adler, Marcus Nathan, ed. *The Itinerary of Benjamin of Tudela*. London: P. Feld-heim, 1964.

Aeschylus. *The Libation Bearers*. Translated by Herbert Weir Smyth. Cambridge, Mass.: Harvard University Press, 1983.

Aesopus. *Fables of Aesop*. Translated by S. A. Handford. Harmondsworth, Middlesex: Penguin Books, 1979.

Aharoni, Yohanan. "Expedition B: 'Cave of Horror'" (in Hebrew). In *The Judean Desert Caves 1961*. Jerusalem: Israel Exploration Society, 1962.

Alexander, Tamar. "The Judeo-Spanish Legend about Rabbi Kalonymus in Jerusalem: A Study of Processes of Folktale Adaptation" (in Hebrew). *Jerusalem Studies in Jewish Folklore* 5–6 (1984): 139–56.

——. "A Sephardic Version of a Blood-Libel Story in Jerusalem." *International Folklore Review* 6 (1986): 131–52.

——. "A 'Saint' and a 'Sage': Ha-Ari and Maimonides in Jewish Folktales" (in Hebrew). *Jerusalem Studies in Hebrew Literature* 13 (1992): 29–64.

——. "The Woman Demon in Jewish Customs and Folktales" (in Hebrew). *Dappim: Research in Literature* 8 (1992): 203–19.

Alexander-Frizer, Tamar. *The Pious Sinner: Ethics and Aesthetics in the Medieval Hassidic Narrative*. Tübingen: J. C. B. Mohr, 1992.

Alexander, Tamar, and Galit Hasan-Rokem. "Spatial Elements in the Proverbs of the Jews of Turkey" (in Hebrew). *Pe'amim* 41 (1990): 112–32.

——. "The Multivalent Construction of Ethos in the Proverbs of a Sephardic Woman" (in Hebrew). *Jerusalem Studies in Jewish Folklore* 17 (1995): 63–87.

Alexiou, Margaret. *The Ritual Lament in Greek Tradition*. Cambridge: Cambridge University Press, 1974.

Almoli, Shlomo. *Pitron Halomot*. 1623. Reprinted in *Pitron Halomot ha-Shalem* (Jerusalem: Bakal, 1997).

Alon, Gedalyah. *Jews, Judaism and the Classical World: Studies in Jewish History in the Times of the Second Temple and Talmud*. Jerusalem: Magnes Press, 1977.

——. "R. Johanan B. Zakkai's Removal to Jabneh." In *Jews, Judaism and the Classical World: Studies in Jewish History in the Times of the Second Temple and Talmud*, translated by Israel Abrahams. Jerusalem: Magnes Press, 1977.

——. *The Jews in their Land in the Talmudic Age (70–640 C.E.)*. Translated and edited by Gershon Levi. 2 vols. Jerusalem: Magnes Press, 1980–1984; Cambridge, Mass.: Harvard University Press, 1989.

——. "The Bar Kokhba War." In vol. 2 of *The Jews in Their Land in the Talmudic Age (70–640 C.E.)*, translated and edited by Gershon Levi. Jerusalem: Magnes Press, 1984.

Amit, Moshe. "Worlds that Did Not Meet" (in Hebrew). In *The Jews in the Hellenistic Roman World: Studies in Memory of Menahem Stern*, edited by Isaiah M. Gafni, Aaron Oppenheimer, and Daniel R. Schwartz. Jerusalem: Zalman Shazar Center for Jewish History, 1996.

Amram, David Werner. *The Makers of Hebrew Books in Italy*. Philadelphia: Julius H. Greenstone, 1909.

Anderson, Walter. *Kaiser und Abt: Die Geschichte eines Schwanks*. Folklore Fellows Communications, no. 42. Helsinki: Academia Scientiarum Fennica, 1923.

Aptowizer, Avigdor. "The Heavenly Temple in the Aggada" (in Hebrew). *Tarbiz* 2 (1931). Reprinted in *The Aggadic Literature: A Reader* (in Hebrew), edited by Avigdor Shinan (Jerusalem: Magnes Press, 1983).

Aristotle. *Poetics*. Translated by W. H. Fyfe. Cambridge, Mass.: Harvard University Press, 1995.

Asher, Adolf, ed. *The Itinerary of Benjamin of Tudela*. London: Hakesheth, 1840.

Attias, Moshe. *Romancero Sefaradi* (in Hebrew and Judeo-Spanish). Jerusalem: Ben-Zvi Institute, 1961.

Bacher, Wilhelm. "Alter jüdisher Volkswitz in der muhammedanischer Literatur." *Monatsschrift für Geschichte und Wissenschaft des Judentums* 19 (1870): 68–72.

Baer, Yizhak. "Jerusalem in the Times of the Great Revolt" (in Hebrew). *Zion* 36 (1971): 127–90.

Bakan, David. *Sigmund Freud and the Jewish Mystical Tradition*. Boston: Beacon Press, 1975.

Bakhtin, Mikhail. *Problems of Dostoevsky's Poetics*. Translated by C. Emerson. Minneapolis: University of Minnesota Press, 1984.

———. *Slovo V Romane (Voprosy Literatury I Estetiki)*. Translated into Hebrew by Ari Avneri. Tel Aviv: Sifriat Poalim, 1989.

Bal, Mieke. "The Rape of Narrative and the Narrative of Rape: Speech Acts and Body Language in Judges." In *Essays on Populations and Persons*, edited by Elaine Scarry. Baltimore: Johns Hopkins University Press, 1988.

Barley, Nigel. " 'The Proverb' and Related Problems of Genre-Definition." *Proverbium* 23 (1974): 880–84.

Barthes, Roland. *Writing Degree Zero*. Translated by Annette Lavers and Colin Smith. New York: Hill and Wang, 1968.

———. *S/Z*. Translated by Richard Miller. New York: Hill and Wang, 1974.

Bascom, William R. "Four Functions of Folklore." In *The Study of Folklore*, edited by Alan Dundes. Englewood Cliffs, N.J.: Prentice Hall, 1965.

Bauman, Richard. "Conceptions of Folklore in the Development of Literary Semiotics." *Semiotica* 39 (1982): 1–20.

———. *Let Your Words Be Few: Symbolism of Speaking and Silence Among Seventeenth-Century Quakers*. Cambridge: Cambridge University Press, 1983.

———. *Story, Performance, Event: Contextual Studies of Oral Narrative*. Cambridge: Cambridge University Press, 1986.

———. "Folklore." In *Folklore, Cultural Performances, and Popular Entertainments*, edited by Richard Bauman. New York: Oxford University Press, 1992.

———. "Performance." In vol. 3 of *International Encyclopedia of Communications*, edited by Erik Barnouw. New York: Oxford University Press, 1989. Reprinted in Bauman, ed., *Folklore, Cultural Performances, and Popular Entertainments* (New York: Oxford University Press, 1992).

Bausinger, Hermann. *Formen der Volkspoesie*. Berlin: Eschmidt, 1980.

Ben-Ami, Issachar. *Saint Veneration among the Jews in Morocco*. Detroit: Wayne State University Press, 1998.

Ben-Amos, Dan. "Analytical Categories and Ethnic Genres." *Genre* 3 (1969): 275–301.

———. "Toward a Definition of Folklore in Context." *Journal of American Folklore* 84 (1971): 3–15.

———. "Talmudic Tall-Tales." In *Folklore Today: A Festschrift for Richard M. Dorson*, edited by Linda Dégh, Henry Glassie, and Felix J. Oinas. Bloomington: Research Center for Language and Semiotic Studies at Indiana University, 1976.

———. "Generic Distinctions in the Aggadah." In *Studies in Jewish Folklore*, edited by Frank Talmage. Cambridge, Mass.: Association for Jewish Studies, 1980.

———. "'Context' in Context." *Western Folklore* 52 (1993): 209–26.

Benoit, Pierre, Jozef Tadeusz Milik, and Roland de Vaux, "Hebrew and Aramean Texts in the Caves of Murabbaât" (in Hebrew). In *The Bar Kokhba Revolt*, edited by Aaron Oppenheimer. Jerusalem: Zalman Shazar Center for Jewish History, 1980.

Beth Arié, Malachi. "Ms. Oxford, Bodleian Library, Bodl. Or. 135" (in Hebrew). *Tarbiz* 54 (1985): 631–34.

Bettelheim, Bruno. *The Uses of Enchantment: The Meaning and Importance of Fairytales*. New York: Vintage Books, 1977.

Betti, Emilio. "Hermeneutics as the General Methodology of the Geisteswissenschaften." In *Contemporary Hermeneutics: Hermeneutics as Method, Philosophy, and Critique*, edited by Josef Bleicher. London: Routledge and Kegan Paul, 1980.

Bialik, Hayyim Nahman, and Yehoshua Hana Ravnitzky, eds. *The Book of Legends— Sefer Ha-Aggadah: Legends from the Talmud and Midrash,* translated by William G. Braude, introduction by David Stern (New York: Schocken Books, 1992).

Bilu, Yoram. "Sigmund Freud and Rabbi Yehudah: On a Jewish Mystical Tradition of 'Psychoanalytic' Dream Interpretation." *The Journal of Psychological Anthropology* 2 (1979): 443–63.

———. "Dreams and the Wishes of the Saint." In *Judaism Viewed from Within and from Without: Anthropological Studies*, edited by Harvey Goldberg. Albany, N.Y: State University of New York Press, 1986.

———. *Without Bounds: The Life and Death of R. Ya'acov Wazana* (in Hebrew). Jerusalem: Magnes Press, 1993.

Bin-Gorion, Micha Josef. *Die Sagen der Juden*. 3 vols. Frankfurt am Main: Rütten & Loening, 1913–1927.

Birley, Anthony R. *Hadrian the Restless Emperor*. New York: Routledge, 1997.

Bland, Nathaniel. *On the Muhammedan Science of Tabir, or Interpretation of Dreams*. London: Harrison and Sons, St. Martin's Lane, 1856.

Blank, Sheldon H. "The Death of Zechariah in Rabbinic Literature." *Hebrew Union College Annual* 12–13 (1937–38): 327–46.

Bloch, Ernst. *The Principle of Hope*. Translated by Neville Plaice, Stephen Plaice, and Paul Knight. Cambridge, Mass.: MIT Press, 1986.

Blumenthal, Henry J. "529 and its Sequel: What Happened to the Academy?" *Byzantion* 48 (1978): 369–85.

Bogatyrev, Petr, and Roman Jakobson. "Folklore as a Special Form of Creativity." In *The Prague School: Selected Writings, 1929–1946*, edited by Peter Steiner. Austin: University of Texas Press, 1982.

Bolte, Johannes, and Georg Polívka. *Anmerkungen zu den Kinder und Hausmärchen der Brüder Grimm*. 5 vols. 1913–1932. Reprint, Hildesheim: Georg Olms, 1963.

Bourdieu, Pierre. *Algeria 1960*. Cambridge: Cambridge University Press, 1979.

Boyarin, Daniel. *Intertextuality and the Reading of the Midrash*. Bloomington: Indiana University Press, 1990.

——. *Carnal Israel: Reading Sex in Talmudic Culture*. Berkeley and Los Angeles: University of California Press, 1993.

——. *Dying for God: Martyrdom and the Making of Christianity and Judaism*. Stanford, Calif.: Stanford University Press, 1999.

Brock, Sebastian P., and Susan Ashbrook Harvey, eds. and trans. "Women Martyrs of Najran." Chap. 4 in *Holy Women of the Christian Orient*, 2d updated ed. Berkeley and Los Angeles: University of California Press, 1998.

Brown, Peter. *The Body and Society: Men, Women and Sexual Renunciation in Early Christianity*. New York: Columbia University Press, 1988.

Brown, Raymond E. *The Birth of the Messiah: A Commentary on the Infancy Narratives in Matthew and Luke*. New York: Doubleday, 1993.

Buber, Solomon, ed. *Eikha Rabbah* (in Hebrew). Vilna: Press of Widow and Brothers Romm, 1893.

——. *Midrash Mishle* (in Hebrew). Vilna: Press of Widow and Brothers Romm, 1893.

——. *Midrash Zuta* (in Hebrew). Berlin: Mekizei Nirdamim, 1894.

Büchler, Abraham (Adolf). "The Samaritans' Share in the Bar Kokhba Revolt" (in Hebrew). In *The Bar Kokhba Revolt*, edited by Aaron Oppenheimer. Jerusalem: Zalman Shazar Center for Jewish History, 1980.

Burton, Richard F., ed. *The Book of a Thousand Nights and a Night*. 10 vols. London: H. S. Nichols, 1897.

——. *Supplemental Nights to the Book of a Thousand Nights and a Night*. London: H. S. Nichols, 1897.

Cameron, Averil. *Christianity and the Rhetoric of Empire: The Development of Christian Discourse*. Berkeley: University of California Press, 1994.

——. *The Later Roman Empire—A.D. 284–430*. Cambridge, Mass.: Harvard University Press, 1993.

Cammann, Schuyler V. R. "Christopher the Armenian and the Three Princes of Serendip." *Comparative Literature Studies* 4 (1967): 229–58.

Campbell, Joseph. *The Hero with a Thousand Faces*. London: Abacus, 1975.

de Certeau, Michel. *The Practice of Everyday Life*. Berkeley and Los Angeles: University of California Press, 1988.

Chauvin, Victor. *Bibliographie des ouvrages arabes*. Vol. 7. Liège: H. Vaillant-Carmanne; Leipzig: Otto Harrassowitz, 1901.

Clements, Ronald Ernest. "The Messianic Hope in the Old Testament." *Journal for the Study of the Old Testament* 43 (1989): 3–19.

Cocchiara, Giuseppe. *The History of Folklore in Europe*. Translated by John McDaniel. Philadelphia: Institute for the Study of Human Issues, 1981.

Cohen, Gershon D. "The Story of Hannah and Her Seven Sons in Hebrew Literature" (in Hebrew). In *Mordecai M. Kaplan Jubilee Volume: On the Occasion of His Seventieth Birthday*, edited by Moshe Davis. New York: Jewish Theological Seminary, 1953.

Cohen, Martin S. *The Shiur Qomah: Liturgy and Theurgy in Pre-Kabbalistic Jewish Mysticism*. Lanham, Md.: University Press of America, 1983.

Cohen, Naomi. "The Theological Stratum of the Martha b. Boethus Tradition: An Explication of the Text in Gittin 56a." *Harvard Theological Review* 69 (1976): 187–95.

Cohen, Naomi G. "The Greek and Latin Transliterations *Mariam* and *Maria*: Their Sociological Significance" (in Hebrew). *Leshonenu* 38 (1974): 170–80.

Cohen, Shaye J. D. "Parallel Historical Tradition in Josephus and Rabbinic Literature." In vol. 1, division B, of *Proceedings of the Ninth World Congress of Jewish Studies*. Jerusalem: World Union of Jewish Studies, 1986.

"Contes populaires grecs, recueillis à Smyrne en 1875, et traduits par Emile Legrand." *Revue de l'Histoire des Religions* 10 (1884): 72–93.

Cotton, Hanna M., Walter H. Cockle, and Fergus G. B. Millar, "The Papyrology of the Roman Near East: A Survey." *Journal of Roman Studies* 85 (1995): 214–35.

Cox Miller, Patricia. *Dreams in Late Antiquity: Studies in the Imagination of a Culture*. Princeton: Princeton University Press, 1994.

Crapanzano, Vincent. *Hermes' Dilemma and Hamlet's Desire: On the Epistemology of Interpretation*. Cambridge, Mass.: Harvard University Press, 1992.

Dan, Joseph. "On the Dream Theory of Ashkenaz Pietists" (in Hebrew). *Sinai* 68 (1971): 288–93.

Dan, Yaron. *The City in Eretz Israel During the Late Roman and Byzantine Periods* (in Hebrew). Jerusalem: Yad Izhak Ben-Zvi, 1984.

Dan, Yosef. *The Hebrew Narrative in the Middle Ages* (in Hebrew). Jerusalem: Keter, 1974.

Darnton, Robert. *The Great Cat Massacre and Other Episodes in French Cultural History*. New York: Basic Books, 1984.

Dégh, Linda. *Narratives in Society: A Performer-Centered Study of Narration*. Folklore Fellows Communications, no. 255. Helsinki: Academia Scientiarum Fennica, 1995.

Dégh, Linda, and André Vazsonyi. "Legend and Belief." In *Folklore Genres*, edited by Dan Ben-Amos. Austin: University of Texas Press, 1976.

Delehaye, Hippolyte. *The Legends of the Saints: An Introduction to Hagiography*. Translated by V. M. Crawford. Norwood, Pa.: Norwood Editions, 1962.

Dimant, Devorah. "Election and Laws of History in Apocalyptic Literature" (in Hebrew). In *Chosen People, Elect Nation and Universal Mission: Collected Essays* (in Hebrew), edited by Shmuel Almog and Michael Heyd. Jerusalem: Zalman Shazar Center for Jewish History, 1991.

Dodds, Eric R. *The Greeks and the Irrational*. Berkeley: University of California Press, 1951.

Dömötör, Tekla. "Some Questions Concerning Belief Legend as a Genre." *Studia Fennica* 26 (1981): 11–27.

Doniger O'Flaherty, Wendy. *Dreams, Illusions and Other Realities*. Chicago: University of Chicago Press, 1984.

Dubois, Jean-Daniel. "La mort de Zacharie: mémoire juive et mémoire chrétienne." *Revue des Études Augustiniennes* 40 (1994): 23–38.

Dundes, Alan. "The Hero Pattern and the Life of Jesus." In *Interpreting Folklore*, edited by Alan Dundes. Bloomington: Indiana University Press, 1980.

Efron, Joshua. "Bar Kokhbah in the Light of the Palestinian and Babylonian Talmudic Traditions" (in Hebrew). In *The Bar Kokhba Revolt: A New Approach*, edited by Aaron Oppenheimer and Uriel Rapaport. Jerusalem: Yad Izhak Ben-Zvi, 1984.

Eggan, Dorothy. "The Personal Use of Myth in Dreams." *Journal of American Folklore* 68 (1955): 445–63.

Elbaum, Yaakov. "Female Characters in Rabbinic Legends: A Model for Emulation" (in Hebrew). In *Hagut: The Woman in Jewish Sources*. Jerusalem: The Ministry of Education, 1983.

Eliach, Yaffa, ed. *Hasidic Tales of the Holocaust*. New York: Oxford University Press, 1982.

Eliade, Mircea. *Patterns in Comparative Religion*. Cleveland: World Publishing, 1968.

Enelow, Hyman, ed. *The Mishnah of R. Eliezer* (in Hebrew). 2 vols. New York: Bloch, 1934.

The Fathers According to R. Nathan: Version A. Translated by Judah Goldin. New Haven: Yale University Press, 1955.

The Fathers According to R. Nathan: Version B. Translated by Anthony J. Saldarini. Leiden: E. J. Brill, 1975.

Festugière, A. J. *Personal Religion Among the Greeks*. Berkeley: University of California Press, 1960.

Fick, Richard, and Alfons Hilka, eds. *Die Reise der drei Söhne des Königs von Serendippo*. Translated by Theodor Benfey. Folklore Fellows Communications, no. 98. Helsinki: Academia Scientiarum Fennica, 1932.

Fine, Elizabeth. *The Folklore Text*. Bloomington: Indiana University Press, 1984.

Fishbane, Michael. " 'The Holy One Sits and Roars': Mythopoesis and the Midrashic Imagination." *Jewish Thought and Philosophy* 1 (1991): 1–21.

Fleischer, Ezra. "Christian–Jewish Relations in the Middle Ages Distorted." *Zion* 59 (1994): 267–316.

Flusser, David. *Jewish Sources in Early Christianity: Studies and Essays* (in Hebrew). Jerusalem: Sifriat Hapoalim, 1979.

——. "The Dead of Massada in the Eyes of Their Contemporaries" (in Hebrew). In *Jews and Judaism in the Second Temple, Mishna, and Talmud Period: Studies in Honor of Shmuel Safrai*, edited by Isaiah Gafni, Aaron Oppenheimer, and Menahem Stern. Tel Aviv: Yad Izhak Ben-Zvi, 1993.

Fraade, Steven. *From Tradition to Commentary: Torah and its Interpretation in the Midrash Sifre to Deuteronomy*. Albany: State University of New York Press, 1991.

Fraenkel, Jonah. "Bible Verses Quoted in the Tales of the Sages." *Scripta Hierosolymitana* 22 (1971): 80–99.

———. "Hermeneutic Problems in the Study of the Aggadic Narrative" (in Hebrew). *Tarbiz* 47 (1978): 139–72. Reprinted in *The Aggadic Literature: A Reader*, edited by Avigdor Shinan (Jerusalem: Magnes Press, 1983).

———. "Paranomasia in Aggadic Narratives." *Scripta Hierosolymitana* 27 (1978): 27–51.

———. *Studies on the Spiritual World of the Aggadic Story* (in Hebrew). Tel Aviv: Ha-Kibbutz Ha-Meuhad, 1981.

———. *The Methods of Aggadah and Midrash* (in Hebrew). 2 vols. Givatayyim: Yad la-Talmud, 1991.

Fraenkel, Sigmund. "Die Scharfsinnsproben." *Zeitschrift für vergleichende Literaturgeschichte und Renaissance-Literatur* 3 (1890): 220–35.

Freud, Sigmund. *Totem and Taboo: Resemblances Between the Psychic Lives of Savages and Neurotics*. Translated by A. A. Brill. Middlesex: Pelican Books, 1938.

———. *Moses and Monotheism*. Translated by Katherine Jones. New York: Vintage Books, 1955.

———. *The Interpretation of Dreams*. Translated by James Strachey. New York: Basic Books, 1953. Originally published as *Die Traumdeutung* (1900; Strachey's translation is based on the 8th enl. and rev. ed. [Leipzig and Vienna: Franz Deuticke, 1930]).

———. "The Theme of the Three Caskets." In *Art and Literature*. Middlesex: Pelican Freud Library, 1985.

Frieden, Ken. *Freud's Dream of Interpretation*. Albany: State University of New York Press, 1990.

Friedländer, Saul. *Reflections on Nazism: An Essay on Kitsch and Death*. New York: Harper and Row, 1984.

Funkenstein, Amos. "History, Counterhistory, and Narrative" (in Hebrew). *Alpayim* 4 (1991): 206–23.

Gadamer, Hans Georg. *Wahrheit und Methode*. Tübingen: J. C. B. Mohr, 1975.

Garney, Peter. *Food and Society in Classical Antiquity*. Cambridge: Cambridge University Press, 1999.

Gaster, Moses. *The Exempla of the Rabbis*. 1924. Reprint, New York: Ktav, 1968.

Geertz, Clifford. *The Interpretation of Cultures*. New York: Basic Books, 1973.

Geiger, Joseph. "The Revolt (in Gallus' Times), and Building the Temple (in Julian's Times)" (in Hebrew). In vol. 1 of *Eretz Israel from the Destruction of the Second Temple to the Muslim Conquest*, edited by Zvi Baras, Shmuel Safrai, Menahem Stern, and Yoram Tsafrir. Jerusalem: Yad Izhak Ben-Zvi, 1982.

Ginzberg, Louis. *Yerushalmi Fragments from the Genizah* (in Hebrew). 1908. Reprint, Jerusalem: Maqor, 1969.

———. *On Jewish Law and Lore*. Philadelphia: Jewish Publication Society, 1955.

———. *The Legends of the Jews*. 7 vols. Baltimore: Johns Hopkins University Press, 1999 [orig. Philadelphia: The Jewish Publication Society of America, 1909–38].

Goddard Elliot, Allison. *Roads to Paradise: Reading the Lives of the Early Saints*. Hanover: University Press of New England, 1987.

Goldsmith, Daniel, ed. *Seder Ha-Kinot le-Tish'a be-Av According to the Ashkenazi Ritual*. Jerusalem: Mossad Ha-Rav Kook, 1977.

Goodblatt, David. "The Beruriah Traditions." *Journal of Jewish Studies* 26 (1975): 68–85.

Goody, Jack. *The Interface Between the Written and the Oral*. Cambridge: Cambridge University Press, 1987.

Goshen-Gottstein, Alon. "God and Israel as Father and Son in Tannaitic Literature" (in Hebrew). Ph.D. diss., Hebrew University of Jerusalem, 1986.

———. " 'Mitzva Kalla' (A Lenient Commandment)" (in Hebrew). In *Alei Shefer: Studies in the Literature of Jewish Thought Presented to Alexander Safran*, edited by Moshe Halamish. Ramat Gan: Bar Ilan University Press, 1990.

Green, Thomas. "Riddle." In *Folklore, Cultural Performances, and Popular Entertainments: A Communications-Centered Handbook*, edited by Richard Bauman. New York: Oxford University Press, 1992.

Grene, David, and Richard Lattimore, eds. *Greek Tragedies*. Chicago: University of Chicago Press, 1960.

Gurevitch, Aaron. *Medieval Popular Culture: Problems of Belief and Perception*. Translated by Janos M. Bak and Paul Hollingsworth. Cambridge: Cambridge University Press, 1988.

———. *Historical Anthropology of the Middle Ages*. Chicago: University of Chicago Press, 1993.

Gutmann, Joshua. *The Parable in the Tannaitic Era* (in Hebrew). Jerusalem: n.p., 1940.

———. "The Mother and Her Seven Sons in the Aggadah and in the Book of the Maccabees 2 and 4" (in Hebrew). In *In Memoriam: Johannis Lewy (1901–1945)*, edited by Menahem Schwabe and Joshua Gutmann. Jerusalem: Magnes Press, 1949.

Habermas, Jürgen. *Knowledge and Human Interests*. Translated by Jeremy J. Shapiro. London: Heinemann, 1972.

Hachlili, Rachel. "Changes in Burial Practices in the Late Second Temple Period: The Evidence from Jericho" (in Hebrew). In *Graves and Burial Practices in Israel in the Ancient Period*, edited by Itamar Singer. Jerusalem: Yad Izhak Ben-Zvi and the Israel Exploration Society, 1994.

Halevy, Elimelech. *The Historical-Biographical Legend: From the Great Knesset until R. Judah Hanasi in Light of Greek and Latin Sources* (in Hebrew). Tel Aviv: n.p., 1975.

Halévy, J. "Examen critique de sources relatives a la persécution des chrétiens de Nedjran par le roi juif des Himyarites." *Revue des Etudes Juives* 18 (1889): 16–42.

Handelman, Don. "Traps of Trans-formation: Theoretical Convergences." In *Untying the Knot: On Riddles and Other Enigmatic Modes*, edited by Galit Hasan-Rokem and David Shulman. New York: Oxford University Press, 1996.

Handelman, Susan A. *The Slayers of Moses: The Emergence of Rabbinic Interpretation in Modern Literary Theory*. Albany: State University of New York Press, 1982.

Harris, Monford. "Dreams in Sefer Hasidim." *Proceedings of the American Academy for Jewish Research* 31 (1963): 51–80.

Hasan-Rokem, Galit. "Cognition in the Folktale: Aesthetic Judgements and Symbolic Structures." *Scripta Hierosolymitana* 27 (1978): 192–204.

——. "Sources of Iraqi-Jewish Folk Narratives: Proverbs in Folk Narrative" (in Hebrew). In *Studies in the History and the Culture of the Jews of Iraq*, edited by Shmuel Moreh. Or Yehudah: Babylonian Jewry Heritage Center, 1981.

——. *Proverbs in Israeli Folk Narratives: A Structural Semantic Analysis*. Folklore Fellows Communications, no. 232. Helsinki: Academia Scientiarum Fennica, 1982.

——. "The Study of Processes of Change in the Folk Narrative" (in Hebrew). *Jerusalem Studies in Jewish Folklore* 3 (1982): 129–37.

——. "Ideological and Psychological Messages in 'The Tale about the Two Children of Zadok the Priest': Toward an Interpretation of Aggadic Midrash" (in Hebrew). *Jerusalem Studies in Hebrew Literature* 3 (1983): 122–39.

——. "The Cobbler of Jerusalem in Finnish Folklore." In *The Wandering Jew: Interpretations of a Christian Legend*, edited by Galit Hasan-Rokem and Alan Dundes. Bloomington: Indiana University Press, 1986.

——. "The Rhetoric of Intimacy, the Rhetoric of the Sacred." *Temenos* 23 (1987): 45–57.

——. "The Snake at the Wedding: Semiotic Reconsideration of the Comparative Method of Folk Narrative Research." *ARV: Scandinavian Yearbook of Folklore* 43 (1987): 73–87.

——. "Ekha? . . . Ayeka?: On Riddles in the Stories of Midrash Ekha Rabba" (in Hebrew). *Jerusalem Studies in Hebrew Literature: Essays in Memory of Dan Pagis* 11 (1988): 531–47.

——. " 'To See the Voices': A Functional, Semiotic, and Hermeneutic Approach to Folk-Narrating" (in Hebrew). *Jerusalem Studies in Jewish Folklore* 10 (1988): 20–31.

——. "Perspectives of Comparative Research of Folk Narratives in Aggadic Midrashim: Enigmatic Tales in *Lamentations Rabba* 1" (in Hebrew). *Tarbiz* 59 (1990).

——. "Between Unity and Plurality: Dov Noy's Studies of Folklore in Talmudic-Midrashic Literature" (in Hebrew). *Jerusalem Studies in Jewish Folklore: For Dov Noy* 13–14 (1992): 18–29.

——. *Adam le-Adam Gesher: The Proverbs of Georgian Jews in Israel* (in Hebrew). Jerusalem: Ben-Zvi Institute, 1993.

——. "Within Limits and Beyond: History and Body in Midrashic Texts." *International Folklore Review* 9 (1993): 5–12.

——. "'A Dream Amounts to the Sixtieth Part of Prophecy': On Interaction between Textual Establishment and Popular Context in Dream Interpretation by the Jewish Sages" (in Hebrew). In *Studies in the History of Popular Culture*, edited by Benjamin Z. Kedar. Jerusalem: The Zalman Shazar Center for Jewish History, 1996.

——. "Spinning Threads of Sand: Riddles as Images of Loss in the Midrash on Lamentations." In *Untying the Knot: On Riddles and Other Enigmatic Modes*, edited by Galit Hasan-Rokem and David Shulman. New York: Oxford University Press, 1996.

——. "The Birth of Scholarship out of the Spirit of Oral Tradition: Folk Narrative Publications and National Identity in Modern Israel." *Fabula* 39 (1998): 277–90.

——. "Narratives in Dialogue: A Folk Literary Perspective on Interreligious Contacts in the Holy Land in Rabbinic Literature of Late Antiquity." In *Sharing the Sacred: Religious Contacts and Conflicts in the Holy Land—First–Fifteenth Centuries C.E.*, edited by Arieh Kofsky and Guy G. Stroumsa. Jerusalem: Yad Izhak Ben-Zvi, 1998.

——. "Textualizing the Tales of the People of the Book: Folk Narrative Anthologies and National Identity in Modern Israel." *Prooftexts* 19 (1999): 69–80.

——. "Communication with the Dead in Jewish Dream Culture." In *Dream Cultures: Toward a Comparative History of Dreaming*, edited by David Shulman and Guy Stroumsa. New York: Oxford University Press, in press.

——. "Ökotyp," *Enzyklopädie des Märchen*. Berlin: Walter de Gruyter, in press.

Heffernan, Thomas J. *Sacred Biography: Saints and Their Biographers in the Middle Ages*. New York: Oxford University Press, 1988.

Heinemann, Joseph. *Public Sermons in the Talmudic Era* (in Hebrew). Jerusalem: Bialik Institute, 1970.

Heinemann, Yitzhak. *The Methods of Aggadah* (in Hebrew). Givatayyim: Magnes and Massada, 1970.

Heller, Bernhard. "Das hebräische und arabische Märchen." In vol. 4 of *Anmerkungen zu den Kinder und Hausmärchen der Brüder Grimm*, edited by Johannes Bolte and Georg Polívka. 1930. Reprint, Hildesheim: Georg Olms, 1963.

Higger, Michael, ed. *Semahot* (in Hebrew). Tel Aviv: Ha-Oved Ha-Dati, 1949.

Hirschberg, Haim Z. "Joseph, King of Himyar, and the Coming of Mar Zutra to Tiberias" (in Hebrew). In *All the Land of Naphtali*, edited by Haim Z. Hirschberg. Jerusalem: Israel Exploration Society, 1978.

Hirshman, Marc G. (Menahem). *A Rivalry of Genius: Jewish and Christian Biblical*

Interpretation. Translated by Batya Stein. Albany: State University of New York Press, 1996.

———. "Shifting Sacred Loci: Honi and His Grandchildren" (in Hebrew). *Tura* 1 (1989): 109–18.

Homer. *The Iliad*. Translated by E. V. Rieu. Penguin Books, 1966.

Homer. *The Odyssey*. Translated by A. T. Murray and George E. Dimock. Cambridge, Mass.: Harvard University Press, 1995.

Honko, Lauri. "Four Forms of Adaptation to Tradition." *Studia Fennica* 26 (1981): 19–33.

———. "Folkloristic Theories of Genre." *Temenos* 3 (1966): 48–66.

Hrushovski, Benjamin. "Do Sounds Have Meaning? The Problem of Expressiveness of Sound Patterns in Poetry" (in Hebrew). *Ha-Sifrut* 1 (1968–69): 410–20.

———. "Segmentation and Motivation in the Text Continuum of Literary Prose." In vol. 5 of *Papers on Poetics and Semiotics*, edited by Benjamin Hrushovski and Itamar Even-Zohar. Tel Aviv: Tel Aviv University Press, 1976.

Hunt, Harry. *The Multiplicity of Dreams: Memory, Imagination, and Consciousness*. New Haven: Yale University Press, 1989.

Huth, Georg. "Die Reisen der drei Söhne des Königs von Serendippo: Ein Beitrag zur vergleichender Märchenkunde." *Zeitschrift für Vergleichende Litteraturgeshichte und Renaissance-Litteratur*, Neue Folge, 2 (1889): 404–14.

Hyman, Aaron. *Toldoth Ha-Tannaim Ve-Ha-Amoraim* (in Hebrew). Jerusalem: Boys Town, 1964.

Ilan, Tal. *Jewish Women in Greco Roman Palestine*. Tübingen: J. C. B. Mohr (Paul Siebeck), 1995.

Ingarden, Roman. *The Literary Work of Art*. Translated by George G. Grabowic. Evanston: Northwestern University Press, 1973. Originally published as *Das Literarische Kunstwerk* (Tübingen: M. Niemeyer, 1930).

Irshai, Oded. "Historical Aspects of the Christian-Jewish Polemic Concerning the Church of Jerusalem in the Fourth Century (In The Light of Patristic and Rabbinic Literature)" (in Hebrew). Ph.D. diss., The Hebrew University of Jerusalem, 1993.

———. "The Church of Jerusalem: From 'The Church of the Circumcision' to 'The Church from the Gentiles.'" In *The History of Jerusalem: The Roman and Byzantine Periods (to 638 C.E.)*, edited by Yoram Tsafrir and Shmuel Safrai. Jerusalem: Yad Izhak Ben-Zvi, 1999.

Isaac, Benjamin. "Bandits in Judea and Arabia." *Harvard Studies in Classical Philology* 88 (1984): 171–203.

———. "The Revolt of Bar Kokhba as Described by Cassius Dio and Other Revolts Against the Romans in Greek and Latin Literature" (in Hebrew). In *The Bar Kokhba Revolt: A New Approach*, edited by Aaron Oppenheimer and Uriel Rapaport. Jerusalem: Yad Izhak Ben-Zvi, 1984.

Jaeger, Werner. *Early Christianity and Greek Paideia*. Cambridge, Mass.: Harvard University Press, 1961.

Jakobson, Roman. "Concluding Statement: Linguistics and Poetics." In *Style in Language*, edited by Thomas Sebeok. Cambridge, Mass.: MIT Press, 1960.

Jason, Heda. *Genre: An Essay in Oral Literature*. Tel Aviv: Tel Aviv University Press, 1972.

——. "Concerning the 'Historical' and the 'Local' Legends and Their Relatives." *Journal of American Folklore* 84 (1971): 134–44. Reprinted in Heda Jason, *Studies in Jewish Ethnopoetry* (Taipei: Chinese Association for Folklore, 1975).

Jolles, André. *Einfache Formen*. Halle (Saale): Niemeyer, 1956.

Josephus Flavius. *The Jewish War*. In vol. 2, bk. 3 of *Collected Works*, translated by H. St. J. Thackeray. Cambridge, Mass.: Harvard University Press, Loeb Classical Library; London: Heinemann, 1976.

The Jossipon (Josephus Gorionides) (in Hebrew). Edited by David Flusser. Jerusalem: Bialik Institute, 1978.

Jung, Carl Gustav. *Dreams*. Translated by R. F. C. Hull. Bollingen Series. Princeton: Princeton University Press, 1974.

Jung, Carl Gustav, with Marie L. von Franz, Joseph L. Henderson, Jolande Jacobi, and Aniela Jaffé. *Man and his Symbols*. London: Picador, 1964.

Kafah, Yosef, ed. *The Book of Lamentations with Translations and Interpretations from Ancient Manuscripts* (in Hebrew). Jerusalem: Ha-Agudah le-Hatzalat Ginzei Yehudei Teiman, 1962.

Kaivola-Bregenhøj, Annikki. *Narrative and Narrating: Variation in Juha Oksanen's Storytelling*. Folklore Fellows Communications, no. 261. Helsinki: Academia Scientiarum Fennica, 1996.

——. "Riddles and Their Use." In *Untying the Knot: On Riddles and Other Enigmatic Modes*, edited by Galit Hasan-Rokem and David Shulman. New York: Oxford University Press, 1996.

Kaminka, Aaron. *Studies in Bible, Talmud, and Rabbinical Literature* (in Hebrew). Tel Aviv: Devir, 1951.

Kara, Yehiel. *The Yemenite Manuscripts of the Babylonian Talmud: Studies in their Aramaic Language* (in Hebrew). Jerusalem: Hebrew University of Jerusalem, Institute of Jewish Studies, 1984. First published in *Edah Velashon* 10 (1984): 1–396.

Kaufman, Shirley, Galit Hasan-Rokem, and Tamar Hess, eds. *The Defiant Muse: Hebrew Feminist Poems from Antiquity to the Present*. New York: The Feminist Press at CUNY, 1999.

Keyes, C. W. "Half-Sister Marriage in New Comedy and the Epidicus." *Transactions of the American Philological Association* 71 (1940): 217–29.

Kiefer, Emma Emily. *Albert Wesselski and Recent Folktale Theories*. Bloomington: Indiana University Press, 1945.

Kister, Meir J. "The Interpretation of Dreams: An Unknown Manuscript of Ibn Qutayba's 'Ibarat al-Ru'ya.'" *Israel Oriental Studies* 4 (1974): 67–103.

——. "Legends in Tafsir and Hadith Literature: Creation of Adam and Related Stories." In *Approaches to the History of the Interpretation of the Qur'an*, edited by Andrew Rippin. Oxford: Clarendon Press, 1988.

——. "Adam: A Study of Some Legends in Tafsir and Hadith Literature." *Israel Oriental Studies* 13 (1993): 113–74.

Kister, Meir J., and Menahem Kister. "On the Jews of Arabia: Some Notes" (in Hebrew). *Tarbiz* 48 (1979): 241–42.

Kister, Menahem. "Legends on the Destruction of the Second Temple in Avot de-Rabbi Natan." *Tarbiz* 67 (1998): 483–529.

——. *Studies in Avot de-Rabbi Nathan: Studies in Text, Redaction, and Interpretation* (in Hebrew). Jerusalem: The Hebrew University, Department of Talmud and Yad Izhak Ben-Zvi, The Institute for Research of Eretz Israel, Dissertation Series, 1998.

Kloner, Amos. "Hideout Complexes from the Period of Bar Kokhva in the Judean Plain" (in Hebrew). In *The Bar Kokhba Revolt: A New Approach*, edited by Aaron Oppenheimer and Uriel Rapaport. Jerusalem: Yad Izhak Ben-Zvi, 1984.

Klotz, Volker. *Das Europäische Kunstmärchen.* Stuttgart: J. B. Metzler, 1985.

Krauss, Samuel. *Griechische und lateinische Lehnwörter in Talmud, Midrash, und Targum.* 2 vols. Berlin: S. Calvary, 1898–1899.

——. "Talmudische Nachricthen über Arabien." *Zeitschrift der Deutschen Morgenländischen Gesellschaft* 70 (1916): 321–53.

——. "The Armies of Bar Kokhba" (in Hebrew). In *Alexander Marx Jubilee Volume*, edited by Saul Lieberman. New York: Jewish Theological Seminary, 1950.

Kristeva, Julia. "Revolution in Poetic Language." In *The Kristeva Reader*, edited by Toril Moi. Oxford: Blackwell, 1986.

Kristianpoller, Alexander. *Traum und Traumdeutung.* Vol. 4: *Monumenta Talmudica.* Wien: Benjamin Harz, 1923.

Krohn, Kaarle. *Folklore Methodology.* Translated by Roger L. Welch. Austin: University of Texas Press, 1971.

Kugel, James. *The Idea of Biblical Poetry: Parallelism and its History.* New Haven: Yale University Press, 1981.

——. "Two Introductions to Midrash." In *Midrash and Literature*, edited by Geoffrey H. Hartman and Sanford Budick. New Haven: Yale University Press, 1986.

Lazarus-Yafeh, Hava. "Some Halakhic Differences between Judaism and Islam" (in Hebrew). *Tarbiz* 51 (1982): 207–25.

Lévi, Israël. "Contes Juifs." *Revue des Études Juives* 40 (1885): 209–23.

——. *Le Ravissement du Messie a sa Naissance et Outre Essais.* Edited by Evelyn Patlagean. Paris: Peeters, 1994.

Lévi-Strauss, Claude. *The Scope of Anthropology*. Translated by Sherry O. Paul and Robert A. Paul. London: Jonathan Cape, 1967.

———. "The Story of Asdiwal." In *The Structural Study of Myth and Totemism*, edited by Edmund Leach. London: Tavistock, 1967.

———. *Structural Anthropology*. Translated by Claire Jacobson and Brooke Grundfest Schoepf. New York: Basic Books, 1967.

———. *L'Origine des Maniéres de Table*. Vol. 3. Paris: Plon, 1968.

———. *The Raw and the Cooked*. Translated by John Weightman and Doreen Weightman. New York: Harper and Row, 1969.

———. *From Honey to Ashes*. Translated by John Weightman and Doreen Weightman. New York: Harper and Row, 1973.

———. *The Savage Mind*. Chicago: University of Chicago Press, 1978. Originally published as *La Pensée Sauvage* (Paris: Plon, 1962).

———. *The Naked Man*. Translated by John Weightman and Doreen Weightman. New York: Harper and Row, 1981.

Levinson, Joshua. "The Tragedy of Romance: A Case of Literary Exile." *Harvard Theological Review* 89 (1996): 227–44.

Levy-Zumwalt, Rosemary. *American Folklore Scholarship: A Dialogue of Dissent*. Bloomington: Indiana University Press, 1988.

Lewy, Hans. "Zu dem Traumbuche des Artemidoros." *Rheinische Museum für Philologie*, Neue Folge, 48 (1893): 398–419.

———. *Chaldean Oracles and Theurgy: Mysticism, Magic, and Platonism in the Later Roman Empire*. Paris: Études Augustiniennes, 1978.

Lieberman, Saul. *Greek in Jewish Palestine: Studies in the Life and Manners of Jewish Palestine in the II–IV Centuries C.E.* New York: Jewish Theological Seminary, 1942.

———. *Hellenism In Jewish Palestine: Studies in the Literary Transmission, Beliefs, and Manners of Palestine in the I Century B.C.E.–IV Century C.E.* New York: Jewish Theological Seminary, 1950.

———. *Studies in Palestinian Talmudic Literature* (in Hebrew), edited by David Rosenthal. Jerusalem: Magnes Press, 1991.

Liebes, Yehuda. "Mazmiah Qeren Yeshu'ah" (in Hebrew) (Who Causes the Glory of Salvation to Sprout). *Jerusalem Studies in Jewish Thought* 3 (1984): 313–49.

———. "'De Natura Dei': On the Development of the Jewish Myth." In *Studies in Jewish Myth and Jewish Messianism*, translated by Batya Stein. New York: State University of New York Press, 1993.

Lüdemann, Gerd. "The Successors of the Jerusalem Christianity: A Critical Evaluation of the Pella Tradition." In *Jewish and Christian Self-Definition*, edited by P. Sanders. London: SCM Press, 1980.

Lüthi, Max. *The Fairytale as Art Form and Portrait of Man*. Bloomington: Indiana University Press, 1984.

Maccoby, Hyam, ed. *Judaism on Trial: Jewish-Christian Disputations in the Middle Ages*. East Brunswick, N.J.: Associated University Presses, 1982.

Macrobius, Ambrosius. *Commentary on the Dream of Scipio*. Translated by W. H. Stahl. New York: Columbia University Press, 1952.

Mandel, Paul David. "The Tale in Midrash Lamentations Rabbah: Version and Style" (in Hebrew). Master's thesis, Hebrew University of Jerusalem, 1983.

——. "Midrash Lamentations Rabbati: Prolegomenon, and a Critical Edition to the Third Parasha" (in Hebrew). Ph.D. diss., The Hebrew University of Jerusalem, 1997.

Manuel, Frank E., and Fritzie P. Manuel. *Utopian Thought in the Western World*. Oxford: Basil Blackwell, 1979.

Marcus, Eliezer. "The Confrontation Between Jews and Non-Jews In Folktales of the Jews of Islamic Countries" (in Hebrew). Ph.D. diss., The Hebrew University of Jerusalem, 1978.

——, ed. *Min Ha-Mabua* (From the fountainhead). Haifa: Israel Folktale Archives, 1966.

Marx, Alexander. "Midrasch Eicha Rabbati." *Orientalistische Literatur Zeitung* 5 (1902): 293–95.

Masoudi [al Masudi]. *Les Prairies d'or*. Translated and edited by C. Barbier de Meynard and Pavet de Courteille. Vol. 3. Paris: Societé Asiatique, 1917.

Meir, Ofra. "The Jewish Versions of AT 875" (in Hebrew). *Yeda-Am* 19 (1979): 55–61.

——. "The Continuity of Editing as the Shaping of a World View" (in Hebrew). In *Rabbinic Thought: Proceedings of the First Conference on "Makhshevet Hazal,"* edited by Marc Hirshman and Tsvi Groner. Haifa: University of Haifa, 1989.

——. "'A Garden in Eden': On the Redaction of Genesis Rabba" (in Hebrew). *Dappim: Research in Literature* 5–6 (1989): 309–30.

——. *The Poetics of Rabbinic Stories* (in Hebrew). Tel Aviv: Sifriat Hapoalim, 1993.

Meissner, Bruno. *Neuarabische Geschichten aus dem Iraq*. Leipzig: J. C. Hinrichs, 1903.

Meletinskii, E., S. Nekludov, E. Novik, and D. Segal. "Problems of the Structural Analysis of Fairytales." In *Soviet Structural Folkloristics*, edited by Pierre Maranda. The Hague: Mouton, 1974.

Meyers, Carol. *Discovering Eve: Ancient Israelite Women in Context*. New York: Oxford University Press, 1988.

Miller, Justin. "Interpretations of Freud's Jewishness, 1924–1974." *Journal of the History of Behavioral Sciences* 17 (1981): 357–74.

Mintz, Alan. *Hurban: Responses to Catastrophe in Hebrew Literature*. New York: Columbia University Press, 1984.

Moberg, Axel. *The Book of Himyarites: A Hitherto Unknown Syriac Work on the Himyarite Martyrs*. Lund: Gleerup, 1921.

Momigliano, Arnaldo. *Alien Wisdom: The Limits of Hellenization*. Cambridge: Cambridge University Press, 1975.

Mor, Menachem. *The Bar-Kochba Revolt: Its Extent and Effect* (in Hebrew). Jerusalem: Yad Izhak Ben-Zvi, 1991.

Movinckel, Sigmund. *He That Cometh*. Translated by G. W. Andersson. Oxford: Basil Blackwell, 1954.

Musurillo, Herbert, ed. *The Acts of the Pagan Martyrs: Acta Alexandrinorum*. Oxford: Clarendon Press, 1954.

Nacht, Jacob. *Der Fuss, Eine Folkloristische Studie*. Wien, 1923 (reprinted from *Jahrbuch für Jüdische Volkskunde*, 1923). Published in an abridged English version as "The Symbolism of the Shoe with Special Reference to Jewish Sources." *Jewish Quarterly Review* 6 (1915–16): 1–22.

Nador, Georg. *Jüdische Rätsel aus Talmud und Midrasch*. Köln: J. Hegner, 1967.

Nenola-Kallio, Aili. *Studies in Ingrian Laments*. Folklore Fellows Communications, no. 234. Helsinki: Academia Scientiarum Fennica, 1982.

Neusner, Jacob. *The Development of a Legend: Studies on the Tradition Concerning Yohanan ben Zakkai*. Leiden: E. J. Brill, 1970.

——. *A Life of Yohanan ben Zakkai*. Leiden: E. J. Brill, 1970.

——. *Beyond Historicism, After Structuralism: Story as History in Ancient Judaism*. Brunswick, Me.: Bowdoin College, 1980.

Niehoff, Maren. "A Dream Which Is Not Interpreted Is Like a Letter Which Is Not Read." *Journal of Jewish Studies* 43 (1992): 58–84.

Nissim of Kairuan. *An Elegant Composition for Relief After Adversity*. Translated by William Z. Brinner. New Haven: Yale University Press, 1977.

Nodet, Étienne, and Justin Taylor. *The Origins of Christianity: An Exploration*. Collegeville, Minn.: The Liturgical Press, 1998.

Nora, Pierre. *Realms of Memory: Rethinking the French Past*. Translated by Arthur Goldhammer. 2 vols. New York: Columbia University Press, 1996–1998.

Noy, Dov. "The Daughters of Zelophehad and the Daughters of Jerusalem" (in Hebrew). *Mahanayim* 48 (1960): 20–25.

——. "Riddles at a Wedding-Banquet" (in Hebrew). *Mahanayim* 83 (1963): 64–71.

——. "Rabbi Shalem Shabazi in the Folktales of the Jews of Yemen" (in Hebrew). In *Boi Teman [Come thou south]: Studies and Documents Concerning the Culture of the Yemenite Jews*, edited by Jehuda Ratzaby. Tel Aviv: Afikim, 1967.

——. "Folklore" (in Hebrew). In vol. 4 of *Encyclopedia of Social Sciences*. Merhavia: Sifriat Hapoalim, 1968.

——. "The Messiah as a Jewish Hero" (in Hebrew). *Mahanayim* 124 (1970): 114–25.

——. "The Jewish Versions of the 'Animal Languages' Folktale (AT 670): A Typological-Structural Study." *Scripta Hierosolymitana* 22 (1971): 171–208.

——. "The Death of Rabbi Shalem Shabazi in the Yemenite Folk Legend" (in Hebrew). In *Legacy of the Jews of Yemen: Studies and Researches*, edited by Yosef Tobi. Jerusalem: Boi Teiman, 1976.

——. "Folklore: Definition and Boundaries" (in Hebrew). In *"Forever After . . .": On the Art of the Folk Narrator*, edited by Tamar Alexander. Ramat Gan: Tag, 1993.

——, ed. *A Tale for Every Month* (in Hebrew). Haifa: Israel Folktale Archives, 1973.

Olrik, Axel. "Epic Laws of Folk Narrative." In *The Study of Folklore*, edited by Alan Dundes. Englewood Cliffs, N.J.: Prentice Hall, 1965.

Ong, Walter J. *Orality and Literacy: The Technologizing of the Word*. London: Methuen, 1982.

Oppenheim, A. Leo. "The Interpretation of Dreams in the Ancient Near East with a Translation of an Assyrian Dreambook." *Transactions of the American Philosophical Society* 46 (1956): 179–373.

Oppenheimer, Aaron. "The Bar Kokhva Revolt" (in Hebrew). In vol. 1 of *Eretz Israel from the Destruction of the Second Temple to the Muslim Conquest*, edited by Zvi Baras, Shmuel Safrai, Menahem Stern, and Yoram Tsafrir. Jerusalem: Yad Izhak Ben-Zvi, 1982.

——. "The Reconstruction of Jewish Settlement in the Galilee" (in Hebrew). In vol. 1 of *Eretz Israel from the Destruction of the Second Temple to the Muslim Conquest*, edited by Zvi Baras, Shmuel Safrai, Menahem Stern, and Yoram Tsafrir. Jerusalem: Yad Izhak Ben-Zvi, 1982.

——. *Galilee in the Mishnaic Period*. Jerusalem: Zalman Shazar Center for Jewish History, 1991.

——. "Sanctity of Life and Martyrdom Following the Bar Kokhba Revolt" (in Hebrew). In *Sanctity of Life and Martyrdom: Studies in Memory of Amir Yekutiel*, edited by Isaiah M. Gafni and Aviezer Ravitzky. Jerusalem: Zalman Shazar Center for Jewish History, 1992.

Oppenheimer, Aaron, and Benjamin Isaac. "Research History of the Bar Kokhba War" (in Hebrew). In *Hiding Complexes in Judean Shephelah*, edited by Amos Kloner and Yigal Tepper. Tel Aviv: Hakibbutz Hameuhad and Israel Exploration Society, 1987.

Pack, Roger. "Artemidorus and his Waking World." *Transactions and Proceedings of the American Philological Association* 86 (1955): 280–90.

Pagis, Dan. *A Secret Sealed: Hebrew Baroque Emblem-Riddles from Italy and Holland* (in Hebrew). Jerusalem: Magnes Press, 1986.

——. "Toward a Theory of the Literary Riddle." In *Untying the Knot: On Riddles and Other Enigmatic Modes*, edited by Galit Hasan-Rokem and David Shulman. New York: Oxford University Press, 1996.

Pardes, Ilana. *Countertraditions in the Bible: A Feminist Approach*. Cambridge, Mass.: Harvard University Press, 1992.

Patai, Raphael. "Jus Primae Noctis." *Folklore Research Center Studies* 4 (1974): 177–80.

Patai, Raphael, Francis Lee Utley, and Dov Noy, eds. *Studies in Biblical and Jewish Folklore*. New York: Haskell House, 1960.

Patrich, Joseph. "Graves and Burial Practices in Talmudic Sources" (in Hebrew).

In *Graves and Burial Practices in Israel in the Ancient Period*, edited by Itamar Singer. Jerusalem: Yad Izhak Ben-Zvi and the Israel Exploration Society, 1994.

Penzer, Norman Mosley, ed. *The Ocean of Story: Somadeva's Katha-Sarit Sagara*. Translated by C. H. Tawney. London: Sawyer, 1926. Reprint, Delhi: Motilal Banarsidass, 1968.

Perles, Josef. "Rabbinische Agadas in 1001 Nacht: Ein beitrag zur Geschichte der Wanderung Orientalischen Märchen." *Monatsschrift für Geschichte und Wissenschaft des Judentums* 22 (1873): 61–85.

Pesikta Rabbati. Translated by William G. Braude. New Haven: Yale University Press, 1968.

Price, Jonathan J. *Jerusalem Under Siege: The Collapse of the Jewish State, 66–70 C.E.* Leiden: E. J. Brill, 1992.

Propp, Vladimir. *The Morphology of the Folktale*. Translated by Laurence Scott, revised and edited by Louis A. Wagner. Austin: The University of Texas Press, 1977. Originally published as *Morfologija skazki* (Leningrad: Academia, 1928).

Rabinov, Paul. "Representations are Social Facts: Modernity and Post-Modernity in Anthropology." In *Writing Culture: The Poetics and Politics of Ethnography*, edited by James Clifford and George E. Marcus. Berkeley and Los Angeles: University of California Press, 1986.

Rabinowitz, Zvi M. "Fragments of Midrash Echa Rabba from the Geniza" (in Hebrew). In *Bar-Ilan: Annual of Bar-Ilan University*, edited by Menahem Zevi Kaddari, Nathaniel Katzburg, and Daniel Sperber. Ramat Gan: Bar Ilan University Press, 1973.

——. "Geniza Fragments of Midrash Ekha Rabba" (in Hebrew). In vol. 3 of *Proceedings of the Sixth World Congress of Jewish Studies*, edited by Avigdor Shinan. Jerusalem: World Union of Jewish Studies, 1977.

Raglan, Lord. *The Hero: A Study in Tradition, Myth, and Drama*. 1936. Reprint, New York: Vintage, 1956.

Rank, Otto. *The Myth of the Birth of the Hero and Other Writings*. 1914. Reprint, New York: Vintage, 1964.

——. *The Incest Theme in Literature and Legend: Fundamentals of a Psychology of Literary Creation*. Translated by Gregory C. Richter. Baltimore: Johns Hopkins University Press, 1992. Originally published as *Das Inzest-Motif in Dichtung und Sage* (Leipzig: F. Deuticke, 1912).

Reiner, Elchanan. "From Joshua to Jesus: The Transformation of a Biblical Story to a Local Myth: A Chapter in the Religious Life of the Galilean Jew." In *Sharing the Sacred: Religious Contacts in the Holy Land*, edited by Arieh Kofsky and Guy G. Stroumsa. Jerusalem: Yad Izhak Ben-Zvi, 1998.

Renou, Louis, ed. and trans. *Contes du Vampire*. Paris: Gallimard, 1963.

——. "L'enigme." In *L'Inde Fondamentale*, edited by Charles Malamoud. Paris: Hermann, 1978.

Ricoeur, Paul. *Freud and Philosophy: An Essay in Interpretation*. Translated by Denis Savage. New Haven: Yale University Press, 1970.

——. "The Hermeneutical Function of Distanciation." *Philosophy Today* 17 (1973): 129–41.

Rimmon-Kenan, Shlomith. *Narrative Fiction: Contemporary Poetics*. London: Routledge, 1980.

Rokem, Freddie. "The Beginning of the Hebrew Theater in Erez Israel: An Analysis of the Repertoire Between the Years 1890–1914" (in Hebrew). *Ha-Sifrut* 29 (1979): 76–81.

——. "The Erotic, the Scientific, and the Aesthetic Gazes in the Theatre." *Assaph: Studies in the Theatre* 7 (1991): 61–73.

——. "One Voice and Many Legs: Oedipus and the Riddle of the Sphinx." In *Untying the Knot: On Riddles and Other Enigmatic Modes*, edited by Galit Hasan-Rokem and David Shulman. New York: Oxford University Press, 1996.

Rosenberg, Yehuda Yudel. *The Golem of Prague and Other Tales of Wonder* (in Hebrew). Selected and edited, with an introduction and notes by Eli Yassif. Jerusalem: Bialik Institute, 1991.

Rotunda, Dominic Peter. *Motif Index of the Italian Novella in Prose*. Bloomington: Indiana University Press, 1942.

Rubenstein, Richard L. *The Religious Imagination: A Study in Psychoanalysis and Jewish Theology*. Boston: Beacon Press, 1971.

Sadeh, Pinhas, ed. *The Book of Fantasies of the Jews* (in Hebrew). Tel Aviv: Schocken, 1983.

Salamon, Hagar. *The Hyena People: Ethiopian Jews in Christian Ethiopia*. Berkeley and Los Angeles: University of California Press, 1999.

Saldarini, Anthony J. "Johanan ben Zakkai's Escape from Jerusalem." *Journal for the Study of Judaism* 6 (1975): 189–204.

Salisbury, Joyce E. *Perpetua's Passion: The Death and Memory of a Young Roman Woman*. New York: Routledge, 1997.

Scarry, Elaine. *The Body in Pain: The Making and Unmaking of the World*. New York: Oxford University Press, 1985.

Schaefer, Peter. "Zur Geschichtsauffassung des rabbinischen Judentums." *Journal for the Study of Judaism* 6 (1975): 167–88.

——. "Die Flucht Johanan b. Zakkais aus Jerusalem und die Gründung 'Lehrhauses' in Jabne." *Aufstieg und Niedergang der römischen Welt* 2 (1979): 43–101.

——. *Der Bar-Kokhba Aufstand*. Tübingen: J. C. B. Mohr (Paul Siebeck), 1981.

Schalit, Abraham. "The Prophecies of Josephus and of R. Yohannan ben Zakkai on the Ascent of Vespasian to the Throne" (in Hebrew). In vol. 3 of *Salo Wittmeyer Baron Jubilee Volume*, edited by Saul Lieberman. Jerusalem: American Academy for Jewish Research, 1975.

Scholem, Gershom. *Jewish Gnosticism and Merkabah Mysticism and Talmudic Tradition*. New York: Jewish Theological Seminary, 1965.

——. "The Messianic Idea in Judaism." In *The Messianic Idea in Judaism and Other Essays in Jewish Spirituality*. New York: Schocken Books, 1972.

——. *Elements of the Kabbalah and Its Symbolism* (in Hebrew). Translated by Joseph Ben Shelomoh. Jerusalem: Bialik Institute, 1976.

Schwartz, Daniel R. "On Abraham Schalit, Herod, Josephus, the Holocaust, Horst R. Moehring, and the Study of Ancient Jewish History." *Jewish History* 2 (1987): 9–28.

Schwarzbaum, Haim. "The Jewish and Moslem Versions of Some Theodicy Legends." *Fabula* 3 (1959): 119–69.

——. *Studies in Jewish and World Folklore*. Berlin: Walter de Gruyter, 1968.

——. "The Messiah in Folklore" (in Hebrew). In *Roots and Landscapes: Studies in Folklore*, edited by Eli Yassif. Beer Sheva: Ben Gurion University Press, 1993.

——. "The Prophet Elijah and R. Joshua b. Levi." In *Roots and Landscapes: Studies in Folklore*, edited by Eli Yassif. Beer Sheva: Ben Gurion University Press, 1993.

Sered, Susan Starr. "Rachel's Tomb and the Milk Grotto of the Virgin Mary: Two Women's Shrines in Beth Lehem." *Journal of Feminist Studies in Religion* 2 (1986): 7–22.

——. "A Tale of Three Rachels, Or: The Cultural Herstory of a Symbol." *Nashim— A Journal of Jewish Women's Studies and Gender Issues* 1 (1998): 5–41.

Shahid, Irfan. "'The Martyrs of Najran': Miscellaneous Reflections." *Le Muséon* 9 (1980): 149–61.

Shaw, Brent D. "Bandits in the Roman Empire." *Past and Present* 105 (1984): 3–52.

Shenhar-Alroy, Aliza. *Stories of Yore: Children's Folktales* (in Hebrew). Haifa: University of Haifa, 1986.

Shinan, Avigdor. "A Tale of a Dog and Ten Kids" (in Hebrew). *Sinai* 85 (1979): 138–64.

——. *The World of Aggadic Literature* (in Hebrew). Tel Aviv: Ministry of Defense, 1987.

——. "The Unfolding of a Rabbinical Legend: The Story of Doeg ben Yosef's Son" (in Hebrew). *Mahanayim* 7 (1994): 70–75.

Shulman, David. *Tamil Temple Myths*. Princeton: Princeton University Press, 1980.

——. *Lectures on Indian Poetry* (in Hebrew). Tel Aviv: Ministry of Defense, 1986.

——. "The Yaksa's Questions." In *Untying the Knot: On Riddles and Other Enigmatic Modes*, edited by Galit Hasan-Rokem and David Shulman. New York: Oxford University Press, 1996.

Shulman, David, and Guy Stroumsa, eds.. *Dream Cultures: Toward a Comparative History of Dreaming*. New York: Oxford University Press, 1999.

Smolar, L., and M. Aberbach. "The Golden Calf Episode in Post-Biblical Literature." *Hebrew Union College Annual* 39 (1970): 91–116.

Sokoloff, Michael. *A Dictionary of Jewish Palestinian Aramaic*. Ramat Gan: Bar Ilan University Press, 1990.

Somadeva. *Tales from the Kathasaritsagara*. Translated by Arshia Sattar. Delhi: Penguin Books, 1994.

Sperber, Daniel. *Magic and Folklore in Rabbinic Literature*. Ramat Gan: Bar-Ilan University Press, 1994.

Stein, Dina. "Types of Discourse: The Interweaving of Different Types of Discourse in a Riddling Tale" (in Hebrew). Master's thesis, Hebrew University of Jerusalem, 1992.

——. "The Queen of Sheba vs. Solomon: Riddles and Interpretation in Midrash Mishlei A" (in Hebrew). *Jerusalem Studies in Jewish Folklore* 15 (1993): 7–35.

——. "A King, a Queen, and the Riddle Between: Riddles and Interpretation in a Late Midrashic Text." In *Untying the Knot: On Riddles and Other Enigmatic Modes*, edited by Galit Hasan-Rokem and David Shulman. New York: Oxford University Press, 1996.

——. "Believing is Seeing: A Reading of Baba Bathra 73a–75b" (in Hebrew). *Jerusalem Studies in Hebrew Literature* 17 (1999): 9–32.

Stemberger, Brigitte. "Der Traum in der Rabbinischen Literatur." *Kairos* 18 (1976): 1–42.

Stern, David. *Parables in Midrash: Narrative and Exegesis in Rabbinic Literature*. Cambridge, Mass.: Harvard University Press, 1991.

——. *Midrash and Theory: Ancient Jewish Exegesis and Contemporary Literary Studies*. Evanston, Ill.: Northwestern University Press, 1996.

Stern, Menahem. "Zealots." *Encyclopaedia Judaica Yearbook*, 1973.

——. "Jerusalem, Incomparably Famous Among Cities of the East" (in Hebrew). In *Studies in Jewish History in the Second Temple Period*, edited by Moshe Amit, Isaiah Gafni, and Moshe David Herr. Jerusalem: Yad Izhak Ben-Zvi, 1991.

——. "The Leadership in Freedom Fighters Groups at the End of the Second Temple" (in Hebrew). In *Studies in Jewish History in the Second Temple Period*, edited by Moshe Amit, Isaiah Gafni, and Moshe David Herr. Jerusalem: Yad Izhak Ben-Zvi, 1991.

Stumme, Hans. *Tunisische Märchen und Gedichte*. 2 vols. Leipzig: J. C. Hinrichs, 1893.

Tabari. *Chronique de Tabari*. Vol. 2. Translated by M. Hermann Zotenberg. Paris: Besson et Chantemerle, 1958.

Taylor, Archer. "The Biographical Pattern in Traditional Narrative." *Journal of the Folklore Institute* 1 (1964): 114–29.

Tedlock, Barbara. *Dreaming: Anthropological and Psychological Interpretations*. Cambridge: Cambridge University Press, 1987.

Thompson, Stith. *Motif Index of Folk Literature*. Copenhagen: Rosenkilde and Bagger, 1961.

Todorov, Tzvetan. *The Fantastic: A Structural Approach to Literary Genre*. Translated by Richard Howard. Ithaca, N.Y.: Cornell University Press, 1971.

Trachtenberg, Joshua. *Jewish Magic and Superstition: A Study in Folk Religion*. New York: Atheneum, 1974.

Trible, Phyllis. *God and the Rhetorics of Sexuality*. Philadelphia: Fortress Press, 1978.

Urbach, Ephraim E. *The Sages: Their Concepts and Beliefs*. Translated by Israel Abrahams. Jerusalem: Magnes Press, 1975.

——. "When Did Prophecy Cease?" (in Hebrew). *Tarbiz* 17 (1946): 1–11. Reprinted in Urbach, *The World of the Sages: Collected Studies* (in Hebrew) (Jerusalem: Magnes Press, 1988).

Utley, Francis Lee. "Folk Literature: An Operational Definition." In *The Study of Folklore*, edited by Alan Dundes. Englewood Cliffs, N.J.: Prentice Hall, 1965.

Valler, Shulamit. *Women and Womanhood in the Stories of the Babylonian Talmud* (in Hebrew). Tel Aviv: Hakibbutz Hameuhad, 1993.

Van Henten, Jan Willem. *The Maccabean Martyrs as Saviours of the Jewish People: A Study of 2 & 4 Maccabees*. Leiden: Brill, 1997.

Van Rompay, Lucas. "The Martyrs of Najran: Some Remarks on the Nature of the Sources." *Orientalia Lovaniensia Analecta* 1 (1982): 301–9.

Verheyden, Jozef. "The Flight of the Christians to Pella." *Ephemerides Theologicae Lovanienses* 66 (1990): 368–84.

Virtanen, Leea. "On the Function of Riddles." In *Finnish Riddles*, edited by Leea Virtanen, Annikki Kaivola-Bregenhøj, and Aarre Nyman. Helsinki-Pieksämäki: Finnish Literature Society Publications, 1977.

Visotzky, Burton L. "Most Tender and Fairest of Women: A Study in the Transmission of Aggada." *Harvard Theological Review* 76 (1983): 403–18.

——, ed. *Midrash Mishle: A Critical Edition based on Vatican MS. Ebr. 44* (in Hebrew). New York: Jewish Theological Seminary of America, 1990.

von Gruenebaum, Gustave E., and Roger Caillois. *The Dream and Human Societies*. Berkeley: University of California Press, 1966.

von Sydow, Carl Wilhelm. "Geography and Folktale Oicotypes." In *Selected Papers on Folklore*. Copenhagen: Rosenkilde and Bagger, 1948. First published in *Bealoideas* 4 (1934): 344–55.

Weiss, Zeev, and Ehud Netser. *Promise and Redemption: A Synagogue Mosaic from Sepphoris*. Jerusalem: The Israel Museum, 1996.

White, Hayden. *Metahistory*. Baltimore: Johns Hopkins University Press, 1973.

——. *Tropics of Discourse*. Baltimore: Johns Hopkins University Press, 1978.

Winnicott, Donald W. *Playing and Reality*. Middlesex: Pelican Books, 1985.

Witakowski, Witold. "Mart(y) Shmuni, the Mother of the Maccabean Martyrs in Syriac Tradition." In René Lavenant, ed., *VI Symposium Syriacum*, *Orientalia Christiana Analecta* 247 (1994): 153–68.

Wüstenfeld, Ferdinand, ed. *Die Chroniken der Stadt Mekka*. 4 vols. Leipzig: F. A. Brockhaus, 1857–1861.

Yadin, Yigael. "Bar Kokhba's Letters (From Camp D)" (in Hebrew). In *The Bar Kokhba Revolt*, edited by Aaron Oppenheimer. Jerusalem: Zalman Shazar Center for Jewish History, 1980.

Yassif, Eli. "The Chapbook—Folklore or Popular Culture?" (in Hebrew). *Jerusalem Studies in Jewish Folklore* 1 (1981): 127–33.

——. *The Tales of Ben Sira in the Middle Ages* (in Hebrew). Jerusalem: Magnes Press, 1985.

——. "Folklore Research and Jewish Studies" (in Hebrew). Parts 1 and 2. *World Union of Jewish Studies Newsletter* 27 (1987): 3–26; 28 (1988): 3–26.

——. "Theory and Practice in the Creation of the Hebrew Narrative in the Middle Ages" (in Hebrew). *Kiryat Sefer* 62 (1988–89): 887–905.

——. "The Narrative Chain in Rabbinic Literature" (in Hebrew). *Jerusalem Studies in Hebrew Literature* 12 (1990): 103–45.

——. *The Hebrew Folktale: History, Genre, Meaning* (in Hebrew). Jerusalem: Bialik Institute, 1994. Translated by Jacqueline S. Teitelbaum (Bloomington: Indiana University Press, 1999).

Yisraeli-Taran, Anat. *The Legends of the Destruction* (in Hebrew). Tel Aviv: Hakibbutz Hameuhad, 1997.

Yuval, Israel J. "Vengeance and Damnation, Blood and Defamation: From Jewish Martyrdom to Blood Libel Accusations." *Zion* 58 (1993): 33–90.

——. " 'The Lord Will Take Vengeance, Vengeance for His Temple': Historia Sine Ira et Studio" (in Hebrew). *Zion* 59 (1994): 351–414.

——. "Jews and Christians in the Middle Ages: Shared Myths, Common Language" (Donatio Constantini and Donatio Vespasiani). In *Demonizing the Other: Antisemitism, Racism, and Xenophobia*, edited by Robert S. Wistrich. Amsterdam: Harwood Academic Publishers, 1999.

Zabara, Joseph Ben Meir. *The Book of Delight*. Translated by Moses Hadas. New York: Columbia University Press, 1932.

Zerubavel, Yael. *Recovered Roots: Collective Memory and the Making of Israeli National Tradition*. Chicago: University of Chicago Press, 1995.

Zfatman, Sara. *The Marriage of a Mortal Man and a She-Demon: The Transformation of a Motif in the Folk Narrative of Ashkenazi Jewry in the Sixteenth–Nineteenth Centuries* (in Hebrew). Jerusalem: Magnes Press, 1987.

——. *The Jewish Tale in the Middle Ages: Between Ashkenaz and Sefarad* (in Hebrew). Jerusalem: Magnes Press, 1993.

Ziegler, Ignaz. *Die Königsgleichnisse in der Midrash*. Breslau: Schlesische Verlags-Anstalt, 1903.

Zinberg, Israel. *A History of Jewish Literature*. Vol. 1. Translated and edited by Bernard Martin. Cleveland: Press of Case Western Reserve University, 1972.

GENERAL INDEX

Aarne, Antti, 78

A Thousand Nights and a Night, 73, 75, 83

Abbaye, 100

Abel, 111, 170

Abdimi of Haifa, Rabbi, 135

Abgar (Amgar), 172, 174, 175, 183–84, 187

Abraham, 59, 118, 124, 125, 126; bosom of,
117; Covenant of, 103; in Sodom, 186

Abrahams, Roger, 57

Achilles, 95

Acre, 121

Adab, 84

Adam, 44, 133, 221n. 48

adaptation: cultural 4, 87; local, 157

Aeschylus, *The Libation Bearers*, 28

Aesopus, 42

afterlife and dreams, 92–95

afterworld, 180

age, 6, 11, 56

Aggadah, literary forms of, 1

Akiva, Rabbi: death, 169; interprets dreams,
102; laughs when others weep, 13–15;
method of interpretation, 15; and Bar
Kokhbah, 161, 165

Alexander (-Frizer), Tamar, 223n. 60,
224n. 66, 232n. 47, 235nn. 8, 11, 12

Alexandria, 172

Alexiou, Margaret, 78

Alon, Gedalyah 36, 184

A'mar, Avner, 85

ambiguity/ambivalence, 114, 119, 131, 142, 151,
158; unresolved, 15, 33, 145, 158, 188, 194

amoraim, 2, 91, 152, 172; Babylonian, 92, 100,
105; Palestinian, 108, 164, 169, 189

anagnorisis (recognition), 30–31

androgynous myth of divinity, 128

angel of death, 15, 92–93

angels, 126, 136, 148, 155

anthropological perception of divinity, 136–
37

Antioch, 78

Aptowitzer, Victor, 4, 5

aqalqalon, 185, 187

aqel, 185, 187

Arab, 74, 152–53, 168

Arabs, 75, 159

Arabia: 71; duke of, 172, 175, 187

Arab narrative traditions, 73–77, 83–84, 86–
87

Arab wisdom literature, 84

Aramaic, 22, 23, 29, 33, 44, 46, 98, 119, 120,
125, 139–41, 163

archaeology, 140, 163–64

Artemidorus of Daldis: *Oneirocritica*, 91, 93

Asmodeus, 15

assonance, 22

associative character of Midrash, 141
Athens, 46–52, 78
Athens-Jerusalem: narrative opposition, 56, 63, 96
Athenian: tries to sell sandals in Jerusalem, 50–51, 64
Athenians: go to Jerusalem, 48–51, 56
authority, 7, 15, 74, 105, 121, 158
Avin, Rabbi, 153, 158
Avot, mishnah, 180
Avot de-Rabbi Nathan, 171, 177
axis mundi, 25
Azulai, Avner, 85

Bab a-Tazkin (the study of tracks), 74, 159
Bacher, Wilhelm, 1, 212n. 20
Baer, Yizhak, 184
Baharam, King, 80
Bakhtin, Mikhail, 228n. 9, 234n. 1
Bal, Mieke, 215n. 54
Balaam, 165
Bana'ah, Rabbi, 105
Bar Hedya (Babylonian dream interpreter), 100
Bar Kokhbah, Ben Kosbah, 160–69, 171, 175–77; strength, 161; revolt, 163
Bar-Siqra, 177
Baroque, 81, 86
Barthes, Roland, 16, 149; "mythologies," 5; analysis of literary texts, 17
bastard, 48, 61, 64, 75, 84
Bauman, Richard, 204nn. 12, 13; 211n. 4
Beit Rimon valley, 197
belief, 89, 106, 148, 179, 180
Ben-Ami, Issachar, 223n. 65
Ben Batiah (Avtiah), 172, 176
Ben Kalba Savua, 172
Ben Tsitsit Hakkeset, 172
Ben-Amos, Dan 2, 5, 40
Benjamin, 111, 132–33
Benjamin of Tudela, *Itinerary,* 81
Benfey, Theodor, 71, 79–80; "Indian theory," 71, 78
Berdyczewski (Bin-Gorion), Micha Josef, 2, 3, 4
Berekhiah, Rabbi, 135
Beruriah, 109

Bethar, 161–62, 164, 175
Beth Lehem, 125, 138, 152–54, 165
Bettelheim, Bruno, 211n. 8
Betti, Emilio, 18
Bialik, Hayyim Nahman, 2, 3, 4; "On the Anthologizing of Aggadah," 3; "The Hebrew Book," 3
Bible: as revelation, 130; King James version, 105
biblical dreams, 95; dream interpretations, 91–92
biblical verses, 121, 127, 181, 196; dream interpretation based on, 95–96, 99, 102, 104–5; generative potential of, 60; narrative function of, 26–27, 68; riddle solution based on, 173, 182
Bilu, Yoram, 223n. 65, 225n. 10, 226n. 21
Bin-Gorion, Immanuel, 2
binyan av, 44
bird, 46, 167
birth, 48–49, 104, 163, 165, 198; of Messiah, 152–60
Bloch, Ernst: "principle of hope," 184
blood, 169–71
"blood test" motif, 84
body, 24, 29–30, 72, 90, 98–99, 113, 116–18, 123, 139–40, 162, 168, 171, 178, 182–83
Books of Maccabees (2 and 4), 118
Bordeaux, pilgrim from, 170
borrowing (cultural), 69
Bourdieu, Pierre, 7, 232n. 47
Boyarin, Daniel, 205n. 20, 231n. 39
Brahmin, sons of, 72
Briar-rose, 42, 195
Buber, Solomon, 20, 128
burial practices, 180

Cairo Genizah fragment T.S.C. 2 (142), 161
camel, 50, 199
cannibalism, 132, 138–42
canonization, 9
Cappadocia, 94–95, 102–3
captives, 20, 23, 58, 122, 143–44
carpenter's apprentice, story of, 36
Carthage, 121–22
Cassius, Dio, 163
casting lots, 49, 54, 57

Cavafy, Constantine, 191, 199
Certeau, Michel de, 7
chain of stories, 44, 62, 71, 79, 125, 181, 192, 197
chain of transmission, 180
children, 8, 48–49, 55–56, 70–71, 110, 119, 126, 144, 193; of Israel, 127, 136, 167
Christian: approach, 142; Church, 154, 157, 163, 188; faith, 76; -Jewish narrative dialogue, 121–25, 154–57; literature, 4; martyrological ideal, 122; mythology, 188; narrative, 157; tradition, 12, 110
Christianity, 80, 157
Cinderella, 42, 183
class, 6, 11; distinctions, 85; priestly, 25–28, 34, 56
comparative research, 4, 67–87, 83
Constantine, 183
contemporary perspective, author's, 38
context, 57, 101–2, 189–90; comparative, 67–87; cultural, 147; folkloristic, 88–91, 96, 106, 132; genre, 39–66; historical, 112, 145, 146–90, 167, 184, 194; ideological, 157; literary, 16–38; narrative, 108; of meaning, 141; social/sociocultural, 108–29, 158
Coptic, 76
Cristoforo Armeno, 80
critical theory, of literature and culture, 18, 131
Cuthean, Samaritan, 96–101, 161–62, 164, 166

Daniel, 91, 182
Danos, Yehezkel, 83
Darnton, Robert, 6, 234n. 3
David, 154, 161, 168
Davis, Natalie, 6
dead in dreams, 91, 92–93
"dead of the desert," 159
death, 33, 65, 91, 92–93, 104–6, 137, 138–40, 162–63, 176, 187; feigning, 172, 175, 177
Dégh, Linda, 235n. 9
demon, 106, 148
dialogue, 7, 13, 24, 33, 97, 109, 110, 113, 115, 116, 118, 183–85, 197; narrative, 121–25, 154–57
dichotomy, 150

Dido, 122
discourse: cultural, 196; different realms of, 115, 124; forms and types of, 108, 131, 149; multivocal modes of, 7, 110, 144, 148; oral, 9; rabbinic, 110; representative, 151; structure of, 106
doctors, 174, 186
Doniger (O'Flaherty), Wendy, 225n. 10
Dodds, Eric R., 106
Doeg ben Joseph, widow of, 119, 121, 143
dogma, 157
dragon, 185
dream resembles riddle, 90
dreams, 94–104, 132
dream interpretation, 11, 36, 88–107; modern theories of, 103; today, 100
Druze, 84
Dubois, Jean Daniel, 170
Dukes, Leopold, 3
Dundes, Alan, 232n. 41
duration, in narrative, 25

ecclesiastical councils, 157
ecotype, 147, 182, 183
ecotypification, 68
eggs, 81
Egyptian dream interpretation, 91
Eleazar, Rabbi, 199
Eleazar b. Azariah, Rabbi, 14, 181
Eleazar ben R. Zadok, 120
Eleazar ha-Cohen, 164
Eleazar of Modi'in, Rabbi, 161–62, 164, 166–67, 176, 186
Elbaum, Yaacov, 203nn.1, 2; 228n. 8
Electra, 28
Eliezer, Rabbi, 172, 174, 178, 198
Eliezer b. Yose ha-Gelili, his thirty-two rules, 44
Elijah, 15, 43, 160, 198
Emmaus, 138, 144
enigma, 62, 73, 191–92, 195, 197–99
enigmatic: attitude, 56; dialogues, 194; reply, 195; reversal, 55, 56; tasks, 56; will, 54
epimythium, 114
Eros, 37, 65
eschatological motifs, 152, 163
Esther, biblical book, 184

ethnographic: account, 137; context, 96; creative mode, 151; features, 159
etiology, 74, 187
Euripides: *Ifigenia in Tauris*, 77
European tradition, 86, 98
Eusebius, 163
everyday life, 6–7, 8, 89, 137
evolutionary approach, 67
experience: loss and mourning, 12, 52, 62–66; religious, 12
Ezra, Mukhtar, 83

fable, 197
family relations, 97, 46, 70; brothers, 72, 75, 79–81; father and son(s), 46–47, 64, 70, 72, 73, 111–12, 130–45, 160, 174–75; mother and child 48–49, 123, 166, 192, 195; mother and son(s), 47–48, 60–61, 64, 97, 114–25, 143, 152–60; siblings 20–37, 98; sisters 126–27; uncle and nephew, 162, 172, 178
fantastic, 188, 195
Faraj, 84
feminist theory, 108–9
Festugière, A. J., 107
Finnish riddling culture (*Hymylä*), 55
Flusser, David, 237n. 25, 245n. 74
folk art, 89
folk literature, 89, 108, 109, 110; definition of, 7; in rabbinic literature, study of, 3–6; re-creation of, 10; study of, 4, 147, 164
folk narrative: features of, 154; genres, 39–43; tradition, 124, 136, 146; viewpoint, 170
folk religion, study of, 4
folk tradition, 154
folklore, 150; definition, 88–89; Jewish, 2; study of, 3, 4; unique form of expression, 109
folkloristics, structural, 18
folktale: association, 196; genre of, 41–43, 73, 75, 164–65, 182; compared with legend, 147–48; of confrontation, 185; princess, 196; structure, 184
formula, 96; curse, 97–99, 139, 187; editorial, 22, 142, 175
formulaic: gifts, 184; number, 46–47, 175, 182, 186, 188
Foucault, Michel, 19

Fraade, Steven, 17
Fraenkel, Jonah, 5, 151, 158, 160; his literary approach to Aggadah, 7; *The Methods of Aggadah and Midrash*, 150
Fraenkel, Sigmund, 2, 3, 212n. 20
Fraenkel, Zecharia, 1
frame narrative, 79–80, 97, 183
Frazer, James, *The Golden Bough*, 4
Freud, Sigmund, 135; and Jewish tradition, 97, 131, 142; *Interpretation of Dreams*, 97; interpretation of Oedipus story, 19; Oedipal model of interpretation, 131, 142
functionalism, 4, 68

Gadamer, Hans Georg, 18–19
Galilee, 76, 155, 186, 197
Gallus, 76
Gamaliel, Rabbi, 14, 137–38, 144
Geertz, Clifford, 2
gematria, 13, 44, 58, 62, 94–95
Genesis, biblical book of, 129, 165, 182
Genesis Rabbah, 8–9, 93
gender, 6, 11; changes in narrative, 30; distinctions in activity, 27–28, 111, 137; distinctions in language 22–24; genre, 68, 147; rabbi awareness of, 43; coherence in *Lamentations Rabbah*, 51; concept of, 6; context, 11; dominant, 85, 114, 119; especially folktale, 39–43; horror propaganda, 139; lament, 113, 129; legend, 120, 140; mechanism, 151, 167, 188; parable, 111, 136; signs, 140, 171; stylistic uniformity of, 114; swindler novella, 167; trickster novella, 57
geographic-historical school or method, 3, 4, 5, 67–68
Georgian Church, 124
gezerah shavah, 44
Ginzberg, Louis, 2, 3; *The Legends of the Jews*, 4
God, 35, 62–63, 65–66, 91–92, 105, 106, 111, 114, 123–24, 126, 148, 150, 153, 160, 161, 166–67, 173, 198–99; and Israel, 132–45; compassion, 167; mourning, 132–37, 142–43
Gophna, 173, 182
golden calf, 59–60, 198
Goliath, 168

Goshen-Gottstein, Alon, 233n. 1
Greece, 77–78
Greek, 163; alphabet, 94–95; dream inter-
pretation, 91; Jewish texts, 122, 155; lamen-
tations, 78; language, 219n. 37, 227n. 33;
literature, 4, 95; novels, 122; sage, 78; tra-
dition 77, 86; translation, 76
Grimm brothers, 40
Gruenbaum, Max, 3
Grunwald, Max, 3
guilt, 37, 135, 138, 142
Gurevitch, Aaron, 234n. 3

Habermas, Jürgen, 19
habitus, 3
Hadrian, 138–40, 161–62, 164, 168
Haifa, 135
Haim Pinto, Rabbi, 85
Halakha, 150
halakhic: context, 94; issue, 196
Haman, 184
hamartia, 168
Hananiah, Mishael, and Azariah, 116
Handelman, Don, 212n. 23
Hannah, 119, 229n. 21
harlot, 20–21, 26–27, 29
Hasmonean princesses, 121
Hebrew: alphabet, 126; language 22, 44, 45,
68, 105, 153, 163, 198; narrative, 79; poet,
195
Heinemann, Joseph, 5
Heinemann, Yitzhak, 4, 151; *The Methods of
Aggadah*, 150; "organic thinking," 5, 150
Hellenistic world, 78
Hellenistic-Roman world, 95
Heller, Bernhard (Bernát), 2, 4
Herder, Johann von, 37
hermeneutical: approaches, 10; conscious-
ness, 6; discourse, 96; focus, 12; implica-
tions, 195; key, 114, 131; poetics of the
rabbis, 45; system, 164; techniques, 44;
theory, 18–20; hero, 181; pattern, 156, 162–
63; spiritual, 176; tragic, 168
Herod, 155
Hezekiah, 153–55
Hillel's seven rules, 44
Himyarite kingdom and inscriptions, 76

Hirshman, Mark G. (Menahem), 203n. 1,
209n. 35, 231n. 32
Hisda, Rav, 105
historical research, 25, 149, 151, 152, 163, 184,
188
Holland, 191
Holy Spirit, 21
Honko, Lauri, 238n. 32
Hrushovski (Harshav), Benjamin (Binya-
min), 22
human sacrifice, 122, 138, 170
humor, 44
Hungarian school, 4

identity: collective, 148; quest for, 29; riddle
of, 54, 196; ideological context, 157;
dimension 27; foundation, 141; level, 137;
meaning, 62; message, 17, 20, 33–37, 137;
portrayal, 177
Ilan, Tal, 232n. 40
incest, 28–36, 97–98, 131
India, 71
Indian narrative traditions, 71–73
information gaps in narrative, 27
inter-group transmission, 110, 121, 128
inter-cultural communication, 7, 51, 67–87,
77, 86
interpretation, 159; feminist, 109; of different
historical poetics, 45–46; of dreams, 11,
32, 88–107; power of, 106; psychoanalytical, 32, 103; theory of, 17–20; vision of,
159
inter-textuality, 57, 60, 121, 124
Iranian Jewish traditions, 85
Iraq, 75
Iraqi Jewish tradition, 83
irony, 30, 142, 154, 168; dramatic, 27–28;
tragic, 28
Irshai, Oded, 237n. 25
Isaac, 64, 118, 124, 126, 127
Islamic law, 75
Ishmael, Rabbi, his thirteen rules, 44
Ishmael b. Elisha, Rabbi, 34–35
Ishmael ben R. Yose, 95–101
Israel, 144, 159; enemy of, 154
Israel Folktale Archive, 5, 82–87
Israeli myth of heroism, 119

light, 97
longue durée, 6
Luke, 126, 154–55
Lüthi, Max, 41–43
Lydda, 174, 186

Maccabean martyrs, 122
Macrobius, 95
magi, 154–55, 165
magic, 186
Maimonides, 114
Mandel, Paul (Pinhas), 204n. 16, 232n. 48
Martha bat Boethus, 120
martyrdom, in Jewish tradition, 118
martyrological tales, 20–22, 34, 77, 114–25
Marxism, 19, 150
Masoudi, 73, 76
Massada, 163
Matthew, 126, 154–56, 165, 170
Mecca, 75
Media, 196
Meir, Ofra, 203n. 1, 210n. 3, 223n. 64
Menahem, the Messiah, 125–26, 152–56, 162–63
mentalité, historians of, 6, 151
Mesopotamian dream interpretation, 91
Merchant of Venice, 195
Messiah, 74, 125–26, 146–90; birth of, 152–60; King, 161, 166; name of, 153–55
Messianic: hope, 152; idea, 156, 166; images, 155; perspective, 171; plot 168; theme, 152; vision, 147
Messianism: Jewish, 154, 160; political, 168
metaphor, 151, 159, 177, 185, 191
methodological question (of women's voices), 128
metonymy, 151
Meyers, Carol, 228n. 8
Midrash: exegetical, 9, 63, 132, 145; homiletic, 9
Midrash on Proverbs (*Midrash Mishle*), 55
Midrash Rabbah, 58
Miriam, 121, 125, 157, 229n. 21
Miriam bat Nakdimon, 120–21
Miriam bat Tanhum, 115–25, 157
"mirror of truth" motif, 81
Mishnah, 180

money, 46–47, 49–51, 80, 94, 100, 144, 153, 160, 174, 187, 200
Mordechai, 182, 184
Moroccan Jewish tradition, 84–85
Moses, 59, 121, 125, 126, 198
motif, 15, 30, 42, 69, 72, 75, 77, 80, 81, 84, 125, 136, 156, 157, 175, 181, 187; F 613.3 "strong man's labor contract: anger bargain," 165; F 614.2 "strong man uproots tree and uses it as weapon," 164–65; reversed, 143–44
Mount Carmel, 59
Mount Sinai, 159
Muhammad, 73, 75, 84
multidimensional model of time, 91
multiple meanings, 139
multivalent system of meanings, 130
multivocal: modes of discourse, 7, 144; monotheistic faith, 148
mystery story, 24
mysticism, 128
myth, 40–41, 147; and ritual, 4, 41; definition, 151–52
mythical knowledge, 159–60

Nahman, Rabbi, 93, 136
Najran, 73, 76–77
Nakdimon ben Gurion, 172, 182
Nathan, Rabbi, 198
Nebuchadnezzar, 91
Nebuzaradan, 169
Nehemiah, Rabbi, 62
Nehmad, Moshe, 85
Nero, 183
New Testament, 154–55
North Africa, 123–24
North African Jewish tradition, 84–85
notarikon, 44, 94
novella, 75, 83, 167
Noy, Dov, 2, 5, 68, 82, 163
nursing, 117, 122

Odysseus, 30
Oedipus: story of, 19, 138; riddle of, 55
olive, 97, 100–101
Olrik, Axel, 207n. 20
ordeal, 175, 187
oracle, 188

oral: creativity, 9, 109; discourse, 9; literary channels, 11; telling, 171, 201; tradition, 73, 75, 83, 86–87, 154; transmission, 9, 16, 22, 51, 68, 79, 82, 109, 155

Orestes, 28

pagan, 110

Pagis, Dan, 53, 65, 81, 191–92, 196

Palmyra, 76

Panchatantra, 71

parable, 62, 111, 136, 138, 142, 174; royal, 111–12, 114, 128, 132–34, 143–44, 167

paradox, 15, 52, 65, 72, 113

Pardes, Ilana, 228n. 8

parody, 116, 125

Patai, Raphael, 2, 4

patriarchs, 127

patriarchal, 109

Patroclus, 95

peah, 192–93

Pella, 188

Penzer, Norman Mosley, 72

Peregrinnagio or *Peregrinaggio di Tre Giovani Figliuoli del re di Serendippo* (*The Voyage of Jaffar's Sons*), 79–82

pepper, 200–201

performance, 4, 5, 7, 22, 88–89; context, 57

Perles, Joseph, 3, 212n. 20

Perpetua, 121–23

Persian, 79

Pesikta de-Rav Kahana, 169–70

Pharaoh, 105

phenomenology of religion, 20, 134

philological research, 3, 8, 17, 67

Phoenician tradition, 122

piyyut(*im*) (liturgical poetry), 37

Plautus, *Epidicus*, 28

play, 44

point of view, 31

polemic, 7, 124, 125, 154, 157

popular culture, 147

praxis, 89, 106

priest, 136, 155, 169

priestly class, 25–28, 34, 56

proem, 111, 114, 126–27, 132, 135, 143, 166, 167, 169

prophecy, 92

Propp, Vladimir, 5, 68

proverb(s), 2, 106, 177, 185, 200

psychoanalysis, 19–20

psychoanalytical discourse and Midrash, 130–32

psychoanalytical interpretation, 32

psychology, 90

psychological: message, 17, 20, 33–36, 137; motivations, 64–65, 132; perspective, 28, 37

ptome (torso), 162, 168

Punic tradition, 122

quotation, 110

Rabbah, 92

Rabbah bar bar Hana, 74, 159–60

rabbinic: academy, 5, 6, 9, 11, 96, 101–6, 108, 110, 150, 159–60; culture (polysystemic character of)8

rabbis, hermeneutical poetics of, 45

Rachel, 126–29, 144

Raglan, Lord, 238n. 30

Ramah, 127

Rank, Otto, 238n. 30

RaShI (Rabbi Shlomo Itzhaki), 92

Rava, 100

Ravnitzky, Yehoshua Hana, 2

Rebecca, 193, 196

regression, 140

Reiner, Elchanan, 237n. 25

Renou, Louis, 72–73

resurrection, 180, 186, 188

retribution, 13, 15, 32, 45, 60, 113, 187

rhyme, 22, 177

Ricoeur, Paul, 19–20, 31, 36–37, 134, 142

riddle(s), 11, 15, 43, 182; allegorical, 184; at weddings, 65, 196; decoding elements, 192, 197; definition of the genre, 52–53, 65, 191–92; dream resembles, 90; encoding elements 192, 197; European, 98; Hebrew literary, 53; neck riddle, 53, 192; of broken mortar 49; of cheese and eggs, 49; of figs, 49; of pregnancy and birth, 48–49, 64; of salt, 49; of serpent, 185; of wood and smoke, 50; narratives, 53; tales, 44, 46–51, 63, 65, 96, 132, 192; true, 53, 192 riddling: mechanism, 70; narratives, 53; situation, 53, 72; test, 46–51, 80, 173, 181

Rimmon-Kenan, Shlomith, 208n. 22

ritual, 89–90, 103, 122, 142, 163, 170

Rokem, Freddie, 213n. 36, 230n. 26

Roman, 164, 166, 200; army, 181; bathing, 182; emperor, 115–18, 173–75, 181; Empire, 76; general, 95; historian, 163; military terminology, 25; oppression, 145; public, 155; ruler, 121; soldiers, 123

Rome, 14, 20, 24, 122, 143, 173, 182, 183

Rubenstein, Richard L., 37, 135

rumor, 178

Sa'adi, 85

sacer, 142

Sage, 147

Salisbury, Joyce E., 122

salt, 80, 201

Samson, riddle of, 53, 55, 57, 71, 73, 192, 196

Sanhedrin, 169

Sanskrit, 71

saying, 75, 80, 83–84, 95, 96, 114, 119, 129, 142, 185

scales, 174

Schalit, Abraham, 184

Scheiber, Alexander (Sandor), 2, 4

Scholem, Gershom, 128, 234n. 2

Schwarzbaum, Haim, 206n. 23, 212n. 20

Scipio Africanus, 95

Sebatini (Sebastia), 172

self-mutilation, motif, 164

self reflection (in interpretation), 19–20, 37, 149

Se'orim, Rabbi, 92

Serendib, Serendippo, 79–80

sermons, 108

sexuality and eros, 23–24, 27, 29, 31, 33, 35, 65, 81, 97–98, 128, 195–97

Shahid, Irfan, 77

Sharvit, Moshe, 85

Shammai, 26

Shangri-La, 189

Sheba, Queen of, 54–55, 57, 64, 71, 196

Shekhinah, 128

Shenhar-Alroy, Aliza, 211n. 11

Shinan, Avigdor, 5, 27

Shiraz, 85

Shiur Qomah, 116, 125

Shulman, David, 213n. 40

signs, 30, 33, 74, 147, 165, 167

Simeon b. Lakish, Rabbi, 111, 132–33

snake, serpent, 162, 164, 167, 185

Solomon, King, 54–55, 57, 64, 71, 196

Song of Songs, biblical book, 116; allegorical tradition of interpretation, 114, 120, 128, 131

sounds, in the text, 22

Spain, 157

star, 95, 99, 155, 161

Stein, Dina, 203n. 2, 213n. 38, 216n. 10, 230n. 23

Stern, David, 205n. 20, 229nn. 12, 17

Stern, Menahem, 220n. 39, 238n. 26

"stiff-necked people," 59–60

structural: analysis, 22–30, 140–45; character of literary text, 16–17; folkloristics, 18; scheme 139

structuralism, 68; literary, 20; theory, 22

structure: of sounds, 22; of the book, 10–12

subject, 194, 196

suicide, 118, 122

supernatural beings, 148

supernatural power, 164–65

Sylvester, bishop, 183

symbols of evil, 134

synagogue, 5, 6, 9, 108

synecdoche, 25

syntactic structure in literary text, 23–24

Tabari, 74

taboos, 42, 122, 131, 140–42

tale type, 67, 68, 72; AT 500 "Rumpelstilzchen," 54; AT 510 "Cinderella," 183; AT 655 "Wise Brothers," 47–48, 69–70, 71–75, 80, 82–86; analysis, 54; AT 655A "The Strayed Camel and the Clever Deductions," 50, 58–59, 64, 70, 73, 82–86; AT 922 "The King and the Abbot," 182; AT 1533 "The Wise Carving of the Fowl," 46–47, 70, 77, 82–86; analysis, 54

Talmud: Babylonian, 34, 58–59, 71, 170, 177, 195; manuscripts, 214n. 47; Munich manuscript, 60–61; Palestinian, 94–96, 166, 170 tannaim, 2, 114, 180

Taya, 74–76, 159

Temple, 119, 169–70; altar, 50; destruction of 12, 14, 25–27, 32, 36–37, 56, 59, 62, 66, 74, 106, 107, 110–11, 137–39, 152–53, 158, 170, 174, 177, 182, 184, 188, 194, 196, 197; Mount, 14

Tendlau, Abraham, 3

Thanatos, 37

theodicy, 13, 15, 32, 45, 121

Thompson, Stith, 211n. 10

"three caskets" motif, 195

tithes, second, 94

Titus, 139, 165, 168, 182, 183, 186

Torah, 44, 102, 104, 105, 117, 126, 144, 181; center, 186; scholars, 179; study, 173, 174, 182, 186

Trajan, 143, 171

Trible, Phyllis, 228n. 8

trickster, 57, 167

Trivikramasena, King, 72

Tunis, 75, 83

Tyre, 200

unconscious: collective, 103; universal categories, 146

Uriah the priest, 170

Urtypus, 86

Usha, 197

utopia, 146–47, 160, 180, 184

Valler, Shulamith, 228n. 8

Valley of Hinnom, 138

Veda, 72

Venice, 79, 81

Vespasian, 171–89

"Vetala stories" (Vampire tales), Indian, 53, 71–72

Virgil, Aeneid, 122

voice(s), 171; androgynous, 169; female, 11, 128–29; heavenly (bat-qol), 162; many, 15, 201; of other, 169, 184; "of the people," 37; Rachel's, 126–29

Wesselski, Albert, 215n. 8

Western gate, 174

Western Wall, 175, 187

widow, 193–94, 196

wild animals, 124

wine, 75

wine merchant, 20–21, 26–27, 47–48, 64

Wissenschaft des Judentums, 4

womb, 50, 140

women, 8, 158, 166; discrimination and oppression of, 109; dreamers, 103–5; lamenters, 24, 111, 113, 141; martyrs, 77; mourning, 111, 129, 138; perspective of, 108–29; redemptive power of, 126–29, 167; victims of violence, 121; voice of, 108–10

Yassif, Eli, 6; The Hebrew Folktale, 149–50

Yazd, 85

Yavneh (Jabneh, Jamnia), 36, 186

Yehozadak, Rabbi, 20–21, 26

Yiddish, 3, 119

Yohannan, Rabbi, 102, 106, 132, 161, 165

Yohannan b. Tortha, Rabbi, 161, 165

Yohannan b. Zakkai, Rabbi (Rabban), 36, 48, 56, 70, 171–89; research on the tale of his exit from Jerusalem 242–45n. 74

Yose ben Halafta, Rabbi, 94, 95, 101

Yuval, Israel, 183, 237n. 25, 245n. 74

Zabara, Joseph Ben Meir, 216n. 10

Zadok, the High Priest, and the children of, 20–34, 177

Zadok, Rabbi, 174–75, 186

Zekhariah, 169–71, 187

Zekhariah ben Berakhyahu, 170

Zekhariah ben Yehoyada, 170

Zekhariah ben Yeverekhyahu, 170

Zerubavel, Yael, 163–64

Zfatman, Sarah, 235n. 5

Zionist Hebrew culture, 3, 119, 163

Zohar, 114

Zotenberg, M. Hermann, 74

Zunz, Leopold, 1

INDEX TO THE BIBLE AND RABBINIC LITERATURE

CONTRAVERSIONS

JEWS AND OTHER DIFFERENCES